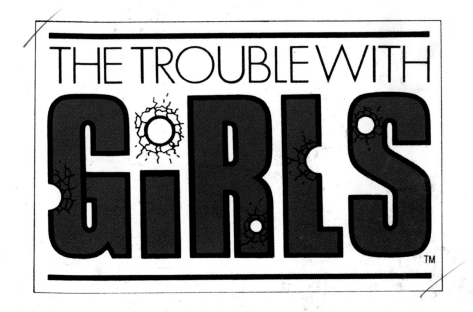

THE TROUBLE WITH GiRLS ™

WILL JACOBS

and

GERARD JONES

CHECKER BOOK PUBLISHING GROUP

"Prepare yourself for a romp,
one with elements of parody,
but with enough internal
consistency to create a world of
its own. It is thoughtfully silly, at
turns droll and nasty and
mockingly dramatic."

Paul Chadwick,
creator of Concrete

THE TROUBLE WITH GIRLS™

Will Jacobs and Gerard Jones

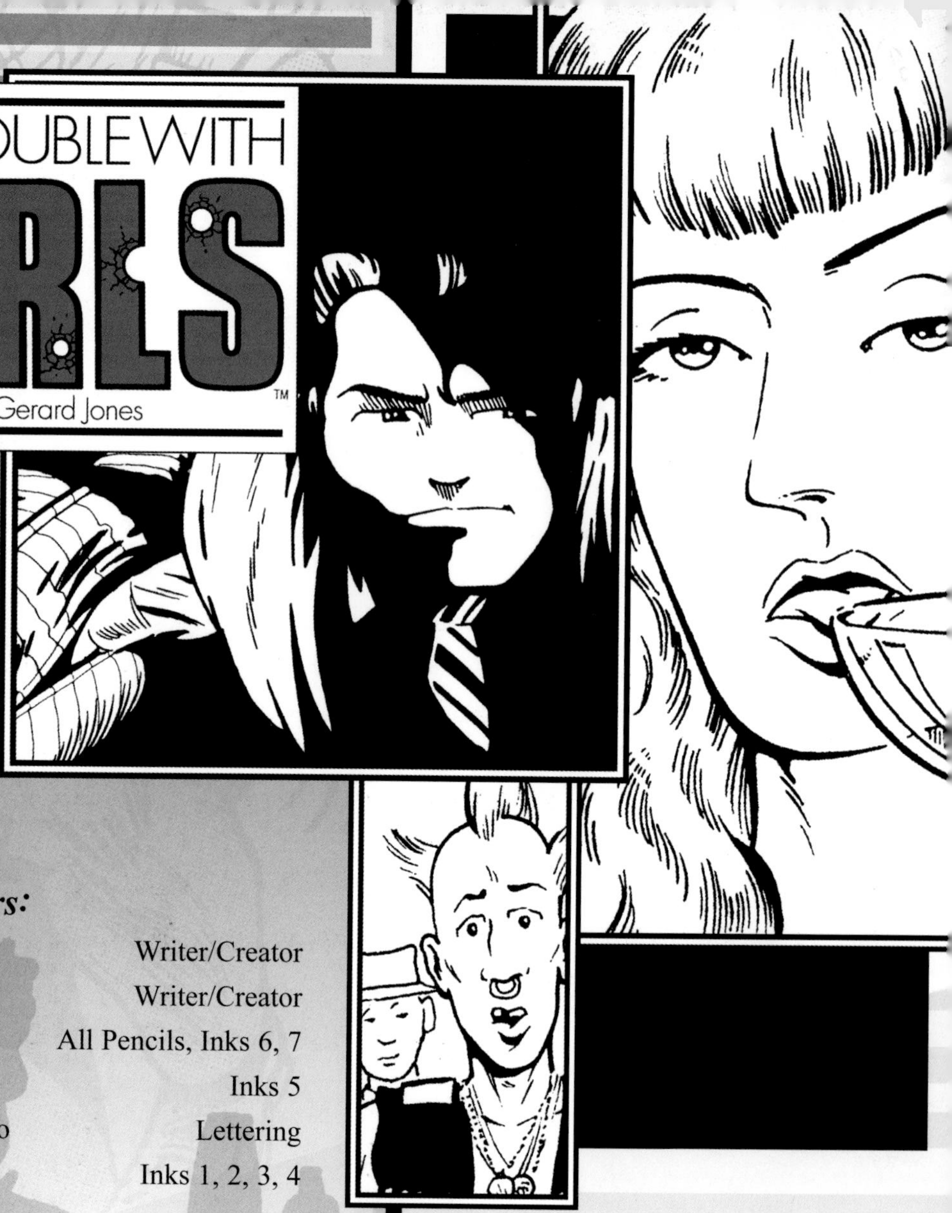

Contributors:

Will Jacobs	Writer/Creator
Gerard Jones	Writer/Creator
Tim Hamilton	All Pencils, Inks 6, 7
Dave Mowry	Inks 5
Diane Valentino	Lettering
Dave Garcia	Inks 1, 2, 3, 4

Compilation:

Mark Thompson	Publisher
Trevor Goodman	Graphic Design
Andrew Paavola	Graphic Design

Checker Book Publishing Group
2044-A South Alex Road
West Carrollton, OH 45449
Visit us online at www.checkerbpg.com

No solicitations accepted

ISBN #1-933160-45-4

Printed in China

Table of Contents

Introduction

The Trouble with Girls was a labor of love. It had to be—there sure wasn't any money in it. When Malibu Comics released it in the summer of 1987, black-and-white "independent" comics were still enjoying a boom. Immediately, as if our creation were the final straw, boom turned to bust. Over the next few years we did everything we could think of—full color, new publishers, pretexts to create new "first issues"—to keep Girls's head above water in an increasingly difficult market. With the support of a loyal body of fans and a few truly committed publishers, we succeeded until 1993, when the next comic-book bust finally pulled us under.

Through it all, we never considered giving up. Sure, we'd have given a kidney or two for Girls to become a huge success, but all we really cared about was the work itself. We'd never had so much fun as writers. If we ever worried about sales it was because we feared cancellation. We wanted to write the adventures of Lester Girls forever. But it looked as though six years was all we'd be given.

Until now.

When Checker told us they wanted to reprint the legendary first fourteen issues of The Trouble with Girls, the first words out of our mouths were, "This could be it." Maybe this, we thought, would be the time when Girls finally garnished the attention it deserved and achieved the glory for which we know it was surely destined. Checker, after all, is no slouch in the world of publishing. Take a glance at its catalogue and some very big names jump out at you. Names like Alan Moore and Milton Caniff, to mention just a couple. Is it really so absurd to imagine a comic book fan picking up an issue of the book you hold in your hands and thinking, "Hey, these people publish Alan Moore. This looks like a fresh take on heroic fiction. You know, it wouldn't surprise me a bit if 'Will Jacobs and Gerard Jones' wasn't a pseudonym for Alan Moore! I think I'll buy it!" Or another potential customer musing, "Hmm. I always thought Milton Caniff's character was named Steve Canyon. I didn't know he was called Lester Girls. But as this black-and-white book is published by Checker, Milton Caniff's publisher, I guess I've been wrong about the name all these years! I'll buy it anyway!"

Advance reports already suggest that the news of the return of this forgotten masterpiece has kindled a bonfire of excitement throughout fandom. Really. We've actually heard some of these reports. From somewhere. And in the midst of such excitement, can a clarion call to bring back ALL-NEW ISSUES of The Trouble with Girls not be far behind?

Ah. But we get ahead of ourselves. Enjoy these first stories of Lester Girls and his friends. We'll say more about those all-new stories in Volume 2…

Will Jacobs & Gerard Jones

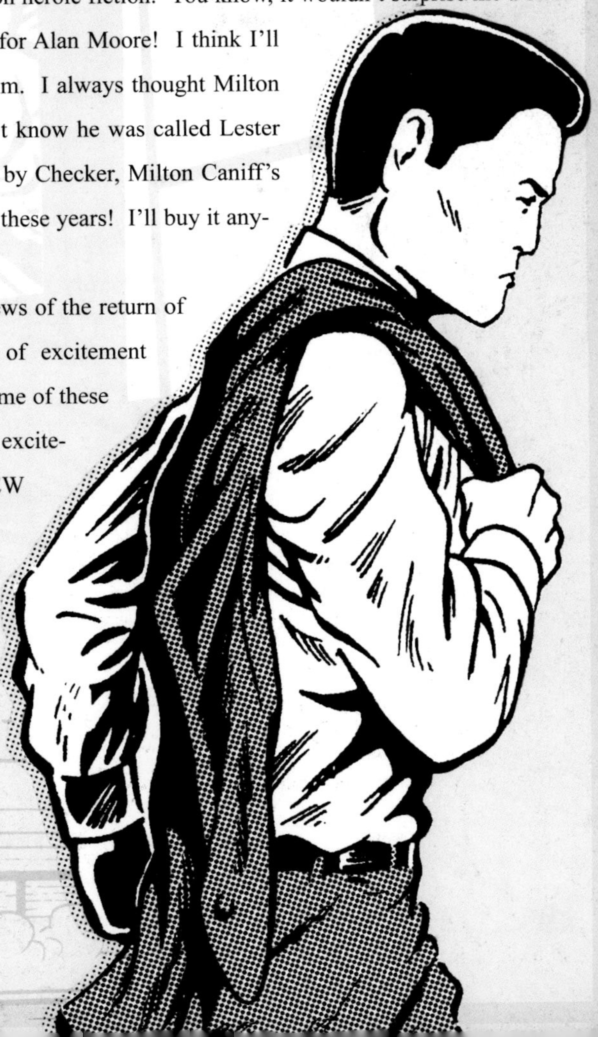

THE TROUBLE WITH GIRLS™

CHAPTER 1

AUGUST 1987

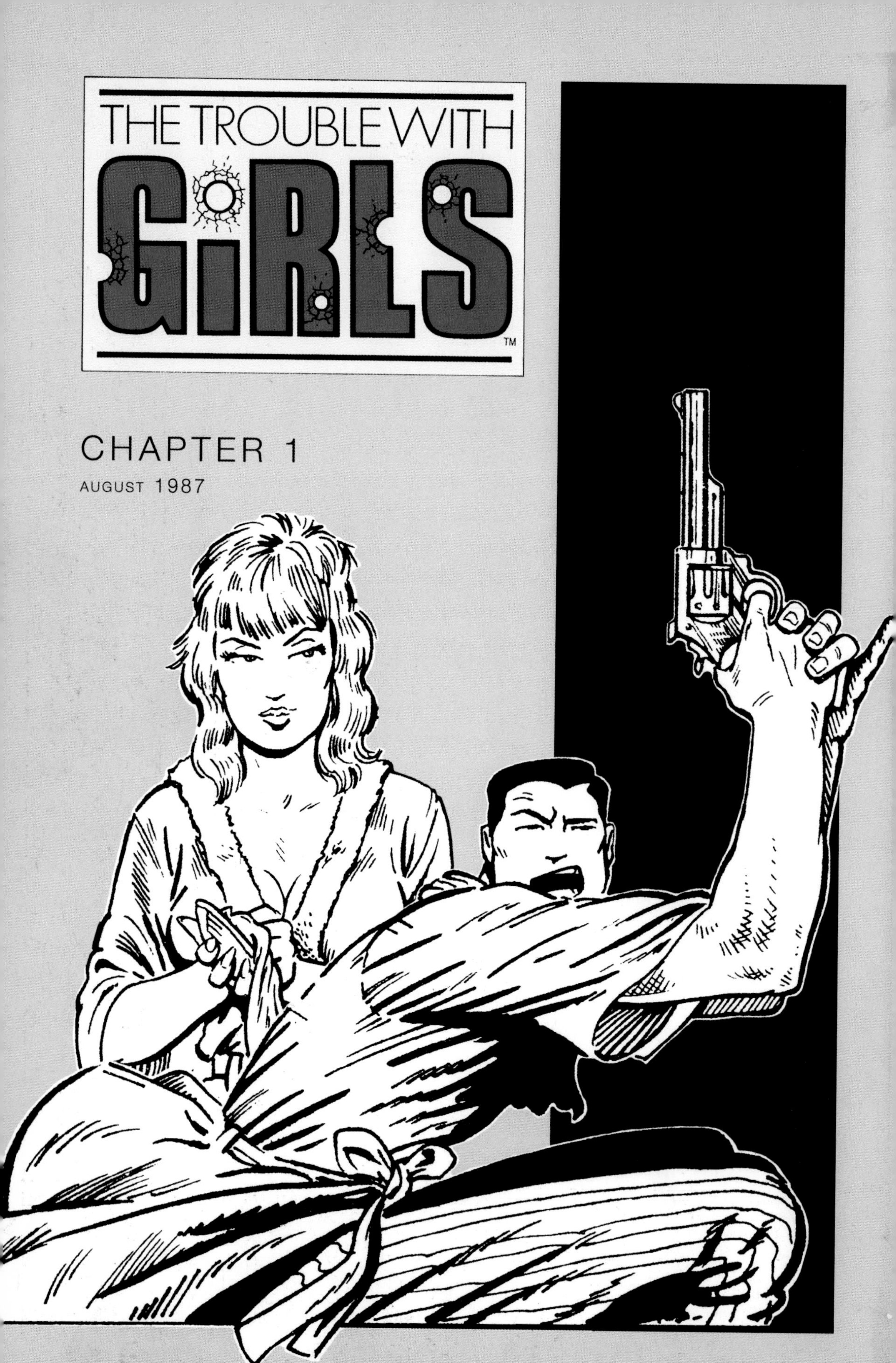

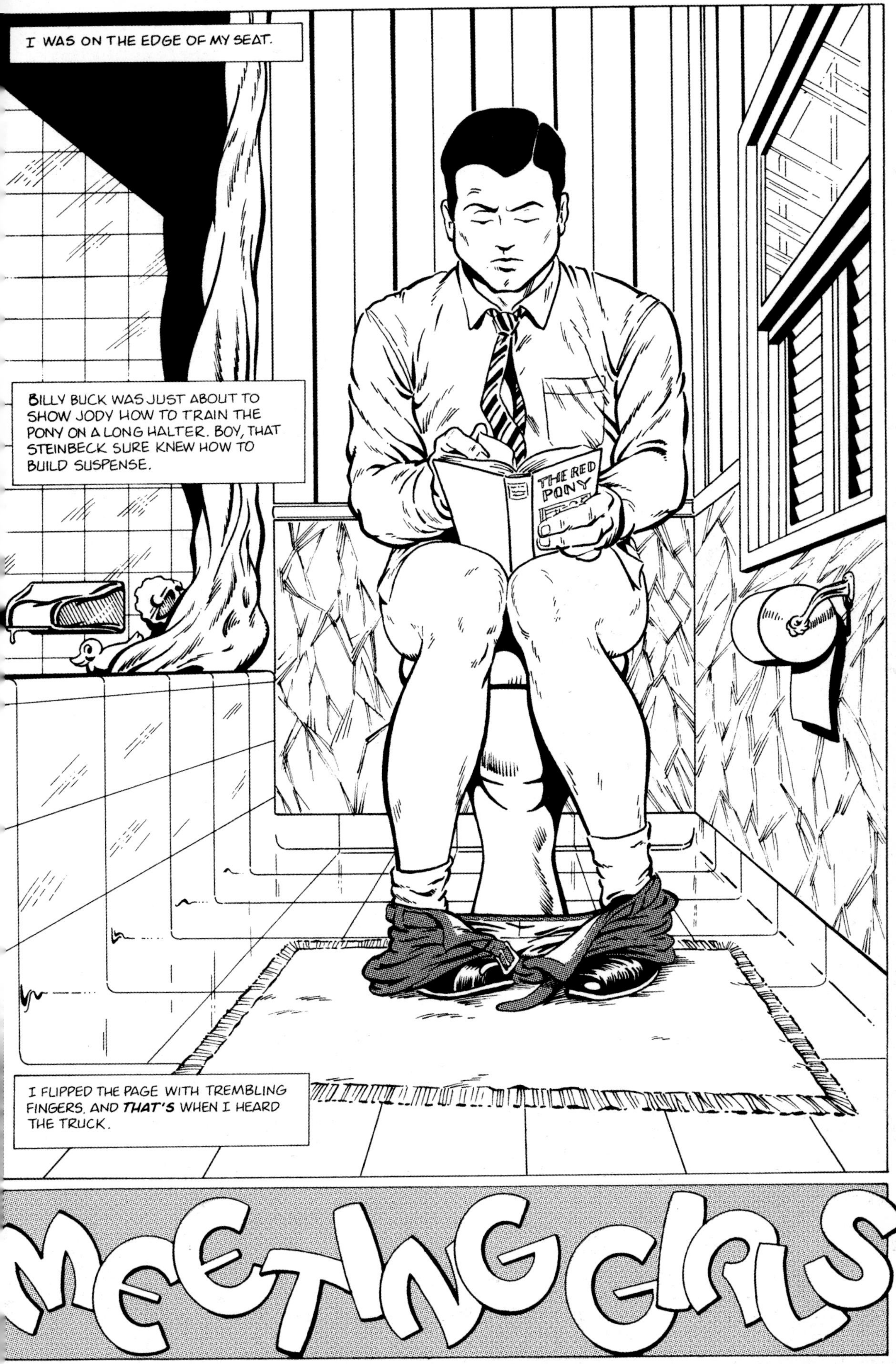
I WAS ON THE EDGE OF MY SEAT.
BILLY BUCK WAS JUST ABOUT TO SHOW JODY HOW TO TRAIN THE PONY ON A LONG HALTER. BOY, THAT STEINBECK SURE KNEW HOW TO BUILD SUSPENSE.
THE RED PONY
I FLIPPED THE PAGE WITH TREMBLING FINGERS, AND *THAT'S* WHEN I HEARD THE TRUCK.
MEETING GIRLS

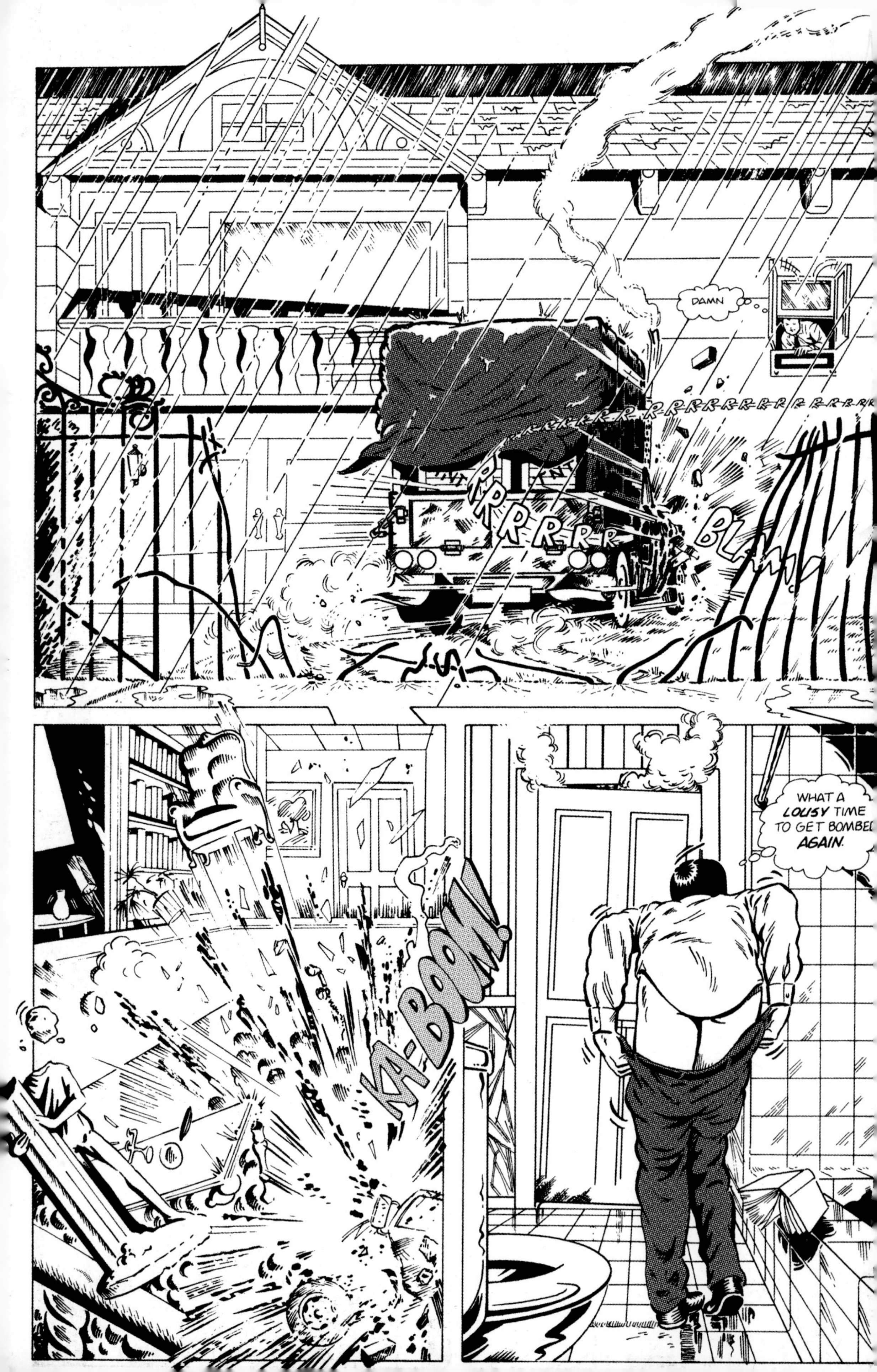
DAMN
RRRRRRR-RRRRRRR
BLAM
KA-BOOM!
WHAT A LOUSY TIME TO GET BOMBED AGAIN.

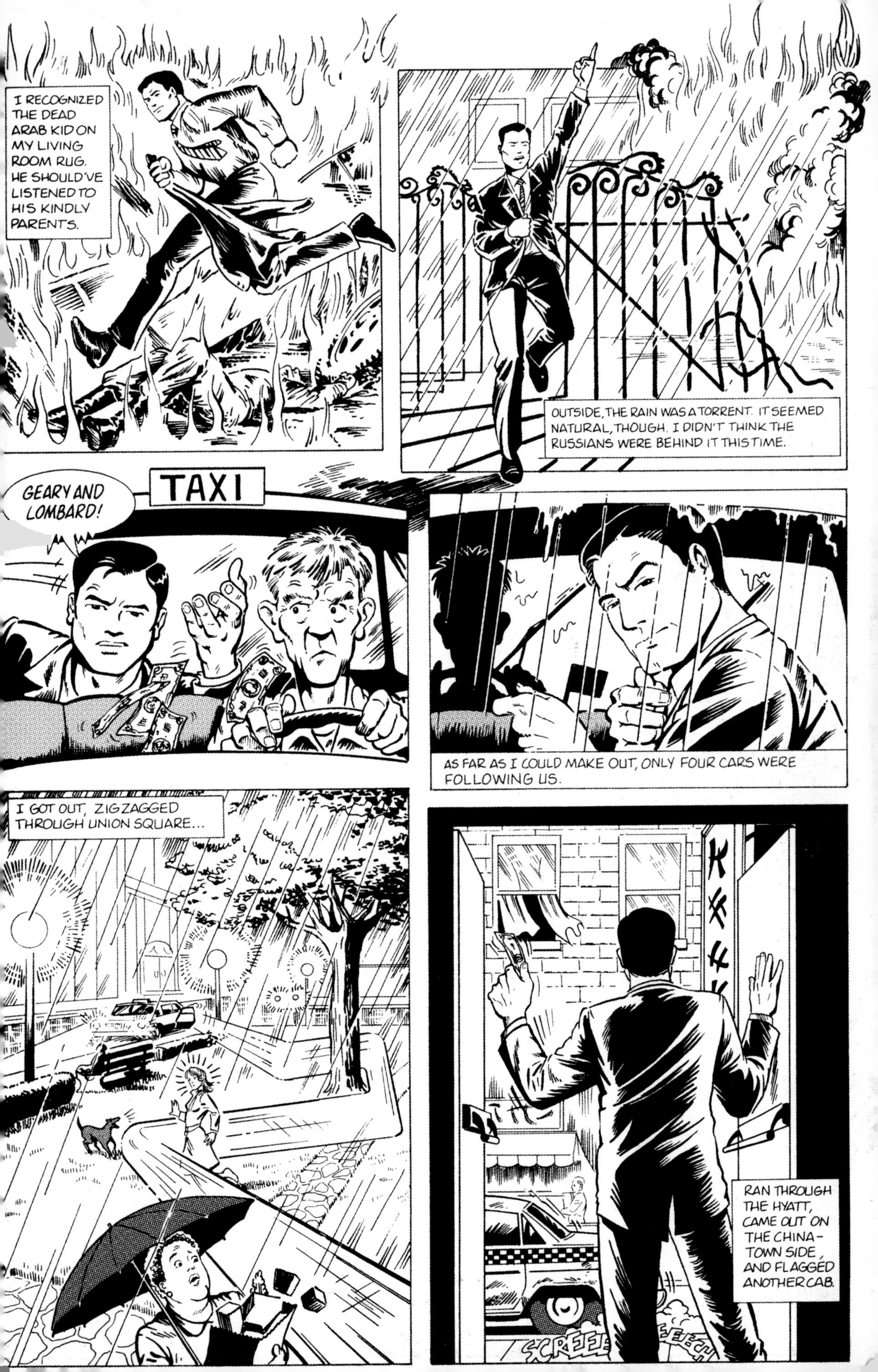
I RECOGNIZED THE DEAD ARAB KID ON MY LIVING ROOM RUG. HE SHOULD'VE LISTENED TO HIS KINDLY PARENTS.
OUTSIDE, THE RAIN WAS A TORRENT. IT SEEMED NATURAL, THOUGH. I DIDN'T THINK THE RUSSIANS WERE BEHIND IT THIS TIME.
GEARY AND LOMBARD!
TAXI
AS FAR AS I COULD MAKE OUT, ONLY FOUR CARS WERE FOLLOWING US.
I GOT OUT, ZIGZAGGED THROUGH UNION SQUARE...
RAN THROUGH THE HYATT, CAME OUT ON THE CHINA-TOWN SIDE, AND FLAGGED ANOTHER CAB.

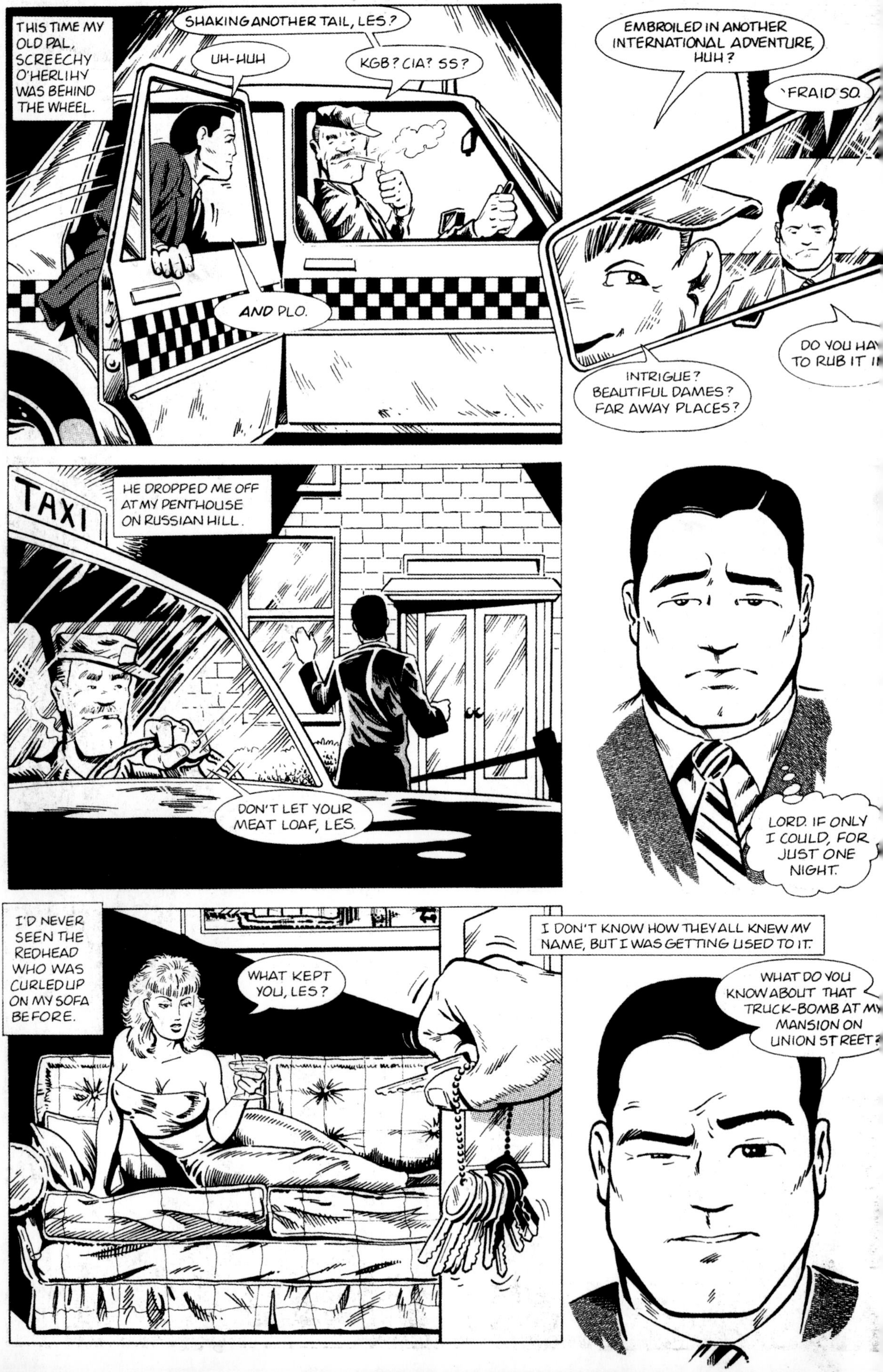
THIS TIME MY OLD PAL, SCREECHY O'HERLIHY WAS BEHIND THE WHEEL.
SHAKING ANOTHER TAIL, LES?
UH-HUH
KGB? CIA? SS?
AND PLO.
EMBROILED IN ANOTHER INTERNATIONAL ADVENTURE, HUH?
`FRAID SO.
INTRIGUE? BEAUTIFUL DAMES? FAR AWAY PLACES?
DO YOU HA
TO RUB IT I
HE DROPPED ME OFF AT MY PENTHOUSE ON RUSSIAN HILL.
TAXI
DON'T LET YOUR MEAT LOAF, LES.
LORD. IF ONLY I COULD, FOR JUST ONE NIGHT.
I'D NEVER SEEN THE REDHEAD WHO WAS CURLED UP ON MY SOFA BEFORE.
WHAT KEPT YOU, LES?
I DON'T KNOW HOW THEY ALL KNEW MY NAME, BUT I WAS GETTING USED TO IT.
WHAT DO YOU KNOW ABOUT THAT TRUCK-BOMB AT MY MANSION ON UNION STREET?

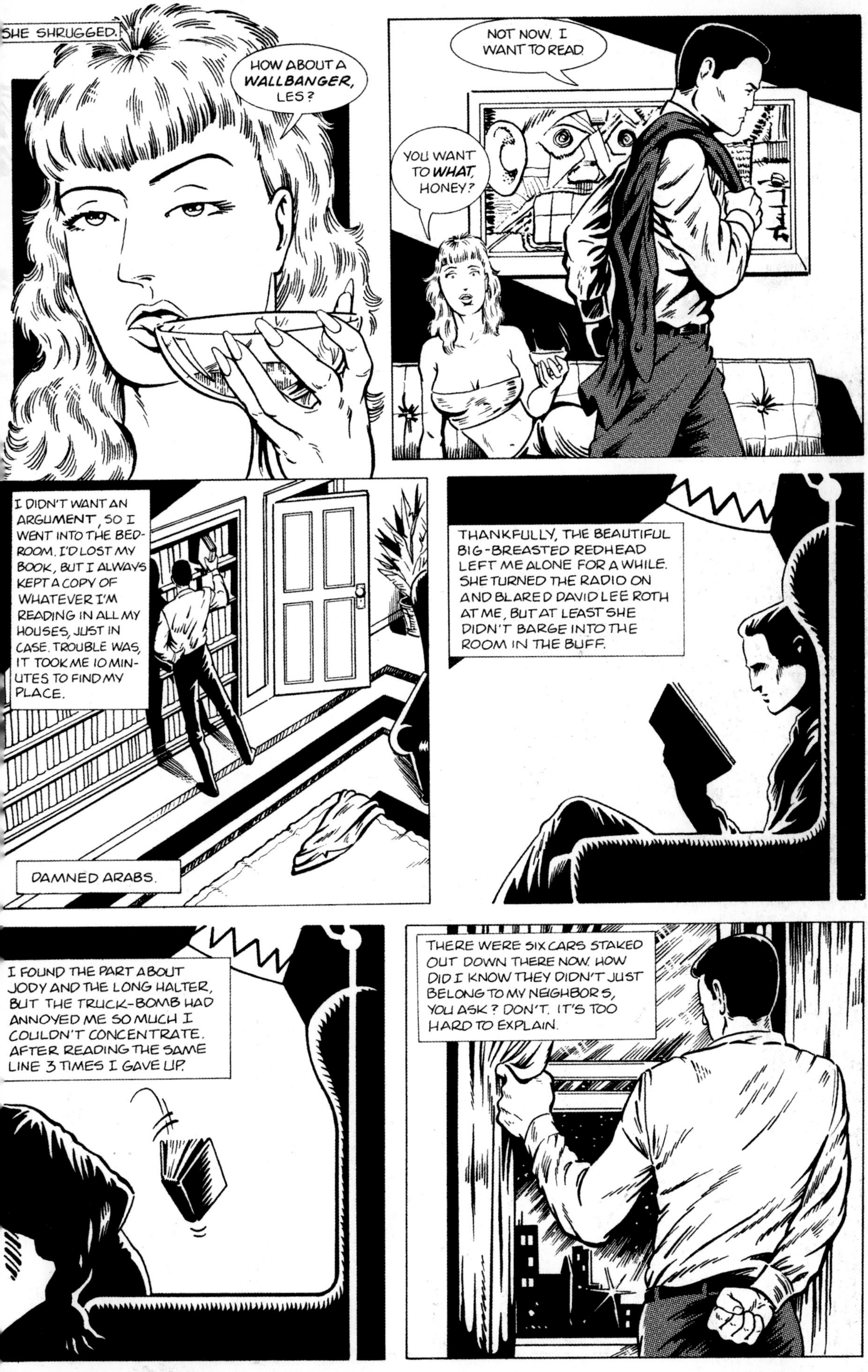
SHE SHRUGGED.
HOW ABOUT A WALLBANGER, LES?
NOT NOW. I WANT TO READ.
YOU WANT TO WHAT, HONEY?
I DIDN'T WANT AN ARGUMENT, SO I WENT INTO THE BEDROOM. I'D LOST MY BOOK, BUT I ALWAYS KEPT A COPY OF WHATEVER I'M READING IN ALL MY HOUSES, JUST IN CASE. TROUBLE WAS, IT TOOK ME 10 MINUTES TO FIND MY PLACE.
DAMNED ARABS.
THANKFULLY, THE BEAUTIFUL BIG-BREASTED REDHEAD LEFT ME ALONE FOR A WHILE. SHE TURNED THE RADIO ON AND BLARED DAVID LEE ROTH AT ME, BUT AT LEAST SHE DIDN'T BARGE INTO THE ROOM IN THE BUFF.
I FOUND THE PART ABOUT JODY AND THE LONG HALTER, BUT THE TRUCK-BOMB HAD ANNOYED ME SO MUCH I COULDN'T CONCENTRATE. AFTER READING THE SAME LINE 3 TIMES I GAVE UP.
THERE WERE SIX CARS STAKED OUT DOWN THERE NOW. HOW DID I KNOW THEY DIDN'T JUST BELONG TO MY NEIGHBORS, YOU ASK? DON'T. IT'S TOO HARD TO EXPLAIN.

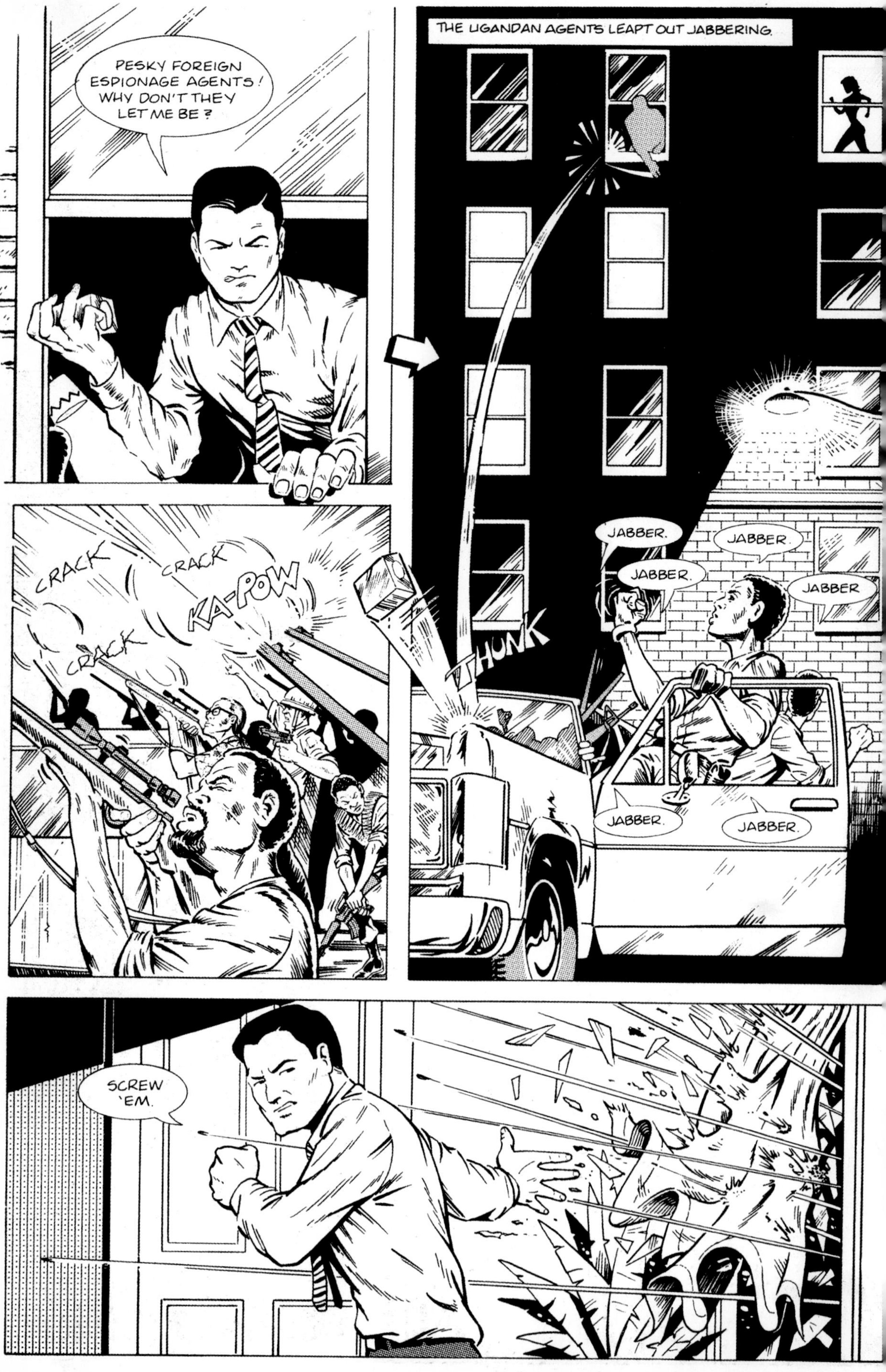

PESKY FOREIGN ESPIONAGE AGENTS! WHY DON'T THEY LET ME BE?
THE UGANDAN AGENTS LEAPT OUT JABBERING.
THUNK
JABBER.
JABBER.
JABBER.
JABBER
JABBER.
JABBER.
CRACK
CRACK
CRACK
KA-POW
SCREW 'EM.

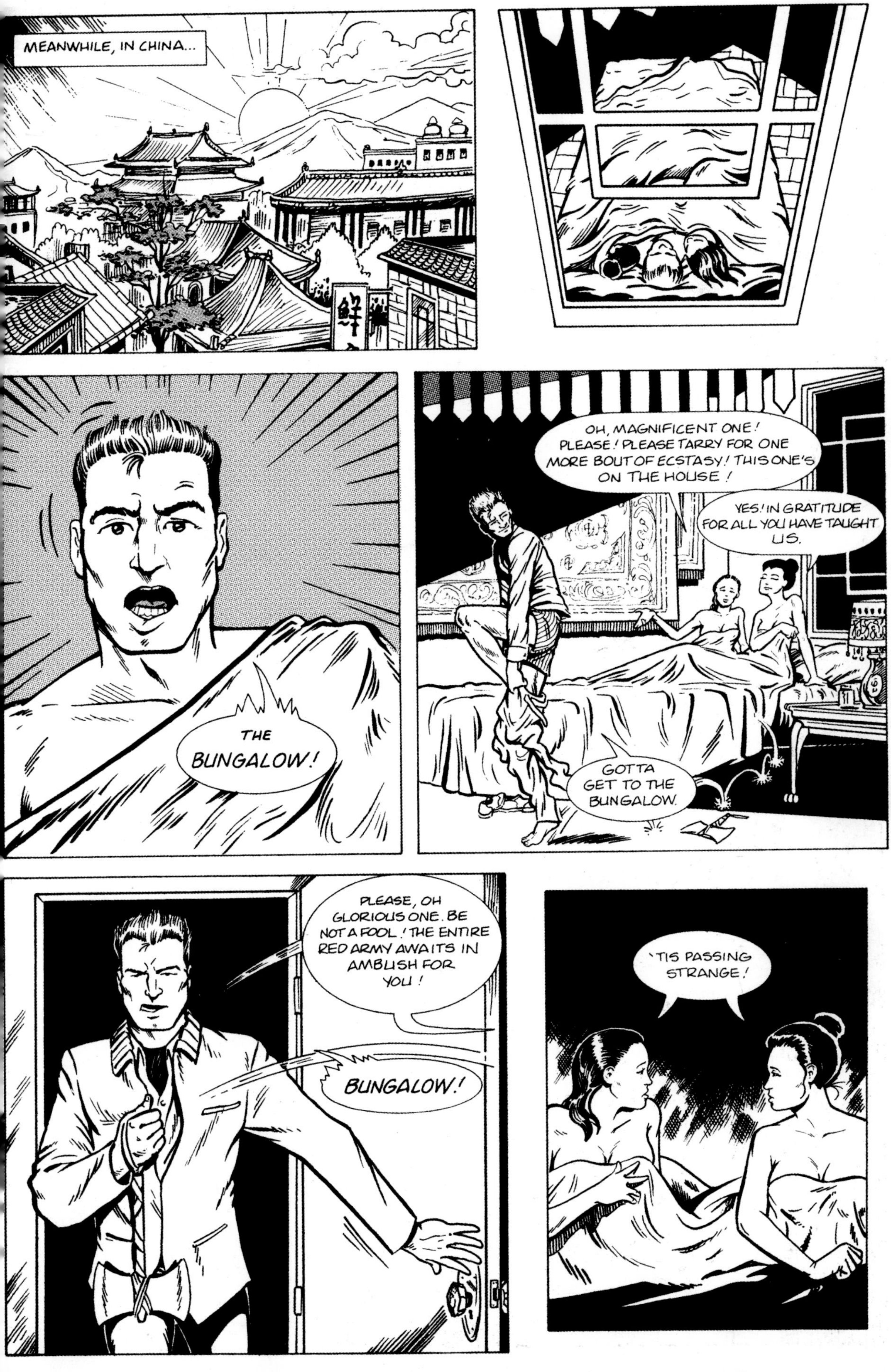

MEANWHILE, IN CHINA...
THE BUNGALOW!
OH, MAGNIFICENT ONE! PLEASE! PLEASE TARRY FOR ONE MORE BOUT OF ECSTASY! THIS ONE'S ON THE HOUSE!
YES! IN GRATITUDE FOR ALL YOU HAVE TAUGHT US.
GOTTA GET TO THE BUNGALOW.
PLEASE, OH GLORIOUS ONE. BE NOT A FOOL! THE ENTIRE RED ARMY AWAITS IN AMBUSH FOR YOU!
BUNGALOW!
'TIS PASSING STRANGE!

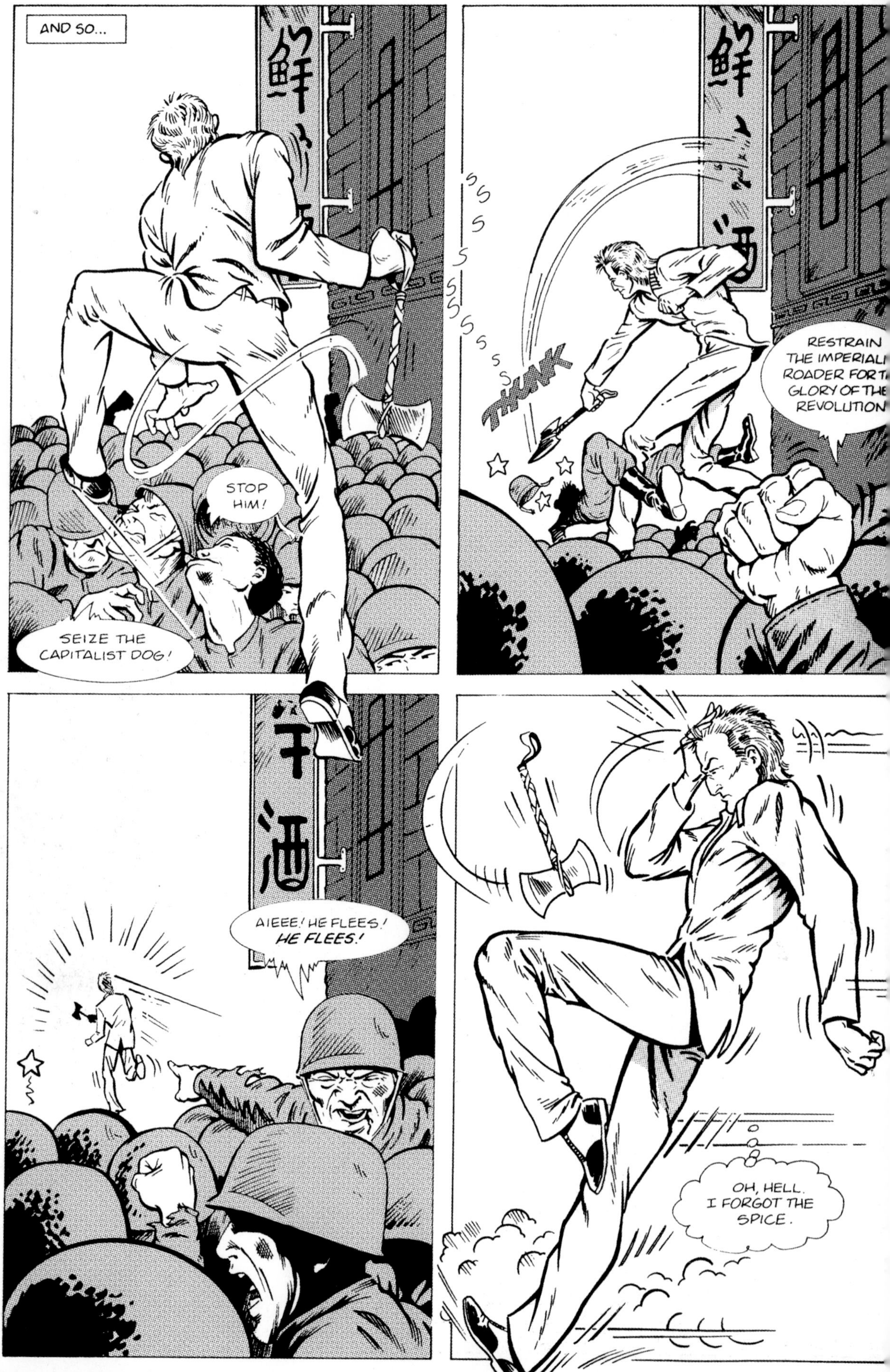
AND SO...
STOP HIM!
SEIZE THE CAPITALIST DOG!
SSSSSSSSSS
THUNK
RESTRAIN THE IMPERIALI ROADER FOR T GLORY OF THE REVOLUTION
AIEEE! HE FLEES! HE FLEES!
OH, HELL. I FORGOT THE SPICE.

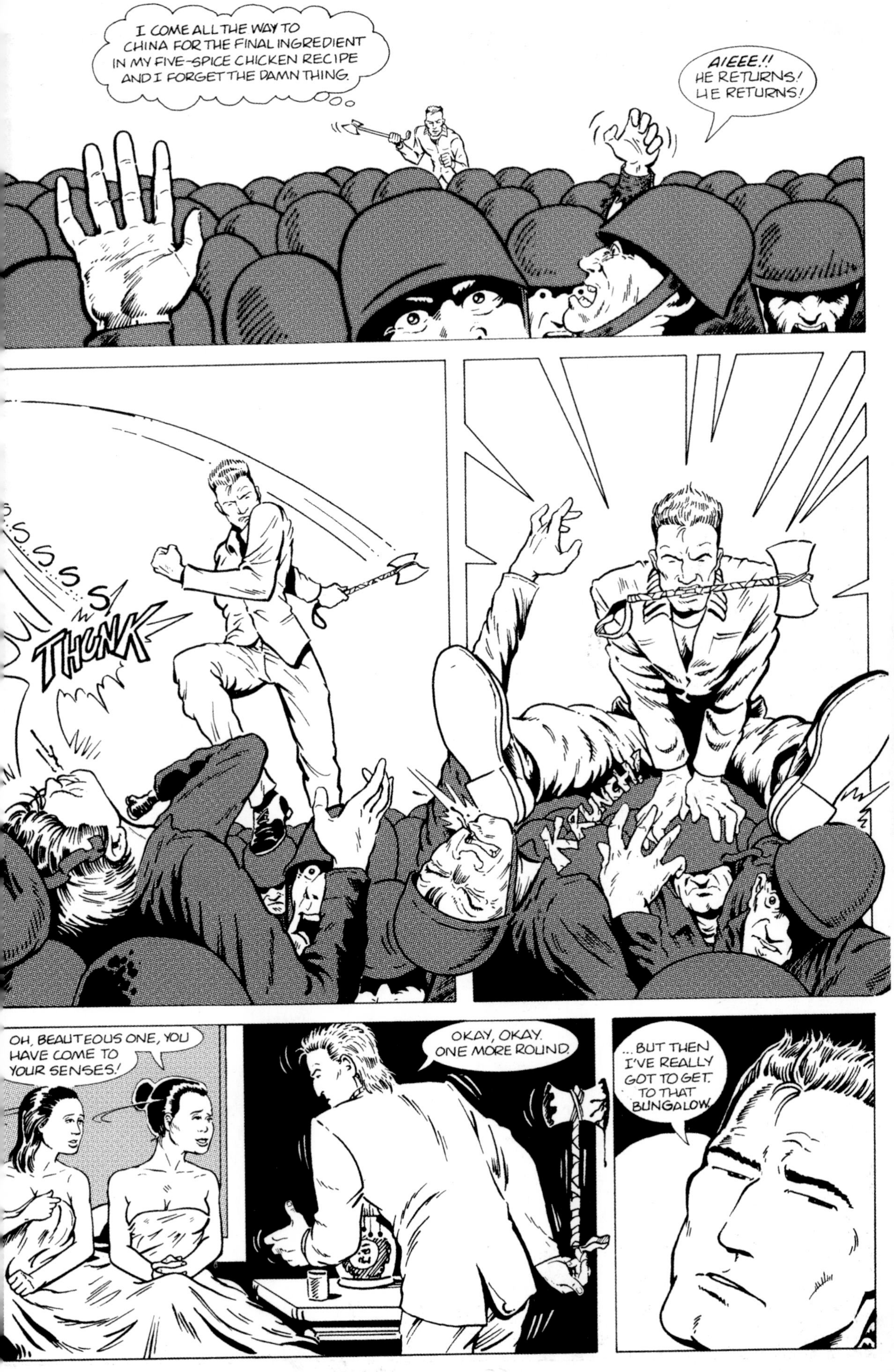

I COME ALL THE WAY TO CHINA FOR THE FINAL INGREDIENT IN MY FIVE-SPICE CHICKEN RECIPE AND I FORGET THE DAMN THING.
AIEEE!! HE RETURNS! HE RETURNS!
SSSSS
THUNK
KRUNCH
OH, BEAUTEOUS ONE, YOU HAVE COME TO YOUR SENSES!
OKAY, OKAY. ONE MORE ROUND.
...BUT THEN I'VE REALLY GOT TO GET TO THAT BUNGALOW.

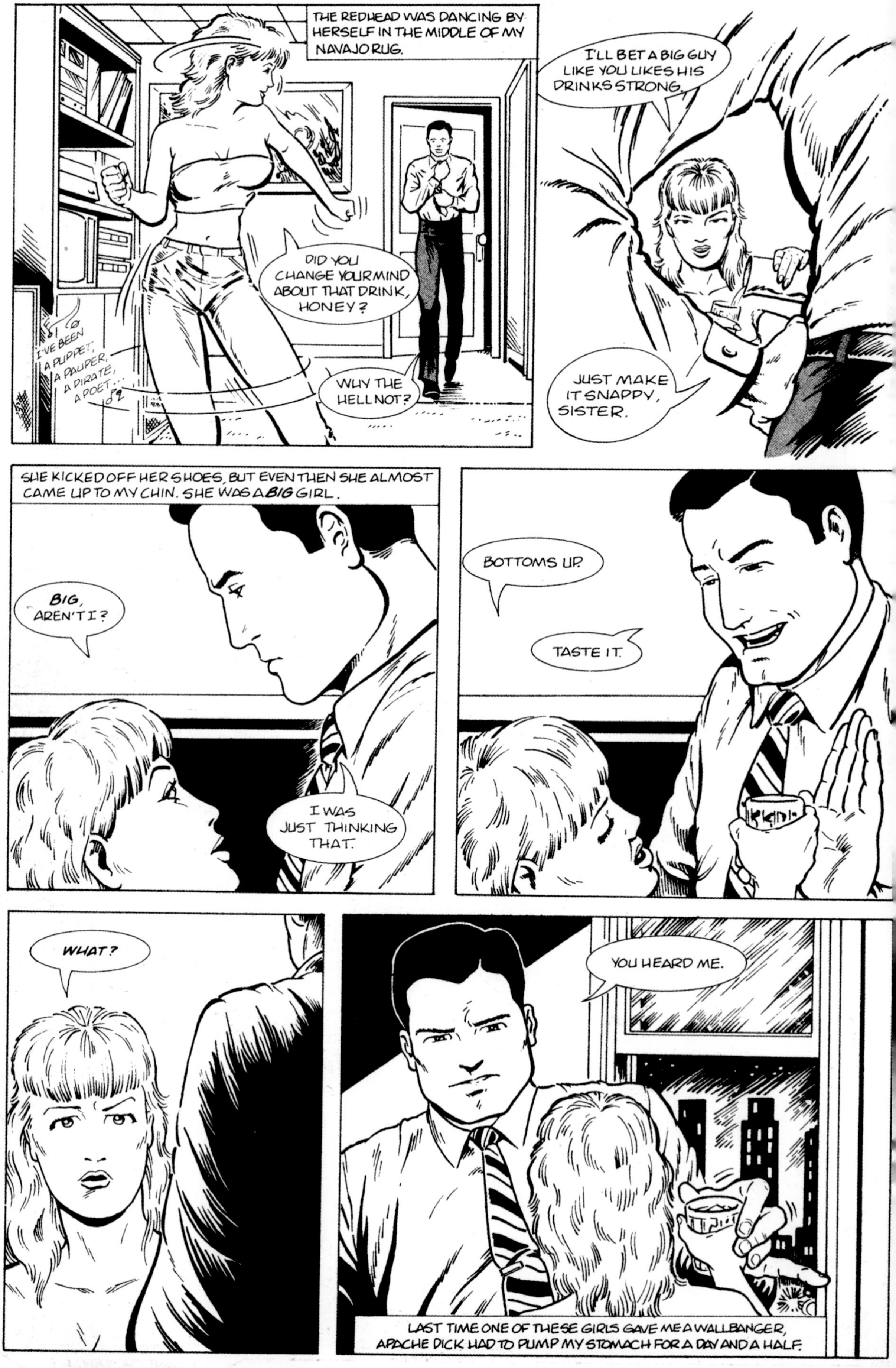
THE REDHEAD WAS DANCING BY HERSELF IN THE MIDDLE OF MY NAVAJO RUG.
I'VE BEEN A PUPPET, A PAUPER, A PIRATE, A POET...
DID YOU CHANGE YOUR MIND ABOUT THAT DRINK, HONEY?
WHY THE HELL NOT?
I'LL BET A BIG GUY LIKE YOU LIKES HIS DRINKS STRONG.
JUST MAKE IT SNAPPY, SISTER.
SHE KICKED OFF HER SHOES, BUT EVEN THEN SHE ALMOST CAME UP TO MY CHIN. SHE WAS A BIG GIRL.
BIG, AREN'T I?
I WAS JUST THINKING THAT.
BOTTOMS UP.
TASTE IT.
WHAT?
YOU HEARD ME.
LAST TIME ONE OF THESE GIRLS GAVE ME A WALLBANGER, APACHE DICK HAD TO PUMP MY STOMACH FOR A DAY AND A HALF.

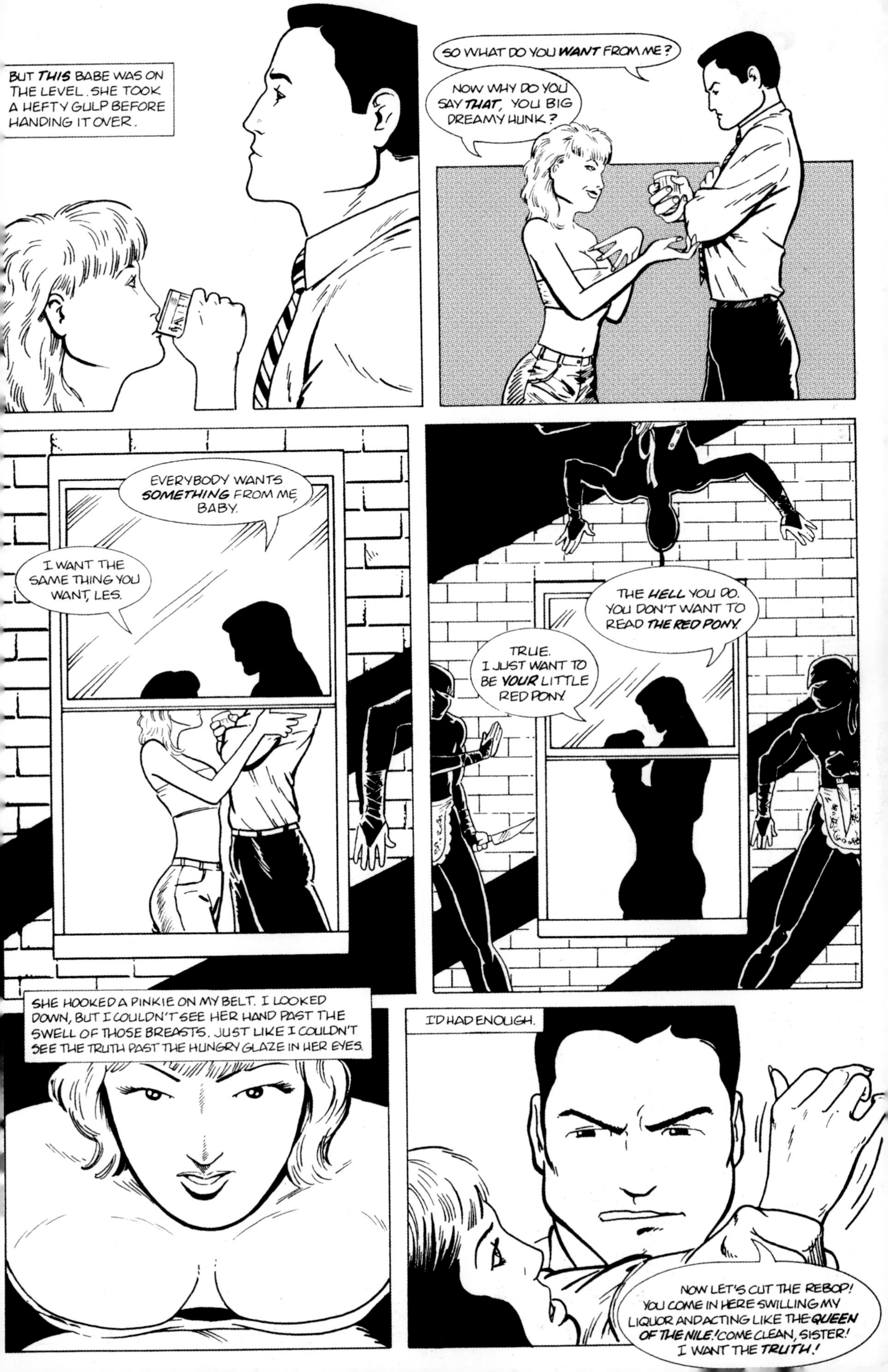
BUT THIS BABE WAS ON THE LEVEL. SHE TOOK A HEFTY GULP BEFORE HANDING IT OVER.
SO WHAT DO YOU WANT FROM ME?
NOW WHY DO YOU SAY THAT, YOU BIG DREAMY HUNK?
EVERYBODY WANTS SOMETHING FROM ME, BABY.
I WANT THE SAME THING YOU WANT, LES.
THE HELL YOU DO. YOU DON'T WANT TO READ THE RED PONY.
TRUE. I JUST WANT TO BE YOUR LITTLE RED PONY.
SHE HOOKED A PINKIE ON MY BELT. I LOOKED DOWN, BUT I COULDN'T SEE HER HAND PAST THE SWELL OF THOSE BREASTS. JUST LIKE I COULDN'T SEE THE TRUTH PAST THE HUNGRY GLAZE IN HER EYES.
I'D HAD ENOUGH.
NOW LET'S CUT THE REBOP! YOU COME IN HERE SWILLING MY LIQUOR AND ACTING LIKE THE QUEEN OF THE NILE! COME CLEAN, SISTER! I WANT THE TRUTH!

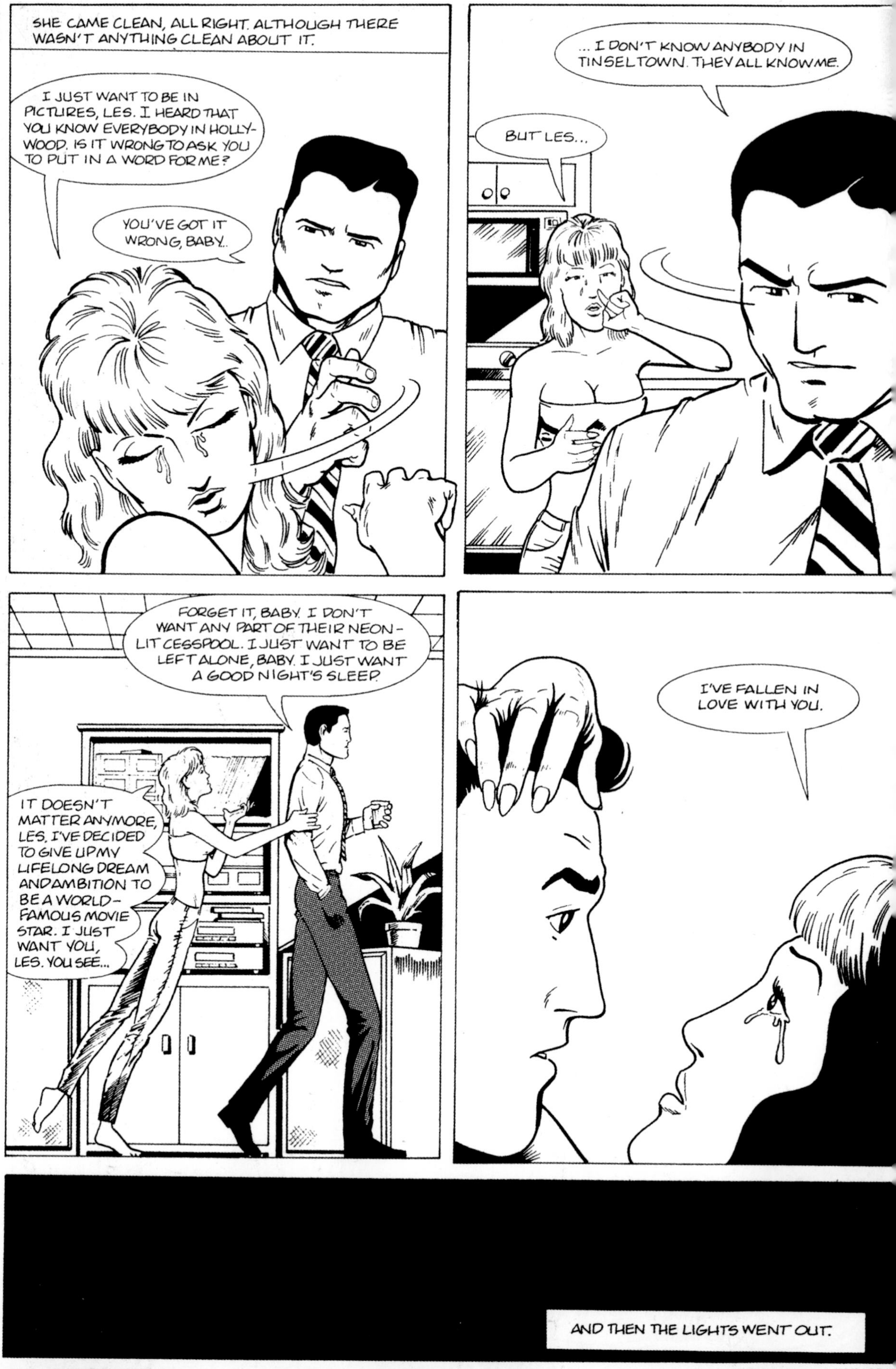
SHE CAME CLEAN, ALL RIGHT. ALTHOUGH THERE WASN'T ANYTHING CLEAN ABOUT IT.
I JUST WANT TO BE IN PICTURES, LES. I HEARD THAT YOU KNOW EVERYBODY IN HOLLY-WOOD. IS IT WRONG TO ASK YOU TO PUT IN A WORD FOR ME?
YOU'VE GOT IT WRONG, BABY...
... I DON'T KNOW ANYBODY IN TINSELTOWN. THEY ALL KNOW ME.
BUT LES...
FORGET IT, BABY. I DON'T WANT ANY PART OF THEIR NEON-LIT CESSPOOL. I JUST WANT TO BE LEFT ALONE, BABY. I JUST WANT A GOOD NIGHT'S SLEEP.
IT DOESN'T MATTER ANYMORE, LES. I'VE DECIDED TO GIVE UP MY LIFELONG DREAM AND AMBITION TO BE A WORLD-FAMOUS MOVIE STAR. I JUST WANT YOU, LES. YOU SEE...
I'VE FALLEN IN LOVE WITH YOU.
AND THEN THE LIGHTS WENT OUT.

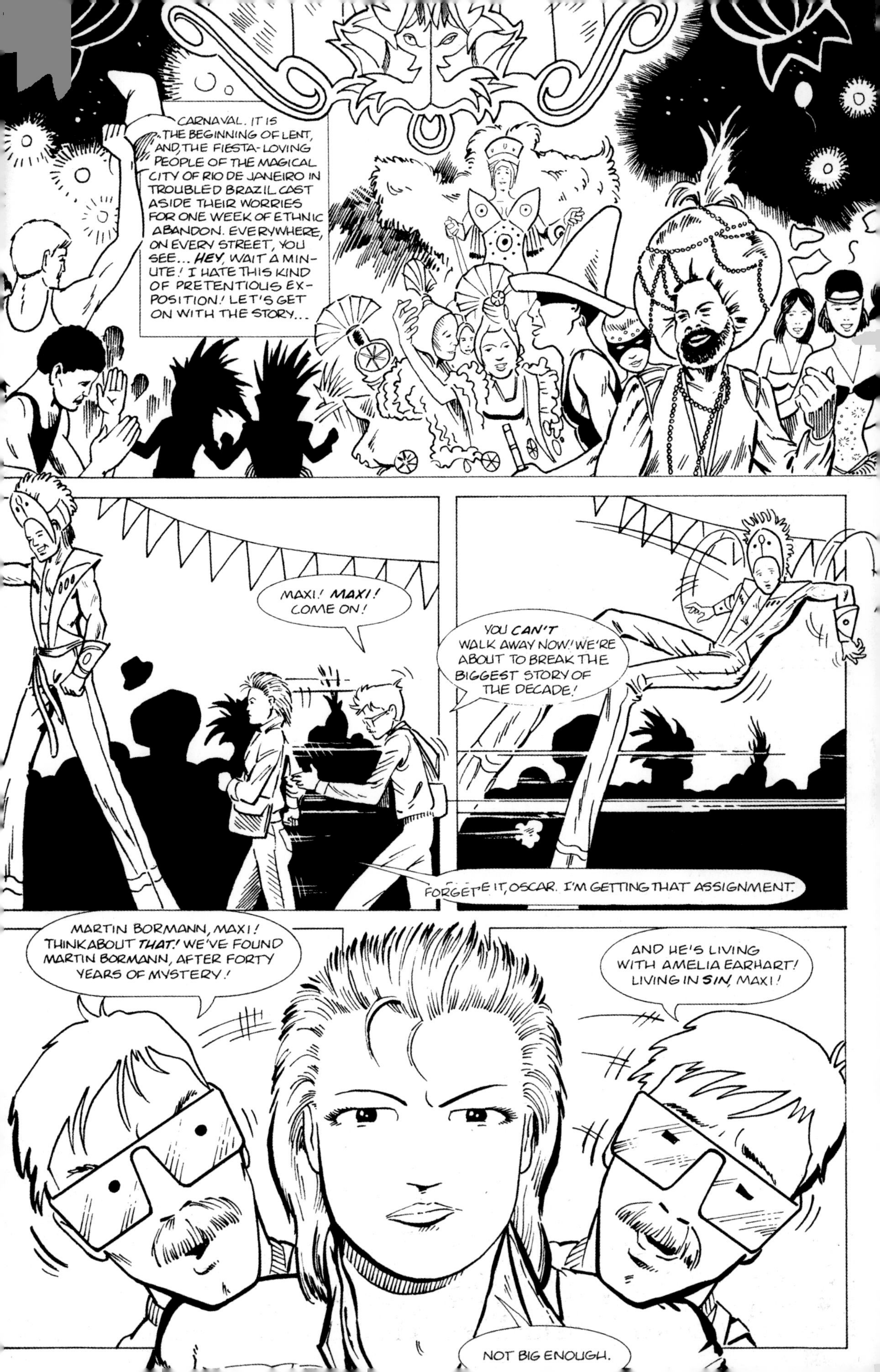

CARNAVAL. IT IS THE BEGINNING OF LENT, AND THE FIESTA-LOVING PEOPLE OF THE MAGICAL CITY OF RIO DE JANEIRO IN TROUBLED BRAZIL CAST ASIDE THEIR WORRIES FOR ONE WEEK OF ETHNIC ABANDON. EVERYWHERE, ON EVERY STREET, YOU SEE... HEY, WAIT A MINUTE! I HATE THIS KIND OF PRETENTIOUS EXPOSITION! LET'S GET ON WITH THE STORY...
MAXI! MAXI! COME ON!
YOU CAN'T WALK AWAY NOW! WE'RE ABOUT TO BREAK THE BIGGEST STORY OF THE DECADE!
FORGET IT, OSCAR. I'M GETTING THAT ASSIGNMENT.
MARTIN BORMANN, MAXI! THINKABOUT THAT! WE'VE FOUND MARTIN BORMANN, AFTER FORTY YEARS OF MYSTERY!
AND HE'S LIVING WITH AMELIA EARHART! LIVING IN SIN, MAXI!
NOT BIG ENOUGH.

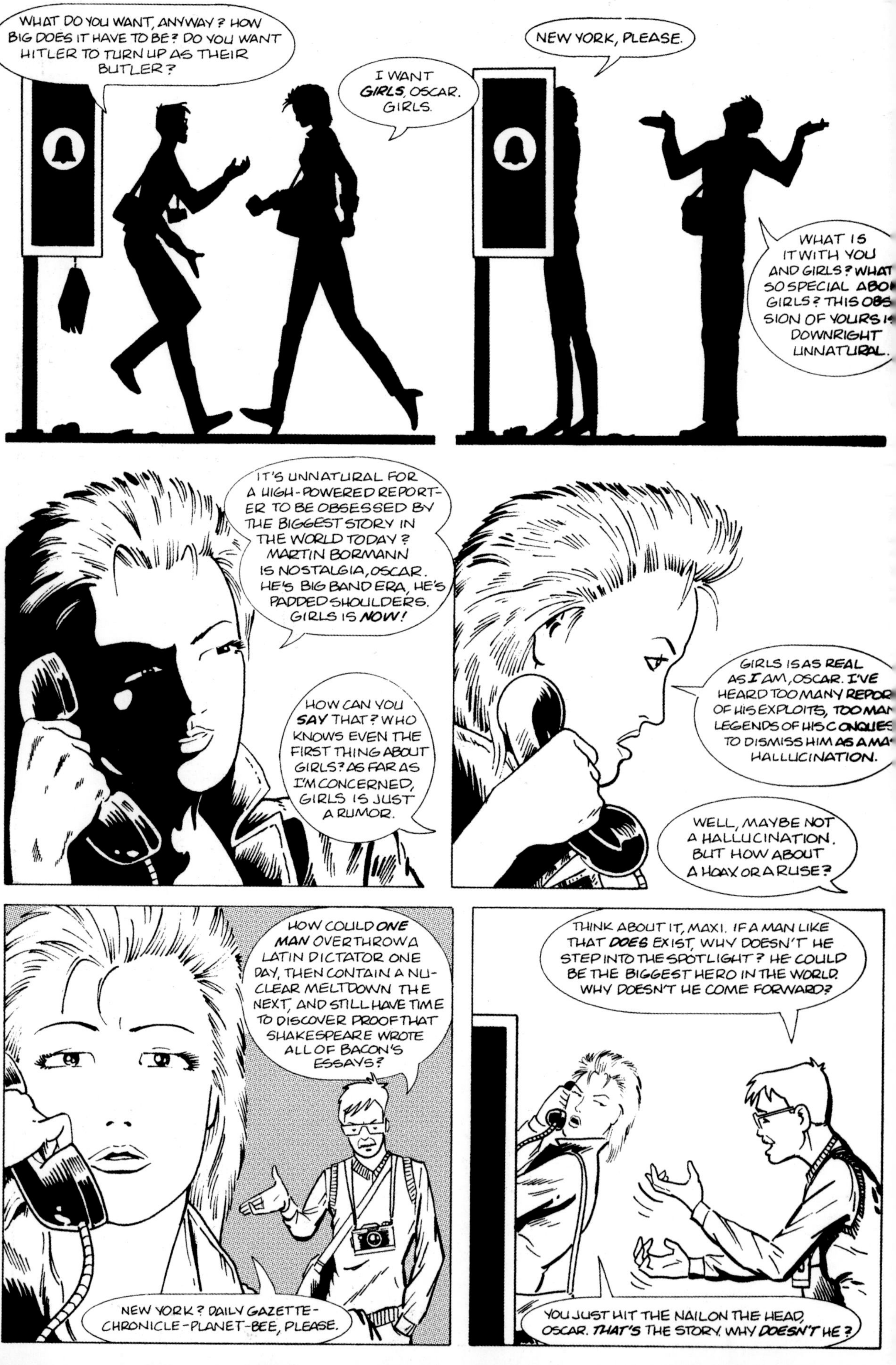
WHAT DO YOU WANT, ANYWAY? HOW BIG DOES IT HAVE TO BE? DO YOU WANT HITLER TO TURN UP AS THEIR BUTLER?
I WANT **GIRLS**, OSCAR. GIRLS.
NEW YORK, PLEASE.
WHAT IS IT WITH YOU AND GIRLS? **WHAT** SO SPECIAL **ABO** GIRLS? THIS **OBS** SION OF **YOURS I** DOWNRIGHT UNNATURAL.
IT'S UNNATURAL FOR A HIGH-POWERED REPORTER TO BE OBSESSED BY THE BIGGEST STORY IN THE WORLD TODAY? MARTIN BORMANN IS NOSTALGIA, OSCAR. HE'S BIG BAND ERA, HE'S PADDED SHOULDERS. GIRLS IS **NOW!**
HOW CAN YOU **SAY** THAT? WHO KNOWS EVEN THE FIRST THING ABOUT GIRLS? AS FAR AS I'M CONCERNED, GIRLS IS JUST A RUMOR.
GIRLS IS AS **REAL** AS **I** AM, OSCAR. **I'VE** HEARD TOO MANY **REPOR** OF HIS EXPLOITS, **TOO MAN** LEGENDS OF HIS **CONQUES** TO DISMISS HIM **AS A MA** HALLUCINATION.
WELL, MAYBE NOT A HALLUCINATION. BUT HOW ABOUT A HOAX OR A RUSE?
HOW COULD **ONE MAN** OVERTHROW A LATIN DICTATOR ONE DAY, THEN CONTAIN A NUCLEAR MELTDOWN THE NEXT, AND STILL HAVE TIME TO DISCOVER PROOF THAT SHAKESPEARE WROTE ALL OF BACON'S ESSAYS?
NEW YORK? DAILY GAZETTE-CHRONICLE-PLANET-BEE, PLEASE.
THINK ABOUT IT, MAXI. IF A MAN LIKE THAT **DOES** EXIST, WHY DOESN'T HE STEP INTO THE SPOTLIGHT? HE COULD BE THE BIGGEST HERO IN THE WORLD. WHY DOESN'T HE COME FORWARD?
YOU JUST HIT THE NAIL ON THE HEAD, OSCAR. **THAT'S** THE STORY. WHY **DOESN'T** HE?

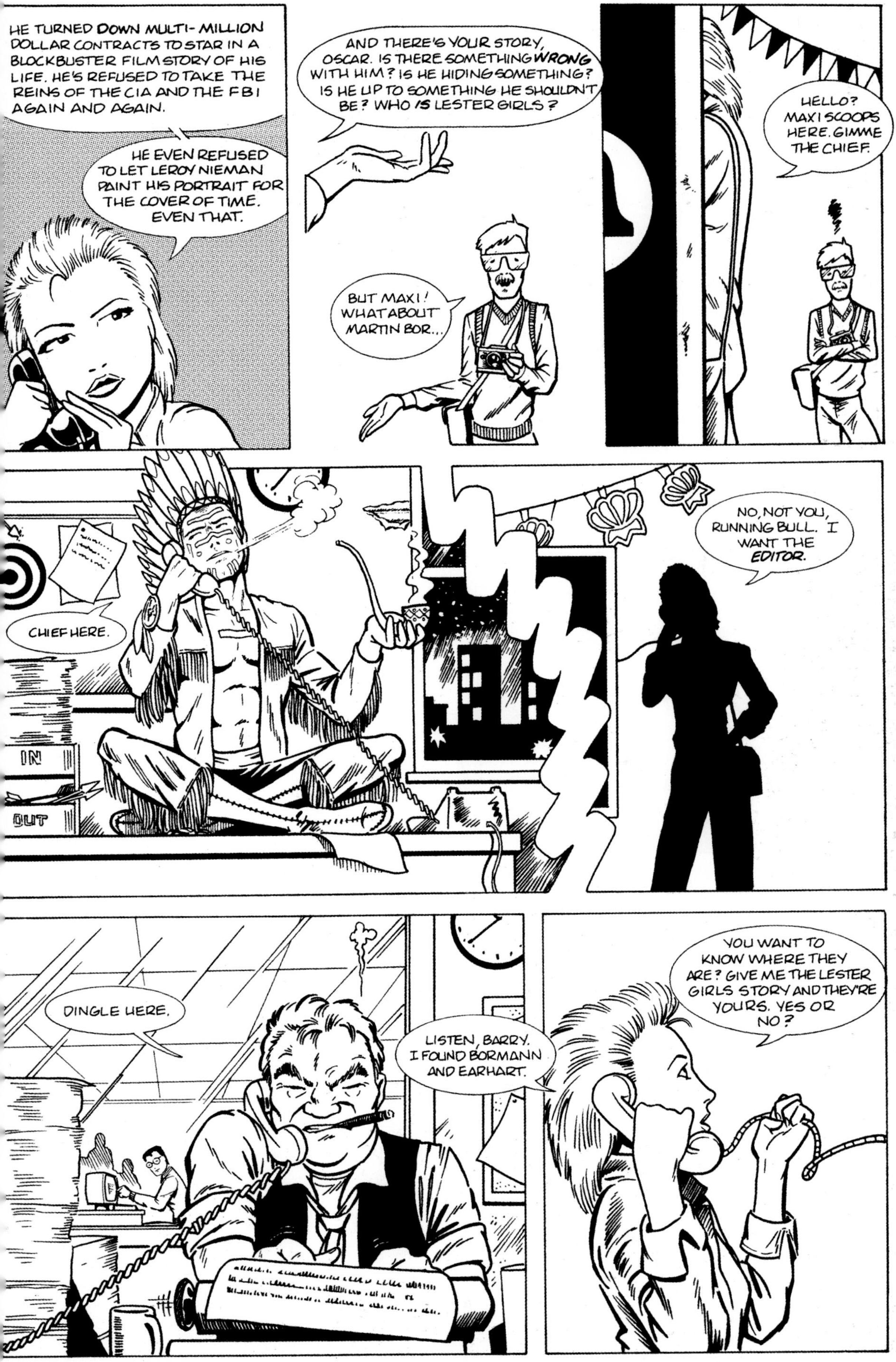
HE TURNED DOWN MULTI-MILLION DOLLAR CONTRACTS TO STAR IN A BLOCKBUSTER FILM STORY OF HIS LIFE. HE'S REFUSED TO TAKE THE REINS OF THE CIA AND THE FBI AGAIN AND AGAIN.
HE EVEN REFUSED TO LET LEROY NIEMAN PAINT HIS PORTRAIT FOR THE COVER OF TIME. EVEN THAT.
AND THERE'S YOUR STORY, OSCAR. IS THERE SOMETHING WRONG WITH HIM? IS HE HIDING SOMETHING? IS HE UP TO SOMETHING HE SHOULDN'T BE? WHO IS LESTER GIRLS?
BUT MAXI! WHAT ABOUT MARTIN BOR...
HELLO? MAXI SCOOPS HERE. GIMME THE CHIEF.
CHIEF HERE.
IN
OUT
NO, NOT YOU, RUNNING BULL. I WANT THE EDITOR.
DINGLE HERE.
LISTEN, BARRY. I FOUND BORMANN AND EARHART.
YOU WANT TO KNOW WHERE THEY ARE? GIVE ME THE LESTER GIRLS STORY AND THEY'RE YOURS. YES OR NO?

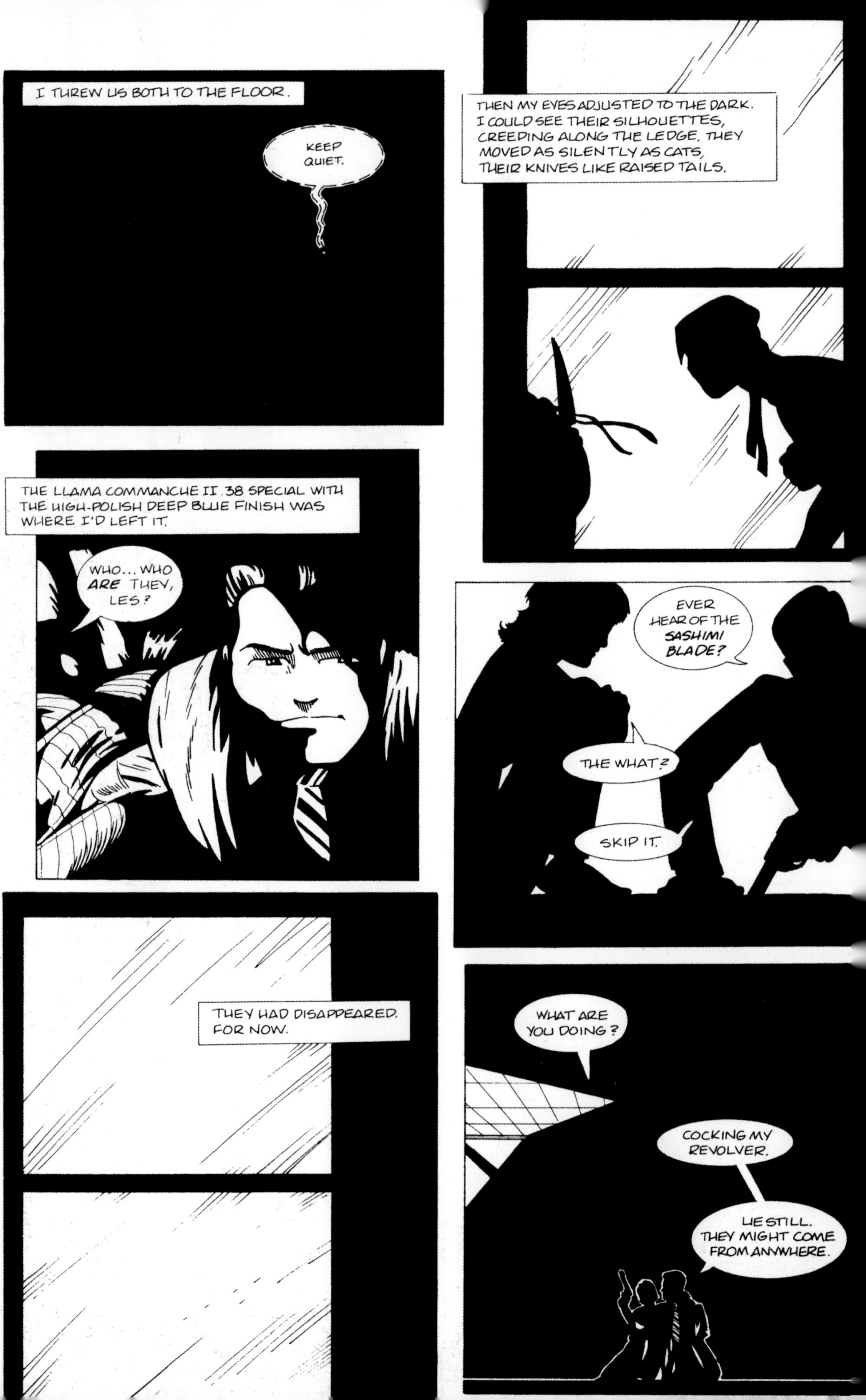
I THREW US BOTH TO THE FLOOR.
KEEP QUIET.
THEN MY EYES ADJUSTED TO THE DARK. I COULD SEE THEIR SILHOUETTES, CREEPING ALONG THE LEDGE. THEY MOVED AS SILENTLY AS CATS, THEIR KNIVES LIKE RAISED TAILS.
THE LLAMA COMMANCHE II .38 SPECIAL WITH THE HIGH-POLISH DEEP BLUE FINISH WAS WHERE I'D LEFT IT.
WHO... WHO ARE THEY, LES?
EVER HEAR OF THE SASHIMI BLADE?
THE WHAT?
SKIP IT.
THEY HAD DISAPPEARED. FOR NOW.
WHAT ARE YOU DOING?
COCKING MY REVOLVER.
LIE STILL. THEY MIGHT COME FROM ANWHERE.

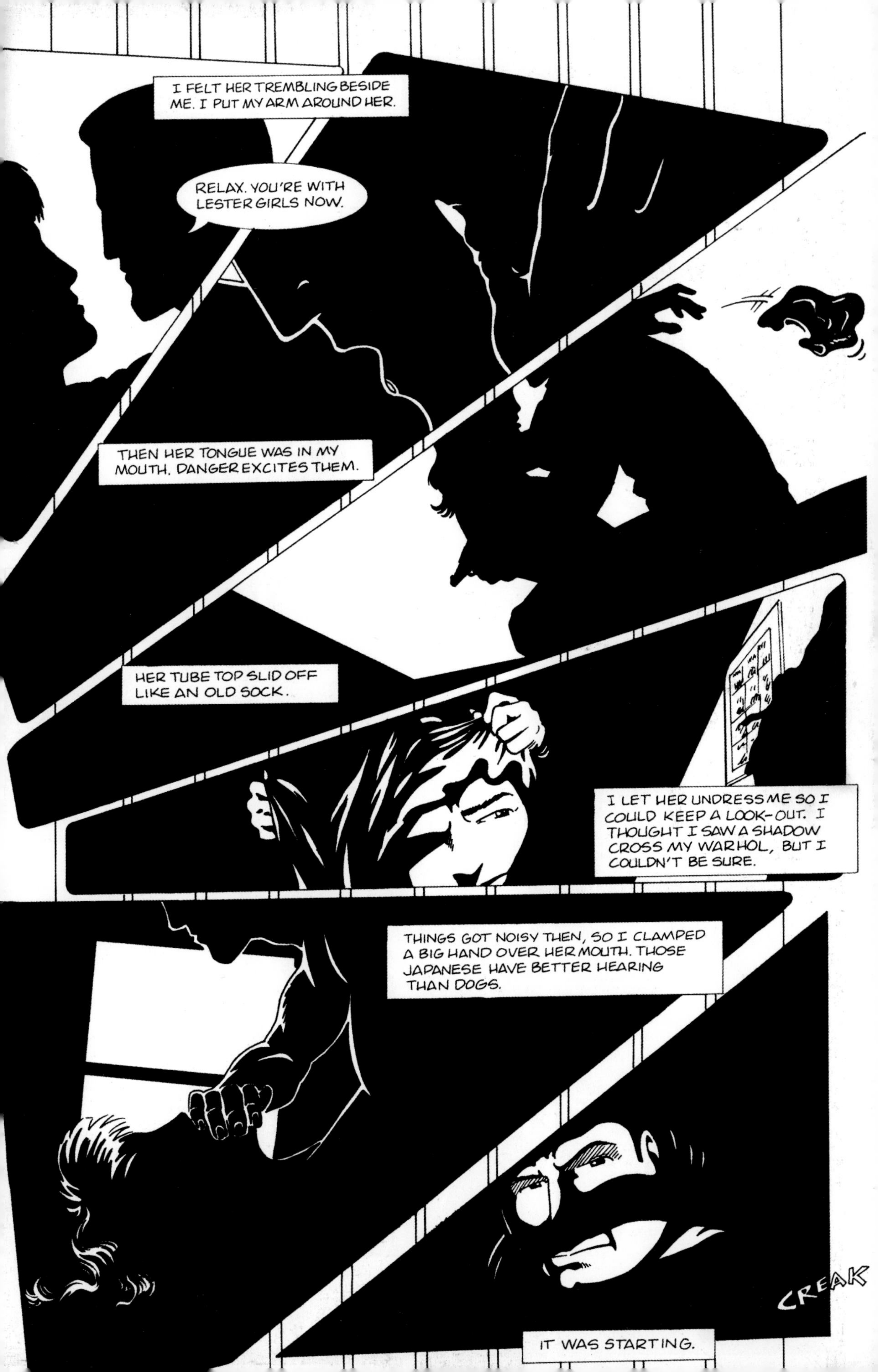
I FELT HER TREMBLING BESIDE ME. I PUT MY ARM AROUND HER.
RELAX. YOU'RE WITH LESTER GIRLS NOW.
THEN HER TONGUE WAS IN MY MOUTH. DANGER EXCITES THEM.
HER TUBE TOP SLID OFF LIKE AN OLD SOCK.
I LET HER UNDRESS ME SO I COULD KEEP A LOOK-OUT. I THOUGHT I SAW A SHADOW CROSS MY WARHOL, BUT I COULDN'T BE SURE.
THINGS GOT NOISY THEN, SO I CLAMPED A BIG HAND OVER HER MOUTH. THOSE JAPANESE HAVE BETTER HEARING THAN DOGS.
CREAK
IT WAS STARTING.

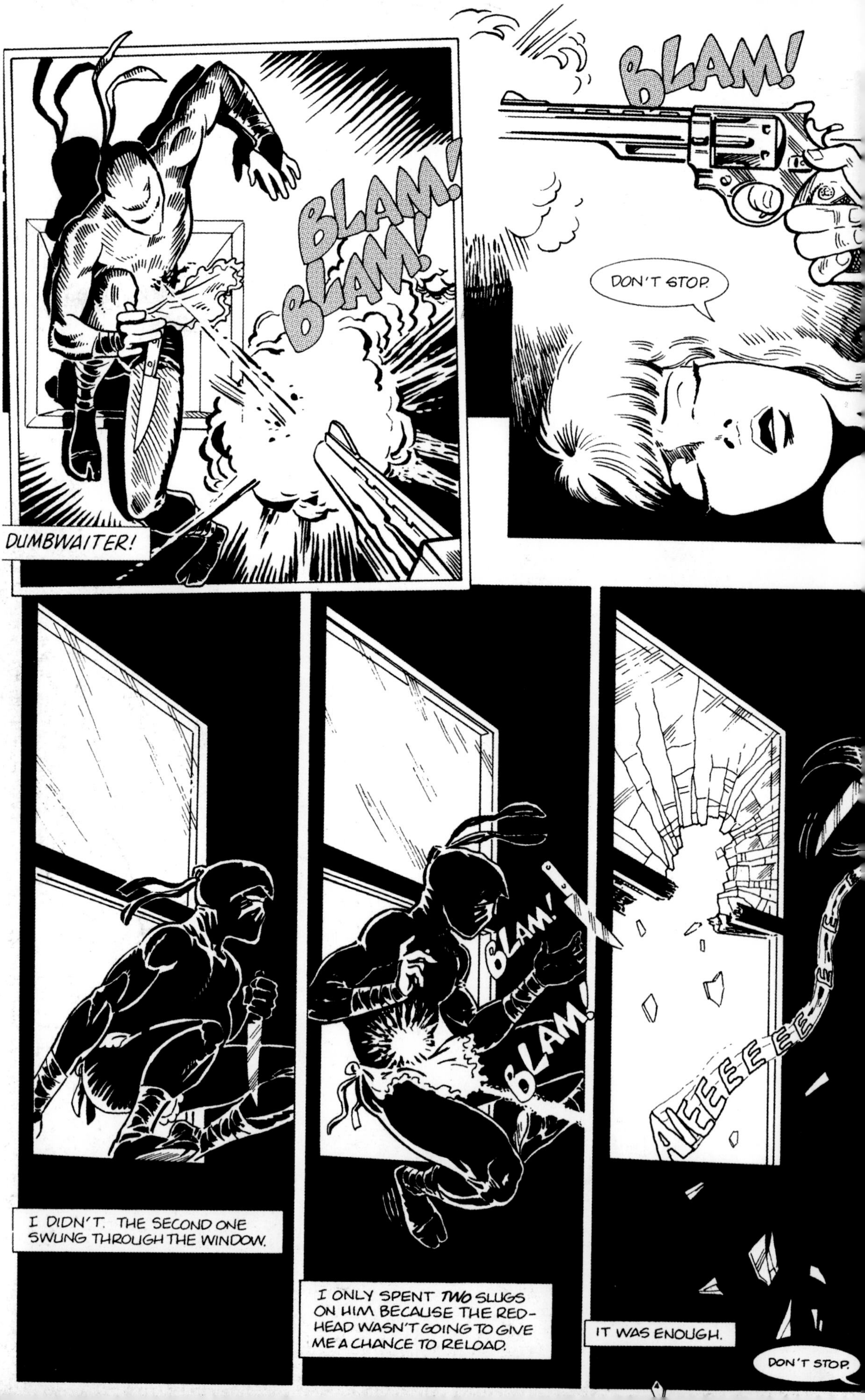

BLAM!
BLAM!
DUMBWAITER!
BLAM!
DON'T STOP.
I DIDN'T. THE SECOND ONE SWUNG THROUGH THE WINDOW.
BLAM!
BLAM!
I ONLY SPENT TWO SLUGS ON HIM BECAUSE THE RED-HEAD WASN'T GOING TO GIVE ME A CHANCE TO RELOAD.
AIEEEEEEEEE
IT WAS ENOUGH.
DON'T STOP.

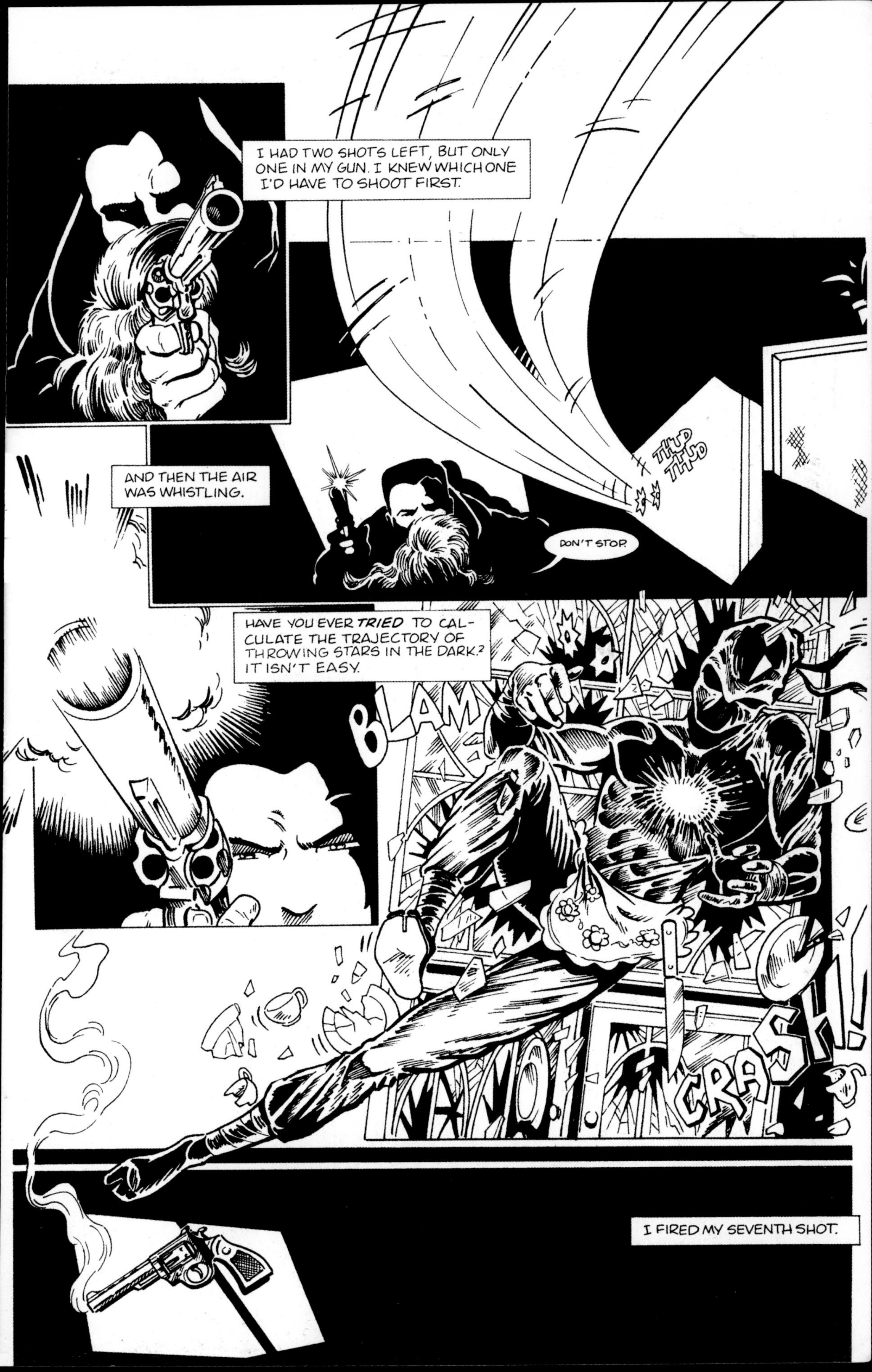
I HAD TWO SHOTS LEFT, BUT ONLY ONE IN MY GUN. I KNEW WHICH ONE I'D HAVE TO SHOOT FIRST.
AND THEN THE AIR WAS WHISTLING.
THUD THUD
DON'T STOP.
HAVE YOU EVER TRIED TO CALCULATE THE TRAJECTORY OF THROWING STARS IN THE DARK? IT ISN'T EASY.
BLAM
CRASH!
I FIRED MY SEVENTH SHOT.

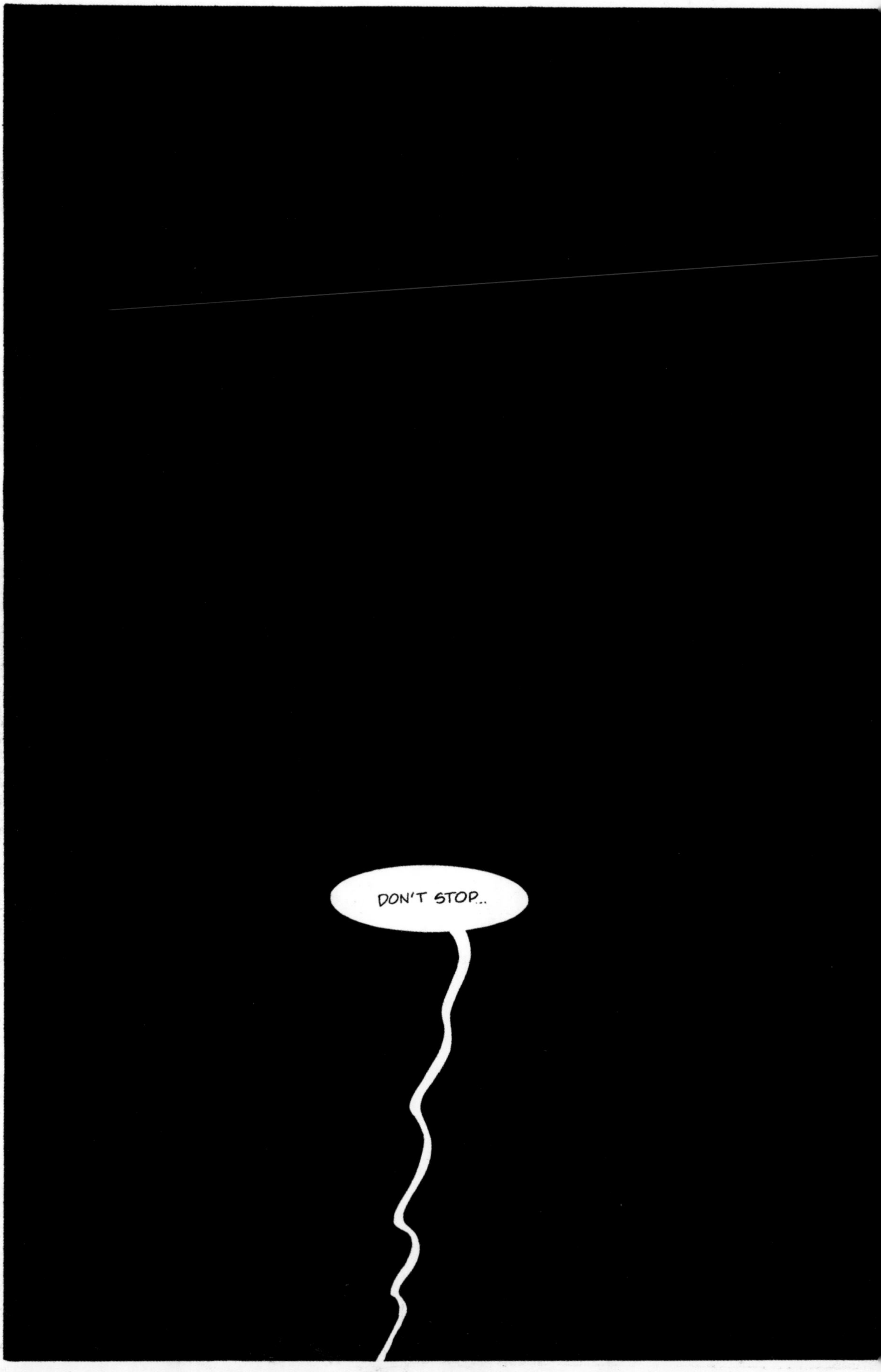
DON'T STOP..

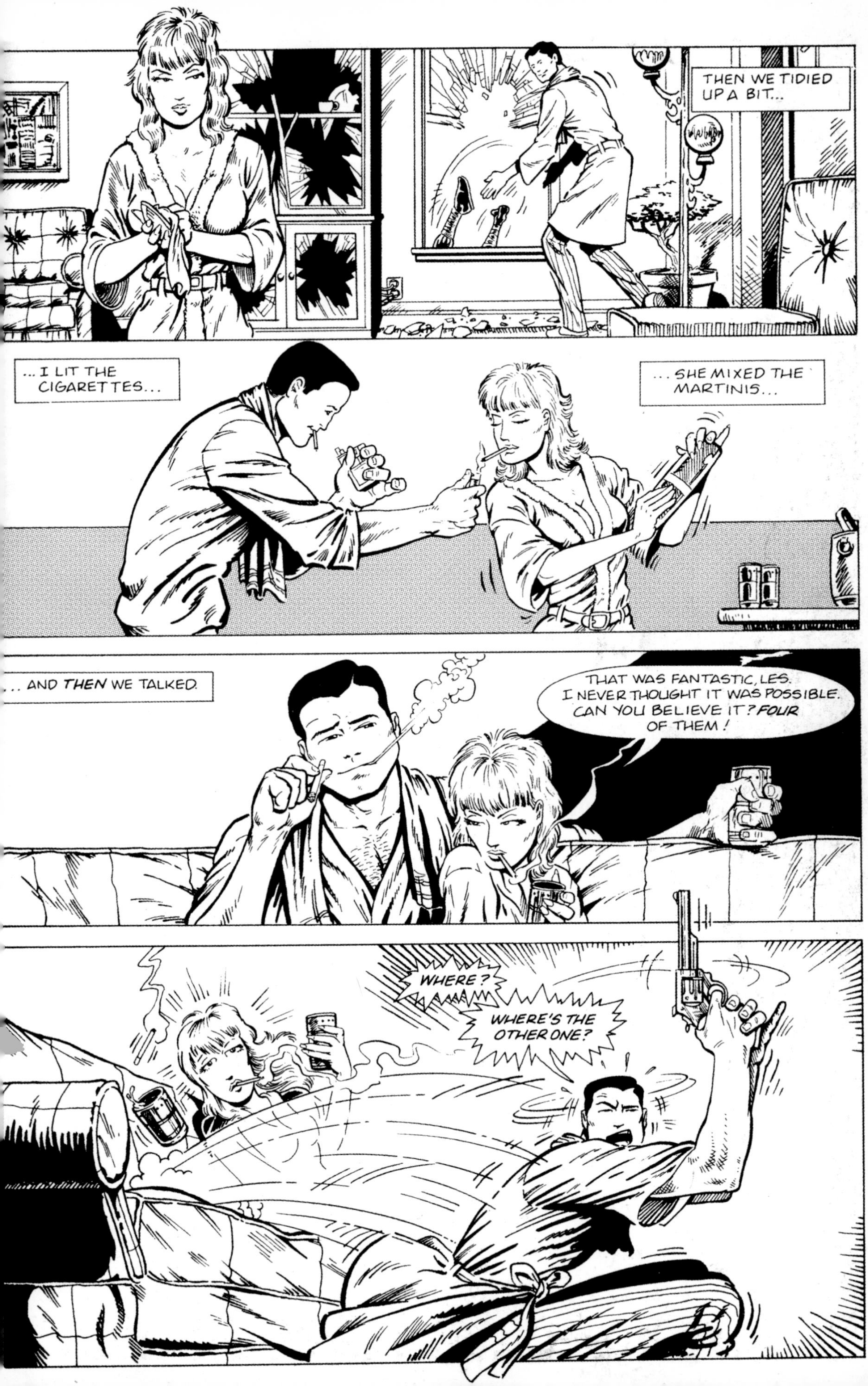
THEN WE TIDIED UP A BIT...
... I LIT THE CIGARETTES...
... SHE MIXED THE MARTINIS...
... AND THEN WE TALKED.
THAT WAS FANTASTIC, LES. I NEVER THOUGHT IT WAS POSSIBLE. CAN YOU BELIEVE IT? FOUR OF THEM!
WHERE?
WHERE'S THE OTHER ONE?

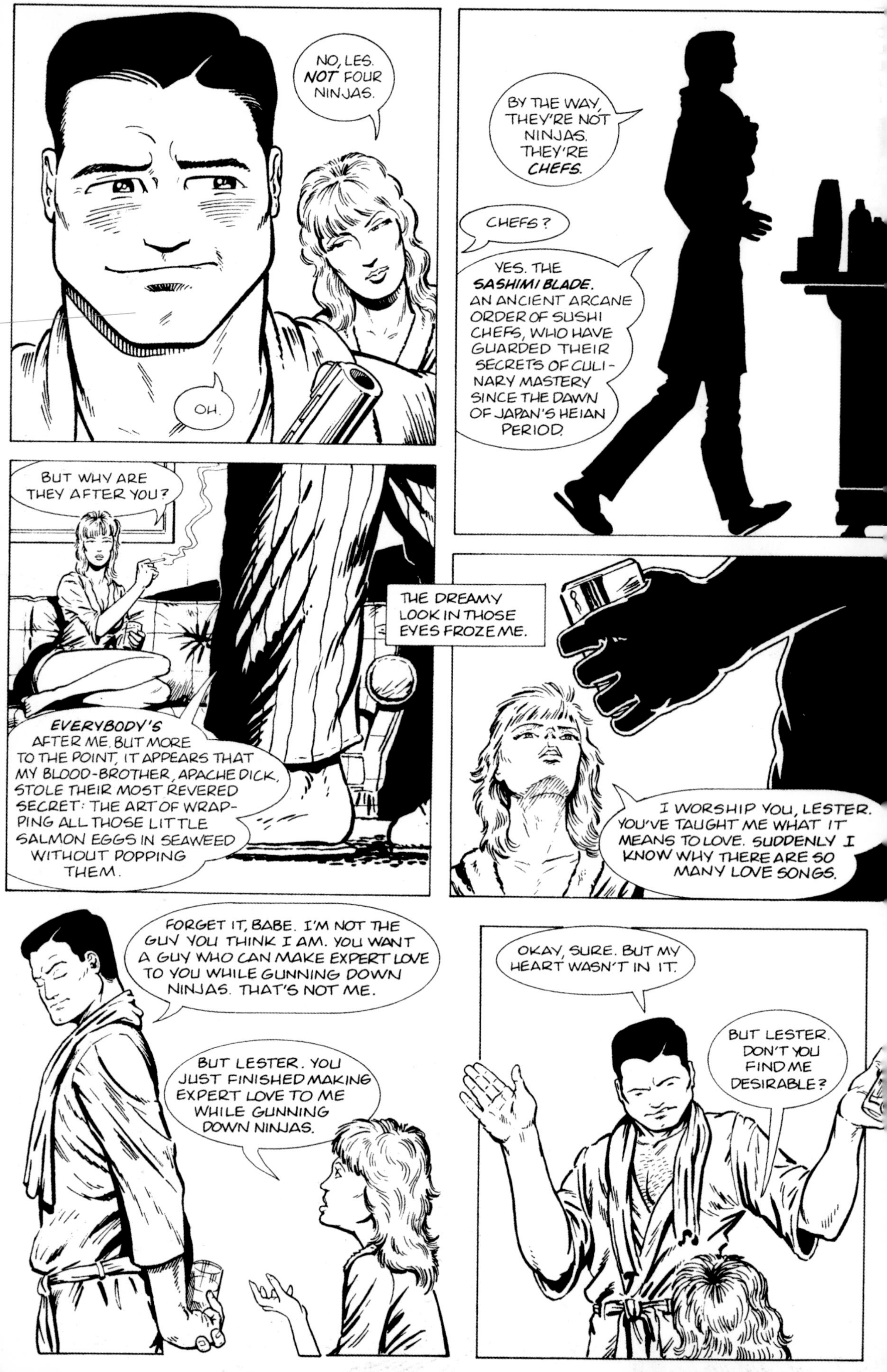
NO, LES. NOT FOUR NINJAS.
OH.
BY THE WAY, THEY'RE NOT NINJAS. THEY'RE CHEFS.
CHEFS?
YES. THE SASHIMI BLADE. AN ANCIENT ARCANE ORDER OF SUSHI CHEFS, WHO HAVE GUARDED THEIR SECRETS OF CULINARY MASTERY SINCE THE DAWN OF JAPAN'S HEIAN PERIOD.
BUT WHY ARE THEY AFTER YOU?
EVERYBODY'S AFTER ME. BUT MORE TO THE POINT, IT APPEARS THAT MY BLOOD-BROTHER, APACHE DICK, STOLE THEIR MOST REVERED SECRET: THE ART OF WRAPPING ALL THOSE LITTLE SALMON EGGS IN SEAWEED WITHOUT POPPING THEM.
THE DREAMY LOOK IN THOSE EYES FROZE ME.
I WORSHIP YOU, LESTER. YOU'VE TAUGHT ME WHAT IT MEANS TO LOVE. SUDDENLY I KNOW WHY THERE ARE SO MANY LOVE SONGS.
FORGET IT, BABE. I'M NOT THE GUY YOU THINK I AM. YOU WANT A GUY WHO CAN MAKE EXPERT LOVE TO YOU WHILE GUNNING DOWN NINJAS. THAT'S NOT ME.
BUT LESTER. YOU JUST FINISHED MAKING EXPERT LOVE TO ME WHILE GUNNING DOWN NINJAS.
OKAY, SURE. BUT MY HEART WASN'T IN IT.
BUT LESTER. DON'T YOU FIND ME DESIRABLE?

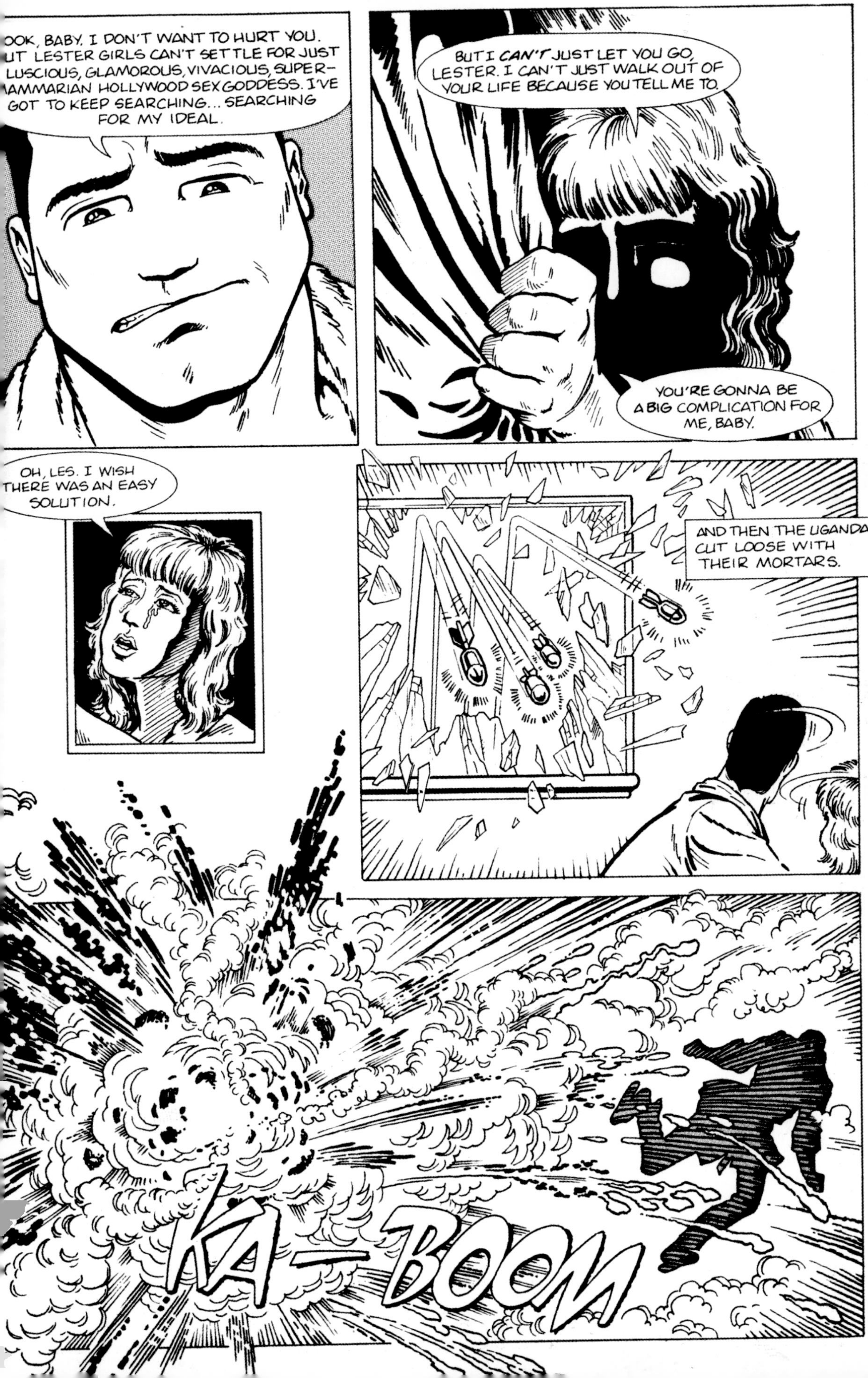
OOK, BABY. I DON'T WANT TO HURT YOU. UT LESTER GIRLS CAN'T SETTLE FOR JUST LUSCIOUS, GLAMOROUS, VIVACIOUS, SUPER-MAMMARIAN HOLLYWOOD SEX GODDESS. I'VE GOT TO KEEP SEARCHING... SEARCHING FOR MY IDEAL.
BUT I CAN'T JUST LET YOU GO, LESTER. I CAN'T JUST WALK OUT OF YOUR LIFE BECAUSE YOU TELL ME TO.
YOU'RE GONNA BE A BIG COMPLICATION FOR ME, BABY.
OH, LES. I WISH THERE WAS AN EASY SOLUTION.
AND THEN THE UGANDANS CUT LOOSE WITH THEIR MORTARS.
KA-BOOM

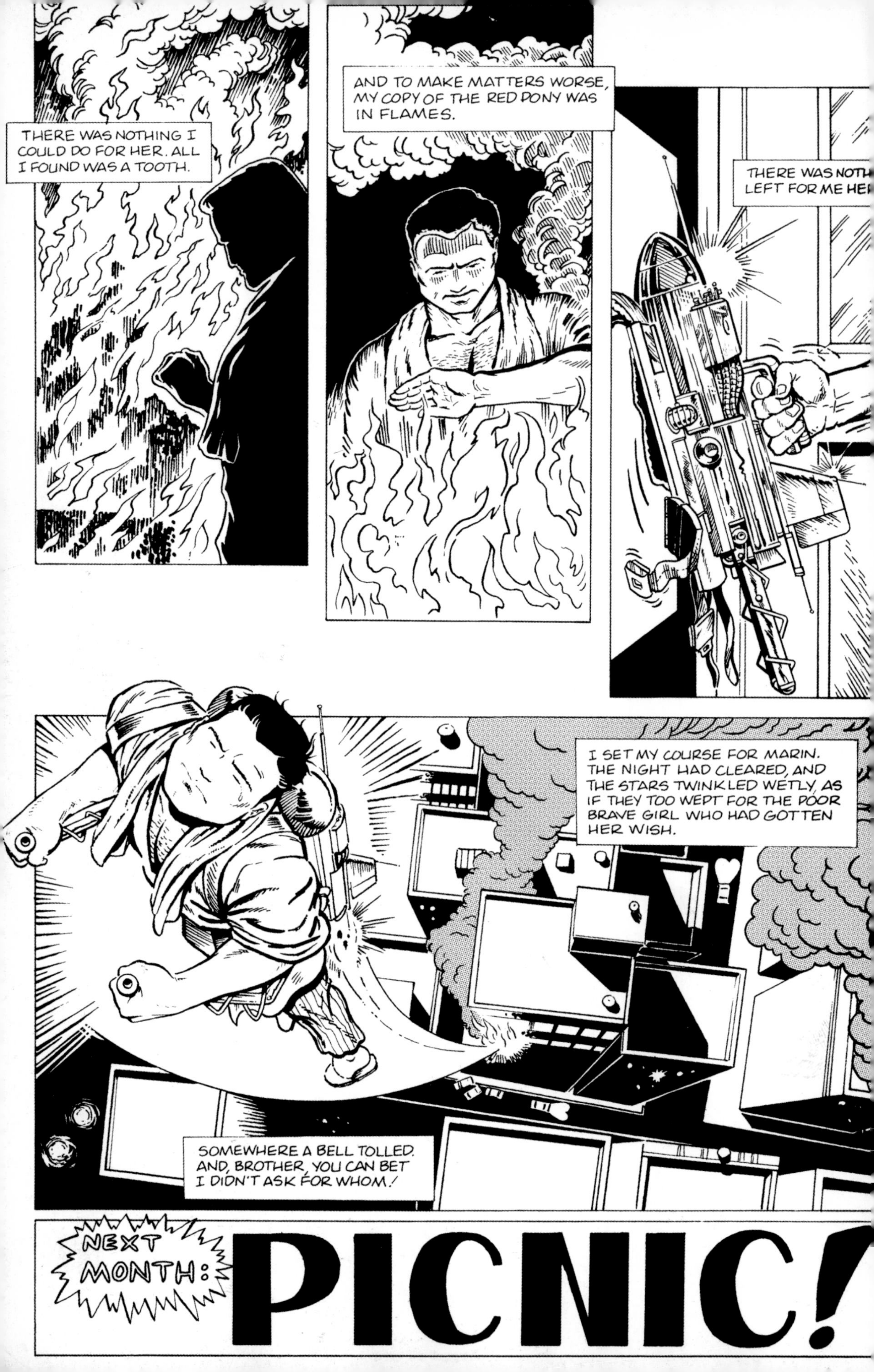
THERE WAS NOTHING I COULD DO FOR HER. ALL I FOUND WAS A TOOTH.
AND TO MAKE MATTERS WORSE, MY COPY OF THE RED PONY WAS IN FLAMES.
THERE WAS NOTH LEFT FOR ME HER
I SET MY COURSE FOR MARIN. THE NIGHT HAD CLEARED, AND THE STARS TWINKLED WETLY, AS IF THEY TOO WEPT FOR THE POOR BRAVE GIRL WHO HAD GOTTEN HER WISH.
SOMEWHERE A BELL TOLLED. AND, BROTHER, YOU CAN BET I DIDN'T ASK FOR WHOM!
NEXT MONTH: PICNIC!

THE TROUBLE WITH GIRLS™

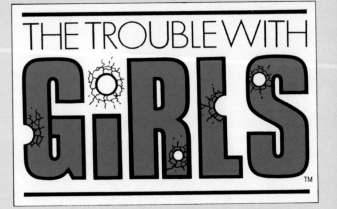

CHAPTER 2

SEPTEMBER 1987

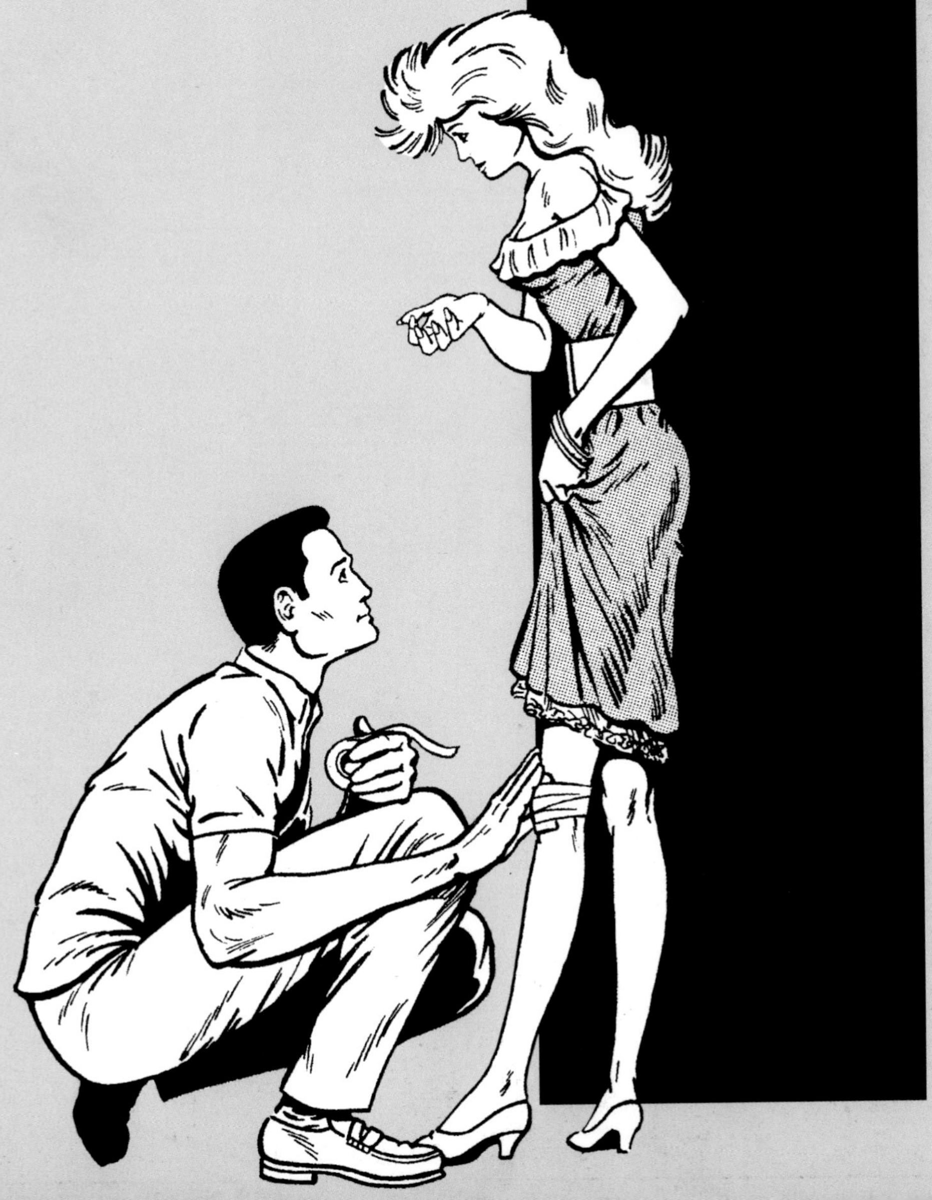

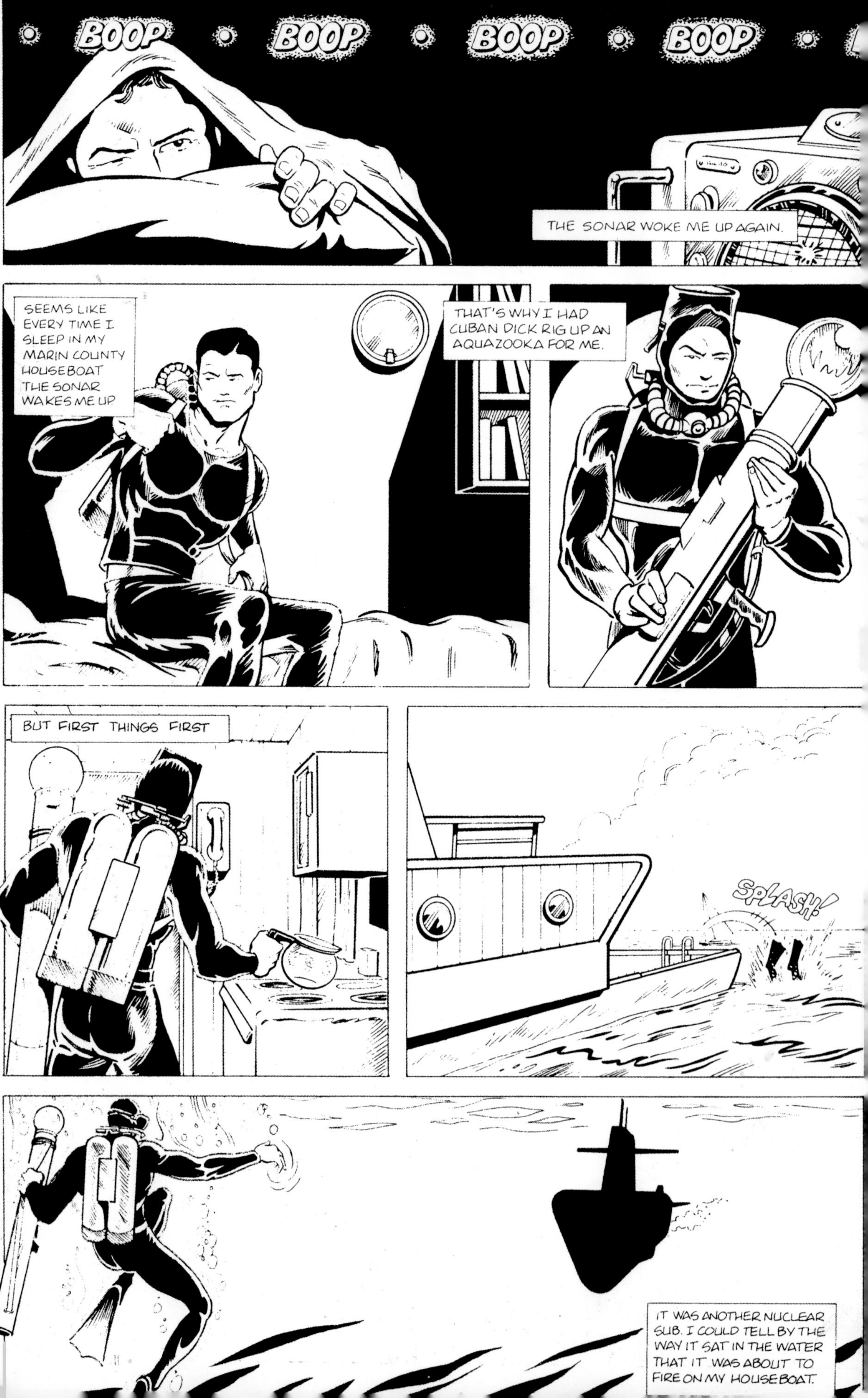
BOOP BOOP BOOP BOOP
THE SONAR WOKE ME UP AGAIN.
SEEMS LIKE EVERY TIME I SLEEP IN MY MARIN COUNTY HOUSEBOAT THE SONAR WAKES ME UP
THAT'S WHY I HAD CUBAN DICK RIG UP AN AQUAZOOKA FOR ME.
BUT FIRST THINGS FIRST
SPLASH!
IT WAS ANOTHER NUCLEAR SUB. I COULD TELL BY THE WAY IT SAT IN THE WATER THAT IT WAS ABOUT TO FIRE ON MY HOUSEBOAT.

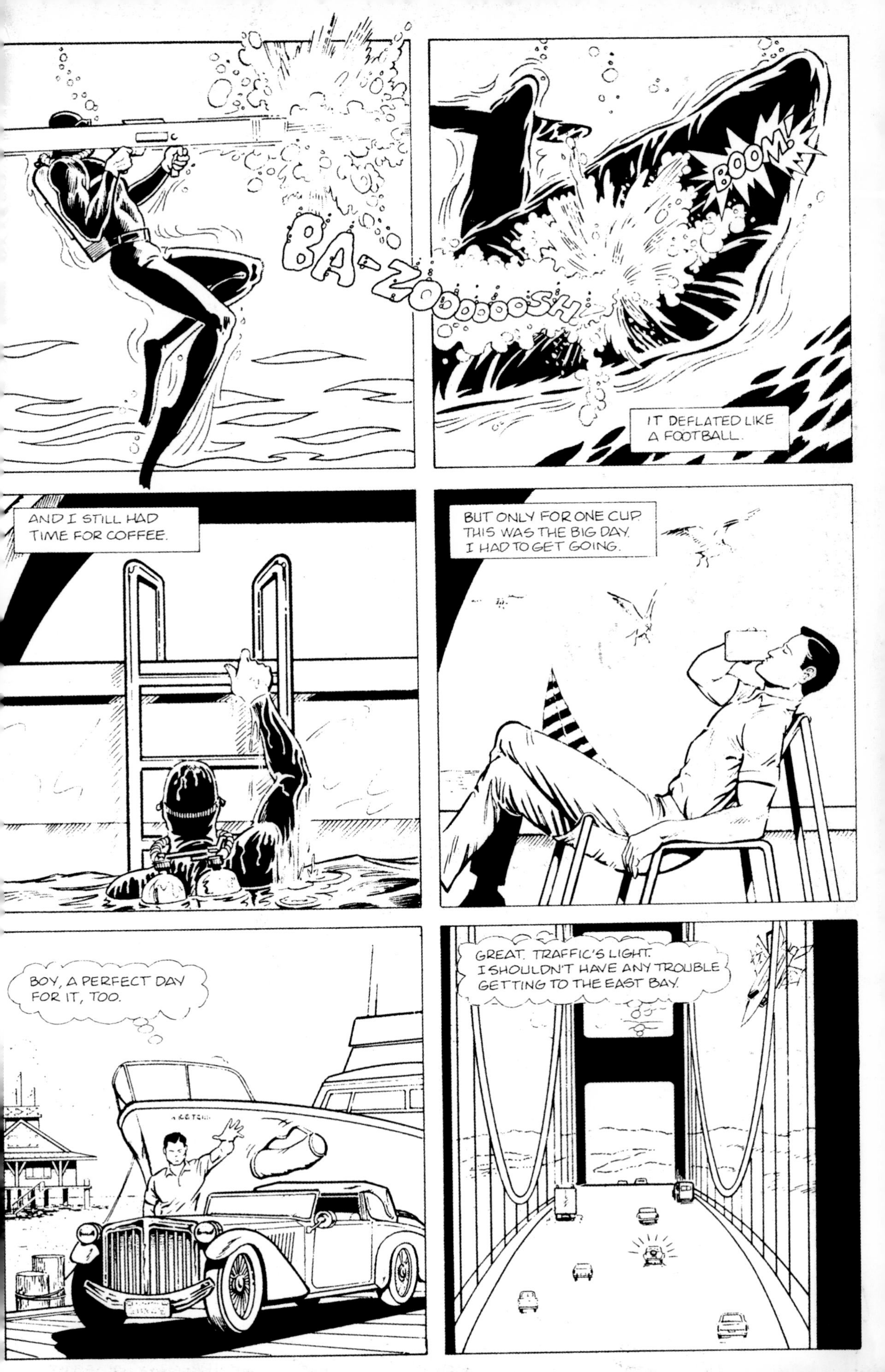
BA-ZOOOOOOSH
BOOM!
IT DEFLATED LIKE A FOOTBALL.
AND I STILL HAD TIME FOR COFFEE.
BUT ONLY FOR ONE CUP. THIS WAS THE BIG DAY. I HAD TO GET GOING.
BOY, A PERFECT DAY FOR IT, TOO.
GREAT. TRAFFIC'S LIGHT. I SHOULDN'T HAVE ANY TROUBLE GETTING TO THE EAST BAY.

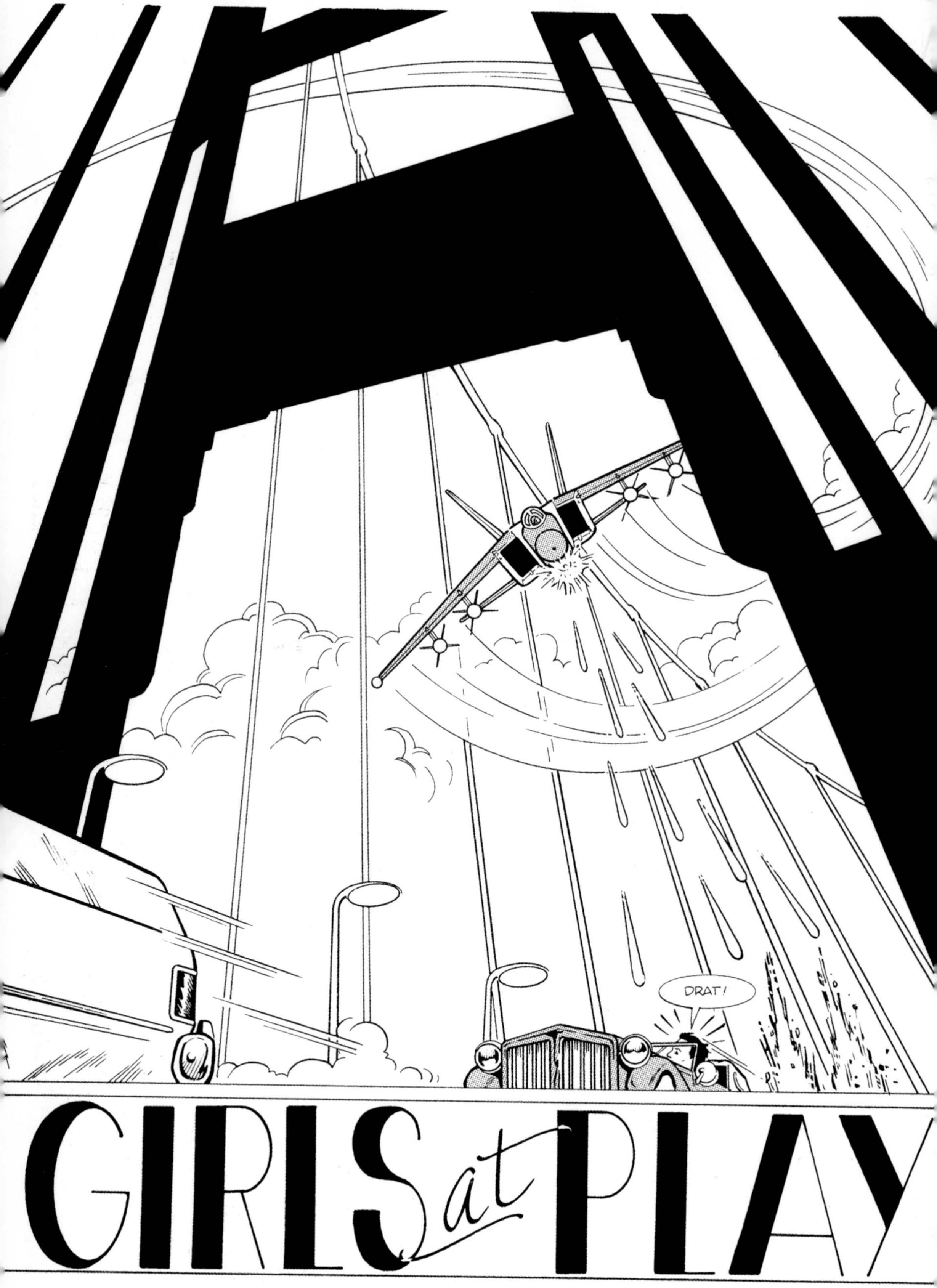
DRAT!

GIRLS at PLAY

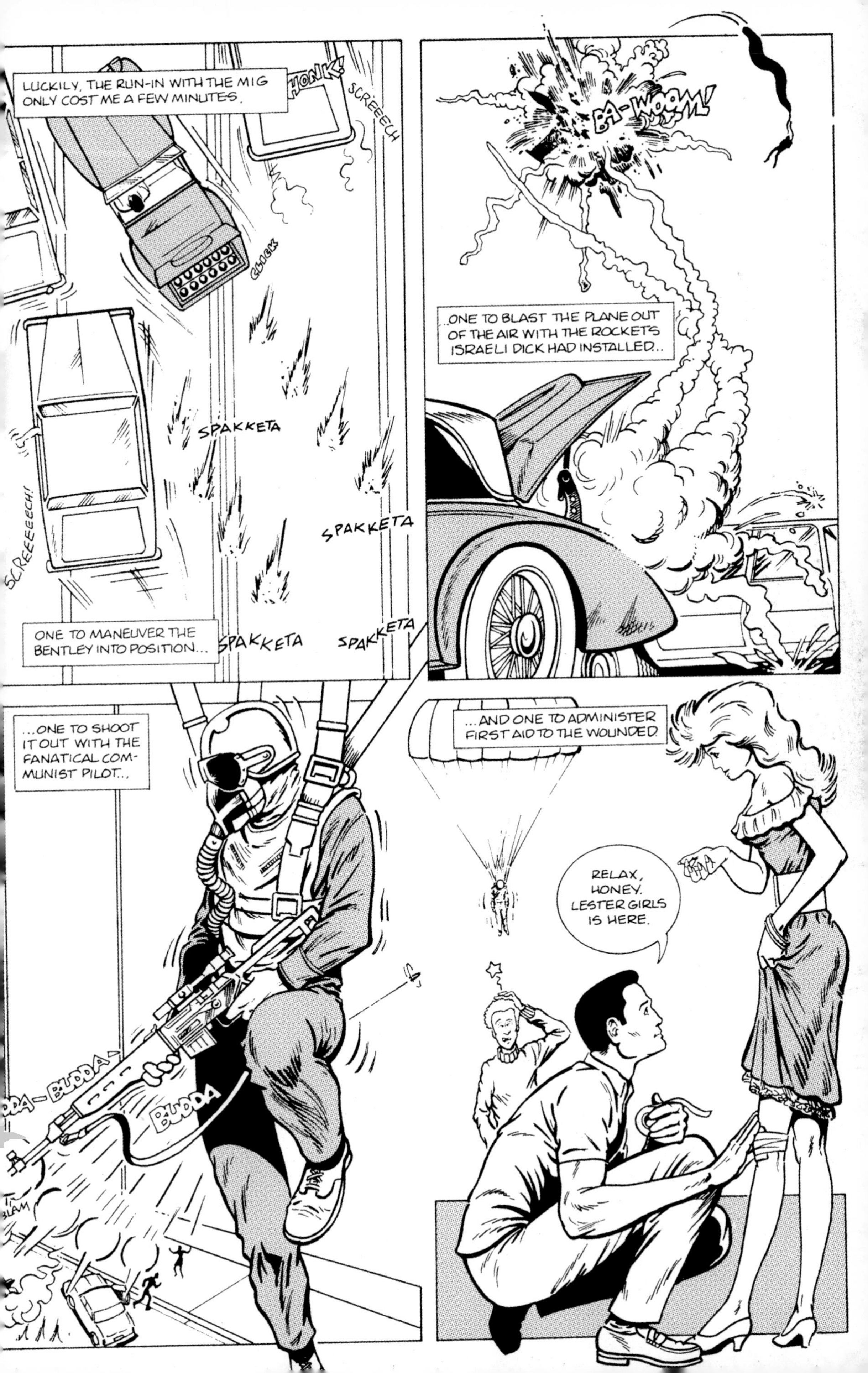
LUCKILY, THE RUN-IN WITH THE MIG ONLY COST ME A FEW MINUTES.
HONK!
SCREEEECH
CLICK
SPAKKETA
SPAKKETA
SCREEEEEECH!
ONE TO MANEUVER THE BENTLEY INTO POSITION...
SPAKKETA
SPAKKETA
BA-WOOM!
...ONE TO BLAST THE PLANE OUT OF THE AIR WITH THE ROCKETS ISRAELI DICK HAD INSTALLED...
...ONE TO SHOOT IT OUT WITH THE FANATICAL COM-MUNIST PILOT...
BUDDA-BUDDA-
BUDDA
...AND ONE TO ADMINISTER FIRST AID TO THE WOUNDED.
RELAX, HONEY. LESTER GIRLS IS HERE.

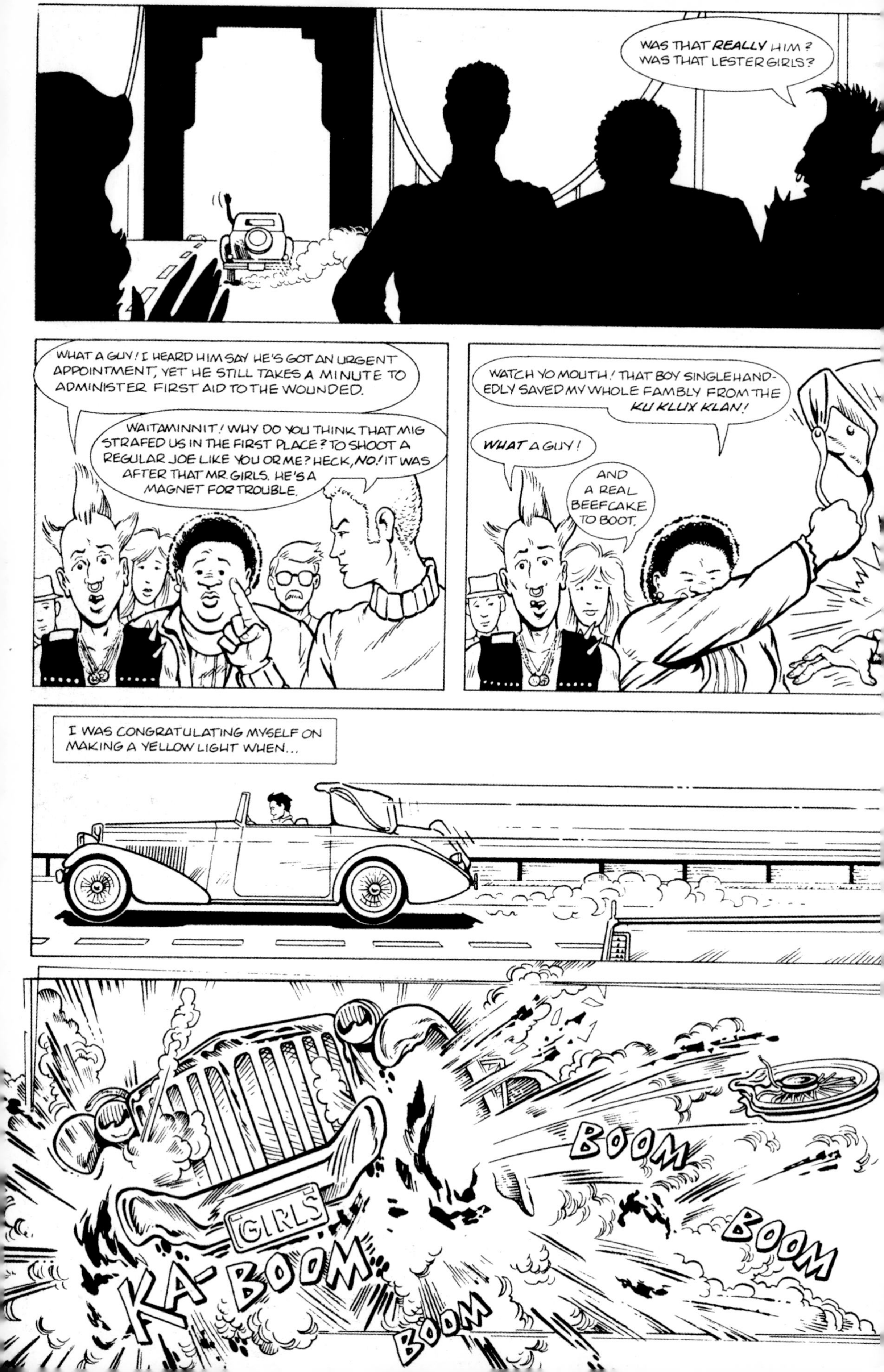
WAS THAT REALLY HIM? WAS THAT LESTER GIRLS?
WHAT A GUY! I HEARD HIM SAY HE'S GOT AN URGENT APPOINTMENT, YET HE STILL TAKES A MINUTE TO ADMINISTER FIRST AID TO THE WOUNDED.
WAITAMINNIT! WHY DO YOU THINK THAT MIG STRAFED US IN THE FIRST PLACE? TO SHOOT A REGULAR JOE LIKE YOU OR ME? HECK, NO! IT WAS AFTER THAT MR. GIRLS. HE'S A MAGNET FOR TROUBLE.
WATCH YO MOUTH! THAT BOY SINGLEHANDEDLY SAVED MY WHOLE FAMBLY FROM THE KU KLUX KLAN!
WHAT A GUY!
AND A REAL BEEFCAKE TO BOOT.
I WAS CONGRATULATING MYSELF ON MAKING A YELLOW LIGHT WHEN...
GIRLS
BOOM
BOOM
KA-BOOM
BOOM

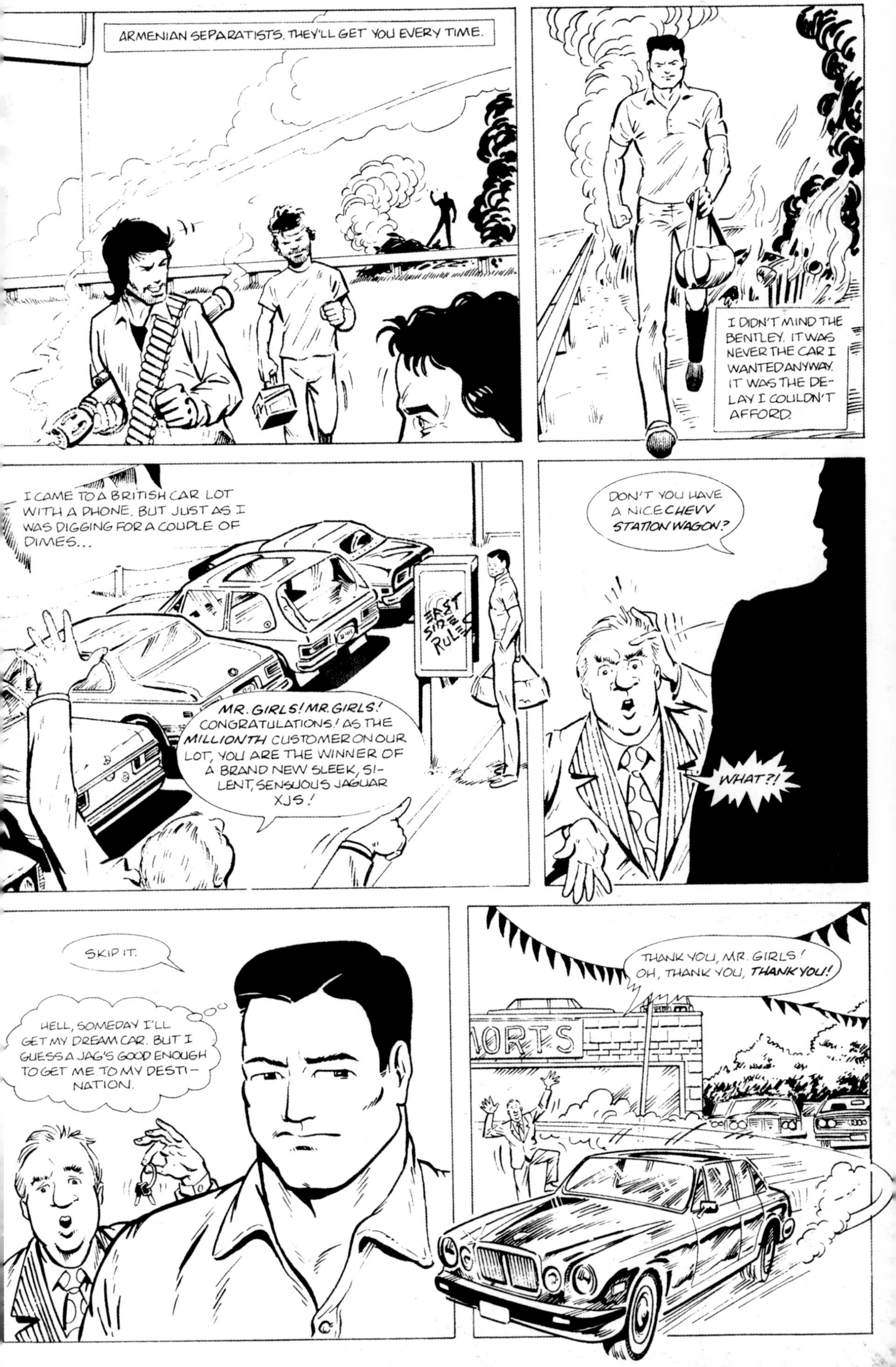

ARMENIAN SEPARATISTS. THEY'LL GET YOU EVERY TIME.
I DIDN'T MIND THE BENTLEY. IT WAS NEVER THE CAR I WANTED ANYWAY. IT WAS THE DELAY I COULDN'T AFFORD.
I CAME TO A BRITISH CAR LOT WITH A PHONE. BUT JUST AS I WAS DIGGING FOR A COUPLE OF DIMES...
EAST SIDE RULES
MR. GIRLS! MR. GIRLS! CONGRATULATIONS! AS THE MILLIONTH CUSTOMER ON OUR LOT, YOU ARE THE WINNER OF A BRAND NEW SLEEK, SILENT, SENSUOUS JAGUAR XJS!
DON'T YOU HAVE A NICE CHEVY STATION WAGON?
WHAT?!
SKIP IT.
HELL, SOMEDAY I'LL GET MY DREAM CAR. BUT I GUESS A JAG'S GOOD ENOUGH TO GET ME TO MY DESTINATION.
THANK YOU, MR. GIRLS! OH, THANK YOU, THANK YOU!
MORTS

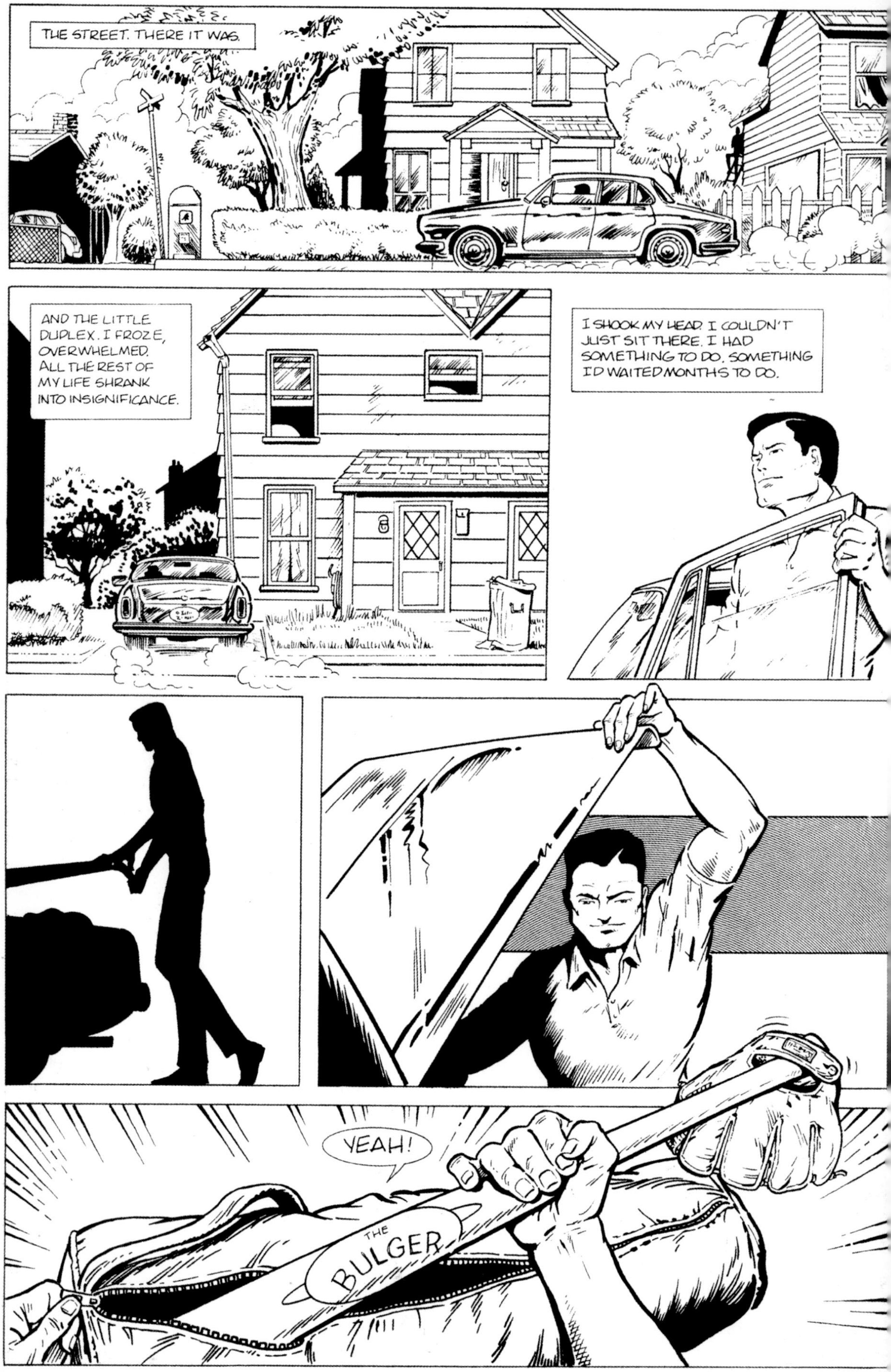
THE STREET. THERE IT WAS.
AND THE LITTLE DUPLEX. I FROZE, OVERWHELMED. ALL THE REST OF MY LIFE SHRANK INTO INSIGNIFICANCE.
I SHOOK MY HEAD. I COULDN'T JUST SIT THERE. I HAD SOMETHING TO DO. SOMETHING I'D WAITED MONTHS TO DO.
YEAH!
THE BULGER

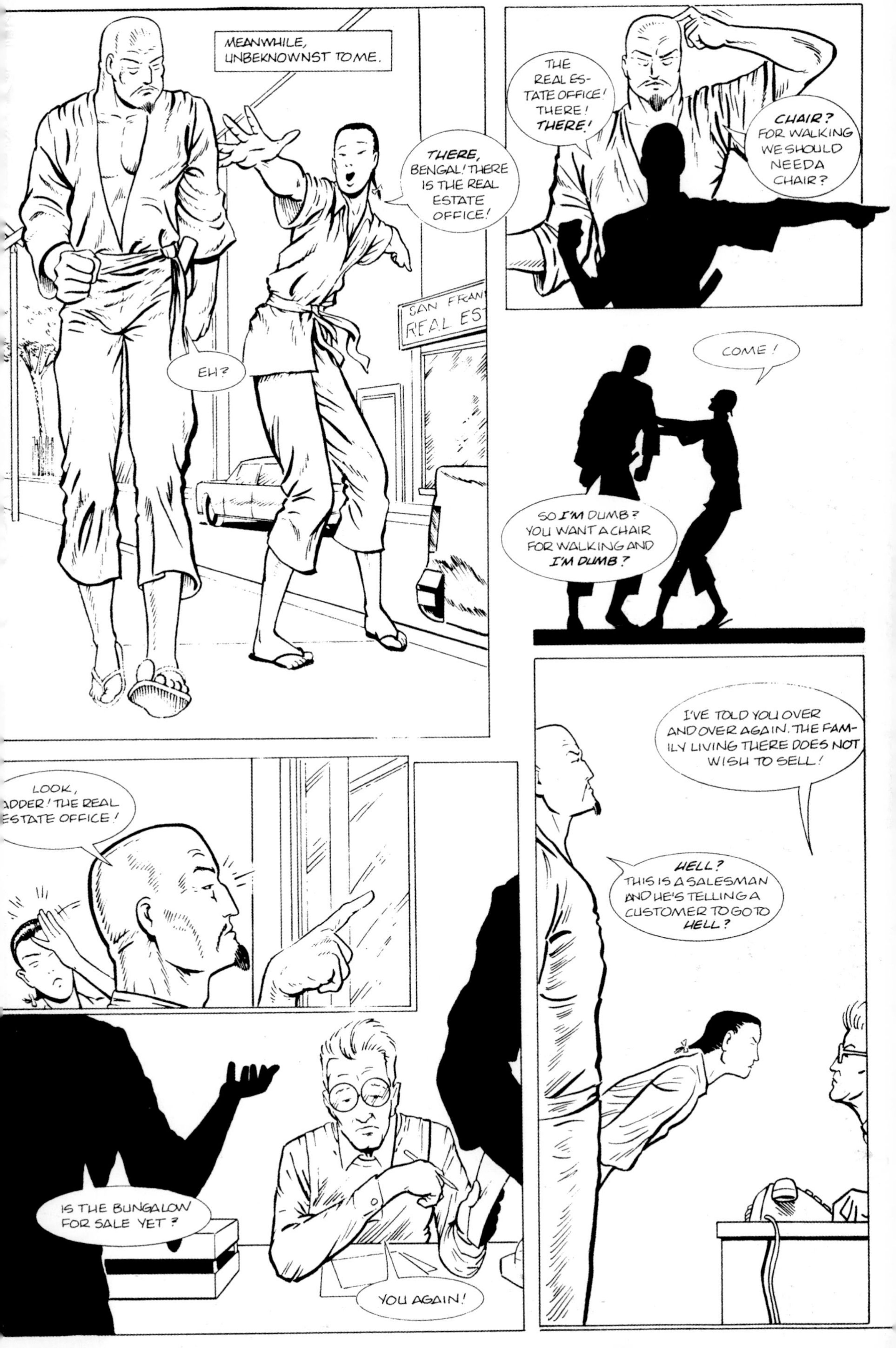
MEANWHILE, UNBEKNOWNST TO ME.
THERE, BENGAL! THERE IS THE REAL ESTATE OFFICE!
EH?
SAN FRAN
REAL EST
THE REAL ES-TATE OFFICE! THERE! THERE!
CHAIR? FOR WALKING WE SHOULD NEEDA CHAIR?
COME!
SO I'M DUMB? YOU WANT A CHAIR FOR WALKING AND I'M DUMB?
LOOK, ADDER! THE REAL ESTATE OFFICE!
IS THE BUNGALOW FOR SALE YET?
YOU AGAIN!
I'VE TOLD YOU OVER AND OVER AGAIN. THE FAM-ILY LIVING THERE DOES NOT WISH TO SELL!
HELL? THIS IS A SALESMAN AND HE'S TELLING A CUSTOMER TO GO TO HELL?

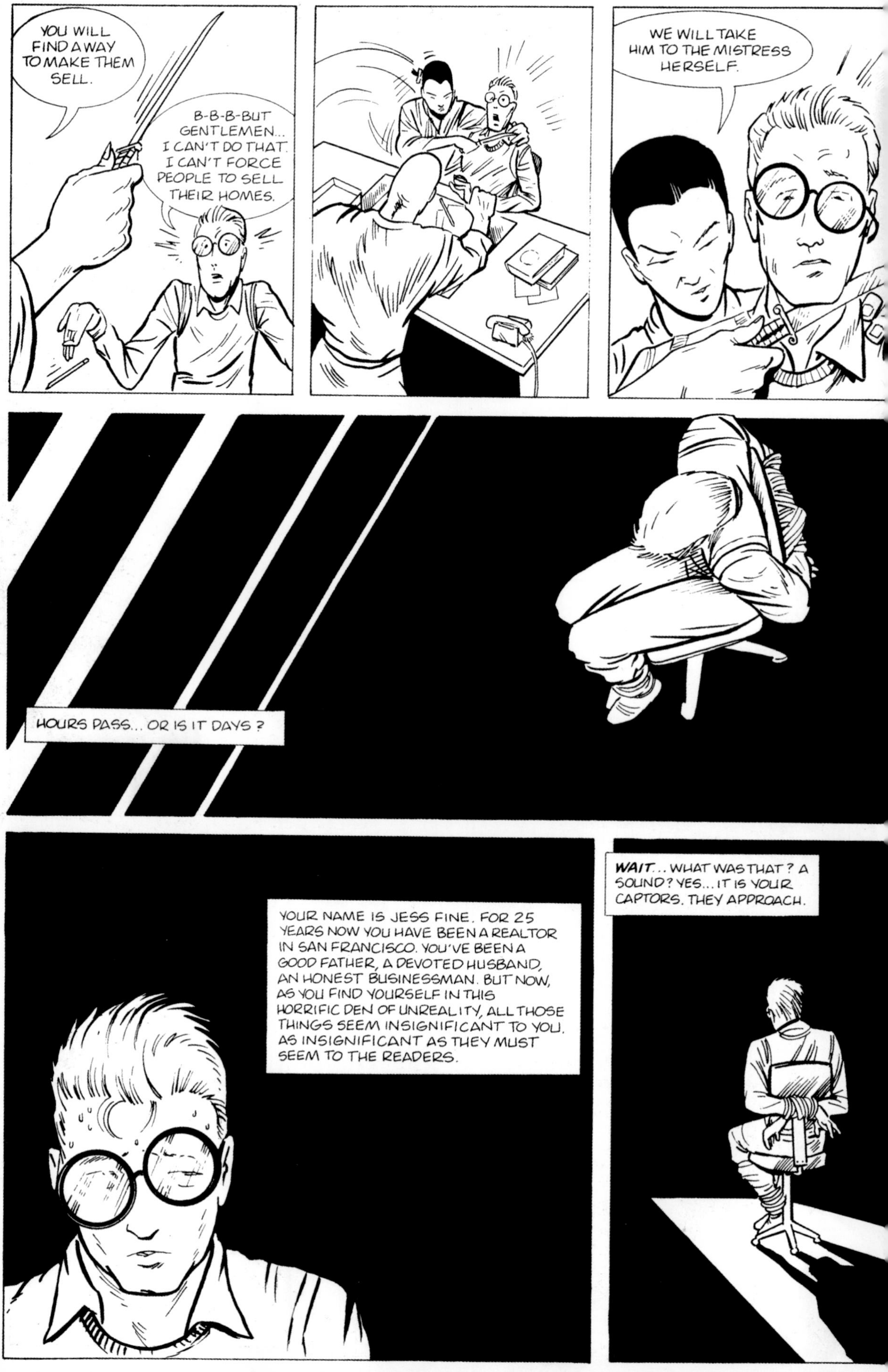

YOU WILL FIND A WAY TO MAKE THEM SELL.
B-B-B-BUT GENTLEMEN... I CAN'T DO THAT. I CAN'T FORCE PEOPLE TO SELL THEIR HOMES.
WE WILL TAKE HIM TO THE MISTRESS HERSELF.
HOURS PASS... OR IS IT DAYS ?
YOUR NAME IS JESS FINE. FOR 25 YEARS NOW YOU HAVE BEEN A REALTOR IN SAN FRANCISCO. YOU'VE BEEN A GOOD FATHER, A DEVOTED HUSBAND, AN HONEST BUSINESSMAN. BUT NOW, AS YOU FIND YOURSELF IN THIS HORRIFIC DEN OF UNREALITY, ALL THOSE THINGS SEEM INSIGNIFICANT TO YOU, AS INSIGNIFICANT AS THEY MUST SEEM TO THE READERS.
WAIT... WHAT WAS THAT ? A SOUND ? YES... IT IS YOUR CAPTORS. THEY APPROACH.

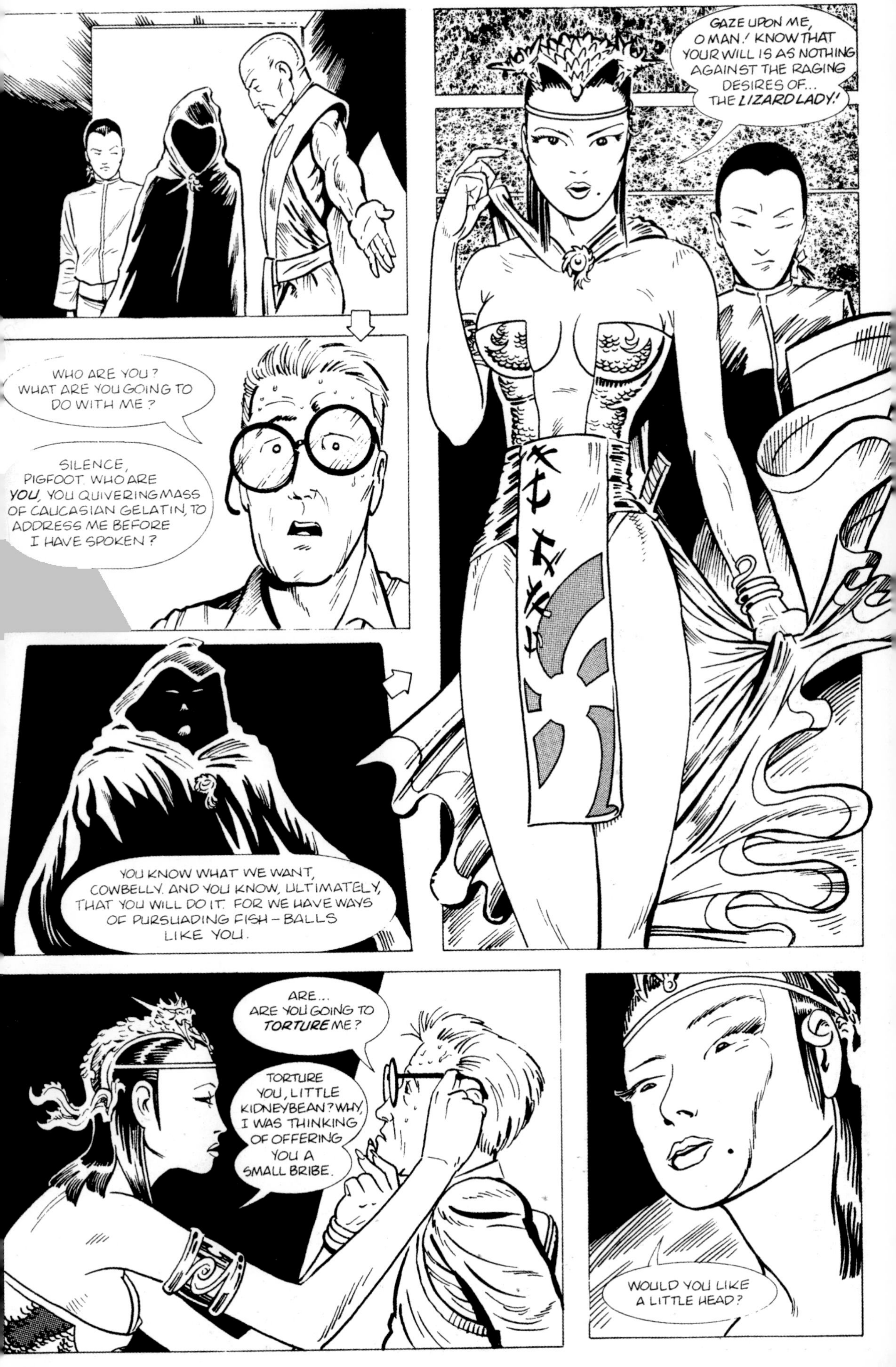
WHO ARE YOU? WHAT ARE YOU GOING TO DO WITH ME?
SILENCE, PIGFOOT. WHO ARE **YOU**, YOU QUIVERING MASS OF CAUCASIAN GELATIN, TO ADDRESS ME BEFORE I HAVE SPOKEN?
YOU KNOW WHAT WE WANT, COWBELLY. AND YOU KNOW, ULTIMATELY, THAT YOU WILL DO IT. FOR WE HAVE WAYS OF PURSUADING FISH-BALLS LIKE YOU.
GAZE UPON ME, O MAN! KNOW THAT YOUR WILL IS AS NOTHING AGAINST THE RAGING DESIRES OF... THE *LIZARD LADY!*
ARE... ARE YOU GOING TO *TORTURE* ME?
TORTURE YOU, LITTLE KIDNEYBEAN? WHY, I WAS THINKING OF OFFERING YOU A SMALL BRIBE.
WOULD YOU LIKE A LITTLE HEAD?

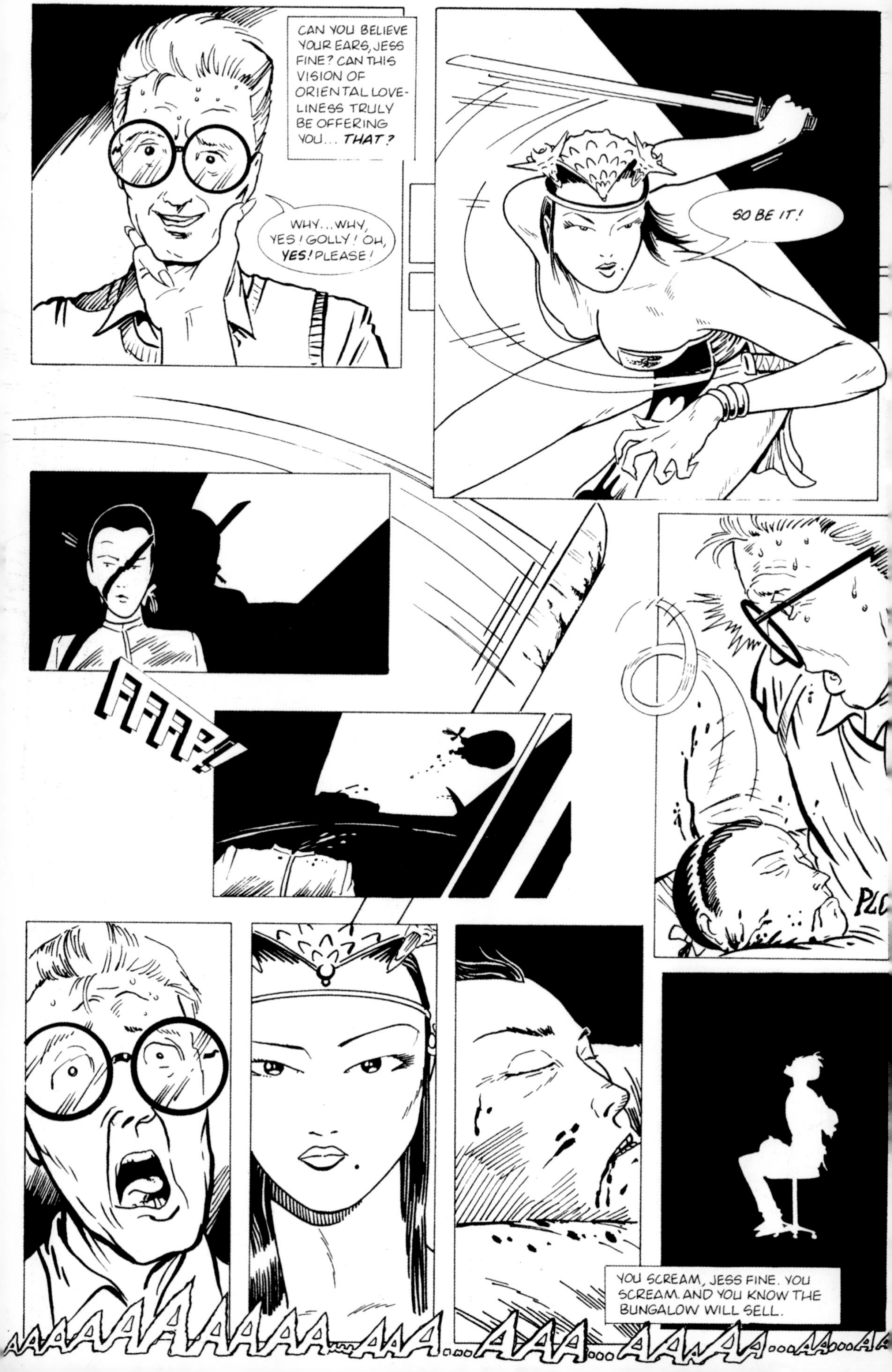
CAN YOU BELIEVE YOUR EARS, JESS FINE? CAN THIS VISION OF ORIENTAL LOVE-LINESS TRULY BE OFFERING YOU... THAT?
WHY...WHY, YES! GOLLY! OH, YES! PLEASE!
SO BE IT!
FFFFP!
PLO
YOU SCREAM, JESS FINE. YOU SCREAM. AND YOU KNOW THE BUNGALOW WILL SELL.
AAAAAAAAAAAA...AAA...AAA...AAAAA...AA...AA

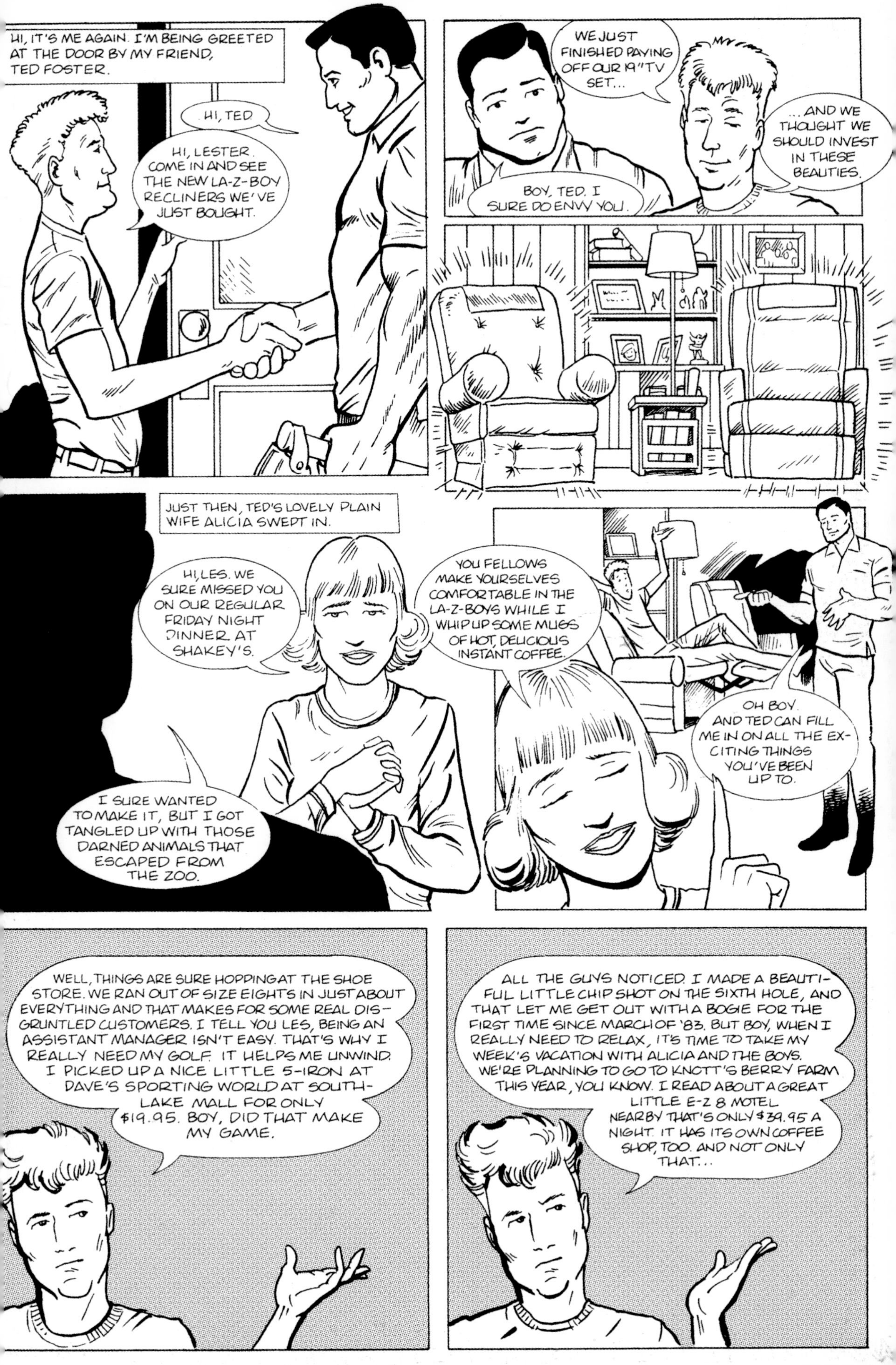
HI, IT'S ME AGAIN. I'M BEING GREETED AT THE DOOR BY MY FRIEND, TED FOSTER.
HI, TED.
HI, LESTER. COME IN AND SEE THE NEW LA-Z-BOY RECLINERS WE'VE JUST BOUGHT.
WE JUST FINISHED PAYING OFF OUR 19" TV SET...
...AND WE THOUGHT WE SHOULD INVEST IN THESE BEAUTIES.
BOY, TED. I SURE DO ENVY YOU.
JUST THEN, TED'S LOVELY PLAIN WIFE ALICIA SWEPT IN.
HI, LES. WE SURE MISSED YOU ON OUR REGULAR FRIDAY NIGHT DINNER AT SHAKEY'S.
I SURE WANTED TO MAKE IT, BUT I GOT TANGLED UP WITH THOSE DARNED ANIMALS THAT ESCAPED FROM THE ZOO.
YOU FELLOWS MAKE YOURSELVES COMFORTABLE IN THE LA-Z-BOYS WHILE I WHIP UP SOME MUGS OF HOT, DELICIOUS INSTANT COFFEE.
OH BOY. AND TED CAN FILL ME IN ON ALL THE EXCITING THINGS YOU'VE BEEN UP TO.
WELL, THINGS ARE SURE HOPPING AT THE SHOE STORE. WE RAN OUT OF SIZE EIGHTS IN JUST ABOUT EVERYTHING AND THAT MAKES FOR SOME REAL DISGRUNTLED CUSTOMERS. I TELL YOU LES, BEING AN ASSISTANT MANAGER ISN'T EASY. THAT'S WHY I REALLY NEED MY GOLF. IT HELPS ME UNWIND. I PICKED UP A NICE LITTLE 5-IRON AT DAVE'S SPORTING WORLD AT SOUTHLAKE MALL FOR ONLY $19.95. BOY, DID THAT MAKE MY GAME.
ALL THE GUYS NOTICED. I MADE A BEAUTIFUL LITTLE CHIP SHOT ON THE SIXTH HOLE, AND THAT LET ME GET OUT WITH A BOGIE FOR THE FIRST TIME SINCE MARCH OF '83. BUT BOY, WHEN I REALLY NEED TO RELAX, IT'S TIME TO TAKE MY WEEK'S VACATION WITH ALICIA AND THE BOYS. WE'RE PLANNING TO GO TO KNOTT'S BERRY FARM THIS YEAR, YOU KNOW. I READ ABOUT A GREAT LITTLE E-Z 8 MOTEL NEARBY THAT'S ONLY $39.95 A NIGHT. IT HAS ITS OWN COFFEE SHOP, TOO. AND NOT ONLY THAT...

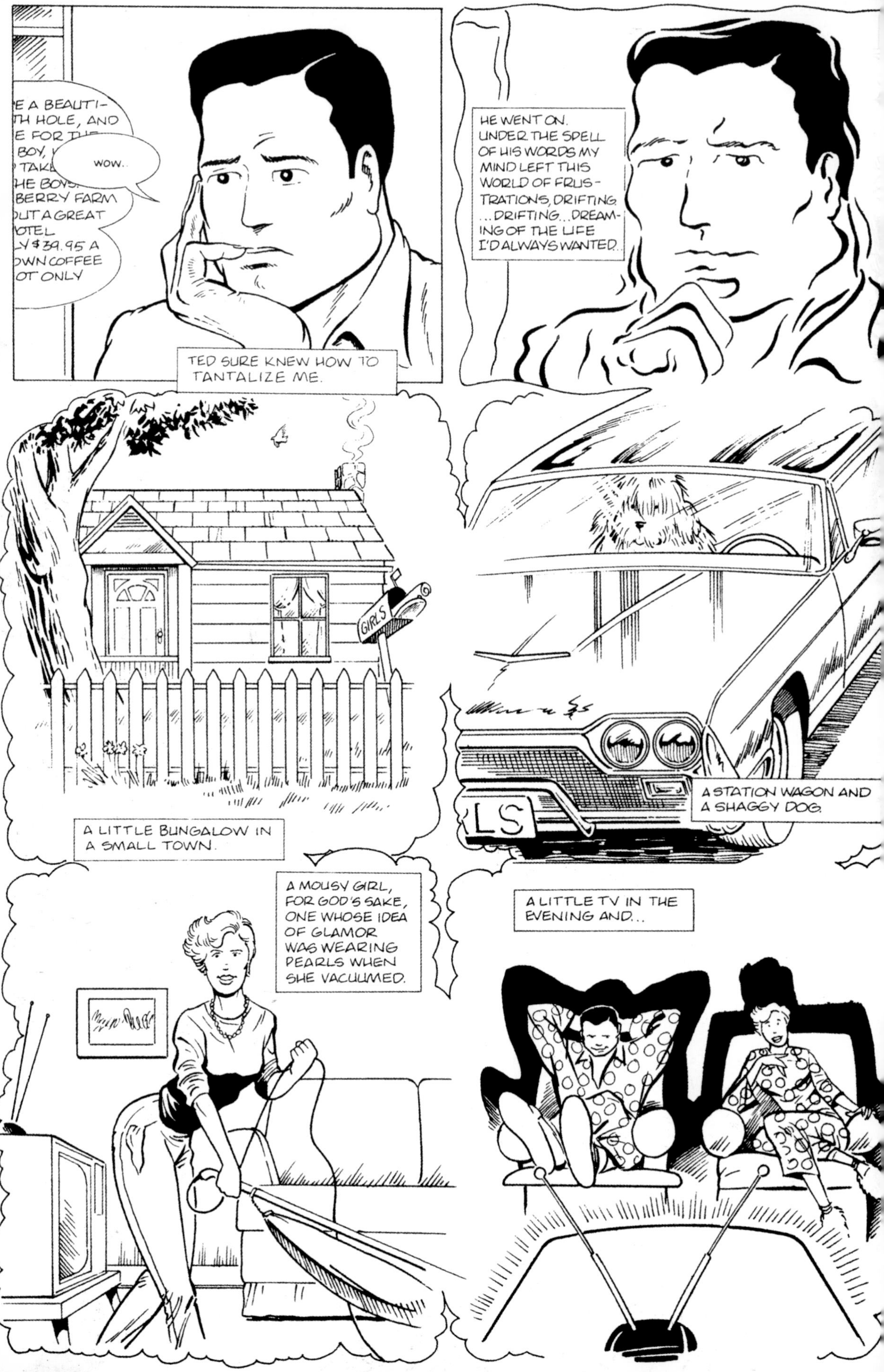

E A BEAUTI-
TH HOLE, AND
E FOR TH
BOY,
TAKE
HE BOYS
BERRY FARM
UT A GREAT
OTEL
LY $39.95 A
WN COFFEE
OT ONLY
WOW..
TED SURE KNEW HOW TO TANTALIZE ME.
HE WENT ON. UNDER THE SPELL OF HIS WORDS MY MIND LEFT THIS WORLD OF FRUS-TRATIONS, DRIFTING. ...DRIFTING...DREAMING OF THE LIFE I'D ALWAYS WANTED..
GIRLS
A LITTLE BUNGALOW IN A SMALL TOWN.
LS
A STATION WAGON AND A SHAGGY DOG.
A MOUSY GIRL, FOR GOD'S SAKE, ONE WHOSE IDEA OF GLAMOR WAS WEARING PEARLS WHEN SHE VACUUMED.
A LITTLE TV IN THE EVENING AND...

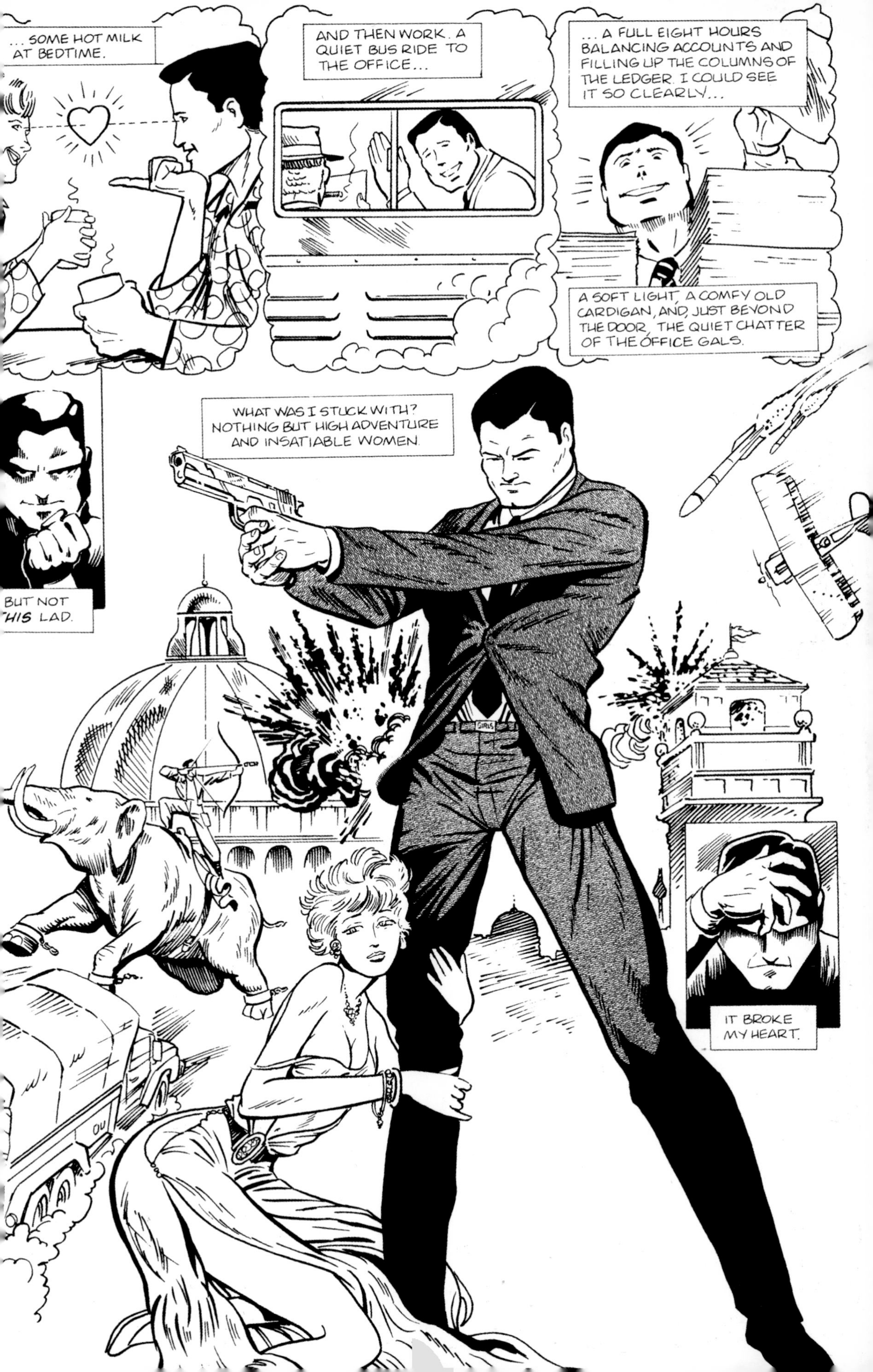

... SOME HOT MILK AT BEDTIME.
AND THEN WORK. A QUIET BUS RIDE TO THE OFFICE...
... A FULL EIGHT HOURS BALANCING ACCOUNTS AND FILLING UP THE COLUMNS OF THE LEDGER. I COULD SEE IT SO CLEARLY...
A SOFT LIGHT, A COMFY OLD CARDIGAN, AND, JUST BEYOND THE DOOR, THE QUIET CHATTER OF THE OFFICE GALS.
BUT NOT THIS LAD.
WHAT WAS I STUCK WITH? NOTHING BUT HIGH ADVENTURE AND INSATIABLE WOMEN.
GIRLS
IT BROKE MY HEART.

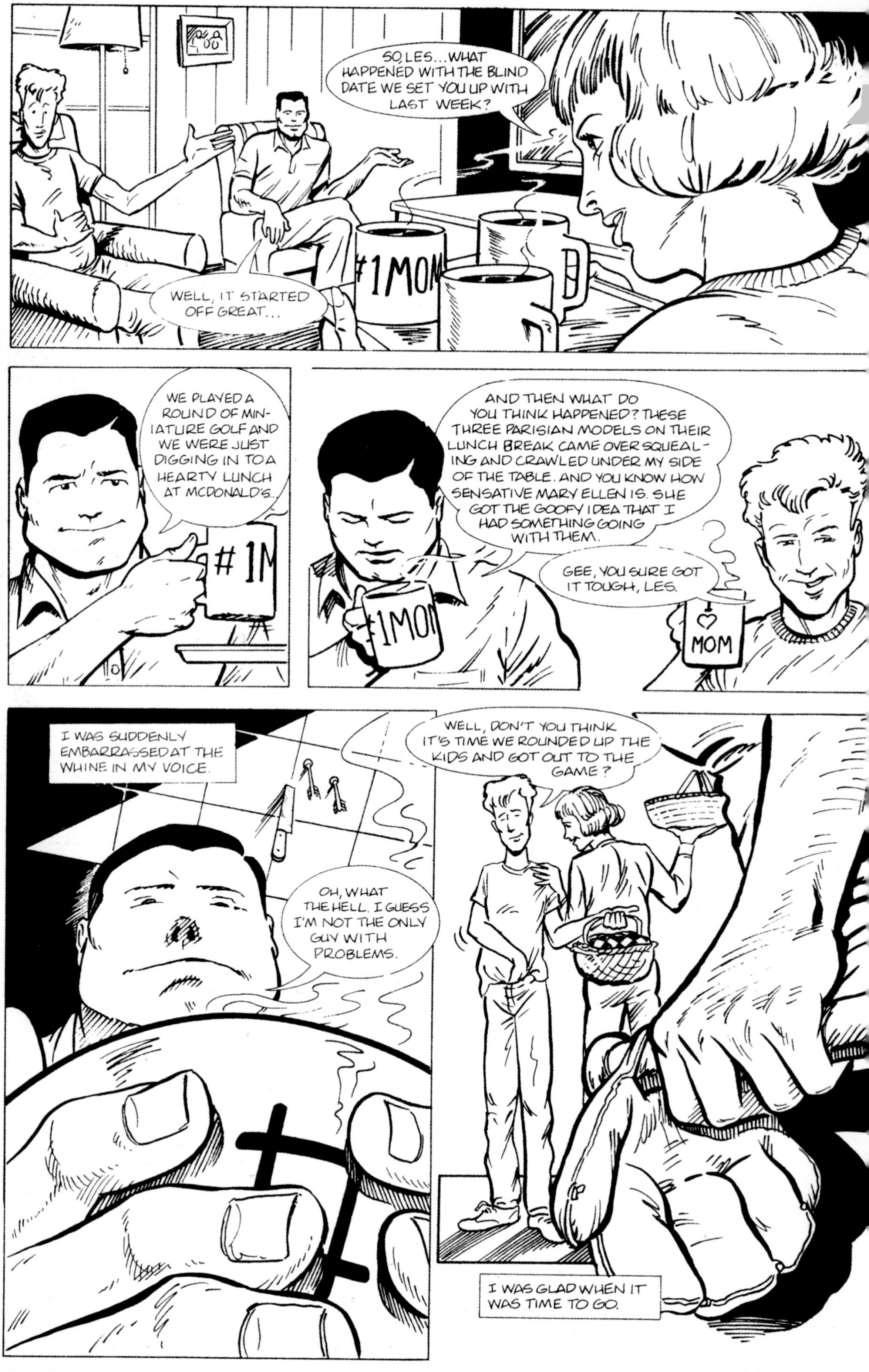
SO, LES... WHAT HAPPENED WITH THE BLIND DATE WE SET YOU UP WITH LAST WEEK?
WELL, IT STARTED OFF GREAT...
#1MOM
WE PLAYED A ROUND OF MINIATURE GOLF AND WE WERE JUST DIGGING IN TO A HEARTY LUNCH AT MCDONALD'S...
#1M
AND THEN WHAT DO YOU THINK HAPPENED? THESE THREE PARISIAN MODELS ON THEIR LUNCH BREAK CAME OVER SQUEALING AND CRAWLED UNDER MY SIDE OF THE TABLE. AND YOU KNOW HOW SENSATIVE MARY ELLEN IS. SHE GOT THE GOOFY IDEA THAT I HAD SOMETHING GOING WITH THEM.
#1MOM
GEE, YOU SURE GOT IT TOUGH, LES.
I ♡ MOM
I WAS SUDDENLY EMBARRASSED AT THE WHINE IN MY VOICE.
OH, WHAT THE HELL. I GUESS I'M NOT THE ONLY GUY WITH PROBLEMS.
WELL, DON'T YOU THINK IT'S TIME WE ROUNDED UP THE KIDS AND GOT OUT TO THE GAME?
I WAS GLAD WHEN IT WAS TIME TO GO.

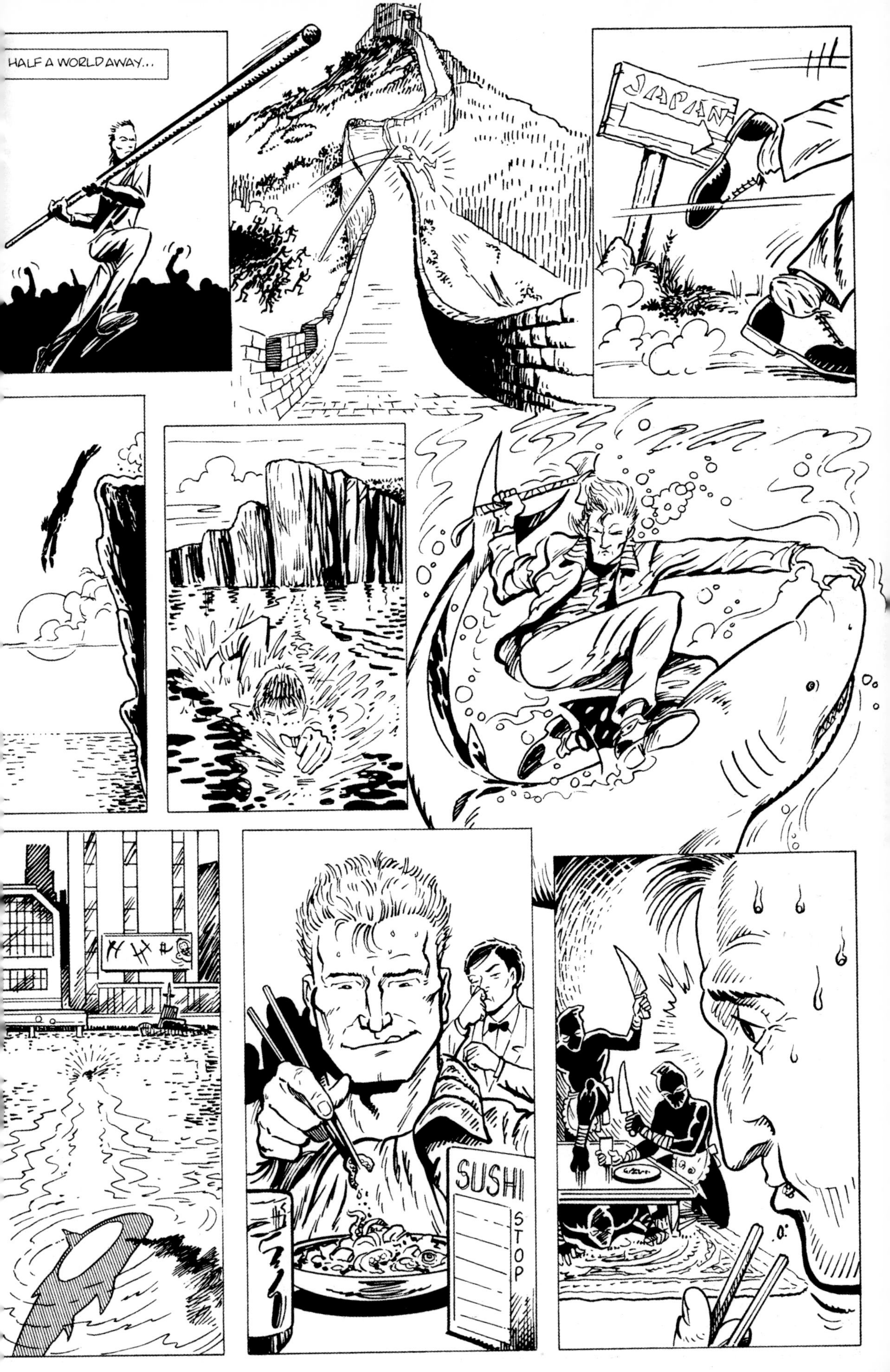

HALF A WORLD AWAY...
JAPAN
SUSHI
STOP

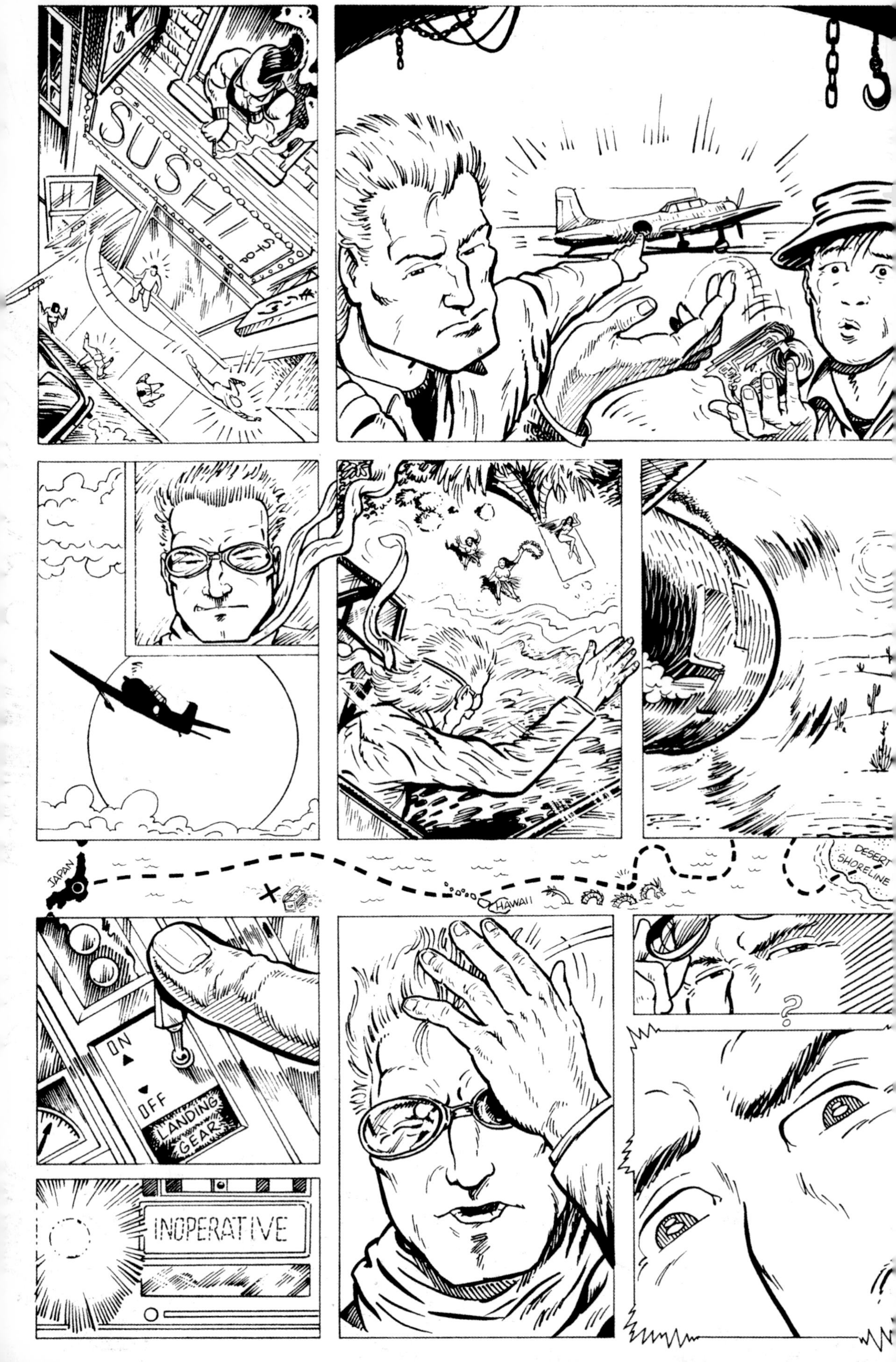
SUSHI
JAPAN
HAWAII
DESERT
SHORELINE
ON
OFF
LANDING
GEAR
INOPERATIVE

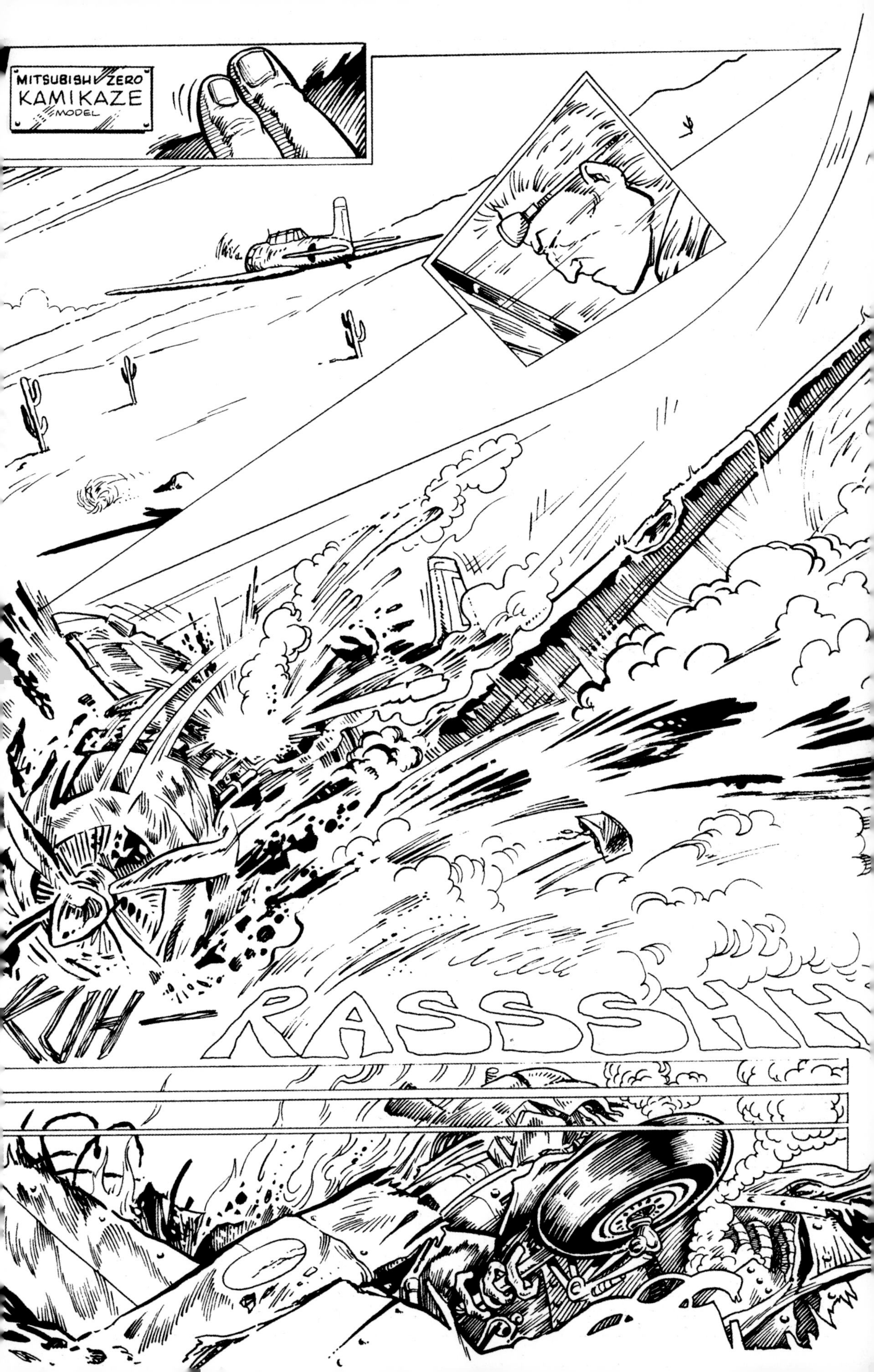
MITSUBISHI ZERO
KAMIKAZE
MODEL
KUH-RASSSHH

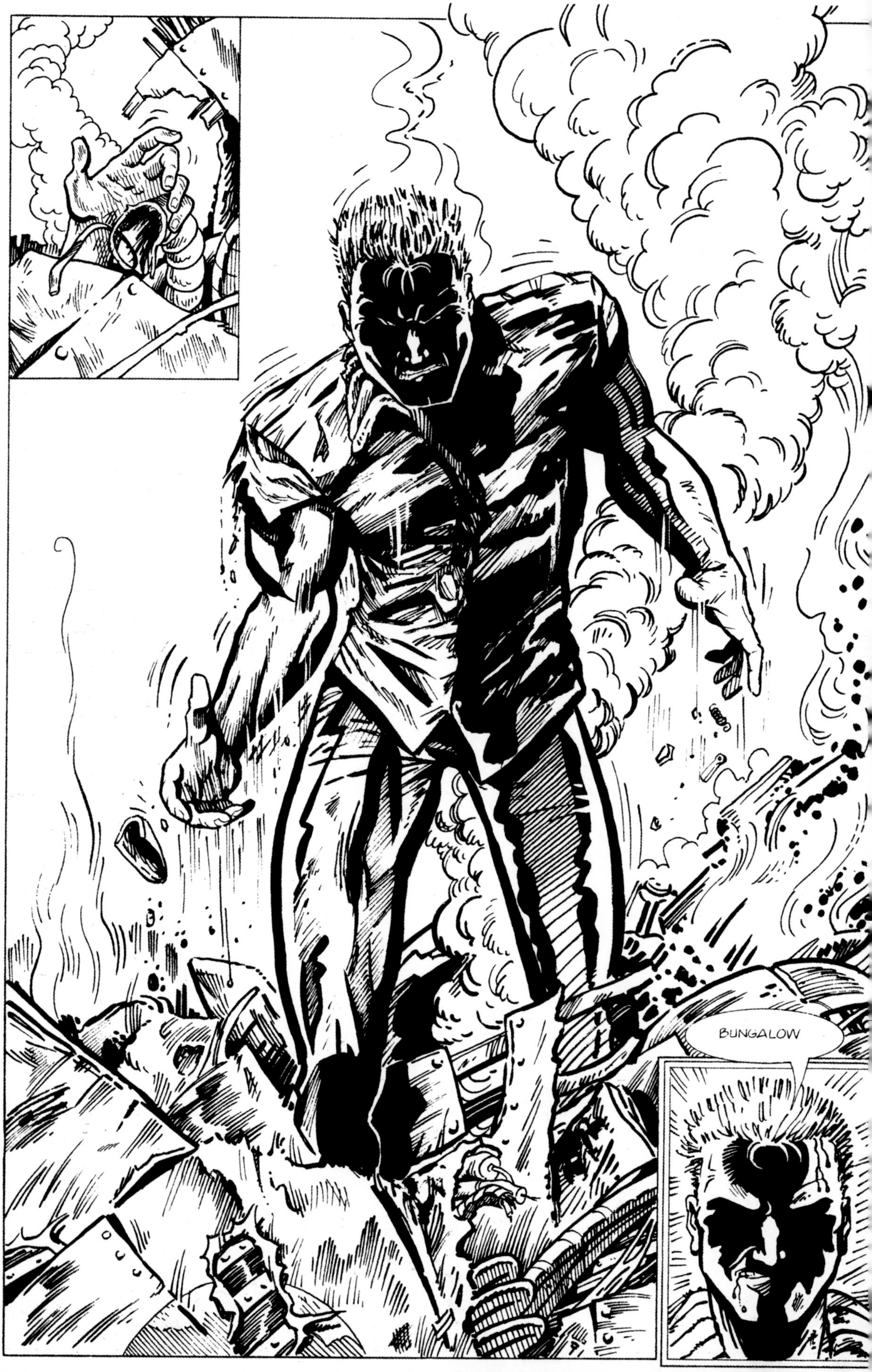
BUNGALOW

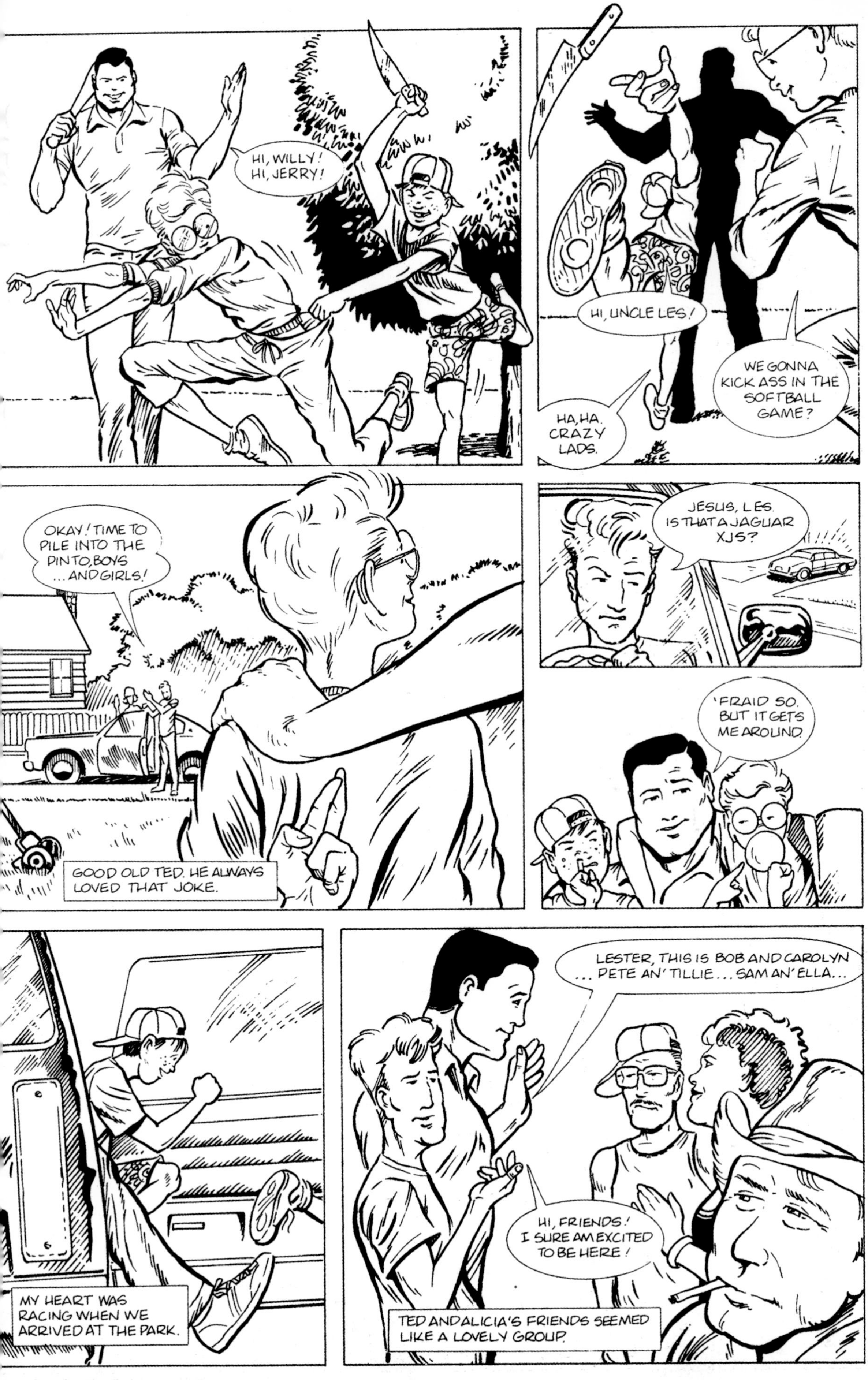

HI, WILLY! HI, JERRY!
HI, UNCLE LES!
WE GONNA KICK ASS IN THE SOFTBALL GAME?
HA, HA. CRAZY LADS.
OKAY! TIME TO PILE INTO THE PINTO, BOYS ...AND GIRLS!
GOOD OLD TED. HE ALWAYS LOVED THAT JOKE.
JESUS, LES. IS THAT A JAGUAR XJS?
'FRAID SO. BUT IT GETS ME AROUND.
MY HEART WAS RACING WHEN WE ARRIVED AT THE PARK.
LESTER, THIS IS BOB AND CAROLYN ... PETE AN' TILLIE ... SAM AN' ELLA...
HI, FRIENDS! I SURE AM EXCITED TO BE HERE!
TED AND ALICIA'S FRIENDS SEEMED LIKE A LOVELY GROUP.

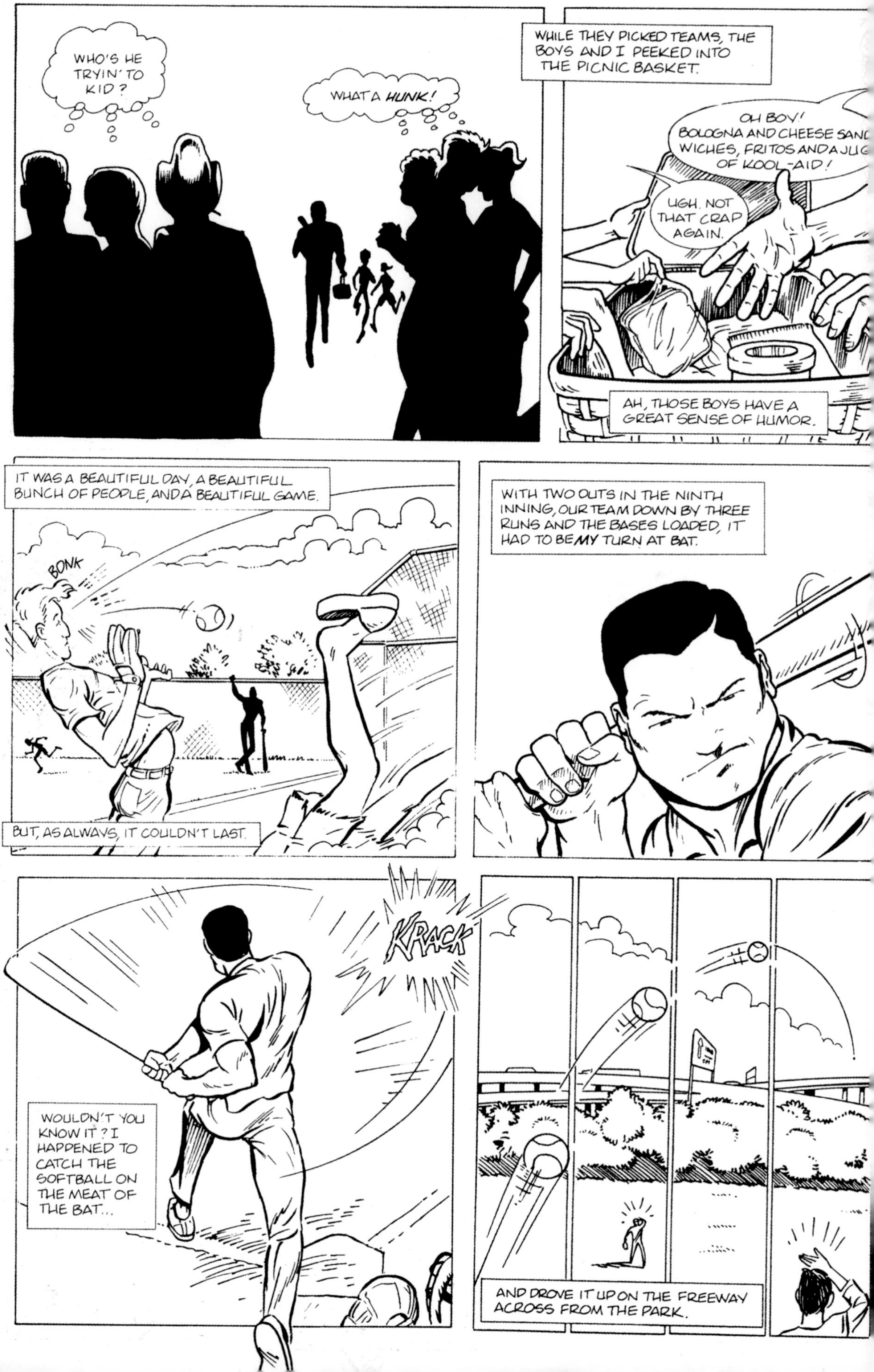
WHO'S HE TRYIN' TO KID?
WHAT A HUNK!
WHILE THEY PICKED TEAMS, THE BOYS AND I PEEKED INTO THE PICNIC BASKET.
OH BOY! BOLOGNA AND CHEESE SAND WICHES, FRITOS AND A JUG OF KOOL-AID!
UGH. NOT THAT CRAP AGAIN.
AH, THOSE BOYS HAVE A GREAT SENSE OF HUMOR.
IT WAS A BEAUTIFUL DAY, A BEAUTIFUL BUNCH OF PEOPLE, AND A BEAUTIFUL GAME.
BONK
BUT, AS ALWAYS, IT COULDN'T LAST.
WITH TWO OUTS IN THE NINTH INNING, OUR TEAM DOWN BY THREE RUNS AND THE BASES LOADED, IT HAD TO BE MY TURN AT BAT.
KRACK
WOULDN'T YOU KNOW IT? I HAPPENED TO CATCH THE SOFTBALL ON THE MEAT OF THE BAT...
AND DROVE IT UP ON THE FREEWAY ACROSS FROM THE PARK.

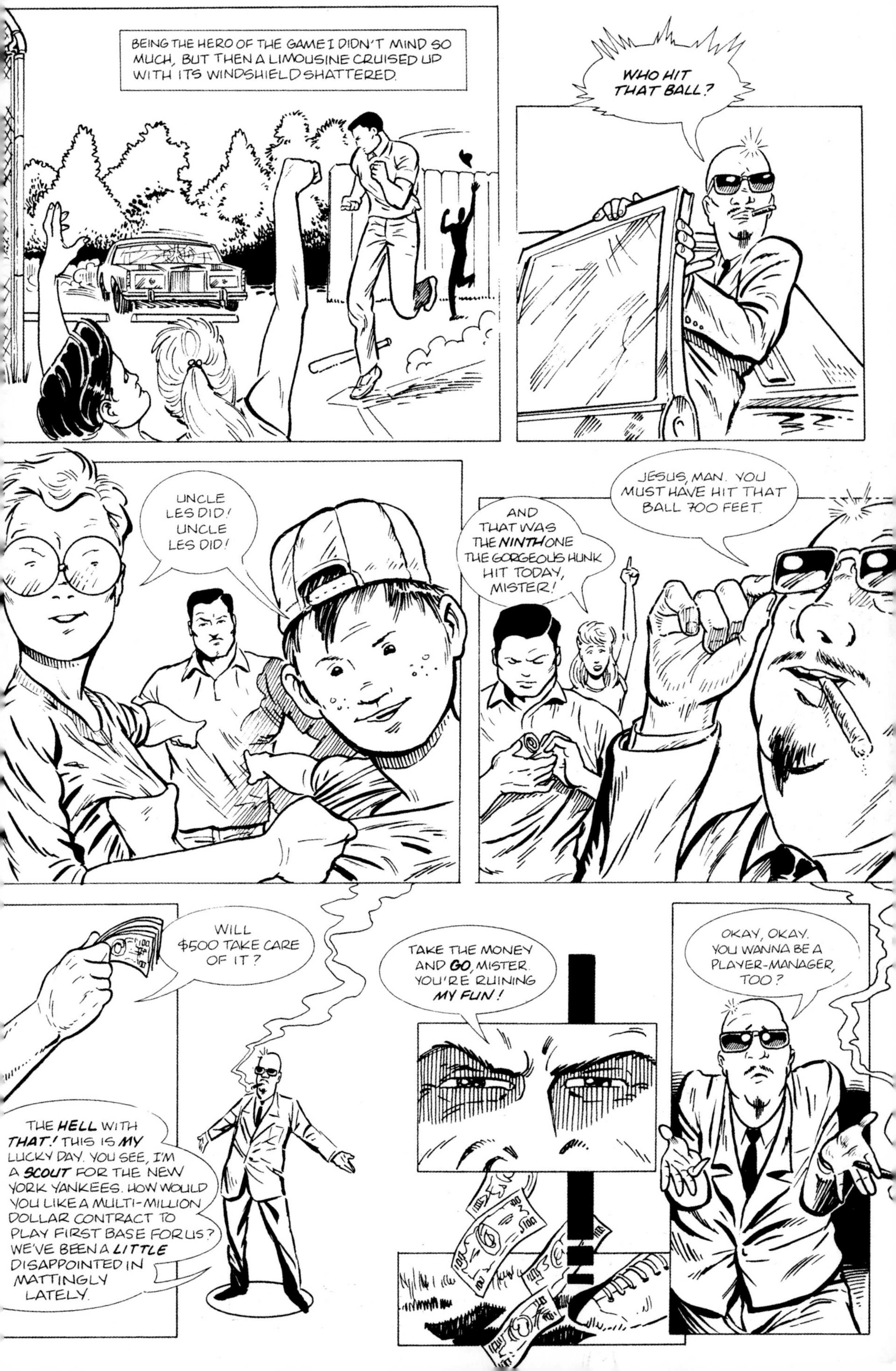
BEING THE HERO OF THE GAME I DIDN'T MIND SO MUCH, BUT THEN A LIMOUSINE CRUISED UP WITH ITS WINDSHIELD SHATTERED.
WHO HIT THAT BALL?
UNCLE LES DID! UNCLE LES DID!
JESUS, MAN. YOU MUST HAVE HIT THAT BALL 700 FEET.
AND THAT WAS THE NINTH ONE THE GORGEOUS HUNK HIT TODAY, MISTER!
WILL $500 TAKE CARE OF IT?
THE HELL WITH THAT! THIS IS MY LUCKY DAY. YOU SEE, I'M A SCOUT FOR THE NEW YORK YANKEES. HOW WOULD YOU LIKE A MULTI-MILLION DOLLAR CONTRACT TO PLAY FIRST BASE FOR US? WE'VE BEEN A LITTLE DISAPPOINTED IN MATTINGLY LATELY.
TAKE THE MONEY AND GO, MISTER. YOU'RE RUINING MY FUN!
OKAY, OKAY. YOU WANNA BE A PLAYER-MANAGER, TOO?

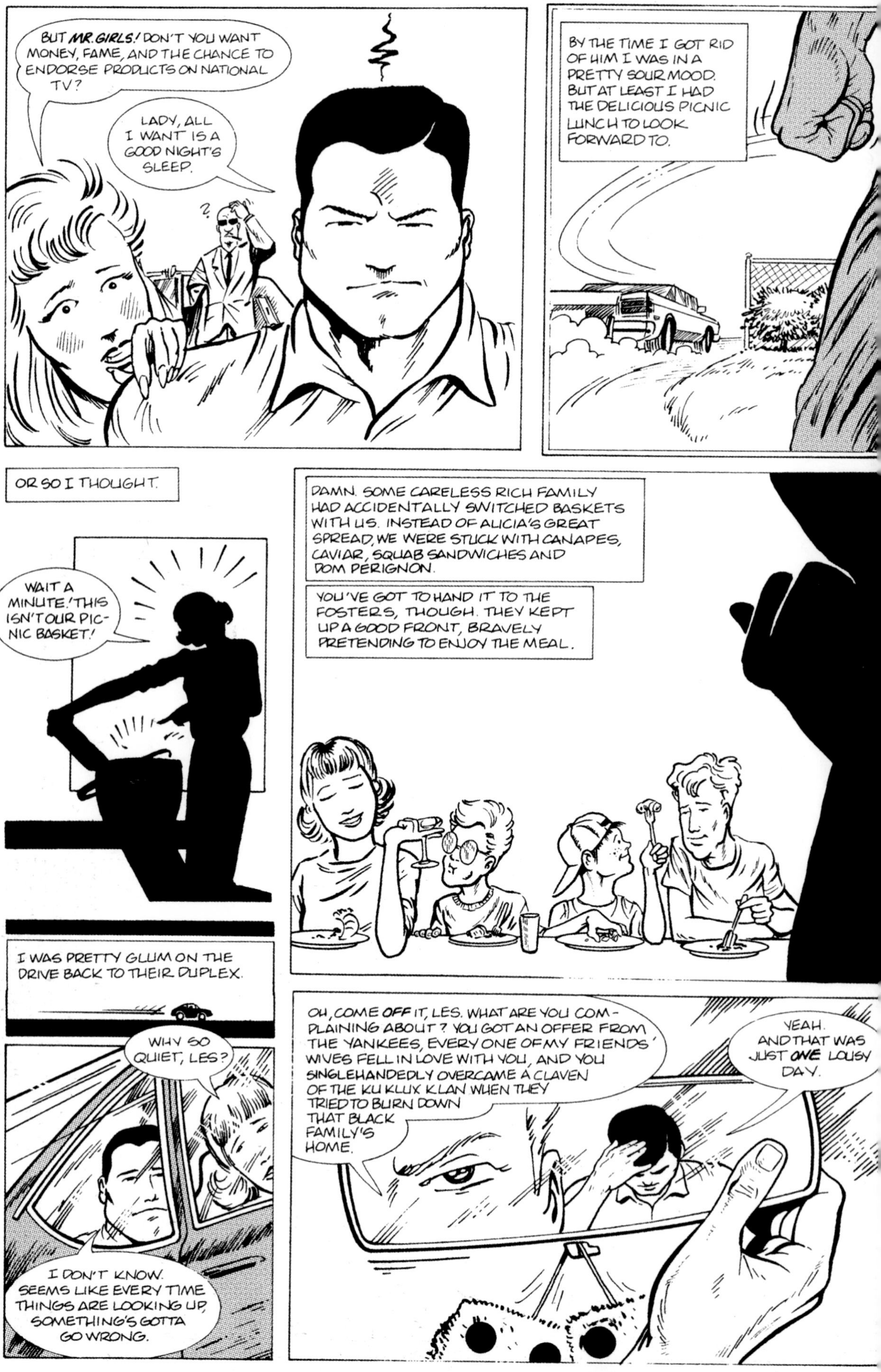
BUT MR. GIRLS! DON'T YOU WANT MONEY, FAME, AND THE CHANCE TO ENDORSE PRODUCTS ON NATIONAL TV?
LADY, ALL I WANT IS A GOOD NIGHT'S SLEEP.
?
BY THE TIME I GOT RID OF HIM I WAS IN A PRETTY SOUR MOOD. BUT AT LEAST I HAD THE DELICIOUS PICNIC LUNCH TO LOOK FORWARD TO.
OR SO I THOUGHT.
WAIT A MINUTE! THIS ISN'T OUR PICNIC BASKET!
DAMN. SOME CARELESS RICH FAMILY HAD ACCIDENTALLY SWITCHED BASKETS WITH US. INSTEAD OF ALICIA'S GREAT SPREAD, WE WERE STUCK WITH CANAPES, CAVIAR, SQUAB SANDWICHES AND DOM PERIGNON.
YOU'VE GOT TO HAND IT TO THE FOSTERS, THOUGH. THEY KEPT UP A GOOD FRONT, BRAVELY PRETENDING TO ENJOY THE MEAL.
I WAS PRETTY GLUM ON THE DRIVE BACK TO THEIR DUPLEX.
WHY SO QUIET, LES?
I DON'T KNOW. SEEMS LIKE EVERY TIME THINGS ARE LOOKING UP, SOMETHING'S GOTTA GO WRONG.
OH, COME OFF IT, LES. WHAT ARE YOU COMPLAINING ABOUT? YOU GOT AN OFFER FROM THE YANKEES, EVERY ONE OF MY FRIENDS' WIVES FELL IN LOVE WITH YOU, AND YOU SINGLEHANDEDLY OVERCAME A CLAVEN OF THE KU KLUX KLAN WHEN THEY TRIED TO BURN DOWN THAT BLACK FAMILY'S HOME.
YEAH. AND THAT WAS JUST ONE LOUSY DAY.

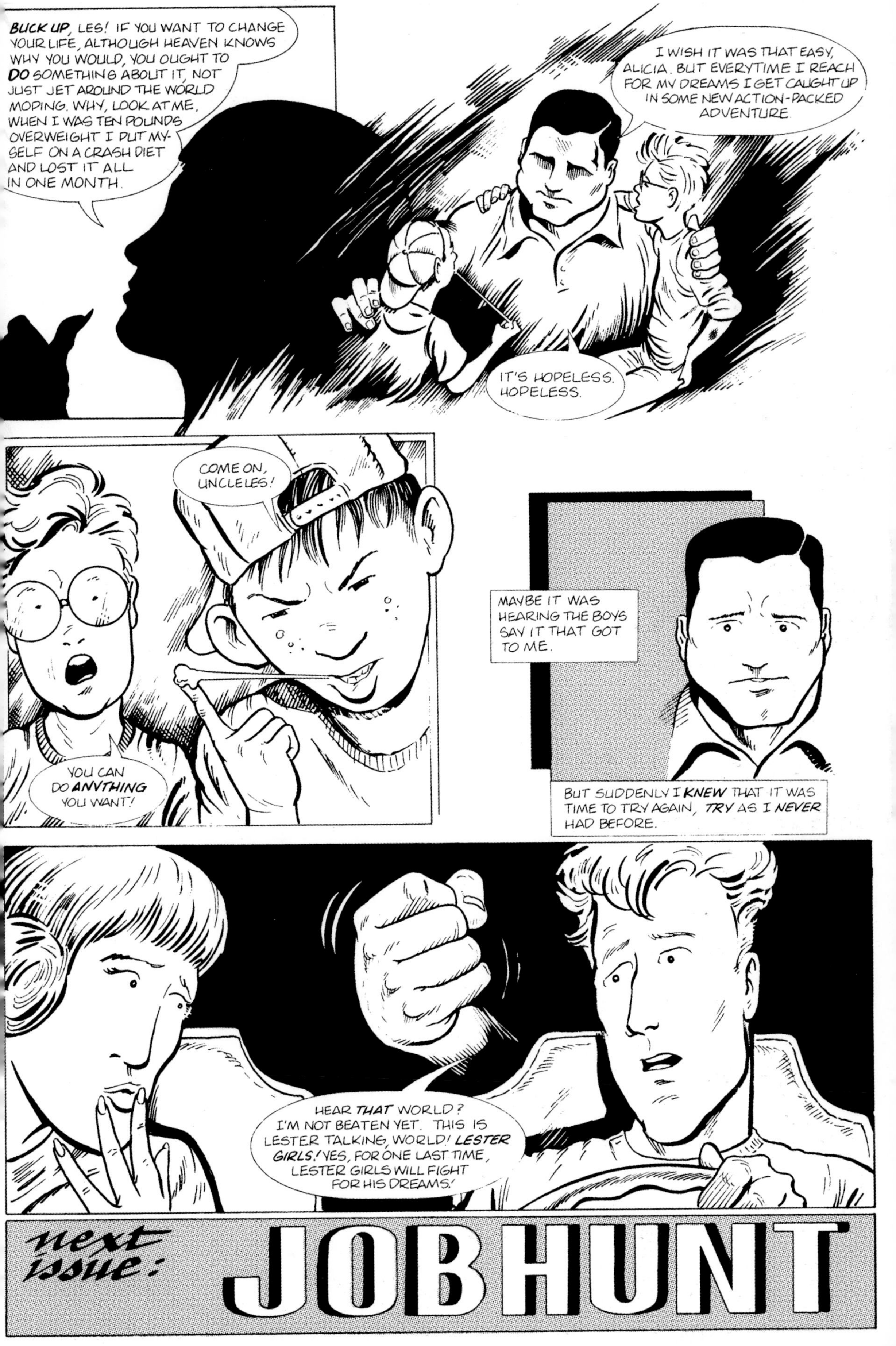

BUCK UP, LES! IF YOU WANT TO CHANGE YOUR LIFE, ALTHOUGH HEAVEN KNOWS WHY YOU WOULD, YOU OUGHT TO DO SOMETHING ABOUT IT, NOT JUST JET AROUND THE WORLD MOPING. WHY, LOOK AT ME, WHEN I WAS TEN POUNDS OVERWEIGHT I PUT MYSELF ON A CRASH DIET AND LOST IT ALL IN ONE MONTH.
I WISH IT WAS THAT EASY, ALICIA. BUT EVERYTIME I REACH FOR MY DREAMS I GET CAUGHT UP IN SOME NEW ACTION-PACKED ADVENTURE.
IT'S HOPELESS. HOPELESS.
COME ON, UNCLE LES!
YOU CAN DO ANYTHING YOU WANT!
MAYBE IT WAS HEARING THE BOYS SAY IT THAT GOT TO ME.
BUT SUDDENLY I KNEW THAT IT WAS TIME TO TRY AGAIN, TRY AS I NEVER HAD BEFORE.
HEAR THAT WORLD? I'M NOT BEATEN YET. THIS IS LESTER TALKING, WORLD! LESTER GIRLS! YES, FOR ONE LAST TIME, LESTER GIRLS WILL FIGHT FOR HIS DREAMS!
next issue: JOB HUNT

THE TROUBLE WITH GIRLS™

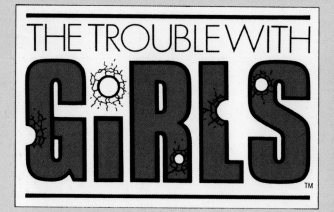

CHAPTER 3

OCTOBER 1987

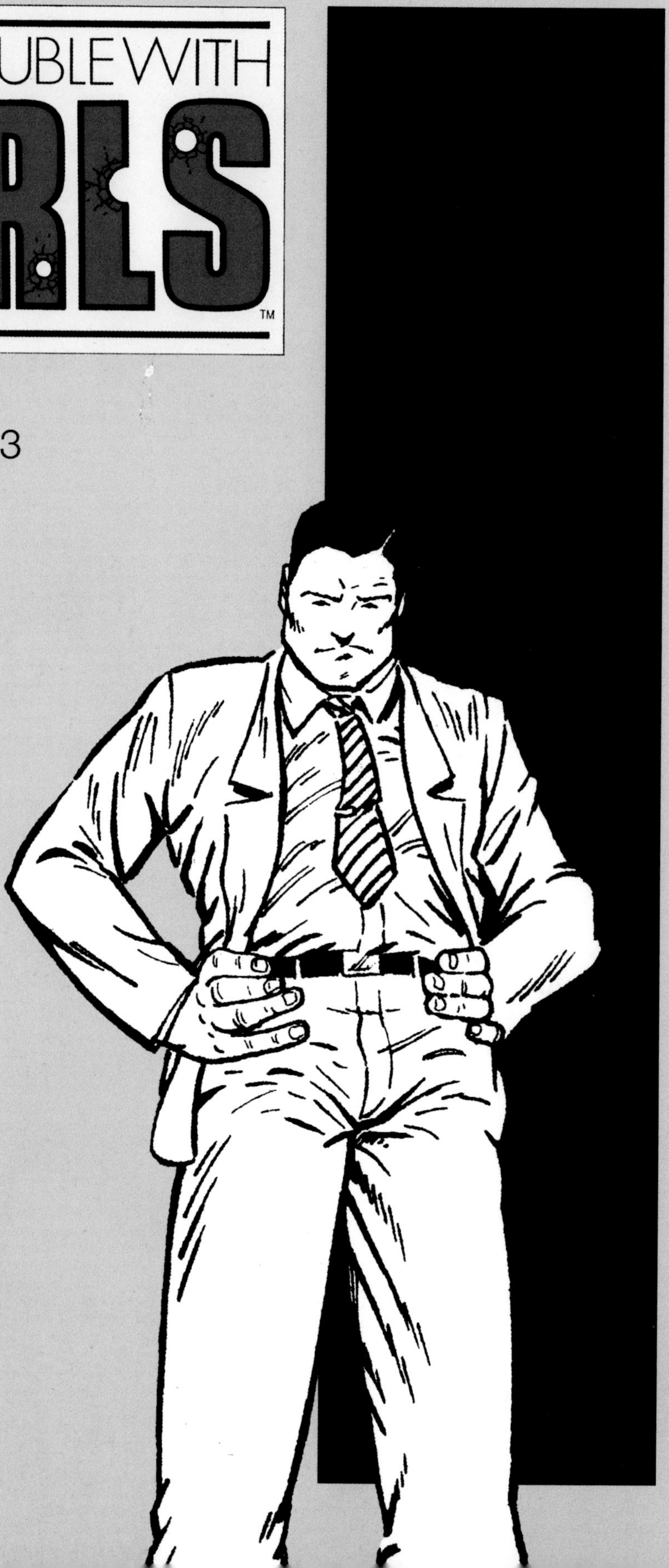

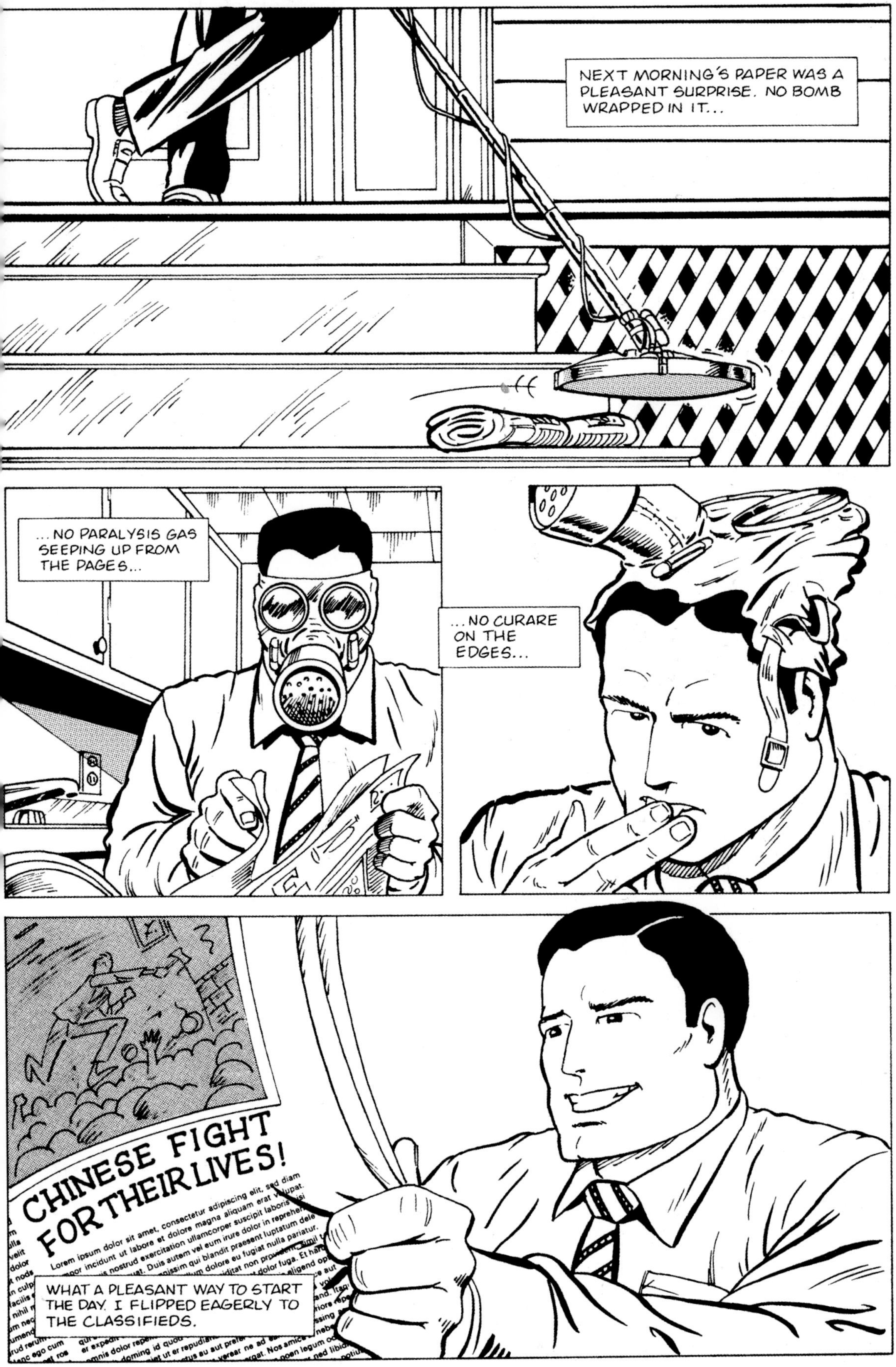
NEXT MORNING'S PAPER WAS A PLEASANT SURPRISE. NO BOMB WRAPPED IN IT...
...NO PARALYSIS GAS SEEPING UP FROM THE PAGES...
...NO CURARE ON THE EDGES...
CHINESE FIGHT FOR THEIR LIVES!
WHAT A PLEASANT WAY TO START THE DAY. I FLIPPED EAGERLY TO THE CLASSIFIEDS.

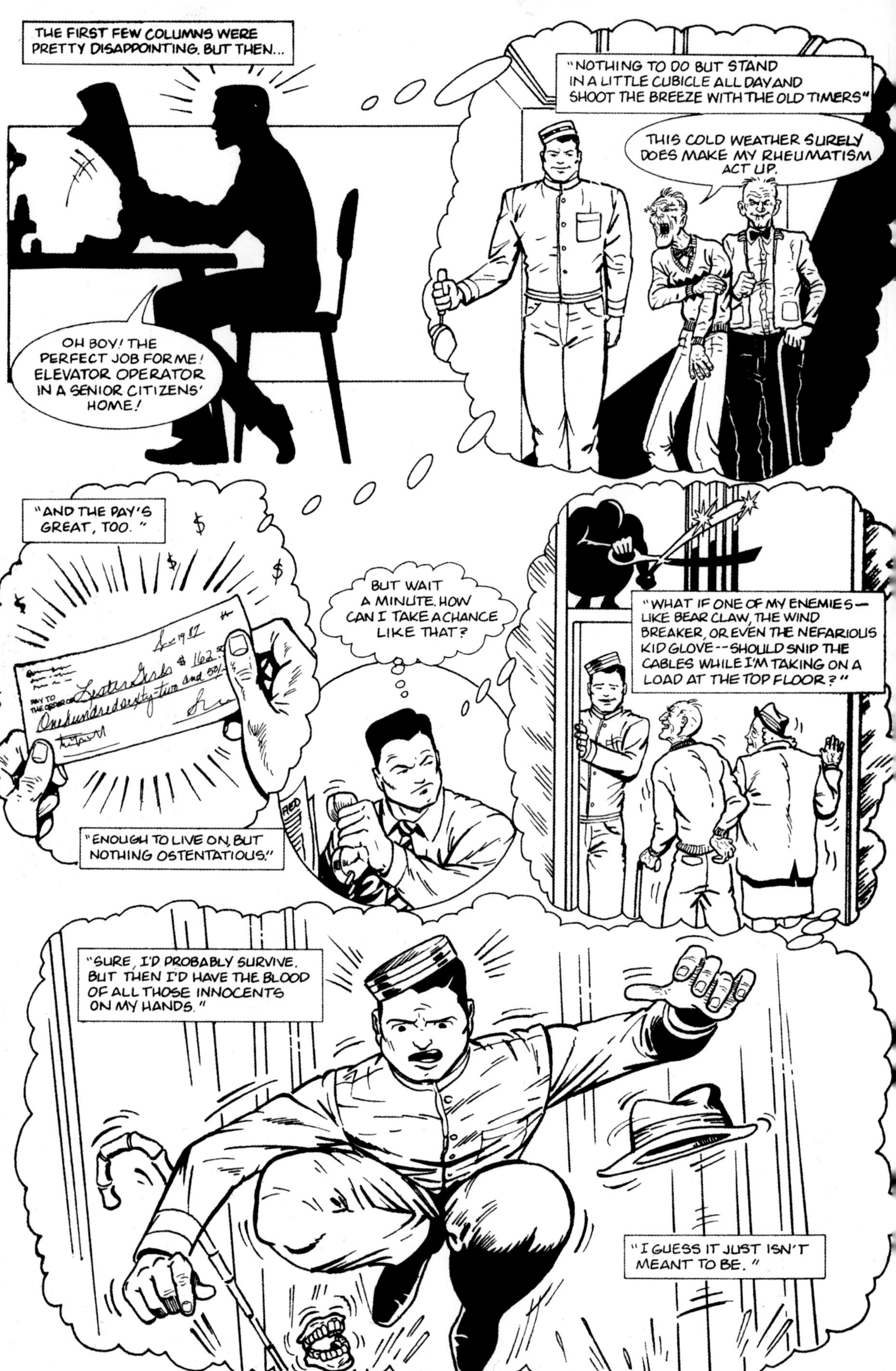
THE FIRST FEW COLUMNS WERE PRETTY DISAPPOINTING. BUT THEN...
OH BOY! THE PERFECT JOB FOR ME! ELEVATOR OPERATOR IN A SENIOR CITIZENS' HOME!
"NOTHING TO DO BUT STAND IN A LITTLE CUBICLE ALL DAY AND SHOOT THE BREEZE WITH THE OLD TIMERS"
THIS COLD WEATHER SURELY DOES MAKE MY RHEUMATISM ACT UP.
"AND THE PAY'S GREAT, TOO."
"ENOUGH TO LIVE ON, BUT NOTHING OSTENTATIOUS."
BUT WAIT A MINUTE. HOW CAN I TAKE A CHANCE LIKE THAT?
"WHAT IF ONE OF MY ENEMIES— LIKE BEAR CLAW, THE WIND BREAKER, OR EVEN THE NEFARIOUS KID GLOVE--SHOULD SNIP THE CABLES WHILE I'M TAKING ON A LOAD AT THE TOP FLOOR?"
"SURE, I'D PROBABLY SURVIVE. BUT THEN I'D HAVE THE BLOOD OF ALL THOSE INNOCENTS ON MY HANDS."
"I GUESS IT JUST ISN'T MEANT TO BE."

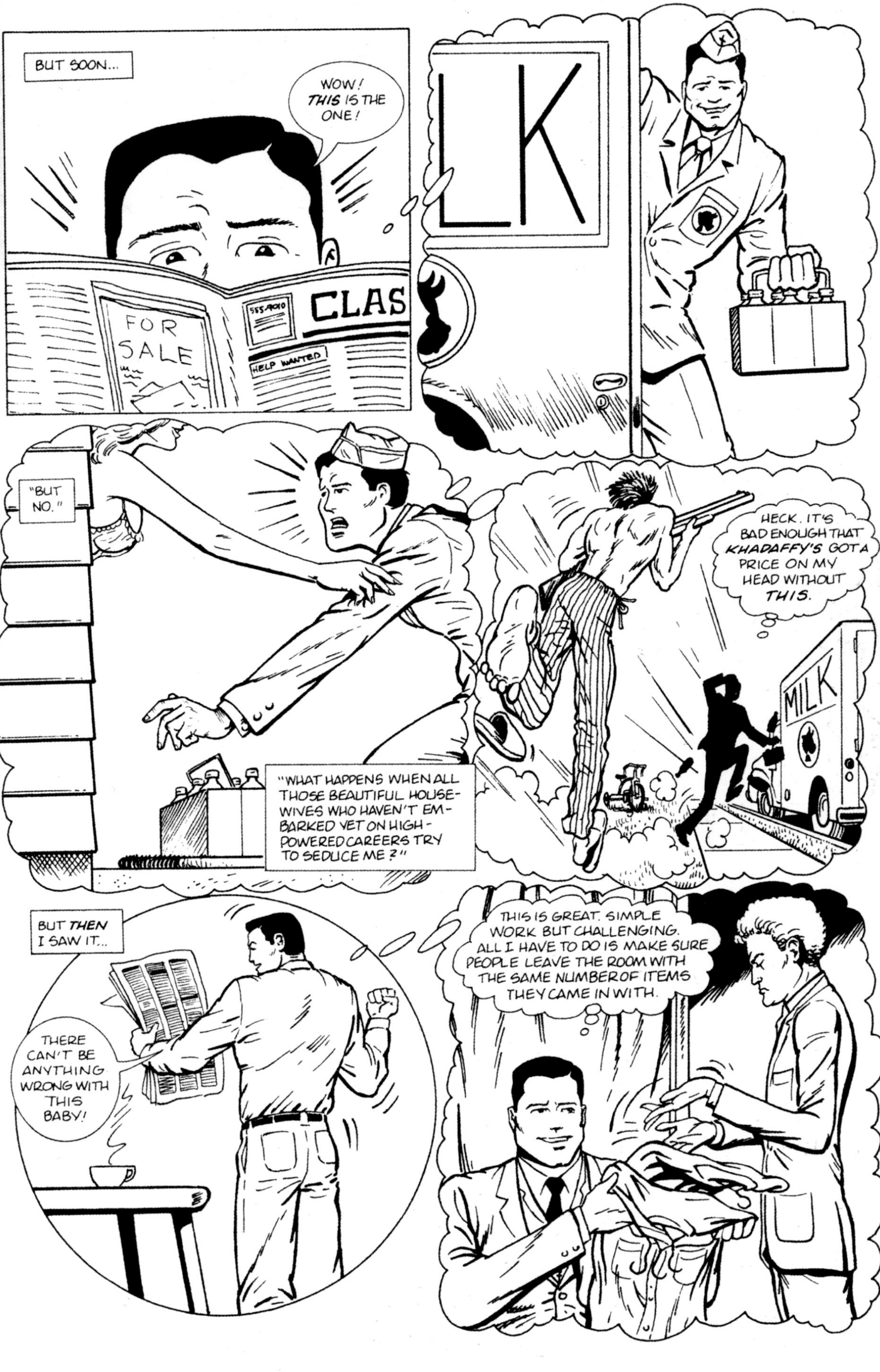
BUT SOON...
WOW! THIS IS THE ONE!
CLAS
FOR SALE
555-9010
HELP WANTED
LK
"BUT NO."
"WHAT HAPPENS WHEN ALL THOSE BEAUTIFUL HOUSE-WIVES WHO HAVEN'T EM-BARKED YET ON HIGH-POWERED CAREERS TRY TO SEDUCE ME?"
HECK. IT'S BAD ENOUGH THAT KHADAFFY'S GOT A PRICE ON MY HEAD WITHOUT THIS.
MILK
BUT THEN I SAW IT...
THERE CAN'T BE ANYTHING WRONG WITH THIS BABY!
THIS IS GREAT. SIMPLE WORK BUT CHALLENGING. ALL I HAVE TO DO IS MAKE SURE PEOPLE LEAVE THE ROOM WITH THE SAME NUMBER OF ITEMS THEY CAME IN WITH.

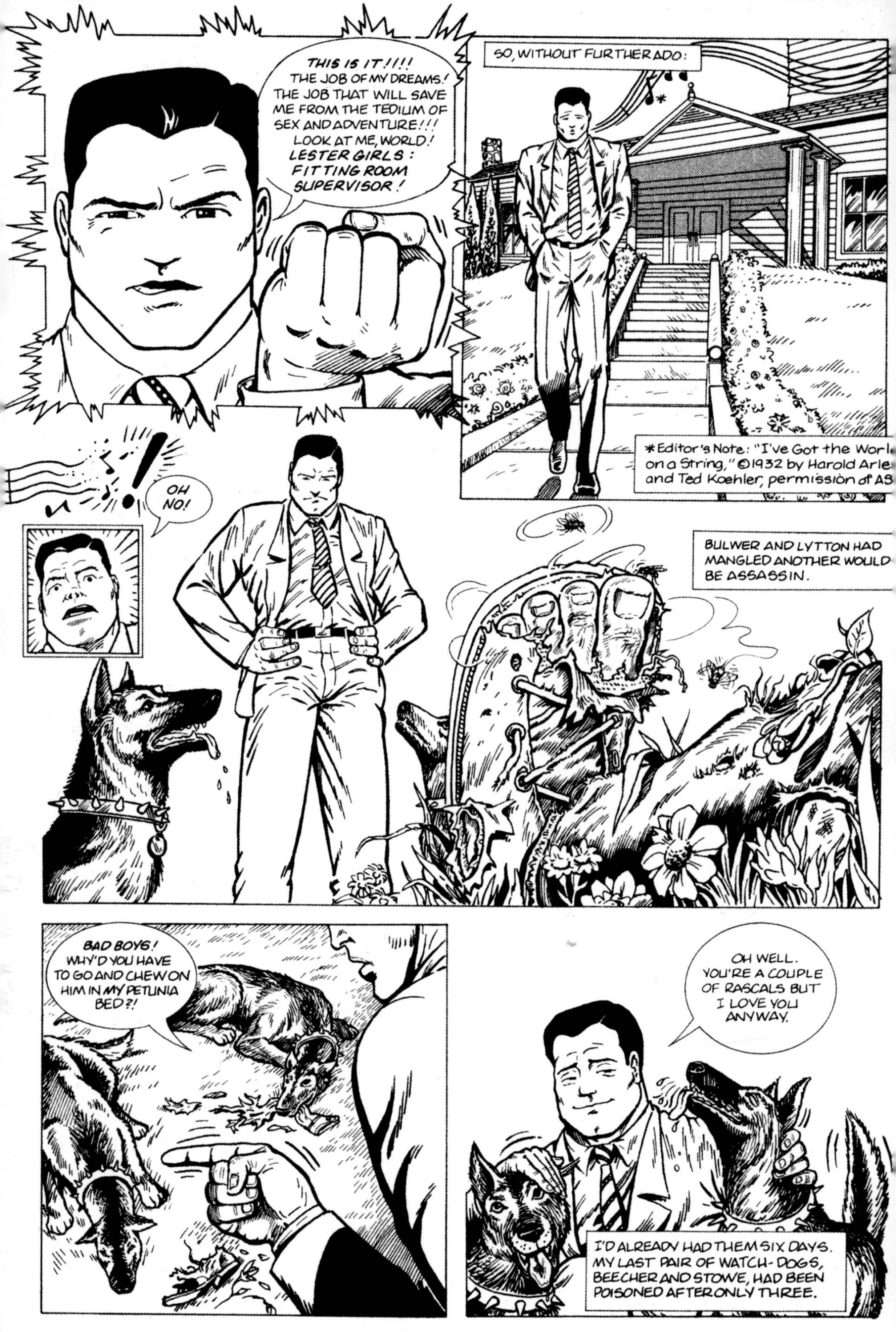

THIS IS IT!!!! THE JOB OF MY DREAMS! THE JOB THAT WILL SAVE ME FROM THE TEDIUM OF SEX AND ADVENTURE!!! LOOK AT ME, WORLD! LESTER GIRLS: FITTING ROOM SUPERVISOR!
SO, WITHOUT FURTHER ADO:
*Editor's Note: "I've Got the World on a String," ©1932 by Harold Arlen and Ted Koehler, permission of ASCAP
OH NO!
BULWER AND LYTTON HAD MANGLED ANOTHER WOULD-BE ASSASSIN.
BAD BOYS! WHY'D YOU HAVE TO GO AND CHEW ON HIM IN MY PETUNIA BED?!
OH WELL. YOU'RE A COUPLE OF RASCALS BUT I LOVE YOU ANYWAY.
I'D ALREADY HAD THEM SIX DAYS. MY LAST PAIR OF WATCH-DOGS, BEECHER AND STOWE, HAD BEEN POISONED AFTER ONLY THREE.

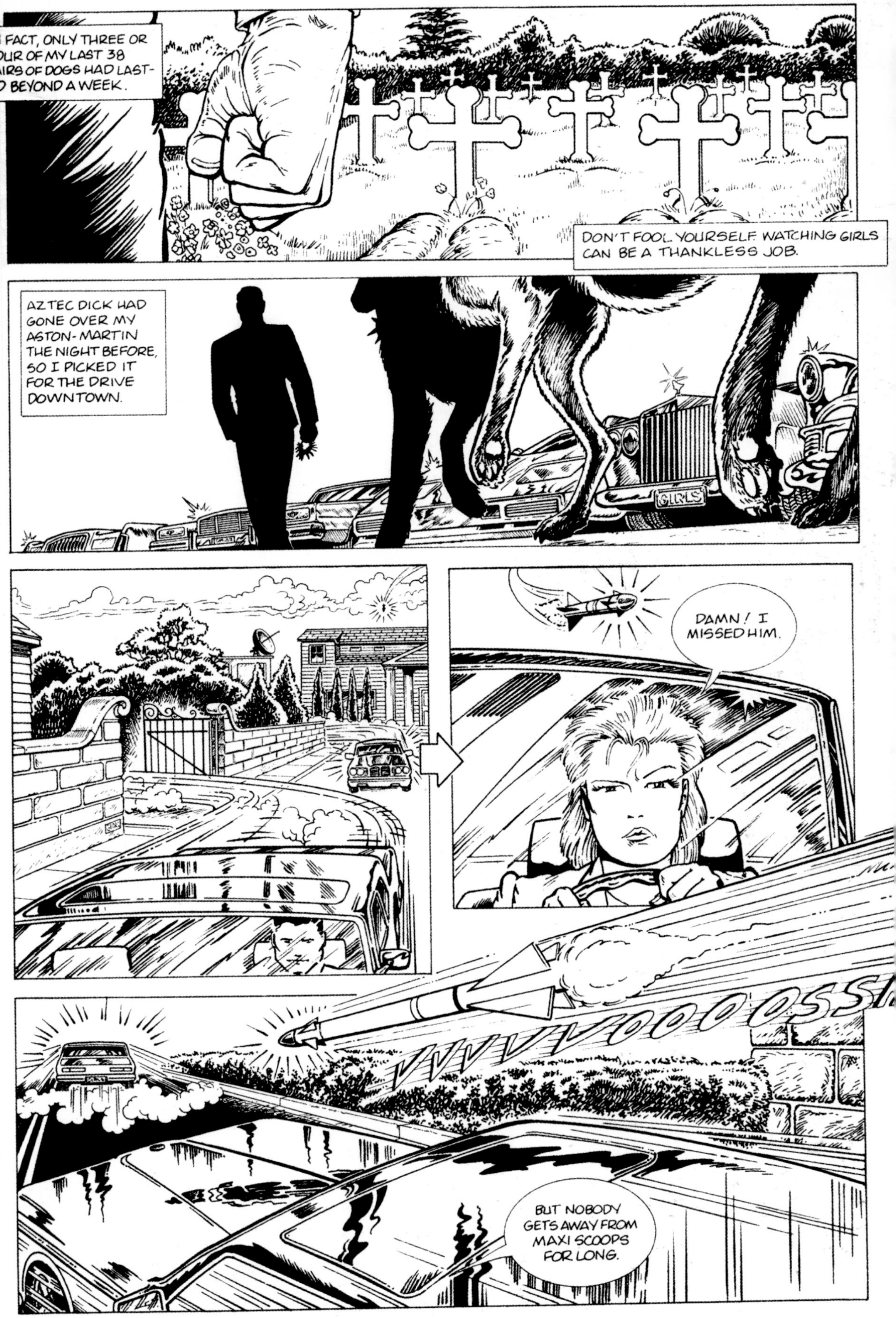

N FACT, ONLY THREE OR OUR OF MY LAST 38 AIRS OF DOGS HAD LAST- D BEYOND A WEEK.
DON'T FOOL YOURSELF. WATCHING GIRLS CAN BE A THANKLESS JOB.
AZTEC DICK HAD GONE OVER MY ASTON-MARTIN THE NIGHT BEFORE, SO I PICKED IT FOR THE DRIVE DOWNTOWN.
GIRLS
DAMN! I MISSED HIM.
VVVVVVOOOOOSS
BUT NOBODY GETS AWAY FROM MAXI SCOOPS FOR LONG.

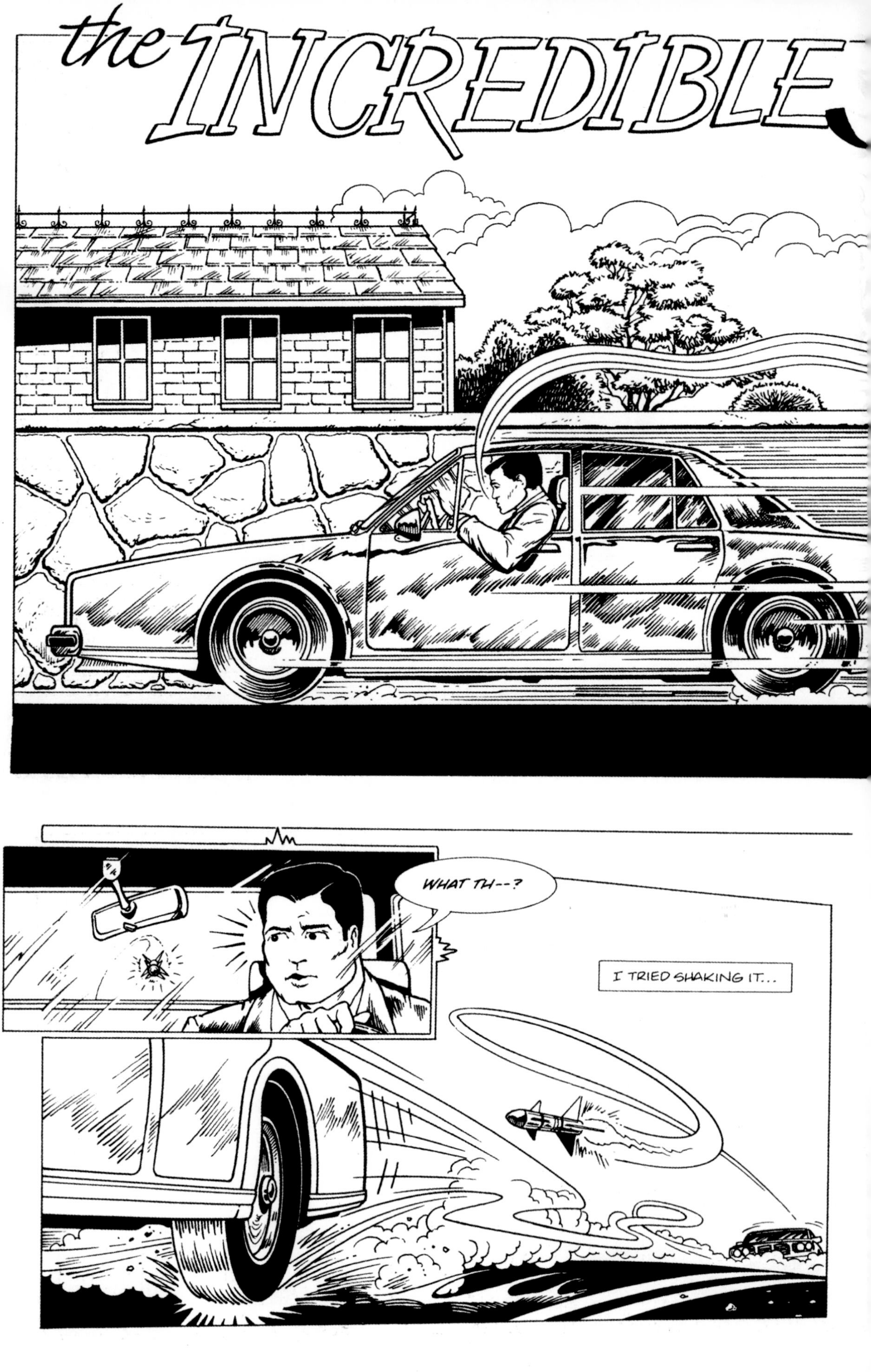
the INCREDIBLE
WHAT TH--?
I TRIED SHAKING IT...

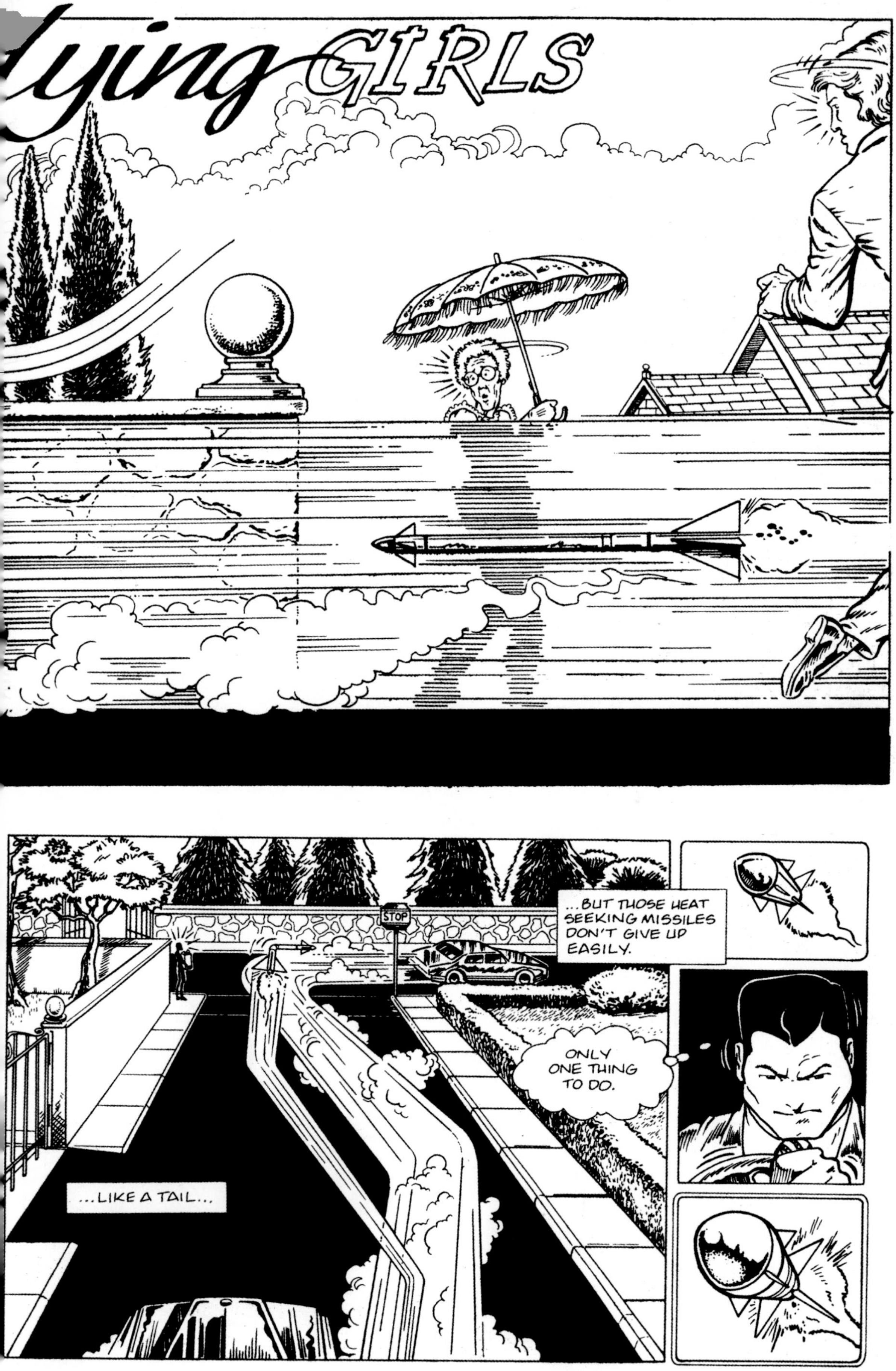
lying GIRLS
STOP
...BUT THOSE HEAT SEEKING MISSILES DON'T GIVE UP EASILY.
ONLY ONE THING TO DO.
...LIKE A TAIL...

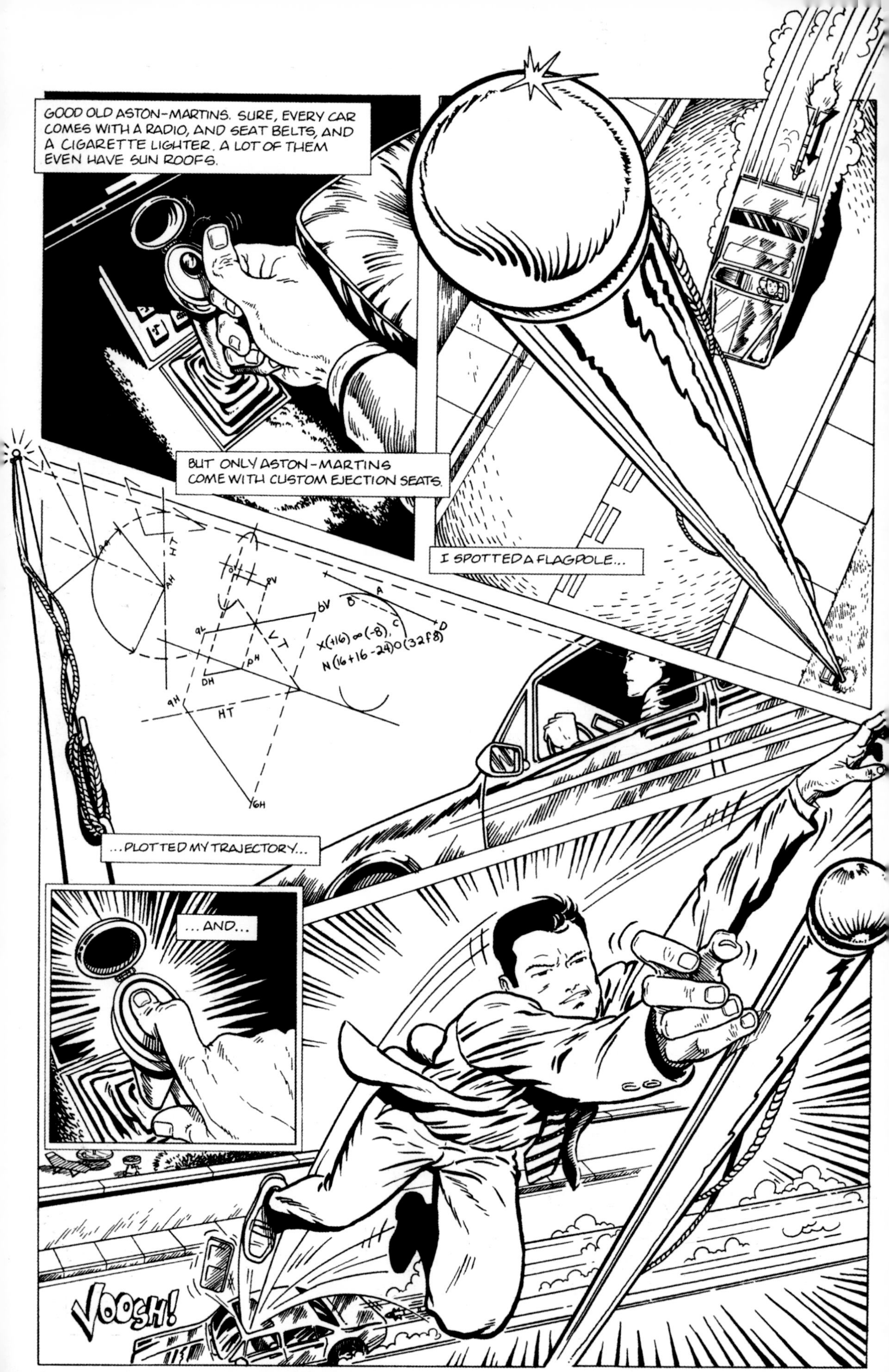
GOOD OLD ASTON-MARTINS. SURE, EVERY CAR COMES WITH A RADIO, AND SEAT BELTS, AND A CIGARETTE LIGHTER. A LOT OF THEM EVEN HAVE SUN ROOFS.
BUT ONLY ASTON-MARTINS COME WITH CUSTOM EJECTION SEATS.
I SPOTTED A FLAGPOLE...
...PLOTTED MY TRAJECTORY...
...AND...
VOOSH!

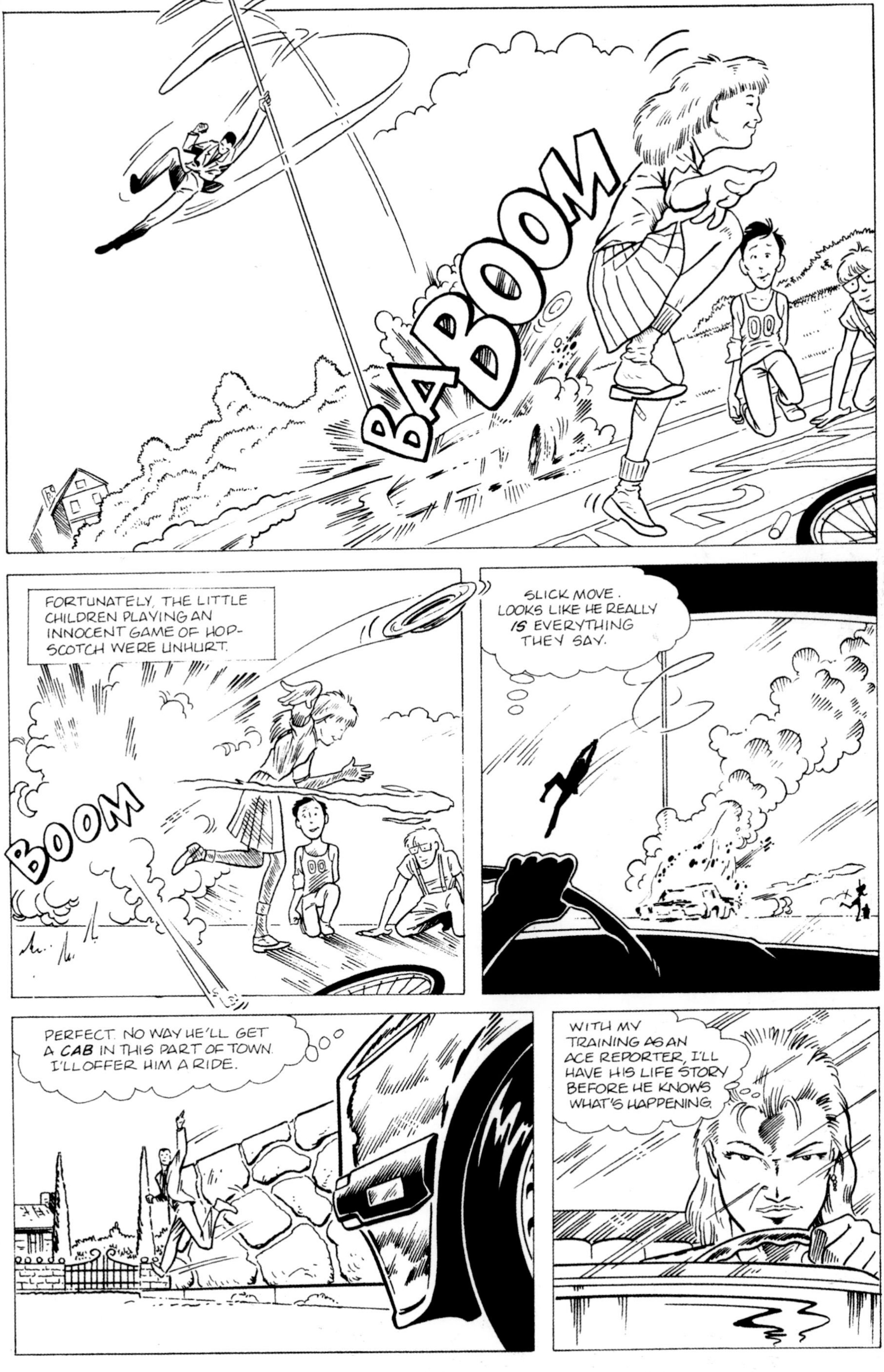
BABOOM
FORTUNATELY, THE LITTLE CHILDREN PLAYING AN INNOCENT GAME OF HOP-SCOTCH WERE UNHURT.
BOOM
SLICK MOVE. LOOKS LIKE HE REALLY IS EVERYTHING THEY SAY.
PERFECT. NO WAY HE'LL GET A CAB IN THIS PART OF TOWN. I'LL OFFER HIM A RIDE.
WITH MY TRAINING AS AN ACE REPORTER, I'LL HAVE HIS LIFE STORY BEFORE HE KNOWS WHAT'S HAPPENING.

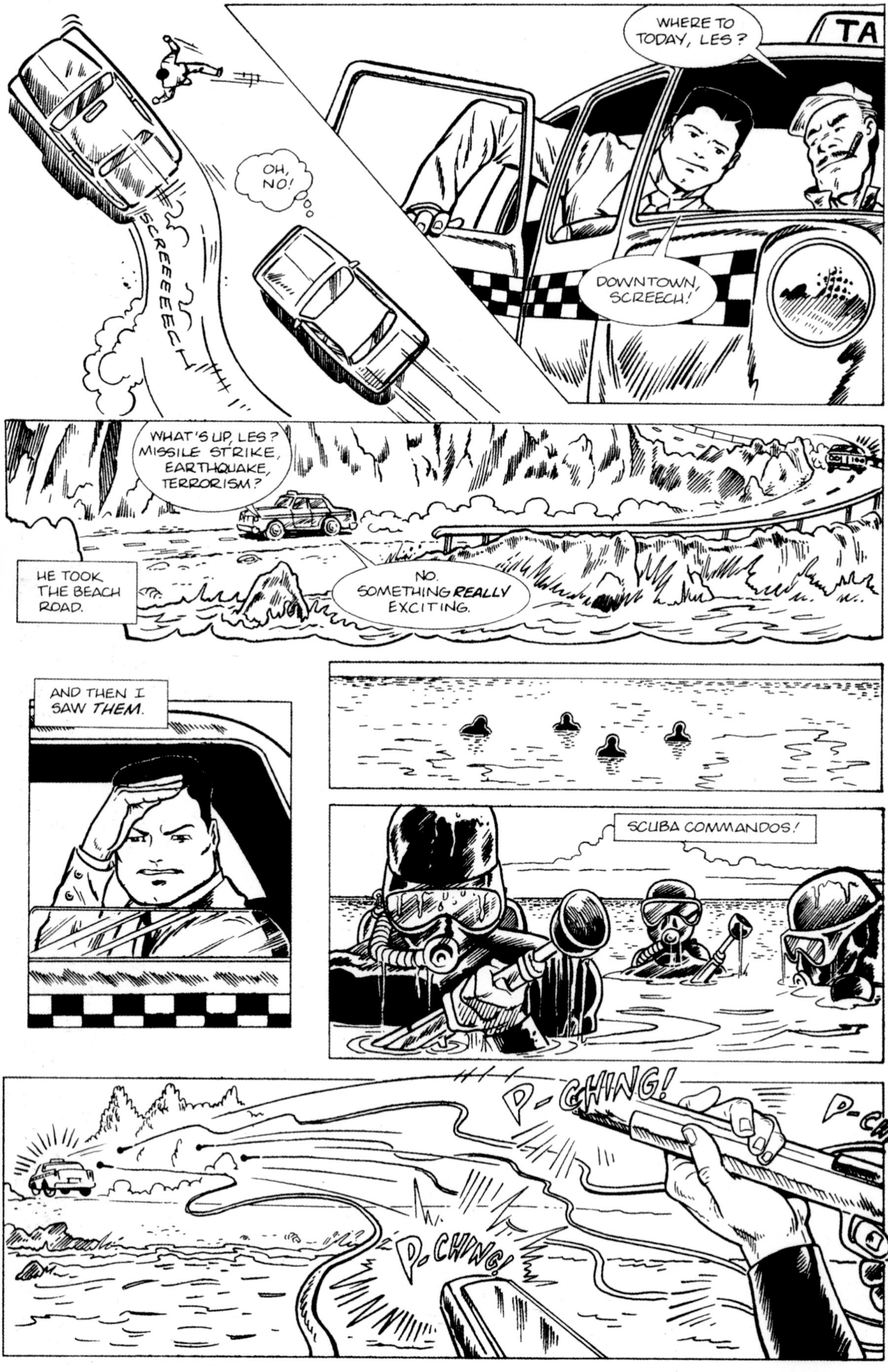
OH, NO!
SCREEEEEECH!
WHERE TO TODAY, LES?
DOWNTOWN, SCREECH!
WHAT'S UP, LES? MISSILE STRIKE, EARTHQUAKE, TERRORISM?
HE TOOK THE BEACH ROAD.
NO. SOMETHING REALLY EXCITING.
AND THEN I SAW THEM.
SCUBA COMMANDOS!
P-CHING!
P-CHING
P-CHING!

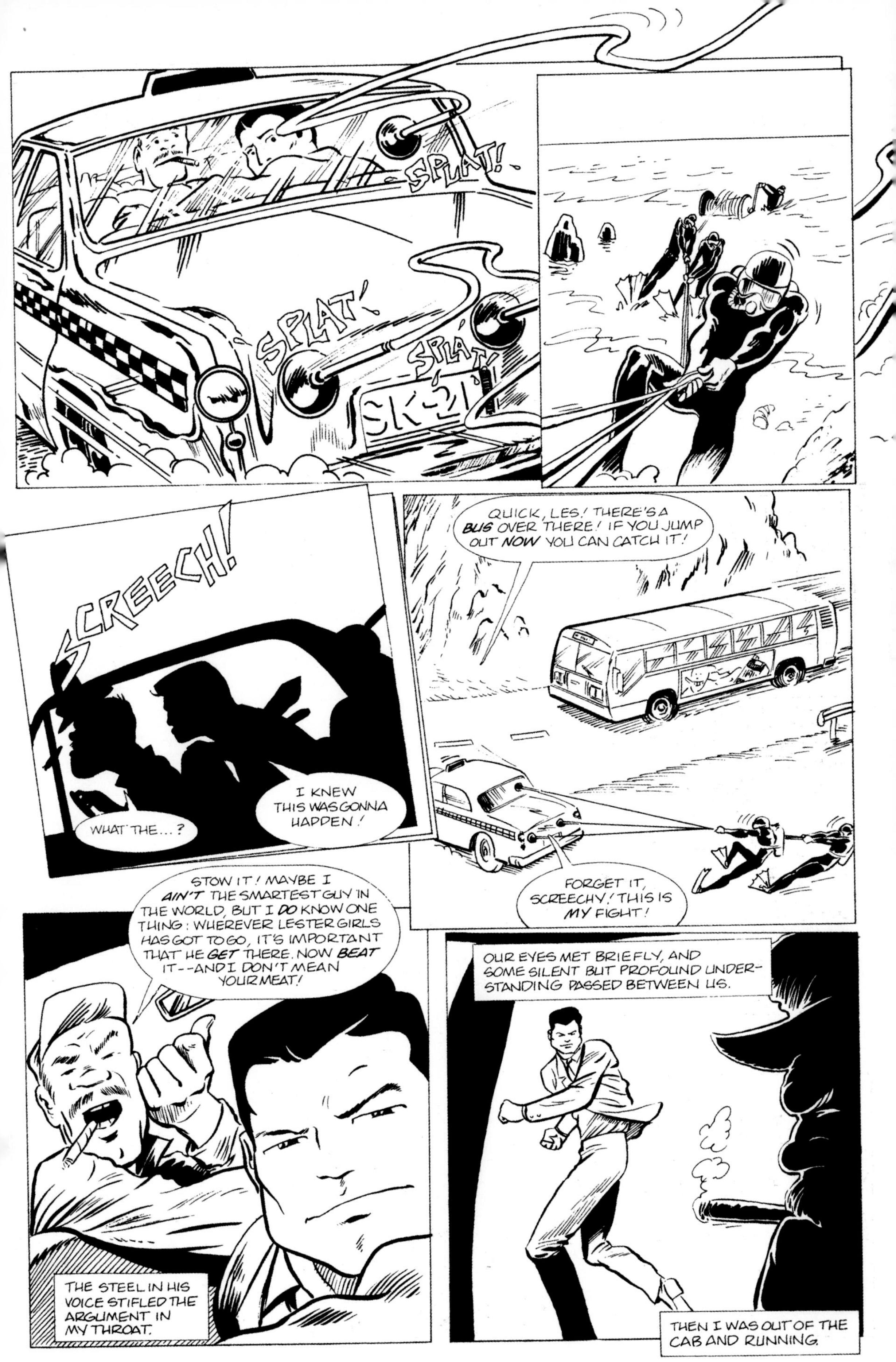
SPLAT!
SPLAT!
SPLAT!
SK-21
SCREECH!
WHAT THE...?
I KNEW THIS WAS GONNA HAPPEN!
QUICK, LES! THERE'S A BUS OVER THERE! IF YOU JUMP OUT NOW YOU CAN CATCH IT!
FORGET IT, SCREECHY! THIS IS MY FIGHT!
STOW IT! MAYBE I AIN'T THE SMARTEST GUY IN THE WORLD, BUT I DO KNOW ONE THING: WHEREVER LESTER GIRLS HAS GOT TO GO, IT'S IMPORTANT THAT HE GET THERE. NOW BEAT IT--AND I DON'T MEAN YOUR MEAT!
THE STEEL IN HIS VOICE STIFLED THE ARGUMENT IN MY THROAT.
OUR EYES MET BRIEFLY, AND SOME SILENT BUT PROFOUND UNDERSTANDING PASSED BETWEEN US.
THEN I WAS OUT OF THE CAB AND RUNNING.

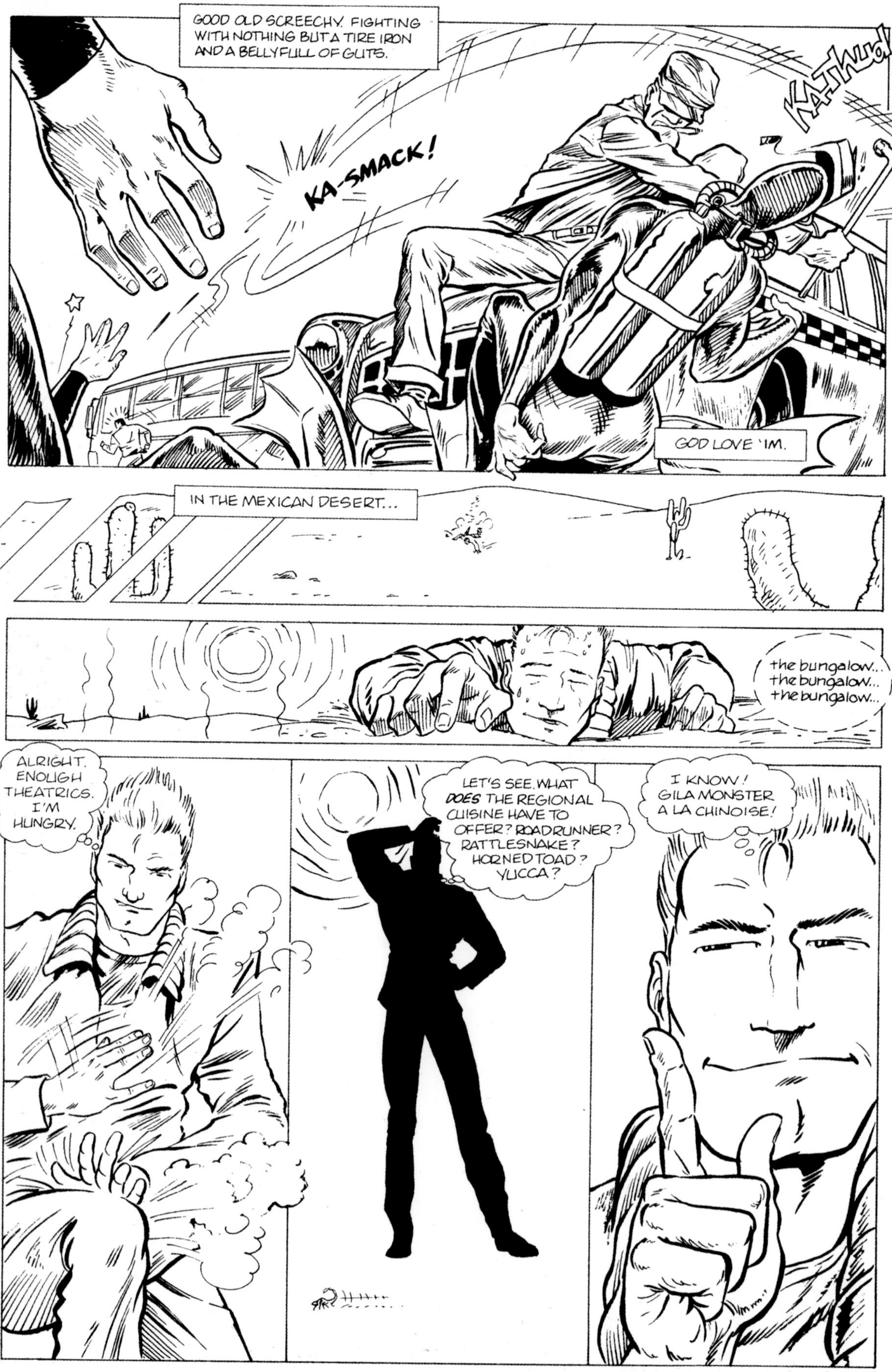

GOOD OLD SCREECHY. FIGHTING WITH NOTHING BUT A TIRE IRON AND A BELLYFULL OF GUTS.
KA-SMACK!
KA-THUD!
GOD LOVE 'IM.
IN THE MEXICAN DESERT...
the bungalow... the bungalow... the bungalow...
ALRIGHT. ENOUGH THEATRICS. I'M HUNGRY.
LET'S SEE. WHAT DOES THE REGIONAL CUISINE HAVE TO OFFER? ROADRUNNER? RATTLESNAKE? HORNED TOAD? YUCCA?
I KNOW! GILA MONSTER A LA CHINOISE!

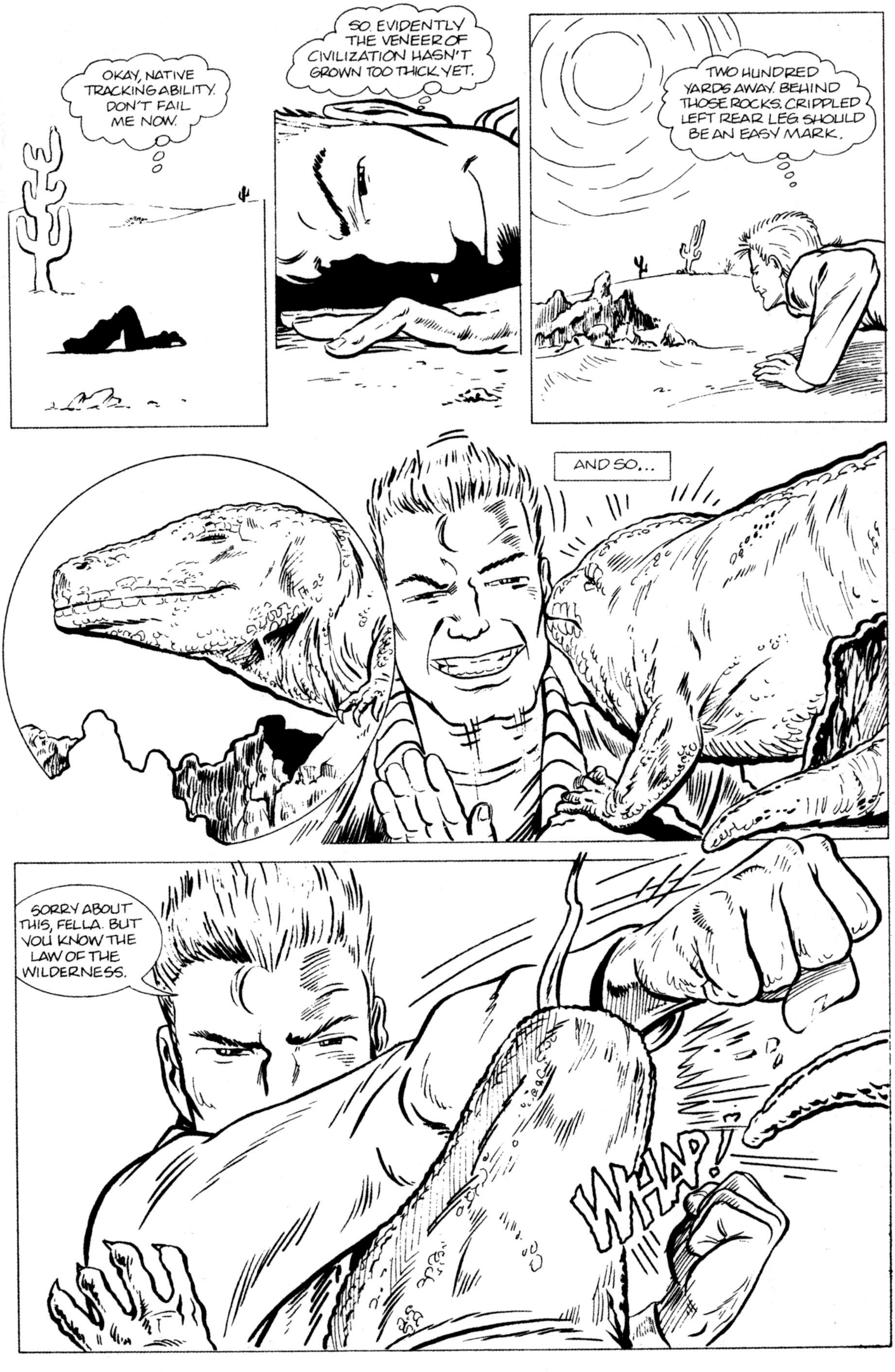
OKAY, NATIVE TRACKING ABILITY. DON'T FAIL ME NOW.
SO. EVIDENTLY THE VENEER OF CIVILIZATION HASN'T GROWN TOO THICK YET.
TWO HUNDRED YARDS AWAY. BEHIND THOSE ROCKS. CRIPPLED LEFT REAR LEG SHOULD BE AN EASY MARK.
AND SO...
SORRY ABOUT THIS, FELLA. BUT YOU KNOW THE LAW OF THE WILDERNESS.
WHAP!

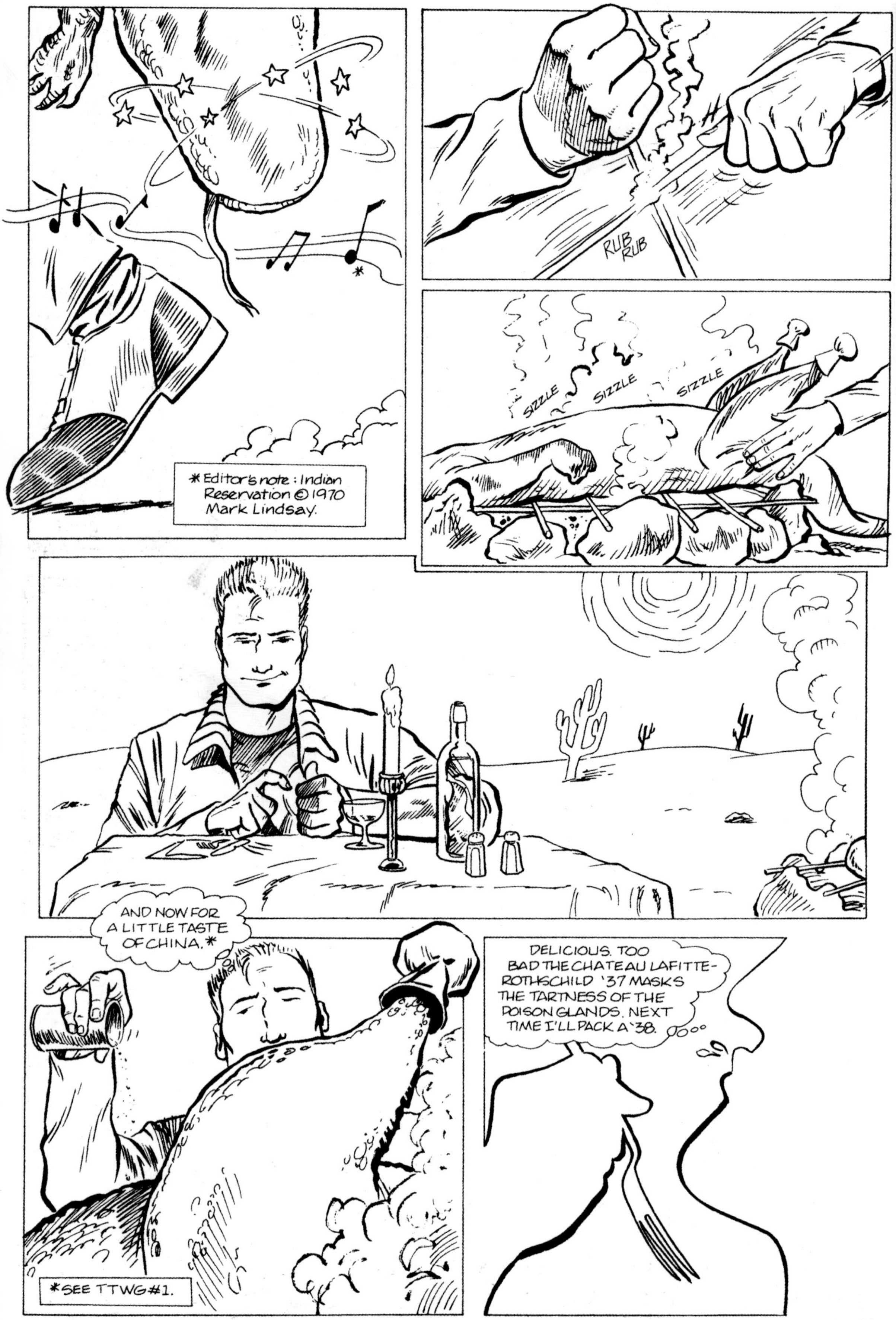
*Editor's note: Indian Reservation © 1970 Mark Lindsay.
RUB RUB
SIZZLE SIZZLE SIZZLE
AND NOW FOR A LITTLE TASTE OF CHINA.*
*SEE TTWG #1.
DELICIOUS. TOO BAD THE CHATEAU LAFITTE-ROTHSCHILD '37 MASKS THE TARTNESS OF THE POISON GLANDS. NEXT TIME I'LL PACK A '38.

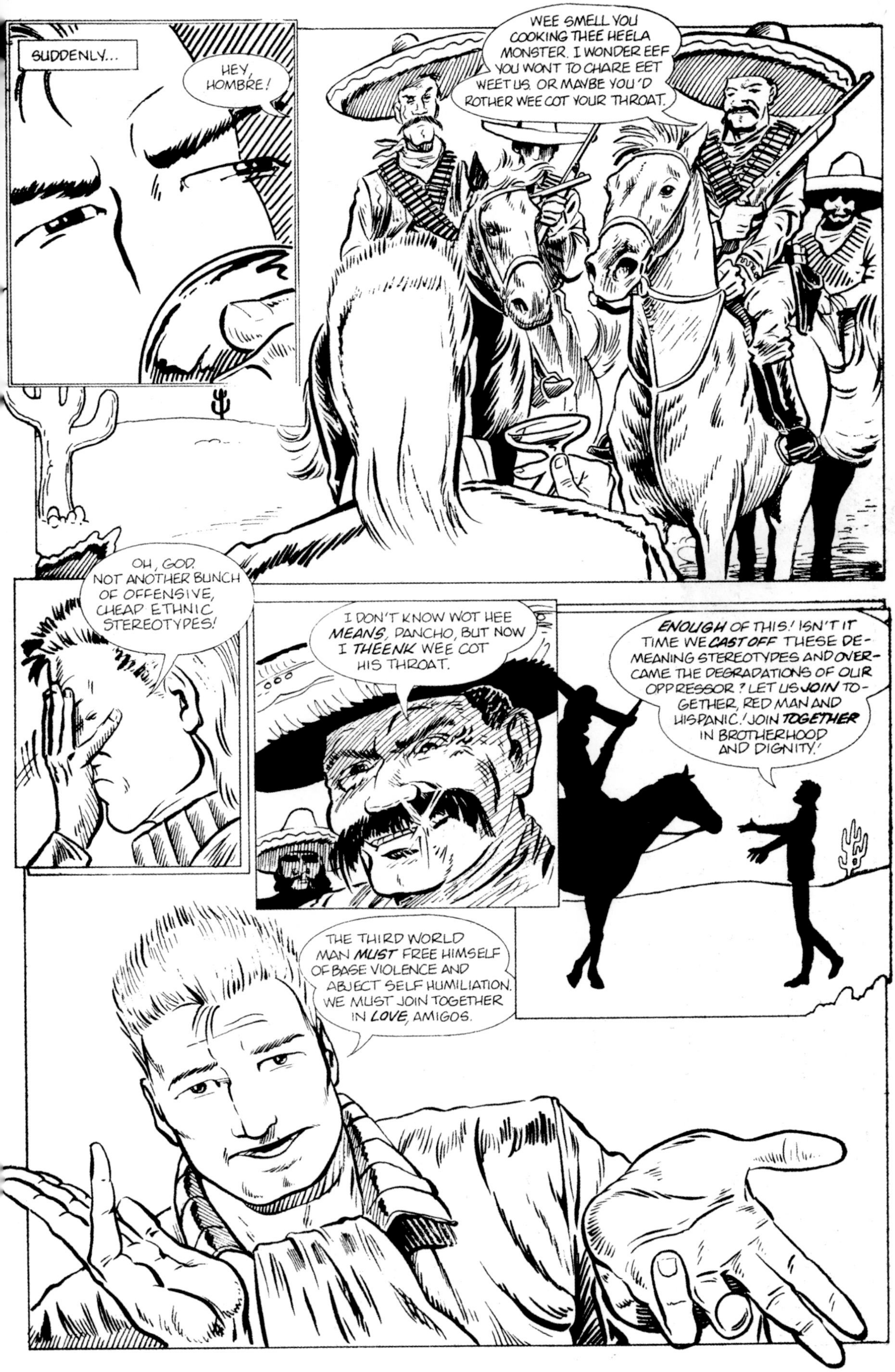
SUDDENLY...
HEY, HOMBRE!
WEE SMELL YOU COOKING THEE HEELA MONSTER. I WONDER EEF YOU WONT TO CHARE EET WEET US. OR MAYBE YOU'D ROTHER WEE COT YOUR THROAT.
OH, GOD. NOT ANOTHER BUNCH OF OFFENSIVE, CHEAP ETHNIC STEREOTYPES!
I DON'T KNOW WOT HEE MEANS, PANCHO, BUT NOW I THEENK WEE COT HIS THROAT.
ENOUGH OF THIS! ISN'T IT TIME WE CAST OFF THESE DEMEANING STEREOTYPES AND OVERCAME THE DEGRADATIONS OF OUR OPPRESSOR? LET US JOIN TOGETHER, RED MAN AND HISPANIC! JOIN TOGETHER IN BROTHERHOOD AND DIGNITY!
THE THIRD WORLD MAN MUST FREE HIMSELF OF BASE VIOLENCE AND ABJECT SELF HUMILIATION. WE MUST JOIN TOGETHER IN LOVE, AMIGOS.

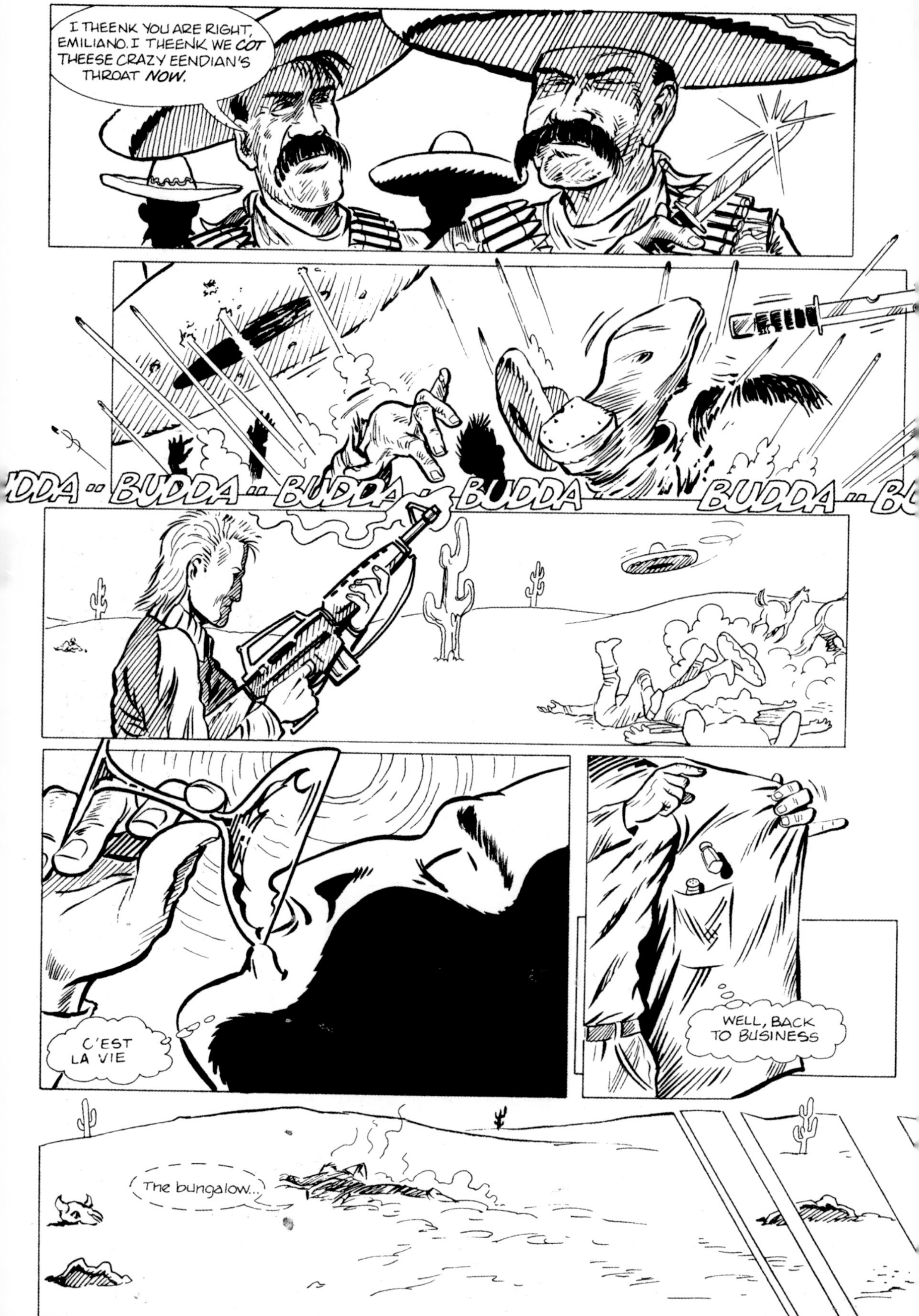
I THEENK YOU ARE RIGHT, EMILIANO. I THEENK WE COT THEESE CRAZY EENDIAN'S THROAT NOW.
BUDDA -- BUDDA -- BUDDA -- BUDDA BUDDA -- BU
C'EST LA VIE
WELL, BACK TO BUSINESS
The bungalow...

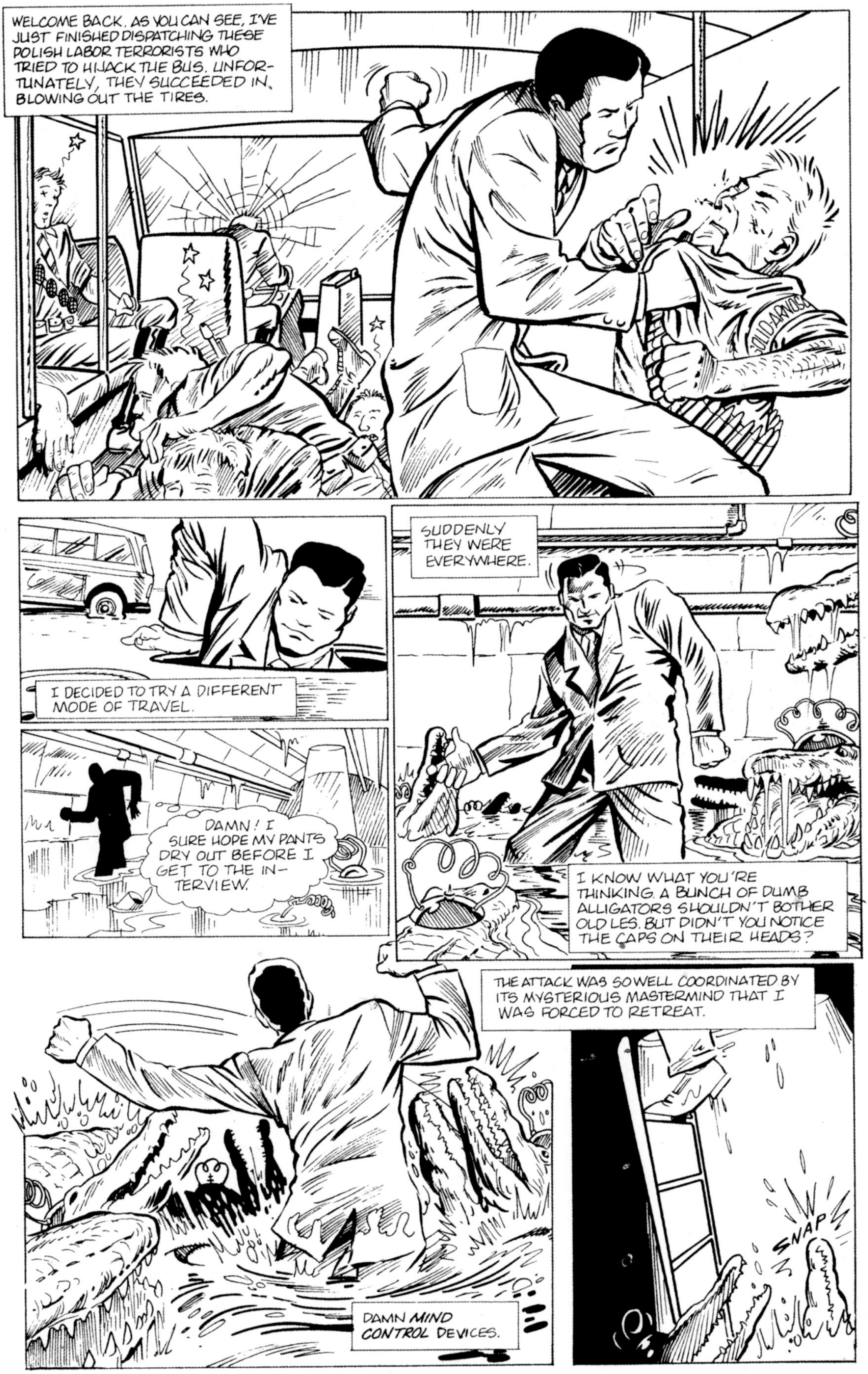
WELCOME BACK. AS YOU CAN SEE, I'VE JUST FINISHED DISPATCHING THESE POLISH LABOR TERRORISTS WHO TRIED TO HIJACK THE BUS. UNFORTUNATELY, THEY SUCCEEDED IN BLOWING OUT THE TIRES.
SOLID-ARNOSC
I DECIDED TO TRY A DIFFERENT MODE OF TRAVEL.
DAMN! I SURE HOPE MY PANTS DRY OUT BEFORE I GET TO THE INTERVIEW.
SUDDENLY THEY WERE EVERYWHERE.
I KNOW WHAT YOU'RE THINKING. A BUNCH OF DUMB ALLIGATORS SHOULDN'T BOTHER OLD LES. BUT DIDN'T YOU NOTICE THE CAPS ON THEIR HEADS?
THE ATTACK WAS SO WELL COORDINATED BY ITS MYSTERIOUS MASTERMIND THAT I WAS FORCED TO RETREAT.
DAMN *MIND CONTROL* DEVICES.
SNAP

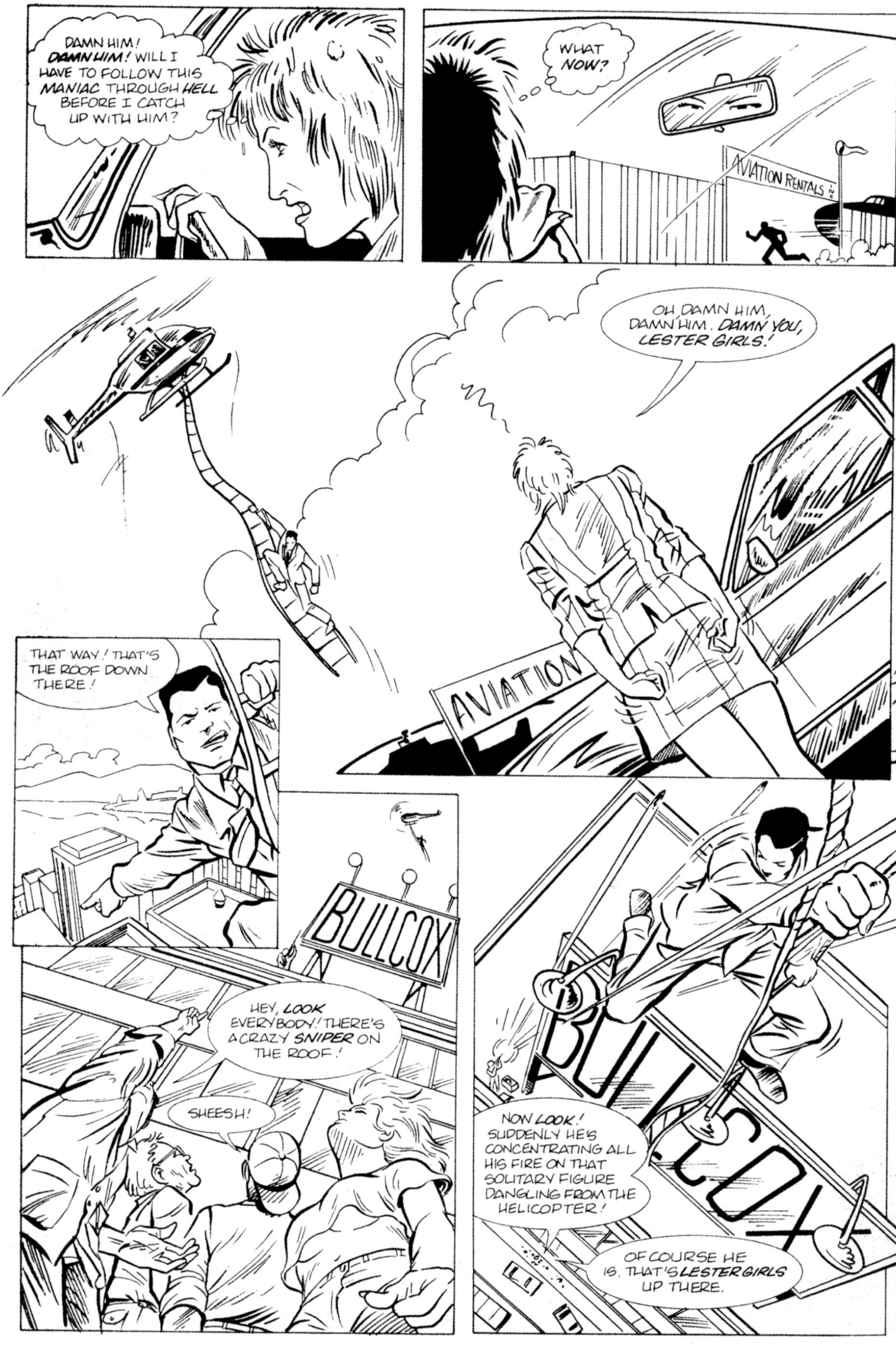
DAMN HIM! DAMN HIM! WILL I HAVE TO FOLLOW THIS MANIAC THROUGH HELL BEFORE I CATCH UP WITH HIM?
WHAT NOW?
AVIATION RENTALS INC
OH DAMN HIM, DAMN HIM. DAMN YOU, LESTER GIRLS!
AVIATION
THAT WAY! THAT'S THE ROOF DOWN THERE!
BULLCOX
HEY, LOOK EVERYBODY! THERE'S A CRAZY SNIPER ON THE ROOF!
SHEESH!
NOW LOOK! SUDDENLY HE'S CONCENTRATING ALL HIS FIRE ON THAT SOLITARY FIGURE DANGLING FROM THE HELICOPTER!
OF COURSE HE IS. THAT'S LESTER GIRLS UP THERE.

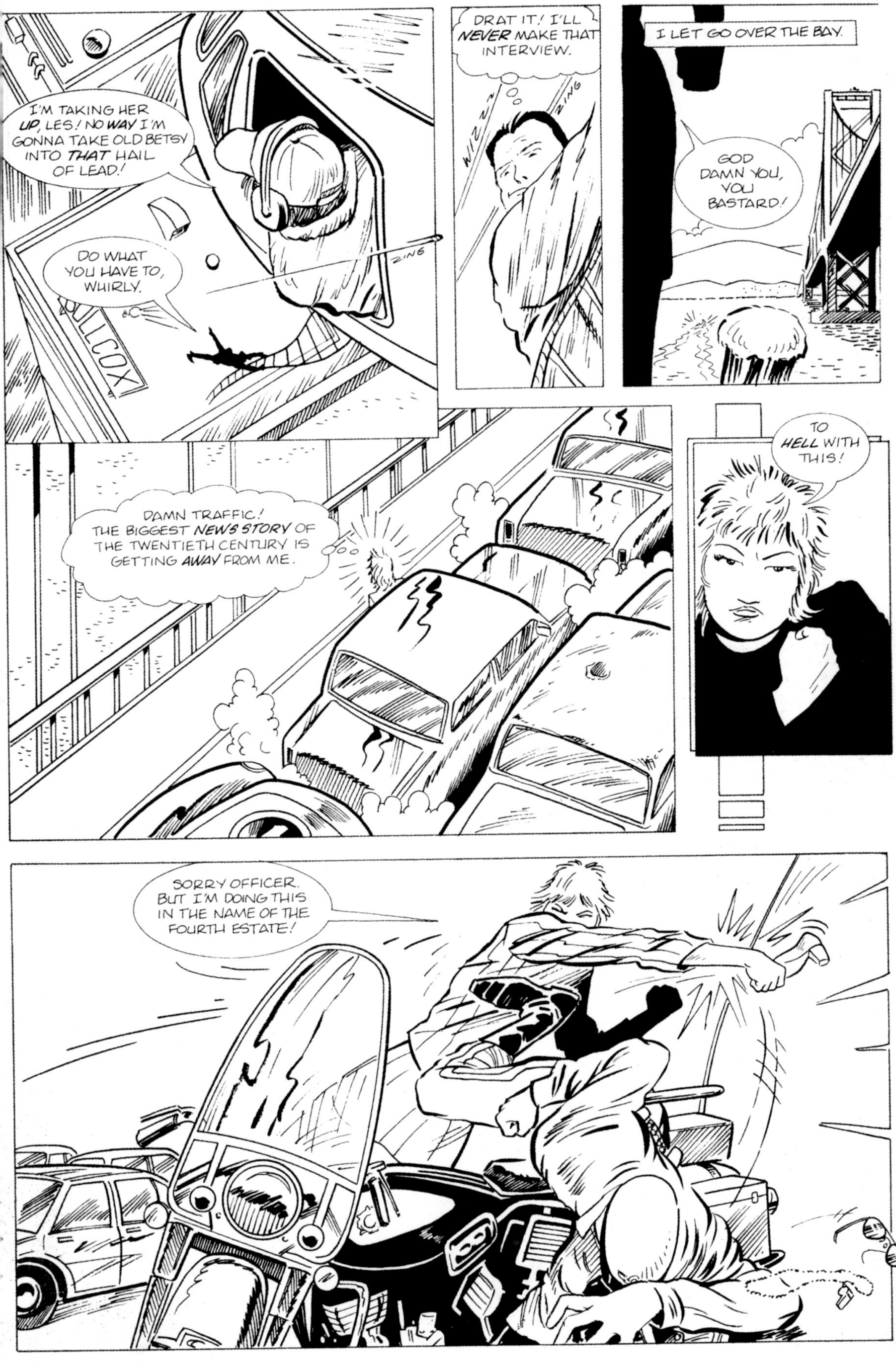
I'M TAKING HER UP, LES! NO WAY I'M GONNA TAKE OLD BETSY INTO THAT HAIL OF LEAD!
DO WHAT YOU HAVE TO, WHIRLY.
ZING
DRAT IT! I'LL NEVER MAKE THAT INTERVIEW.
WIZZZ
ZING
I LET GO OVER THE BAY.
GOD DAMN YOU, YOU BASTARD!
DAMN TRAFFIC! THE BIGGEST NEWS STORY OF THE TWENTIETH CENTURY IS GETTING AWAY FROM ME.
TO HELL WITH THIS!
SORRY OFFICER. BUT I'M DOING THIS IN THE NAME OF THE FOURTH ESTATE!

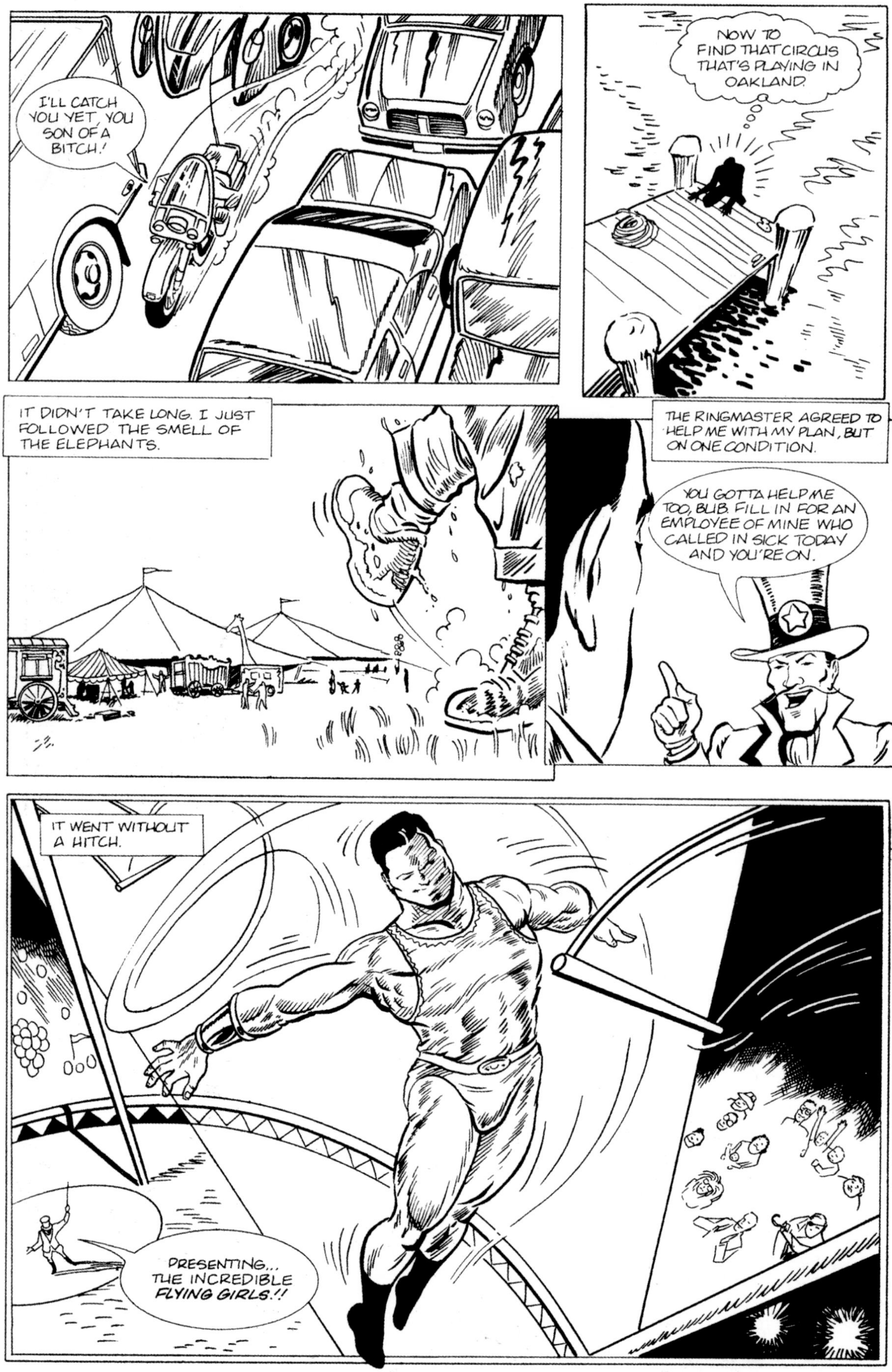
I'LL CATCH YOU YET, YOU SON OF A BITCH!
NOW TO FIND THAT CIRCUS THAT'S PLAYING IN OAKLAND.
IT DIDN'T TAKE LONG. I JUST FOLLOWED THE SMELL OF THE ELEPHANTS.
THE RINGMASTER AGREED TO HELP ME WITH MY PLAN, BUT ON ONE CONDITION.
YOU GOTTA HELP ME TOO, BUB. FILL IN FOR AN EMPLOYEE OF MINE WHO CALLED IN SICK TODAY AND YOU'RE ON.
IT WENT WITHOUT A HITCH.
PRESENTING... THE INCREDIBLE FLYING GIRLS!!

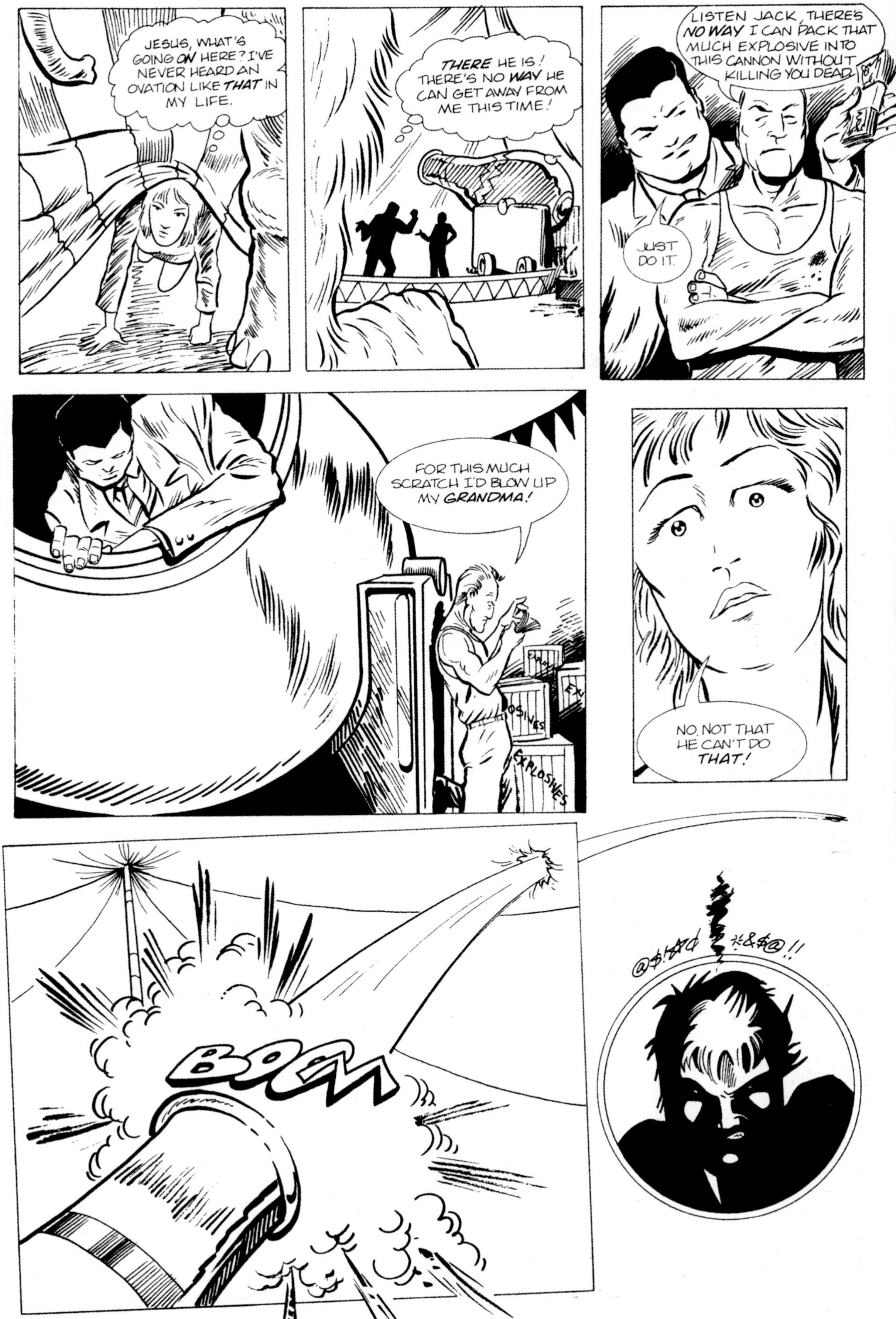
JESUS, WHAT'S GOING ON HERE? I'VE NEVER HEARD AN OVATION LIKE THAT IN MY LIFE.
THERE HE IS! THERE'S NO WAY HE CAN GET AWAY FROM ME THIS TIME!
LISTEN JACK, THERE'S NO WAY I CAN PACK THAT MUCH EXPLOSIVE INTO THIS CANNON WITHOUT KILLING YOU DEAD.
JUST DO IT.
FOR THIS MUCH SCRATCH I'D BLOW UP MY GRANDMA!
EXPLOSIVES
NO, NOT THAT HE CAN'T DO THAT!
BOOM
@$!#¢ *&$@!!

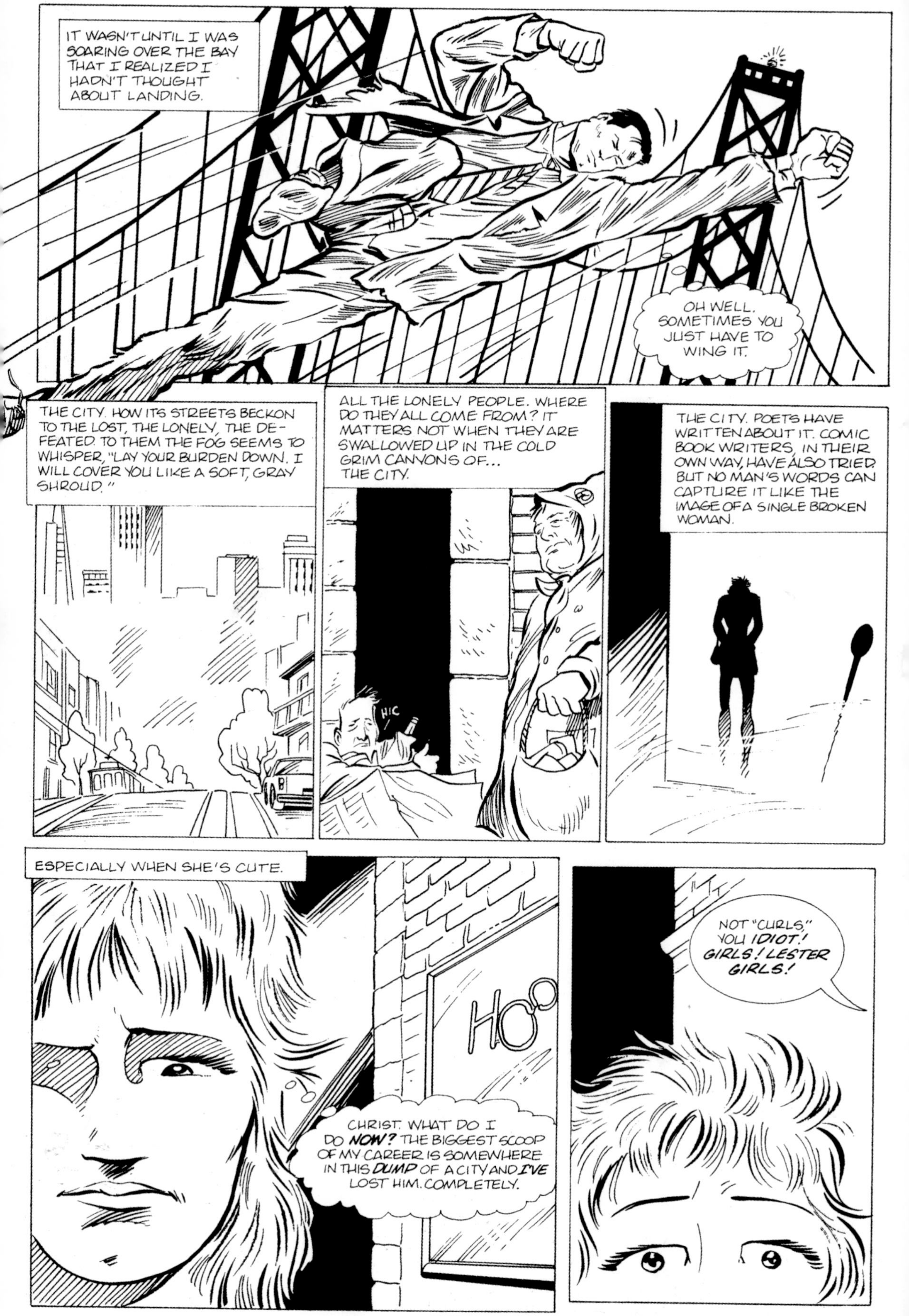
IT WASN'T UNTIL I WAS SOARING OVER THE BAY THAT I REALIZED I HADN'T THOUGHT ABOUT LANDING.
OH WELL. SOMETIMES YOU JUST HAVE TO WING IT.
THE CITY. HOW ITS STREETS BECKON TO THE LOST, THE LONELY, THE DEFEATED. TO THEM THE FOG SEEMS TO WHISPER, "LAY YOUR BURDEN DOWN. I WILL COVER YOU LIKE A SOFT, GRAY SHROUD."
ALL THE LONELY PEOPLE. WHERE DO THEY ALL COME FROM? IT MATTERS NOT WHEN THEY ARE SWALLOWED UP IN THE COLD GRIM CANYONS OF... THE CITY.
HIC
THE CITY. POETS HAVE WRITTEN ABOUT IT. COMIC BOOK WRITERS, IN THEIR OWN WAY, HAVE ALSO TRIED. BUT NO MAN'S WORDS CAN CAPTURE IT LIKE THE IMAGE OF A SINGLE BROKEN WOMAN.
ESPECIALLY WHEN SHE'S CUTE.
HO
CHRIST. WHAT DO I DO *NOW?* THE BIGGEST SCOOP OF MY CAREER IS SOMEWHERE IN THIS *DUMP* OF A CITY AND *I'VE* LOST HIM. COMPLETELY.
NOT "CURLS," YOU *IDIOT!* *GIRLS! LESTER GIRLS!*

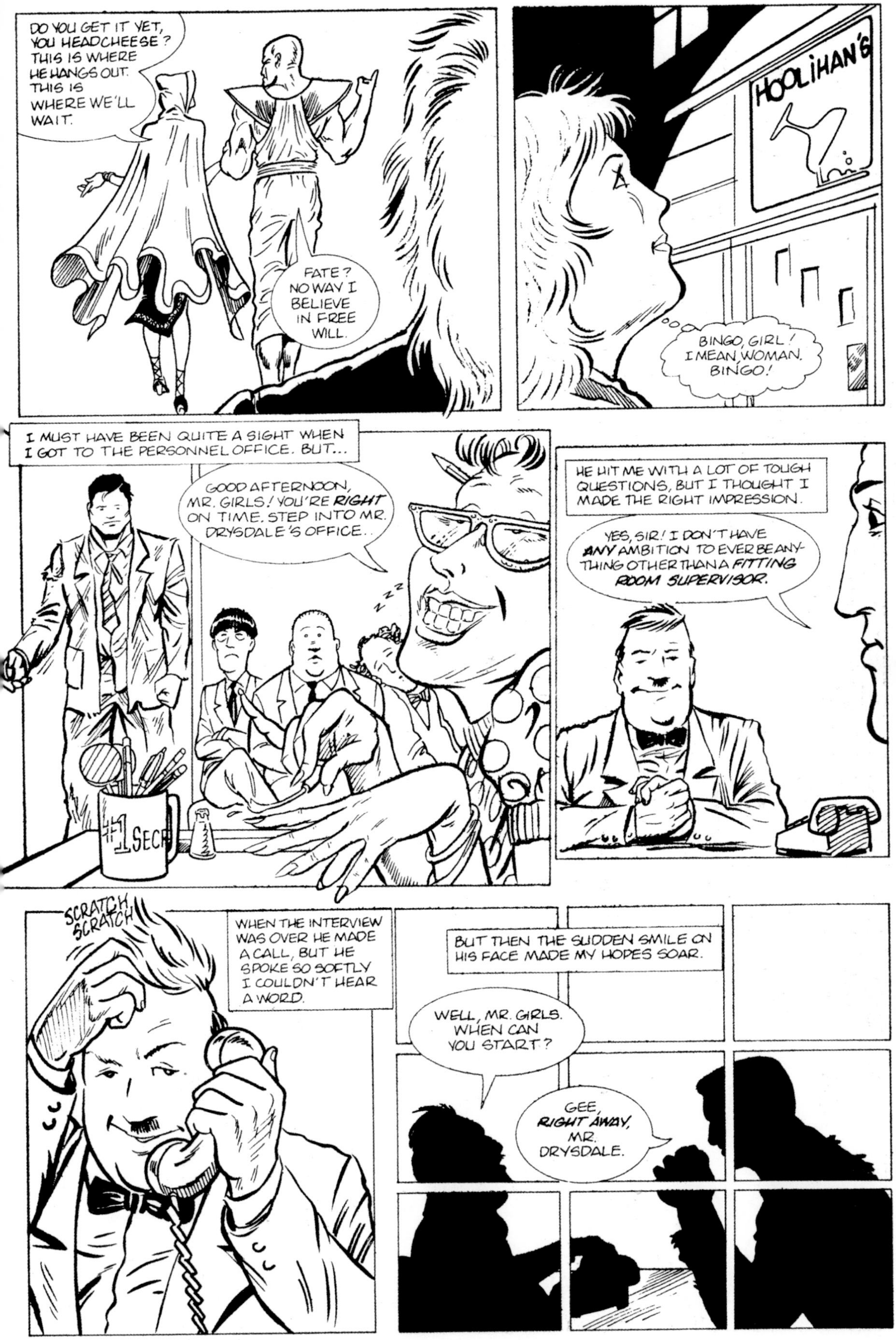

DO YOU GET IT YET, YOU HEADCHEESE? THIS IS WHERE HE HANGS OUT. THIS IS WHERE WE'LL WAIT.
FATE? NO WAY I BELIEVE IN FREE WILL.
HOOLIHAN'S
BINGO, GIRL! I MEAN, WOMAN. BINGO!
I MUST HAVE BEEN QUITE A SIGHT WHEN I GOT TO THE PERSONNEL OFFICE. BUT...
GOOD AFTERNOON, MR. GIRLS! YOU'RE RIGHT ON TIME. STEP INTO MR. DRYSDALE'S OFFICE..
ZZZ
#1 SECR
HE HIT ME WITH A LOT OF TOUGH QUESTIONS, BUT I THOUGHT I MADE THE RIGHT IMPRESSION.
YES, SIR! I DON'T HAVE ANY AMBITION TO EVER BE ANYTHING OTHER THAN A FITTING ROOM SUPERVISOR.
SCRATCH SCRATCH
WHEN THE INTERVIEW WAS OVER HE MADE A CALL, BUT HE SPOKE SO SOFTLY I COULDN'T HEAR A WORD.
BUT THEN THE SUDDEN SMILE ON HIS FACE MADE MY HOPES SOAR.
WELL, MR. GIRLS. WHEN CAN YOU START?
GEE, RIGHT AWAY, MR. DRYSDALE.

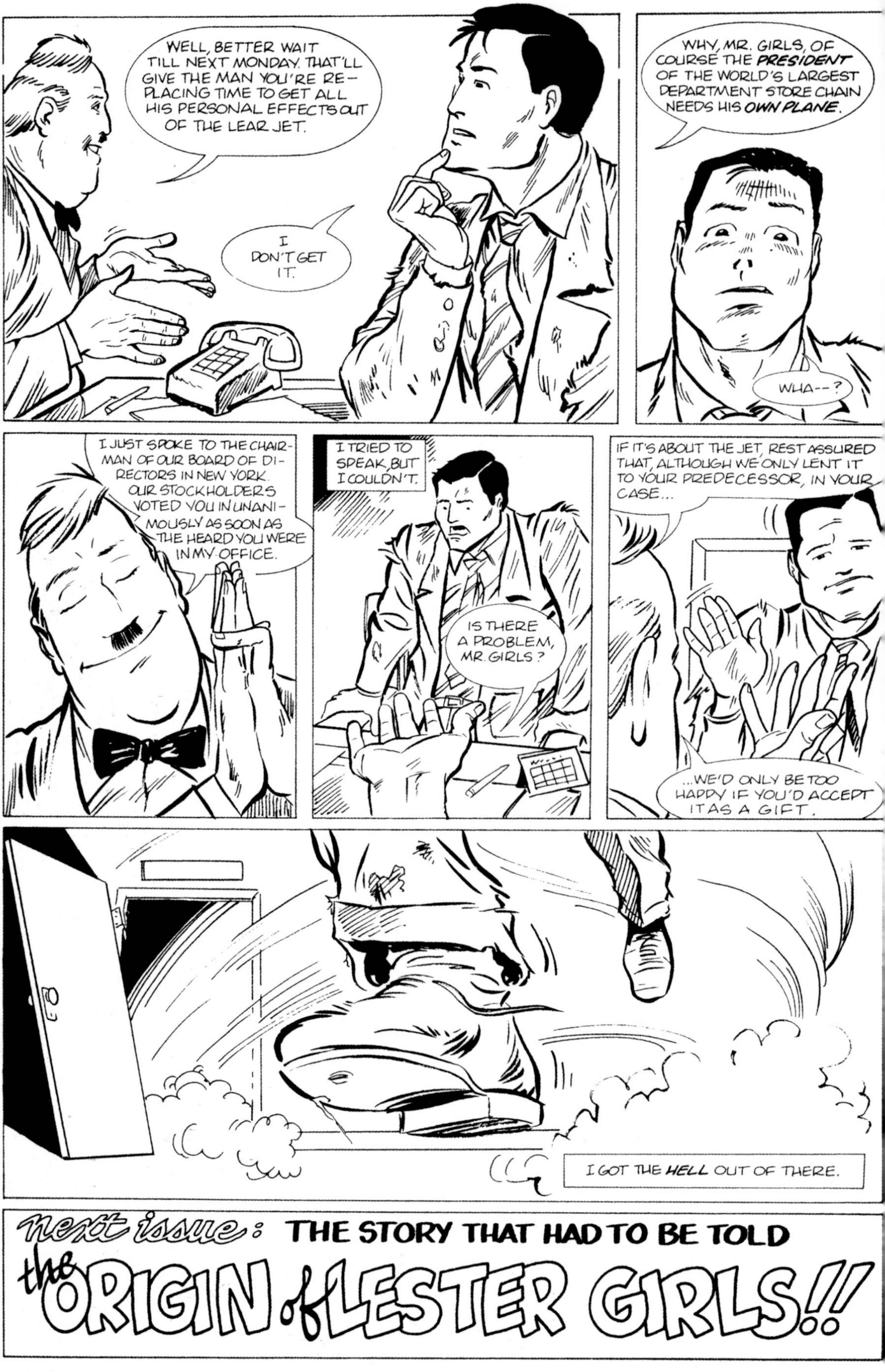
WELL, BETTER WAIT TILL NEXT MONDAY. THAT'LL GIVE THE MAN YOU'RE RE-PLACING TIME TO GET ALL HIS PERSONAL EFFECTS OUT OF THE LEAR JET.
I DON'T GET IT.
WHY, MR. GIRLS, OF COURSE THE PRESIDENT OF THE WORLD'S LARGEST DEPARTMENT STORE CHAIN NEEDS HIS OWN PLANE.
WHA--?
I JUST SPOKE TO THE CHAIR-MAN OF OUR BOARD OF DI-RECTORS IN NEW YORK. OUR STOCKHOLDERS VOTED YOU IN UNANI-MOUSLY AS SOON AS THE HEARD YOU WERE IN MY OFFICE.
I TRIED TO SPEAK, BUT I COULDN'T.
IS THERE A PROBLEM, MR. GIRLS?
IF IT'S ABOUT THE JET, REST ASSURED THAT, ALTHOUGH WE ONLY LENT IT TO YOUR PREDECESSOR, IN YOUR CASE...
...WE'D ONLY BE TOO HAPPY IF YOU'D ACCEPT IT AS A GIFT.
I GOT THE HELL OUT OF THERE.
next issue: THE STORY THAT HAD TO BE TOLD
the ORIGIN of LESTER GIRLS!!

THE TROUBLE WITH GIRLS

CHAPTER 4
NOVEMBER 1987

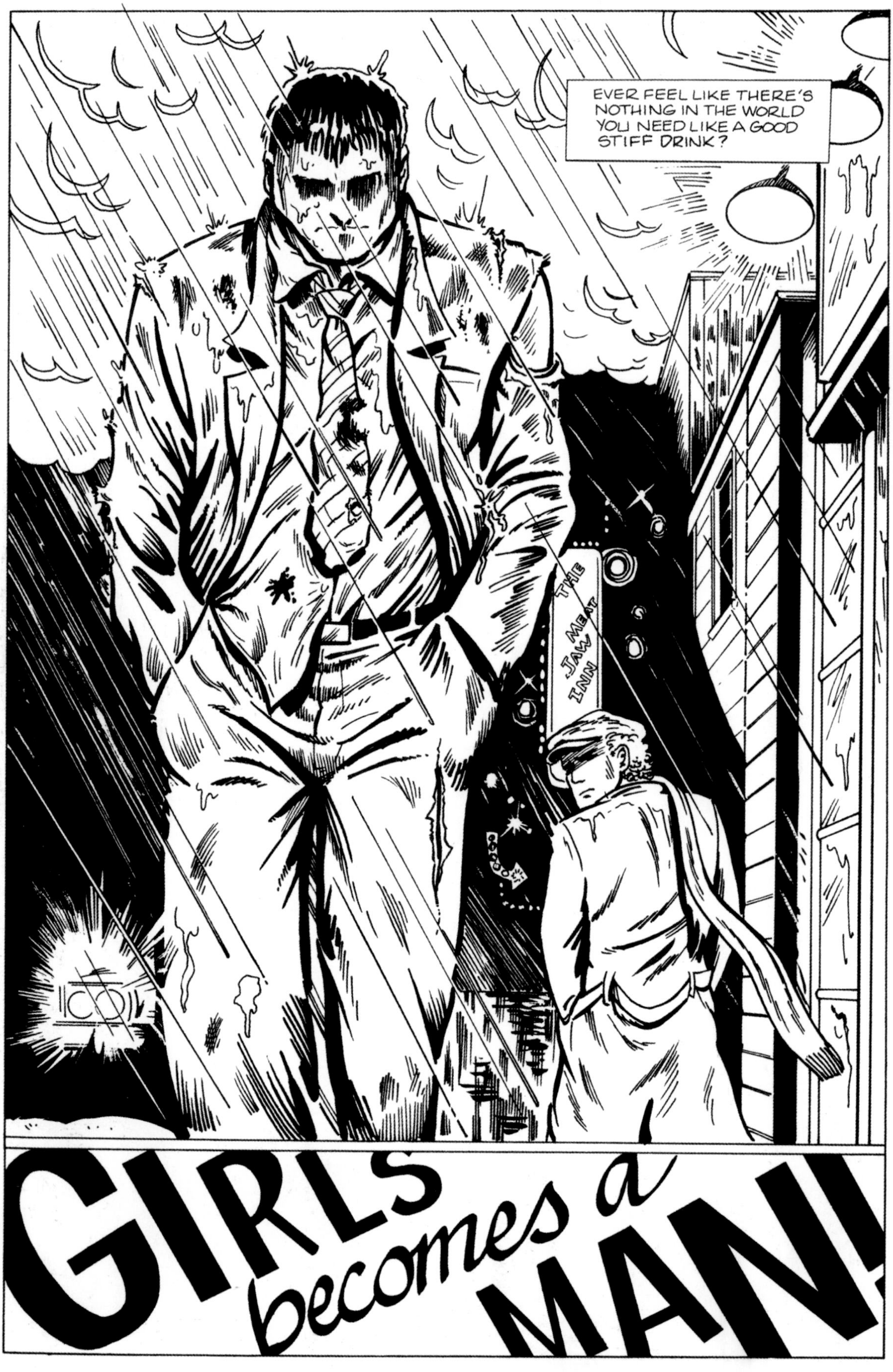
EVER FEEL LIKE THERE'S NOTHING IN THE WORLD YOU NEED LIKE A GOOD STIFF DRINK?
THE JAW MEAT INN
GIRLS becomes a MAN!

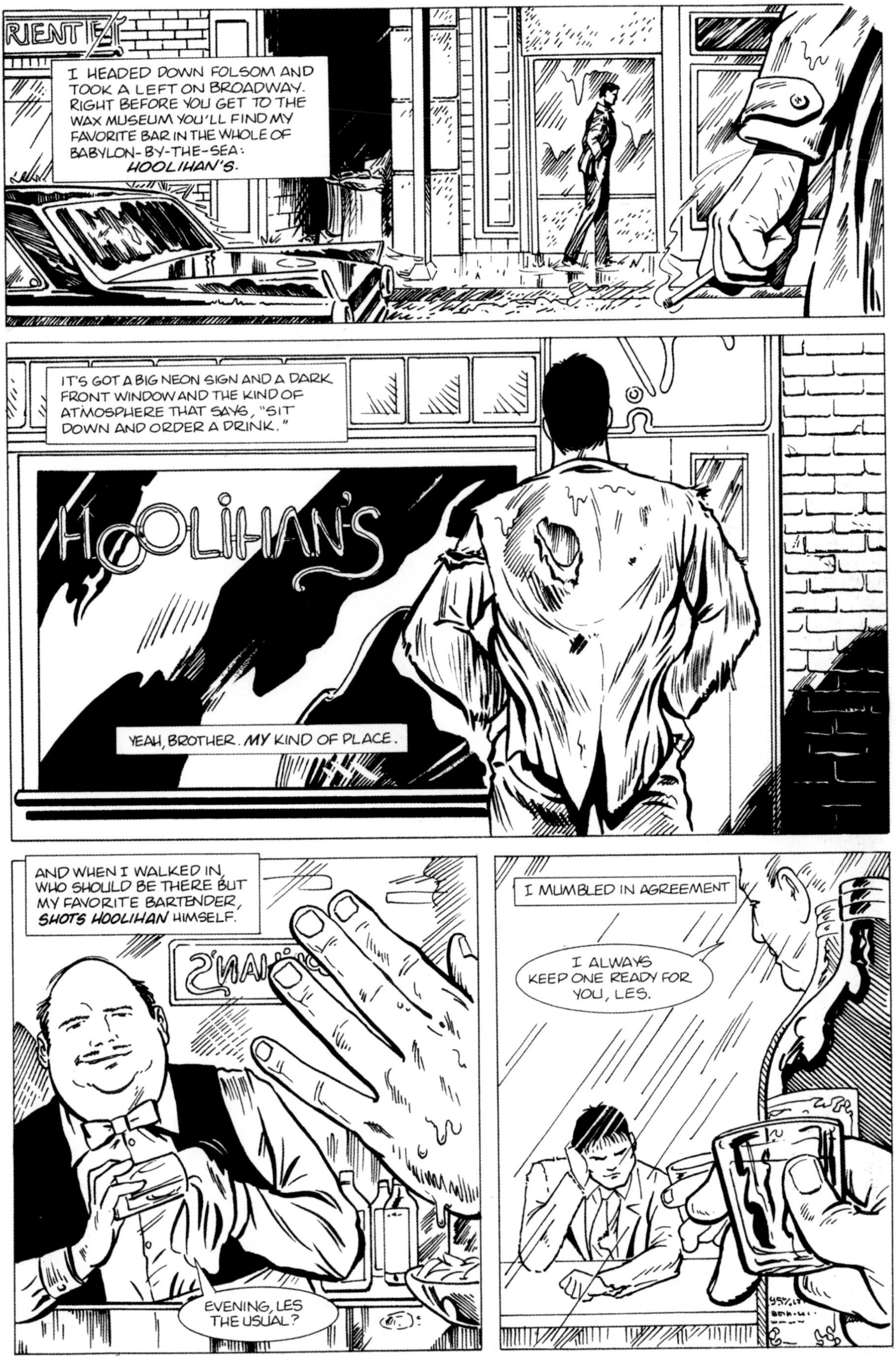
I HEADED DOWN FOLSOM AND TOOK A LEFT ON BROADWAY. RIGHT BEFORE YOU GET TO THE WAX MUSEUM YOU'LL FIND MY FAVORITE BAR IN THE WHOLE OF BABYLON-BY-THE-SEA: HOOLIHAN'S.
IT'S GOT A BIG NEON SIGN AND A DARK FRONT WINDOW AND THE KIND OF ATMOSPHERE THAT SAYS, "SIT DOWN AND ORDER A DRINK."
HOOLIHAN'S
YEAH, BROTHER. MY KIND OF PLACE.
AND WHEN I WALKED IN, WHO SHOULD BE THERE BUT MY FAVORITE BARTENDER, SHOTS HOOLIHAN HIMSELF.
EVENING, LES THE USUAL?
I MUMBLED IN AGREEMENT
I ALWAYS KEEP ONE READY FOR YOU, LES.

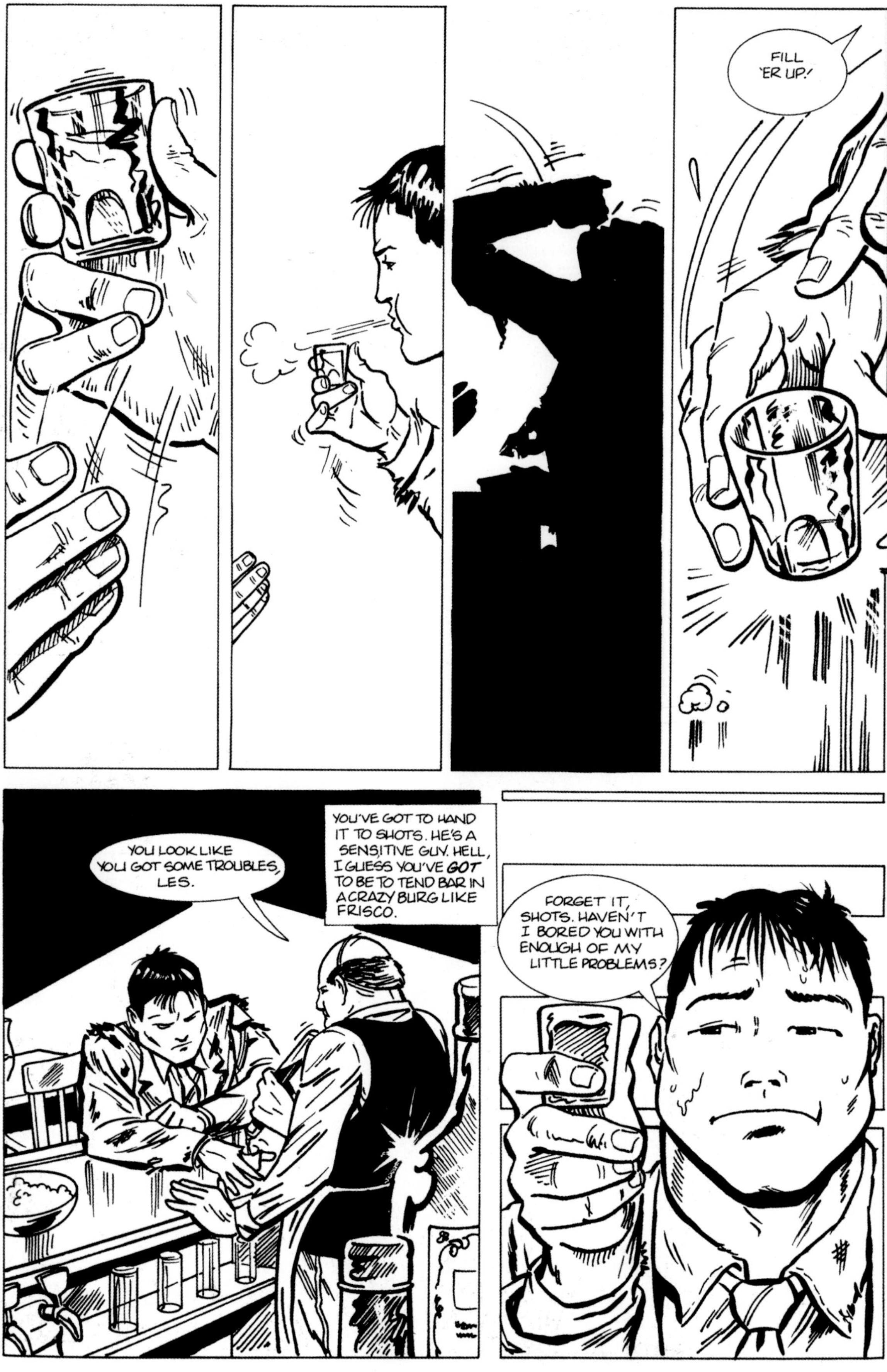
FILL 'ER UP!
YOU LOOK LIKE YOU GOT SOME TROUBLES, LES.
YOU'VE GOT TO HAND IT TO SHOTS. HE'S A SENSITIVE GUY. HELL, I GUESS YOU'VE GOT TO BE TO TEND BAR IN A CRAZY BURG LIKE FRISCO.
FORGET IT, SHOTS. HAVEN'T I BORED YOU WITH ENOUGH OF MY LITTLE PROBLEMS?

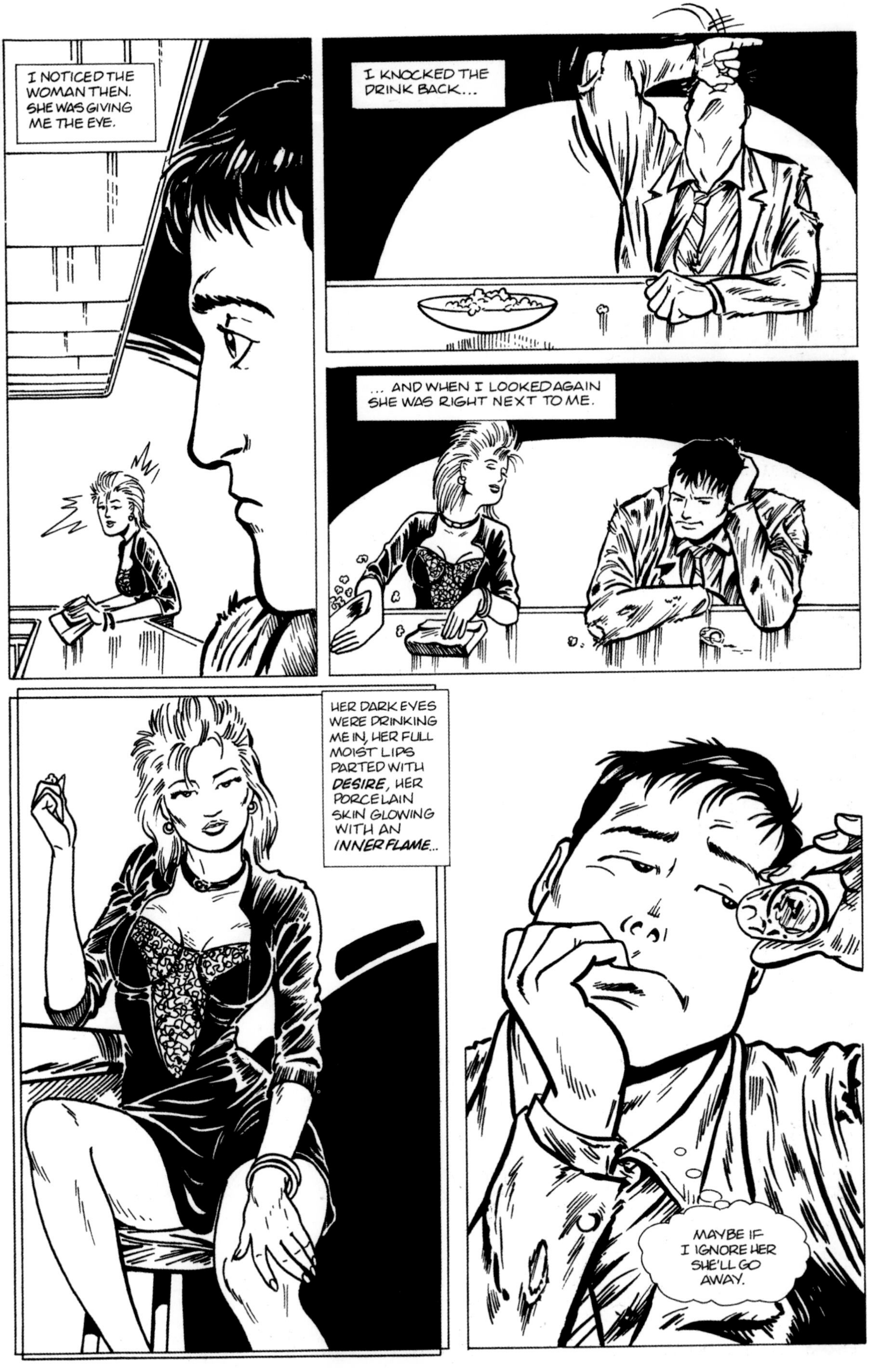
I NOTICED THE WOMAN THEN. SHE WAS GIVING ME THE EYE.
I KNOCKED THE DRINK BACK...
... AND WHEN I LOOKED AGAIN SHE WAS RIGHT NEXT TO ME.
HER DARK EYES WERE DRINKING ME IN, HER FULL MOIST LIPS PARTED WITH DESIRE, HER PORCELAIN SKIN GLOWING WITH AN INNER FLAME...
MAYBE IF I IGNORE HER SHE'LL GO AWAY.

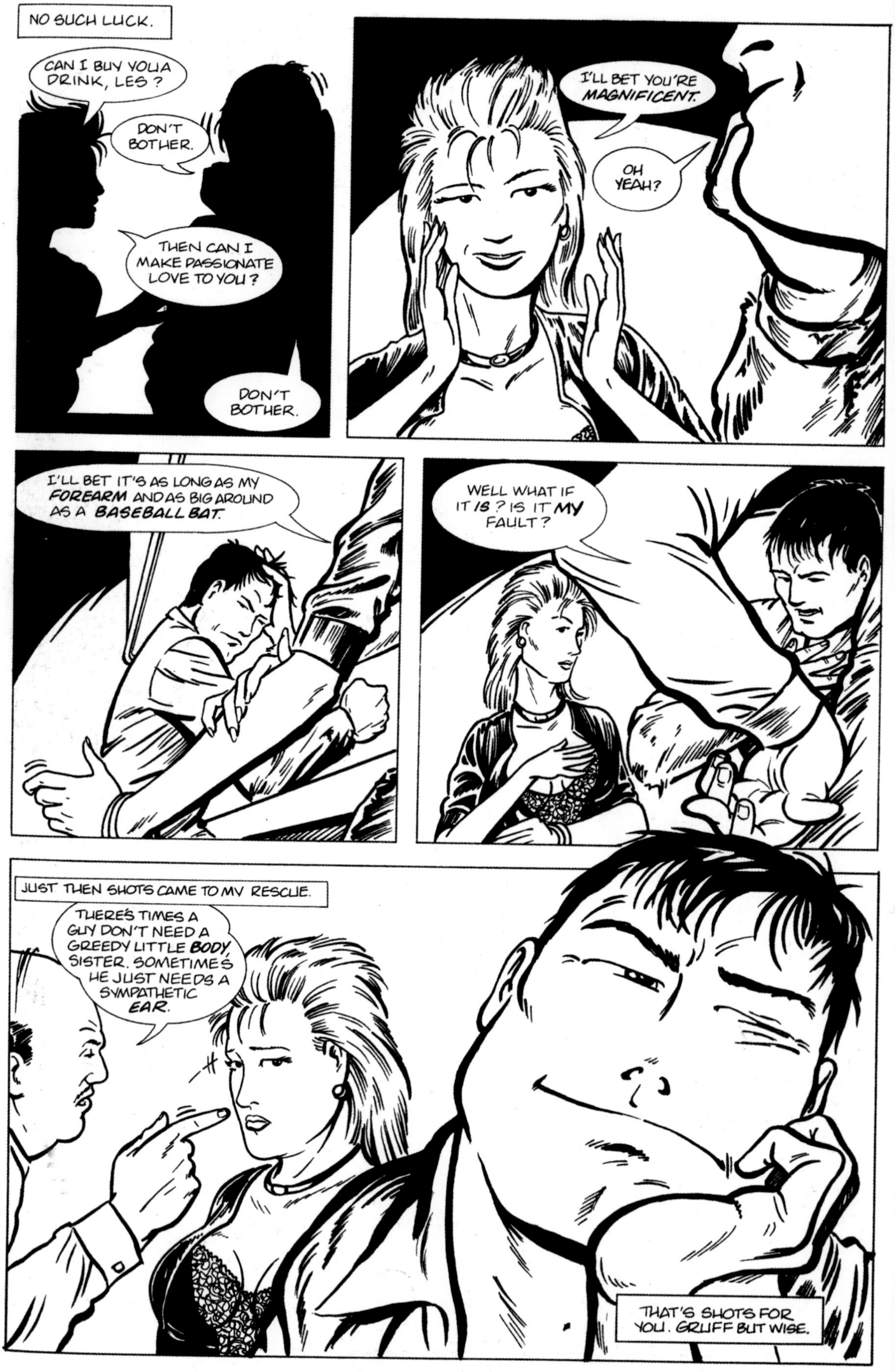
NO SUCH LUCK.
CAN I BUY YOU A DRINK, LES?
DON'T BOTHER.
THEN CAN I MAKE PASSIONATE LOVE TO YOU?
DON'T BOTHER.
I'LL BET YOU'RE MAGNIFICENT.
OH YEAH?
I'LL BET IT'S AS LONG AS MY FOREARM AND AS BIG AROUND AS A BASEBALL BAT.
WELL WHAT IF IT IS? IS IT MY FAULT?
JUST THEN SHOTS CAME TO MY RESCUE.
THERE'S TIMES A GUY DON'T NEED A GREEDY LITTLE BODY, SISTER. SOMETIMES HE JUST NEEDS A SYMPATHETIC EAR.
THAT'S SHOTS FOR YOU. GRUFF BUT WISE.

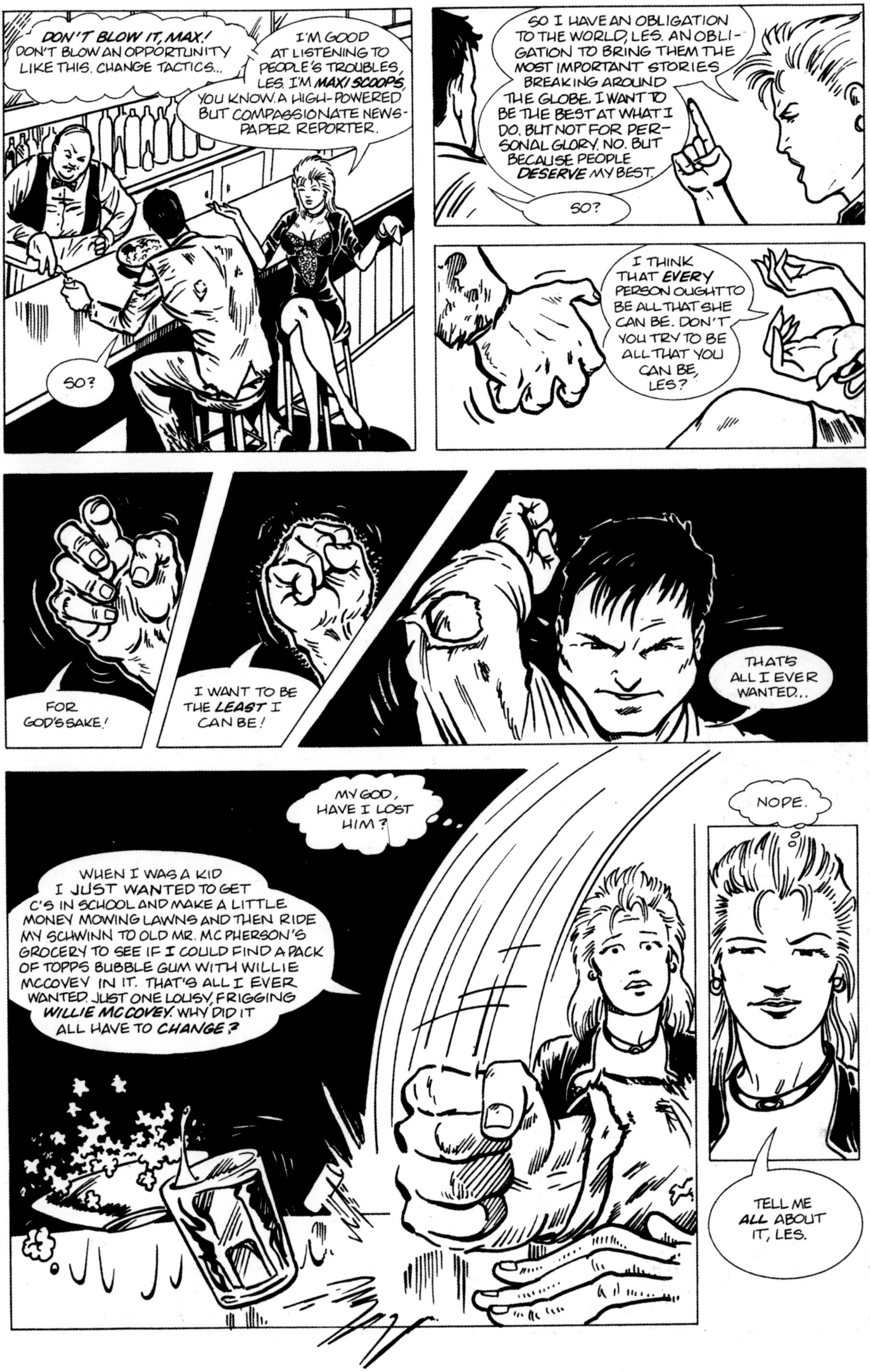
DON'T BLOW IT, MAX! DON'T BLOW AN OPPORTUNITY LIKE THIS. CHANGE TACTICS...
I'M GOOD AT LISTENING TO PEOPLE'S TROUBLES, LES. I'M MAXI SCOOPS, YOU KNOW. A HIGH-POWERED BUT COMPASSIONATE NEWSPAPER REPORTER.
SO?
SO I HAVE AN OBLIGATION TO THE WORLD, LES. AN OBLIGATION TO BRING THEM THE MOST IMPORTANT STORIES BREAKING AROUND THE GLOBE. I WANT TO BE THE BEST AT WHAT I DO. BUT NOT FOR PERSONAL GLORY. NO. BUT BECAUSE PEOPLE DESERVE MY BEST.
SO?
I THINK THAT EVERY PERSON OUGHT TO BE ALL THAT SHE CAN BE. DON'T YOU TRY TO BE ALL THAT YOU CAN BE, LES?
FOR GOD'S SAKE!
I WANT TO BE THE LEAST I CAN BE!
THAT'S ALL I EVER WANTED...
MY GOD, HAVE I LOST HIM?
WHEN I WAS A KID I JUST WANTED TO GET C'S IN SCHOOL AND MAKE A LITTLE MONEY MOWING LAWNS AND THEN RIDE MY SCHWINN TO OLD MR. MCPHERSON'S GROCERY TO SEE IF I COULD FIND A PACK OF TOPPS BUBBLE GUM WITH WILLIE MCCOVEY IN IT. THAT'S ALL I EVER WANTED. JUST ONE LOUSY, FRIGGING WILLIE MCCOVEY. WHY DID IT ALL HAVE TO CHANGE?
NOPE.
TELL ME ALL ABOUT IT, LES.

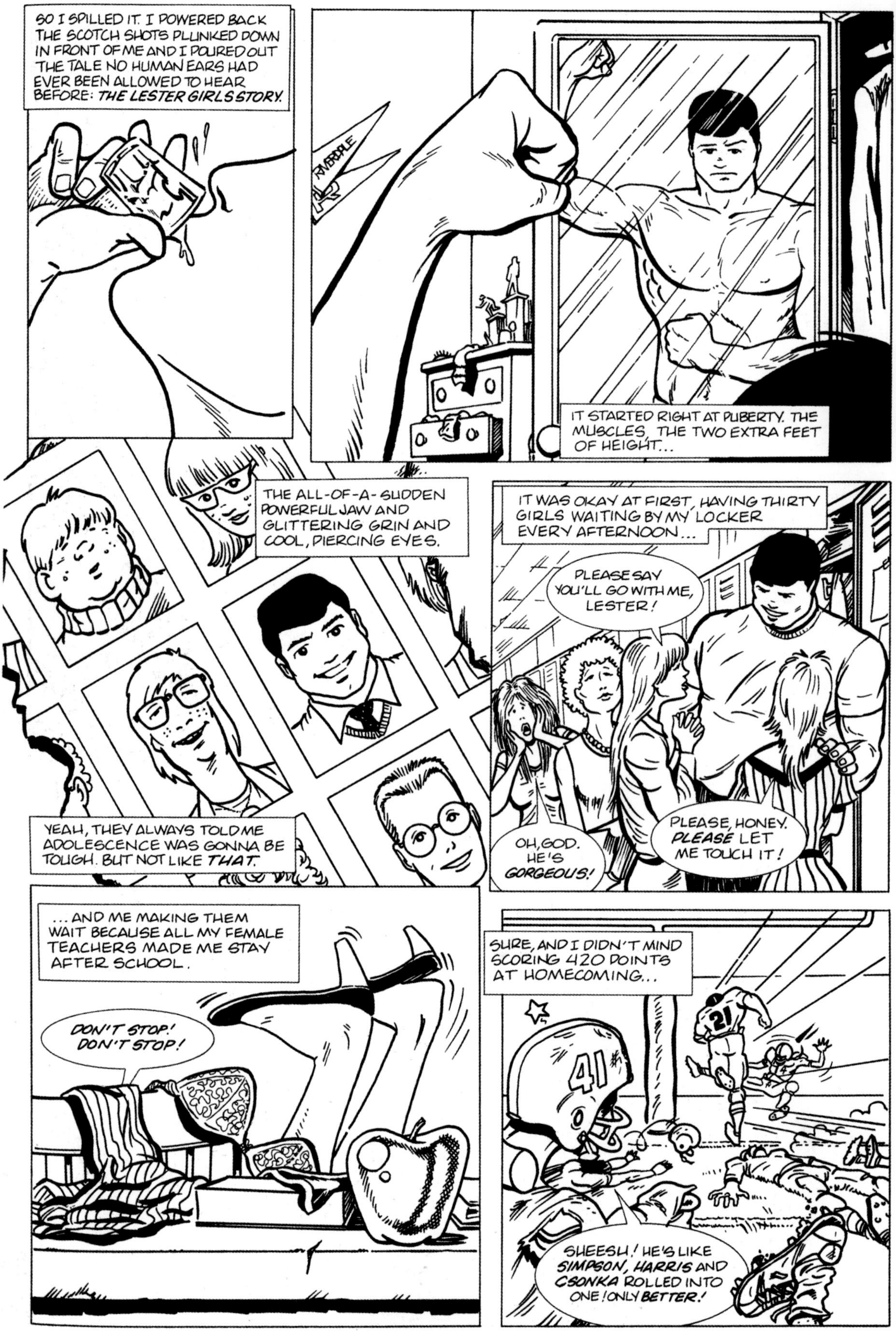
SO I SPILLED IT. I POWERED BACK THE SCOTCH SHOTS PLUNKED DOWN IN FRONT OF ME AND I POURED OUT THE TALE NO HUMAN EARS HAD EVER BEEN ALLOWED TO HEAR BEFORE: THE LESTER GIRLS STORY.
RIVERDALE
IT STARTED RIGHT AT PUBERTY. THE MUSCLES, THE TWO EXTRA FEET OF HEIGHT...
THE ALL-OF-A-SUDDEN POWERFUL JAW AND GLITTERING GRIN AND COOL, PIERCING EYES.
YEAH, THEY ALWAYS TOLD ME ADOLESCENCE WAS GONNA BE TOUGH. BUT NOT LIKE THAT.
IT WAS OKAY AT FIRST, HAVING THIRTY GIRLS WAITING BY MY LOCKER EVERY AFTERNOON...
PLEASE SAY YOU'LL GO WITH ME, LESTER!
OH, GOD. HE'S GORGEOUS!
PLEASE, HONEY. PLEASE LET ME TOUCH IT!
...AND ME MAKING THEM WAIT BECAUSE ALL MY FEMALE TEACHERS MADE ME STAY AFTER SCHOOL.
DON'T STOP! DON'T STOP!
SURE, AND I DIDN'T MIND SCORING 420 POINTS AT HOMECOMING...
41
21
SHEESH! HE'S LIKE SIMPSON, HARRIS AND CSONKA ROLLED INTO ONE! ONLY BETTER!

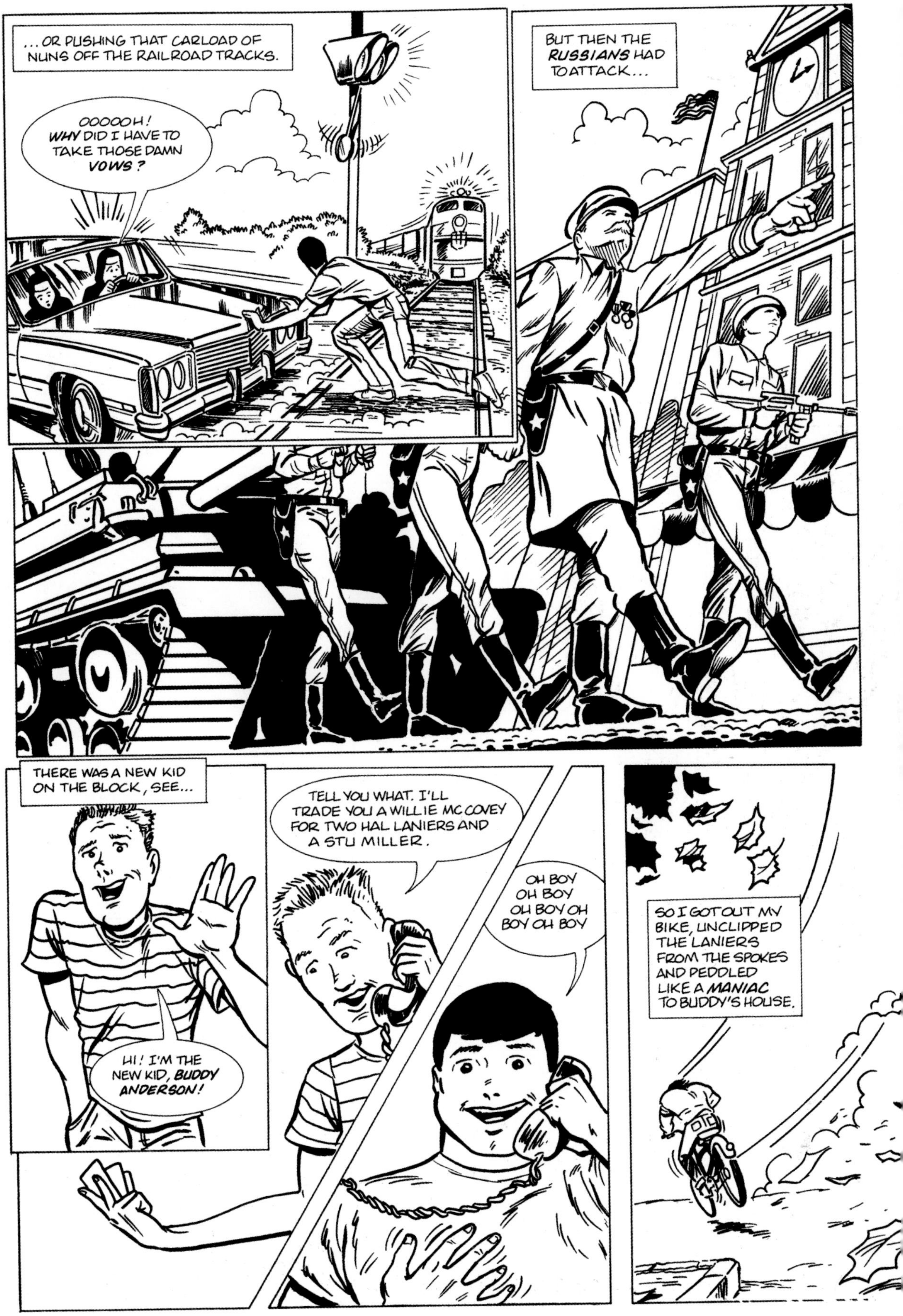
...OR PUSHING THAT CARLOAD OF NUNS OFF THE RAILROAD TRACKS.
OOOOOH! WHY DID I HAVE TO TAKE THOSE DAMN VOWS?
BUT THEN THE RUSSIANS HAD TO ATTACK...
THERE WAS A NEW KID ON THE BLOCK, SEE...
HI! I'M THE NEW KID, BUDDY ANDERSON!
TELL YOU WHAT. I'LL TRADE YOU A WILLIE MC COVEY FOR TWO HAL LANIERS AND A STU MILLER.
OH BOY OH BOY OH BOY OH BOY OH BOY
SO I GOT OUT MY BIKE, UNCLIPPED THE LANIERS FROM THE SPOKES AND PEDDLED LIKE A MANIAC TO BUDDY'S HOUSE.

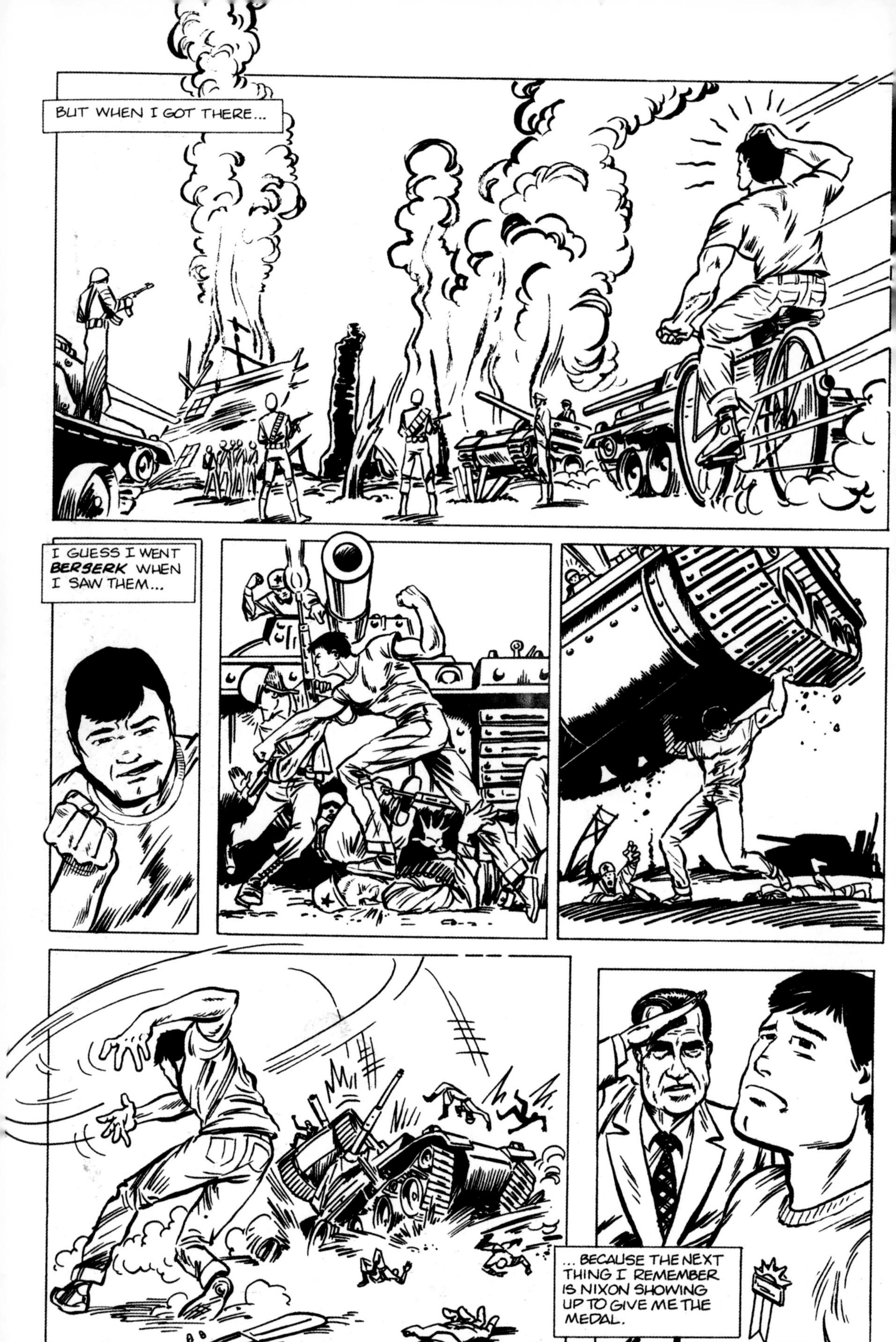
BUT WHEN I GOT THERE...
I GUESS I WENT **BERSERK** WHEN I SAW THEM...
... BECAUSE THE NEXT THING I REMEMBER IS NIXON SHOWING UP TO GIVE ME THE MEDAL.

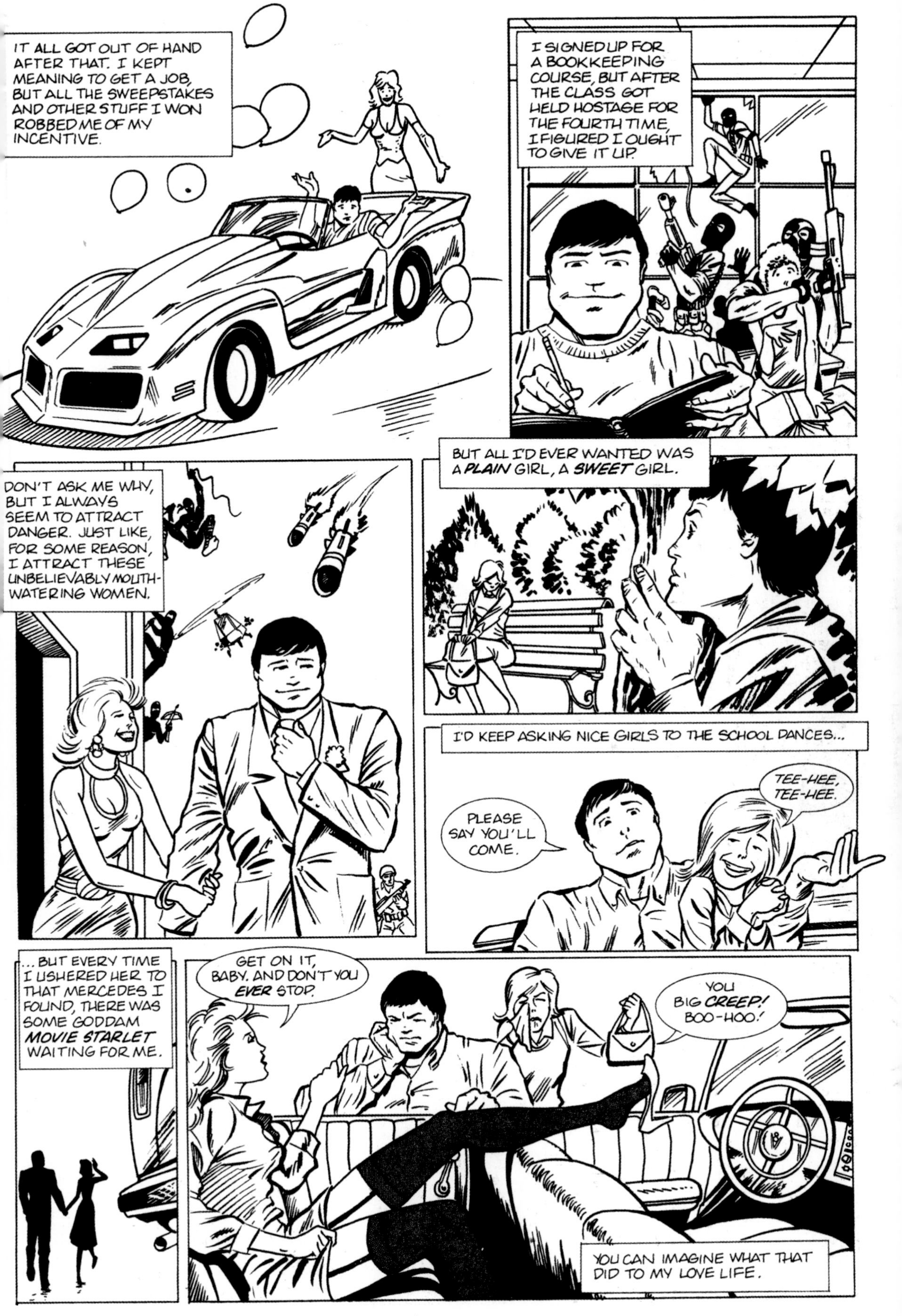
IT ALL GOT OUT OF HAND AFTER THAT. I KEPT MEANING TO GET A JOB, BUT ALL THE SWEEPSTAKES AND OTHER STUFF I WON ROBBED ME OF MY INCENTIVE.
I SIGNED UP FOR A BOOKKEEPING COURSE, BUT AFTER THE CLASS GOT HELD HOSTAGE FOR THE FOURTH TIME, I FIGURED I OUGHT TO GIVE IT UP.
DON'T ASK ME WHY, BUT I ALWAYS SEEM TO ATTRACT DANGER. JUST LIKE, FOR SOME REASON, I ATTRACT THESE UNBELIEVABLY MOUTH-WATERING WOMEN.
BUT ALL I'D EVER WANTED WAS A PLAIN GIRL, A SWEET GIRL.
I'D KEEP ASKING NICE GIRLS TO THE SCHOOL DANCES...
PLEASE SAY YOU'LL COME.
TEE-HEE, TEE-HEE.
...BUT EVERY TIME I USHERED HER TO THAT MERCEDES I FOUND, THERE WAS SOME GODDAM MOVIE STARLET WAITING FOR ME.
GET ON IT, BABY. AND DON'T YOU EVER STOP.
YOU BIG CREEP! BOO-HOO!
YOU CAN IMAGINE WHAT THAT DID TO MY LOVE LIFE.

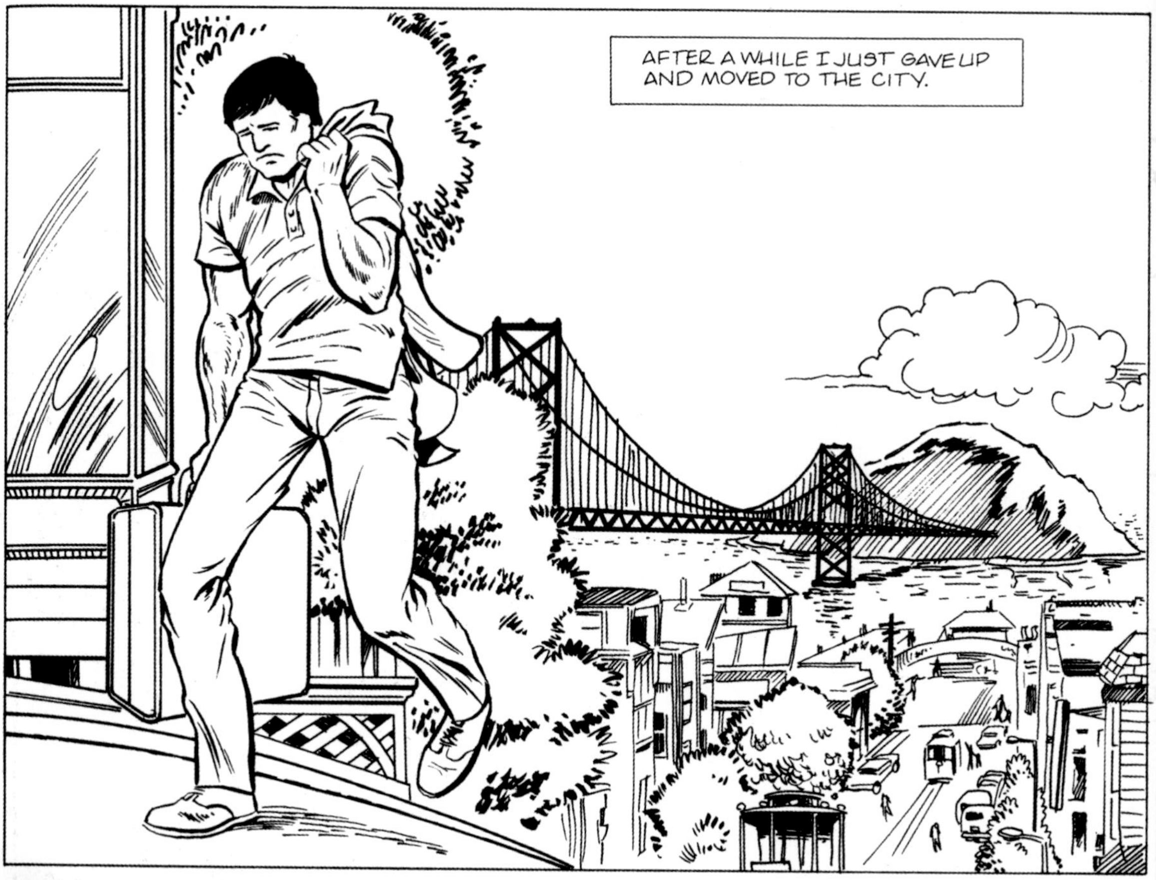
AFTER A WHILE I JUST GAVE UP AND MOVED TO THE CITY.

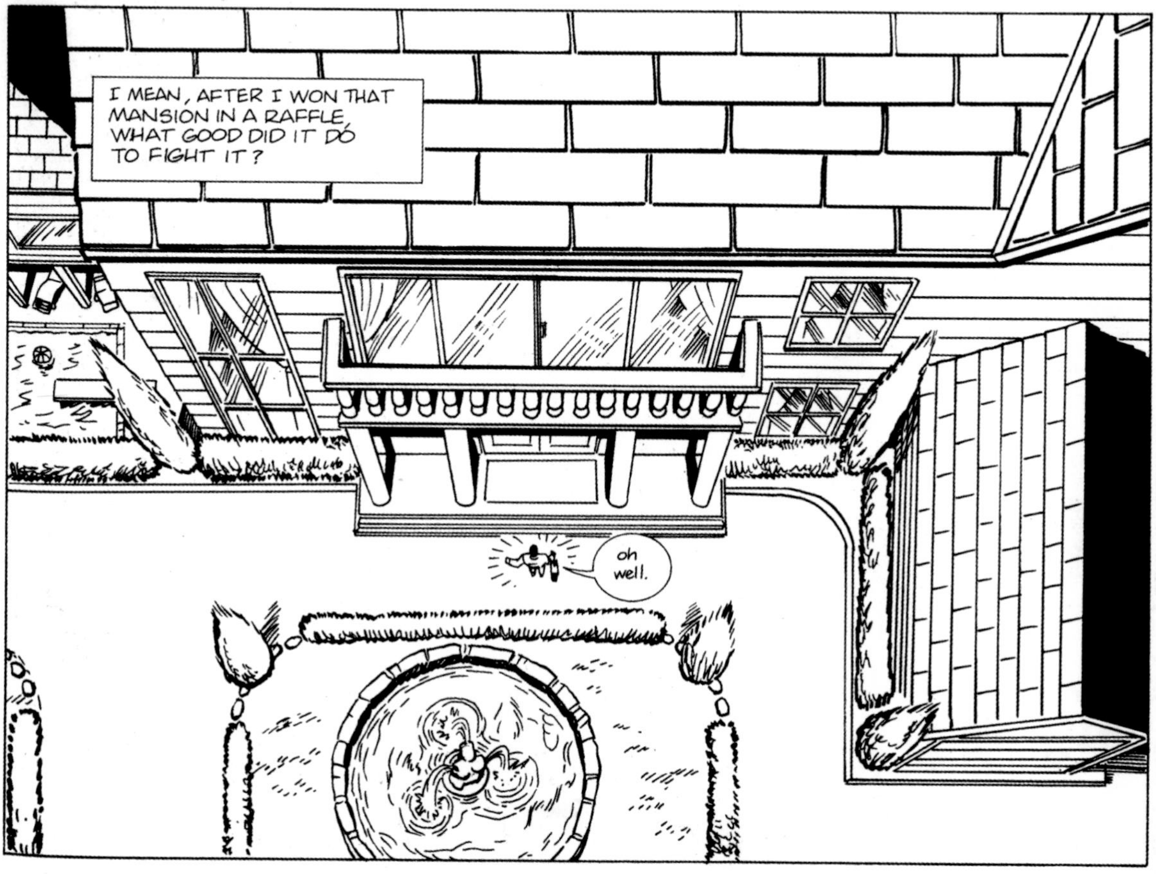
I MEAN, AFTER I WON THAT MANSION IN A RAFFLE, WHAT GOOD DID IT DO TO FIGHT IT?
oh well.

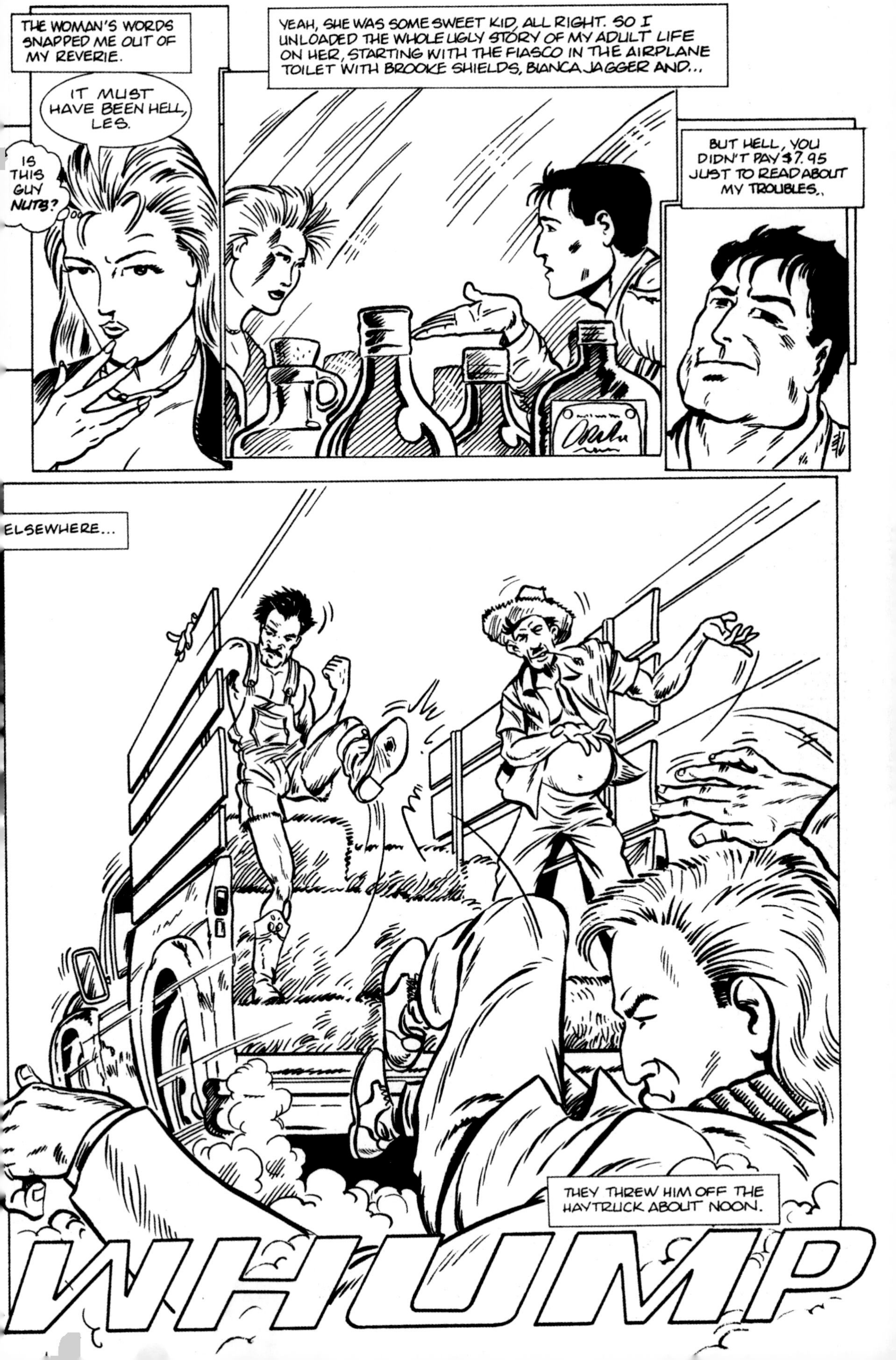
THE WOMAN'S WORDS SNAPPED ME OUT OF MY REVERIE.
IT MUST HAVE BEEN HELL, LES.
IS THIS GUY NUTS?
YEAH, SHE WAS SOME SWEET KID, ALL RIGHT. SO I UNLOADED THE WHOLE UGLY STORY OF MY ADULT LIFE ON HER, STARTING WITH THE FIASCO IN THE AIRPLANE TOILET WITH BROOKE SHIELDS, BIANCA JAGGER AND...
BUT HELL, YOU DIDN'T PAY $7.95 JUST TO READ ABOUT MY TROUBLES..
ELSEWHERE...
THEY THREW HIM OFF THE HAYTRUCK ABOUT NOON.
WHUMP

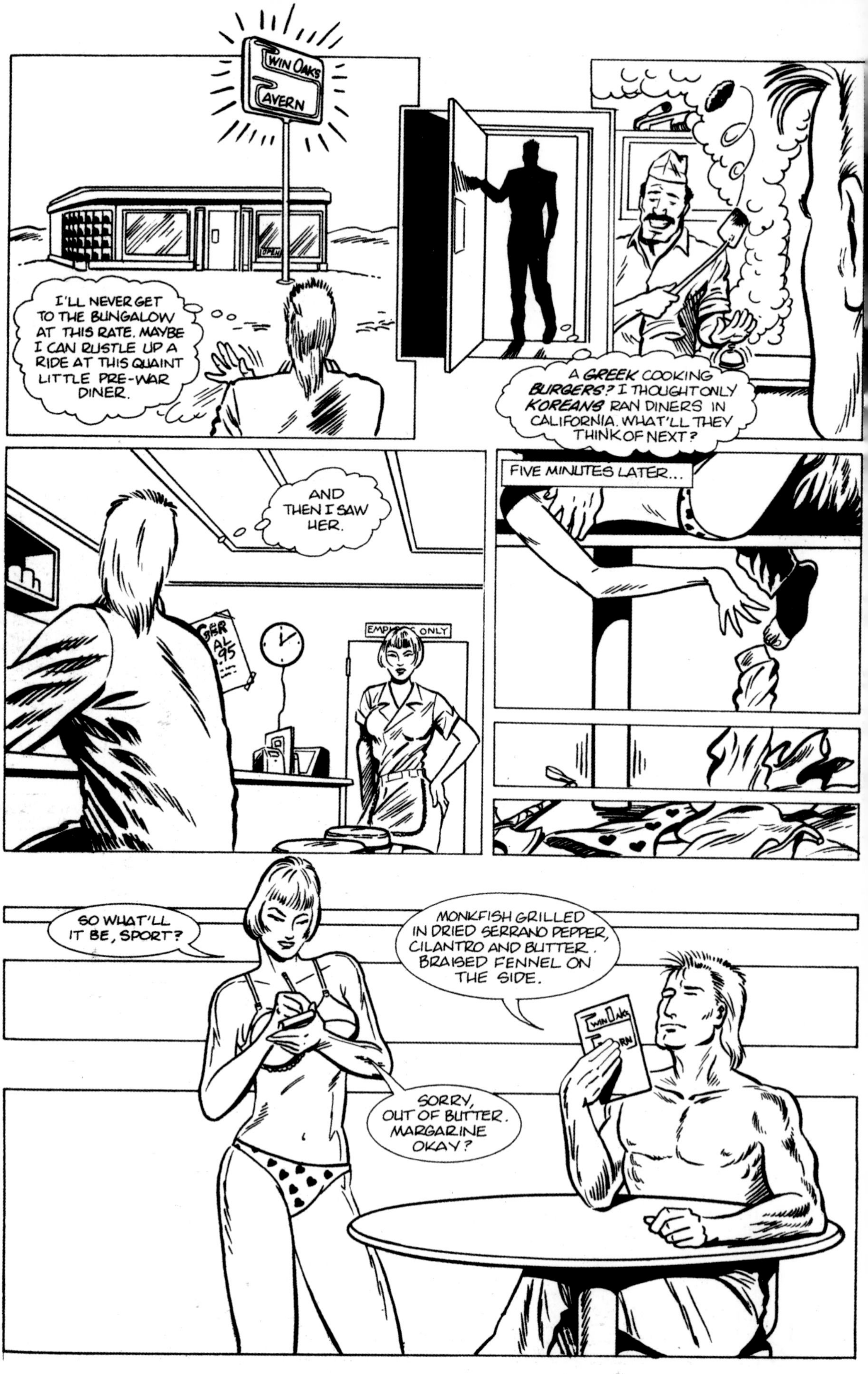
TWIN OAKS TAVERN
OPEN
I'LL NEVER GET TO THE BUNGALOW AT THIS RATE. MAYBE I CAN RUSTLE UP A RIDE AT THIS QUAINT LITTLE PRE-WAR DINER.
A GREEK COOKING BURGERS? I THOUGHT ONLY KOREANS RAN DINERS IN CALIFORNIA. WHAT'LL THEY THINK OF NEXT?
AND THEN I SAW HER.
FIVE MINUTES LATER...
SO WHAT'LL IT BE, SPORT?
MONKFISH GRILLED IN DRIED SERRANO PEPPER, CILANTRO AND BUTTER. BRAISED FENNEL ON THE SIDE.
SORRY, OUT OF BUTTER. MARGARINE OKAY?

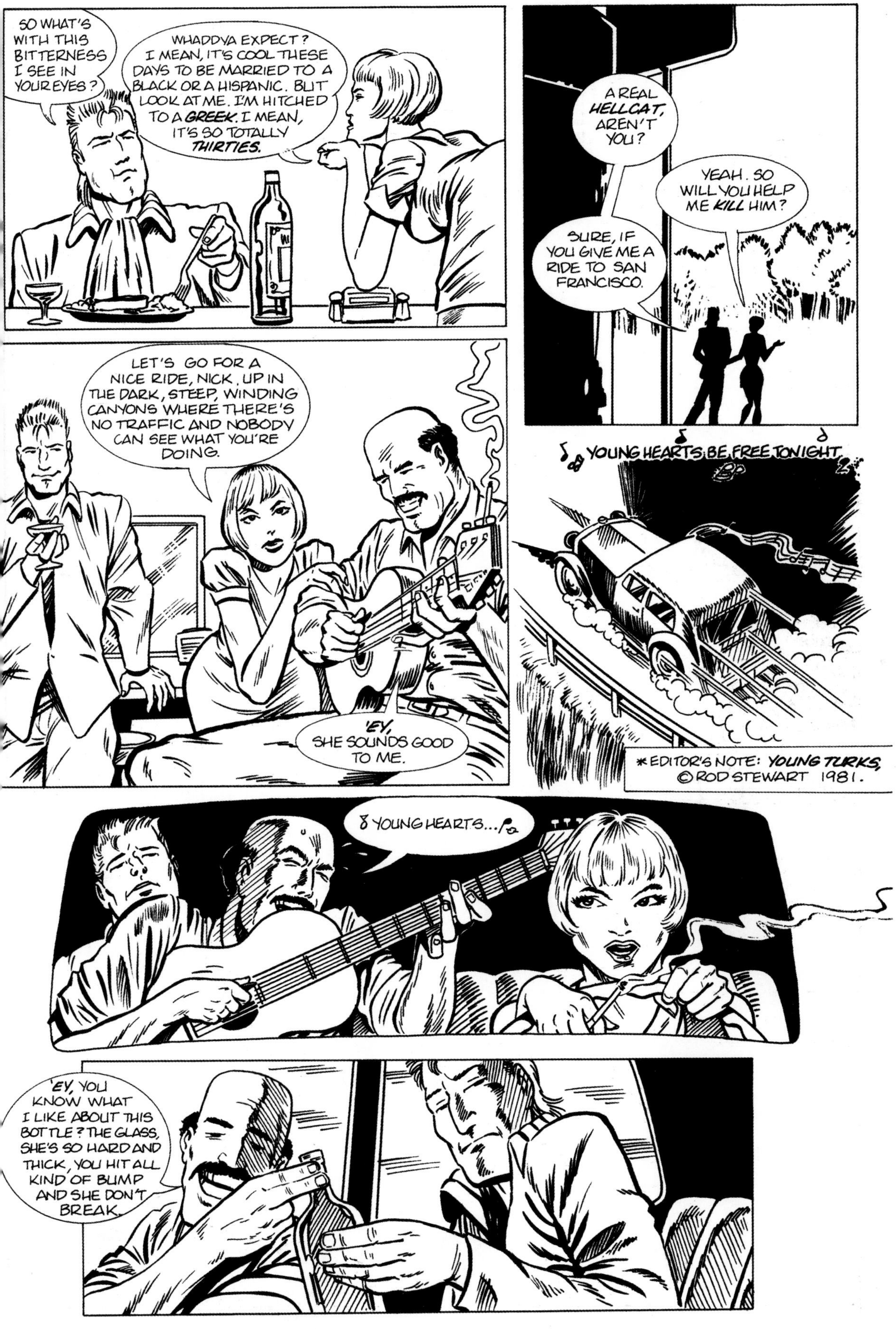

SO WHAT'S WITH THIS BITTERNESS I SEE IN YOUR EYES?
WHADDYA EXPECT? I MEAN, IT'S COOL THESE DAYS TO BE MARRIED TO A BLACK OR A HISPANIC. BUT LOOK AT ME. I'M HITCHED TO A GREEK. I MEAN, IT'S SO TOTALLY THIRTIES.
A REAL HELLCAT, AREN'T YOU?
YEAH. SO WILL YOU HELP ME KILL HIM?
SURE, IF YOU GIVE ME A RIDE TO SAN FRANCISCO.
LET'S GO FOR A NICE RIDE, NICK, UP IN THE DARK, STEEP, WINDING CANYONS WHERE THERE'S NO TRAFFIC AND NOBODY CAN SEE WHAT YOU'RE DOING.
'EY, SHE SOUNDS GOOD TO ME.
YOUNG HEARTS BE FREE TONIGHT
*EDITOR'S NOTE: YOUNG TURKS, © ROD STEWART 1981.
YOUNG HEARTS...
'EY, YOU KNOW WHAT I LIKE ABOUT THIS BOTTLE? THE GLASS, SHE'S SO HARD AND THICK, YOU HIT ALL KIND OF BUMP AND SHE DON'T BREAK.

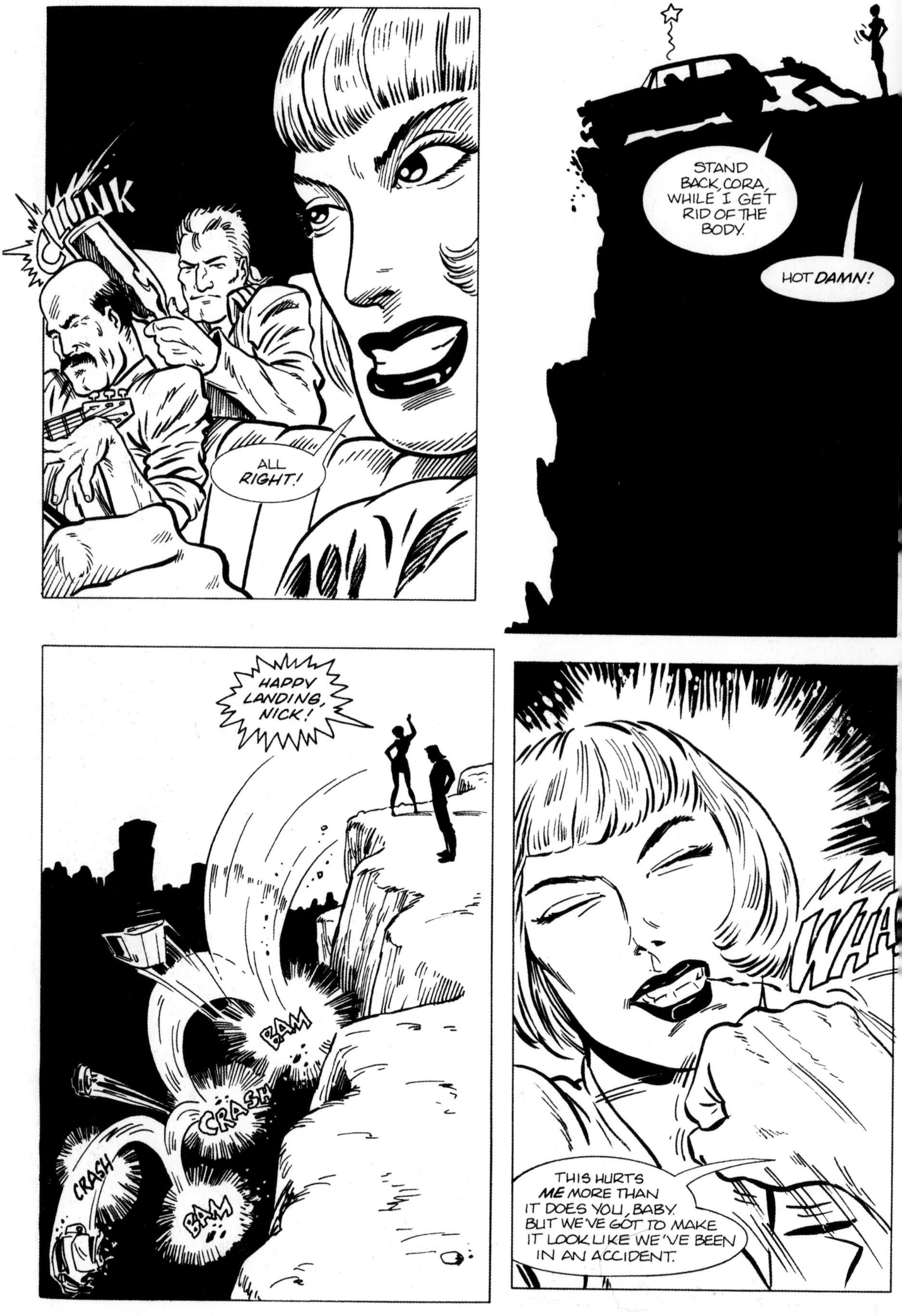
CLUNK
ALL RIGHT!
STAND BACK, CORA, WHILE I GET RID OF THE BODY.
HOT DAMN!
HAPPY LANDING, NICK!
BAM
CRASH
CRASH
BAM
WHA
THIS HURTS ME MORE THAN IT DOES YOU, BABY. BUT WE'VE GOT TO MAKE IT LOOK LIKE WE'VE BEEN IN AN ACCIDENT.

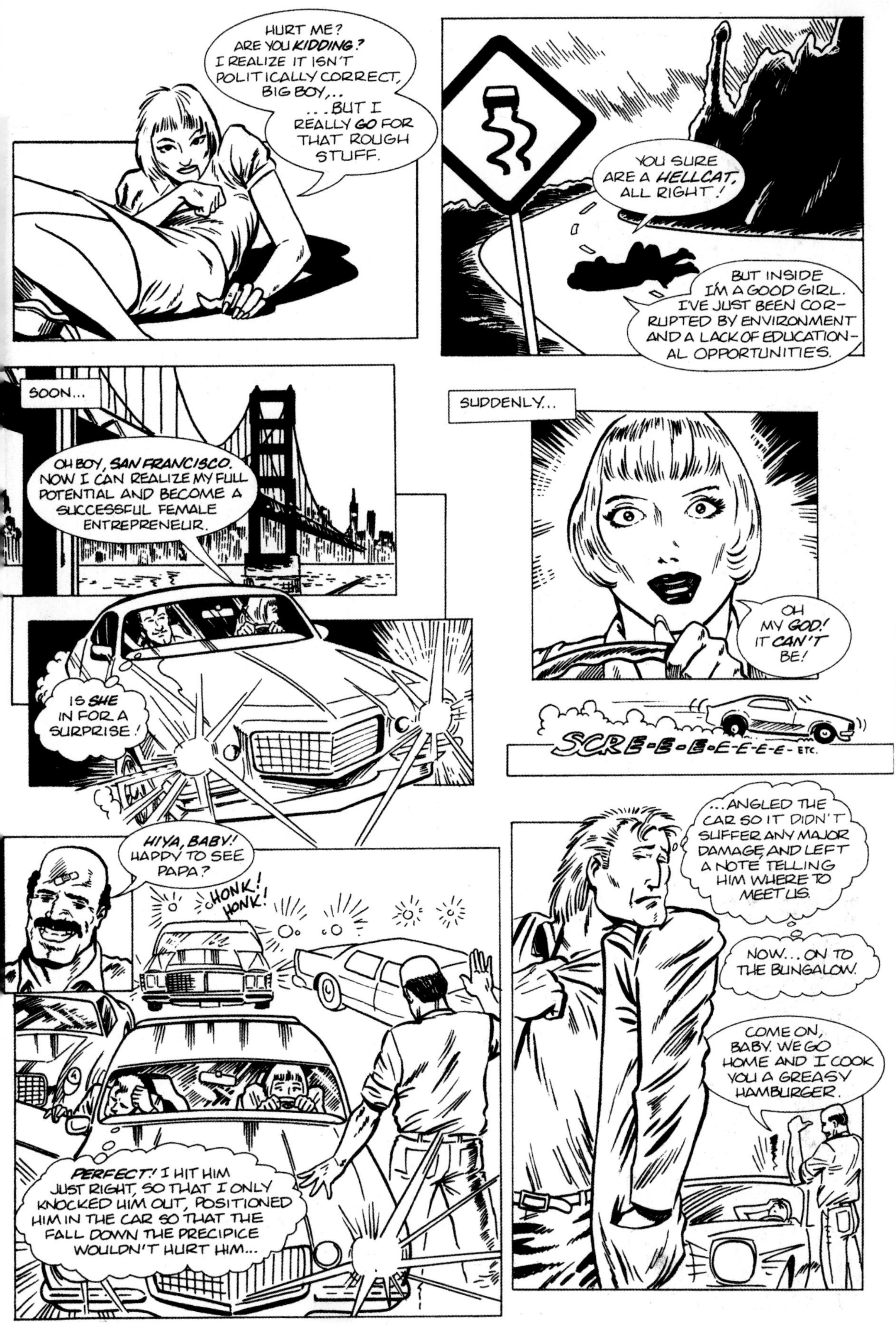

HURT ME? ARE YOU KIDDING? I REALIZE IT ISN'T POLITICALLY CORRECT, BIG BOY,..
. . . BUT I REALLY GO FOR THAT ROUGH STUFF.
YOU SURE ARE A HELLCAT, ALL RIGHT!
BUT INSIDE I'M A GOOD GIRL. I'VE JUST BEEN COR-RUPTED BY ENVIRONMENT AND A LACK OF EDUCATION-AL OPPORTUNITIES.
SOON...
OH BOY, SAN FRANCISCO. NOW I CAN REALIZE MY FULL POTENTIAL AND BECOME A SUCCESSFUL FEMALE ENTREPRENEUR.
IS SHE IN FOR A SURPRISE!
SUDDENLY...
OH MY GOD! IT CAN'T BE!
SCRE-E-E-E-E-E-E ETC.
HIYA, BABY! HAPPY TO SEE PAPA?
HONK! HONK!
PERFECT! I HIT HIM JUST RIGHT, SO THAT I ONLY KNOCKED HIM OUT, POSITIONED HIM IN THE CAR SO THAT THE FALL DOWN THE PRECIPICE WOULDN'T HURT HIM...
...ANGLED THE CAR SO IT DIDN'T SUFFER ANY MAJOR DAMAGE, AND LEFT A NOTE TELLING HIM WHERE TO MEET US.
NOW... ON TO THE BUNGALOW.
COME ON, BABY. WE GO HOME AND I COOK YOU A GREASY HAMBURGER.

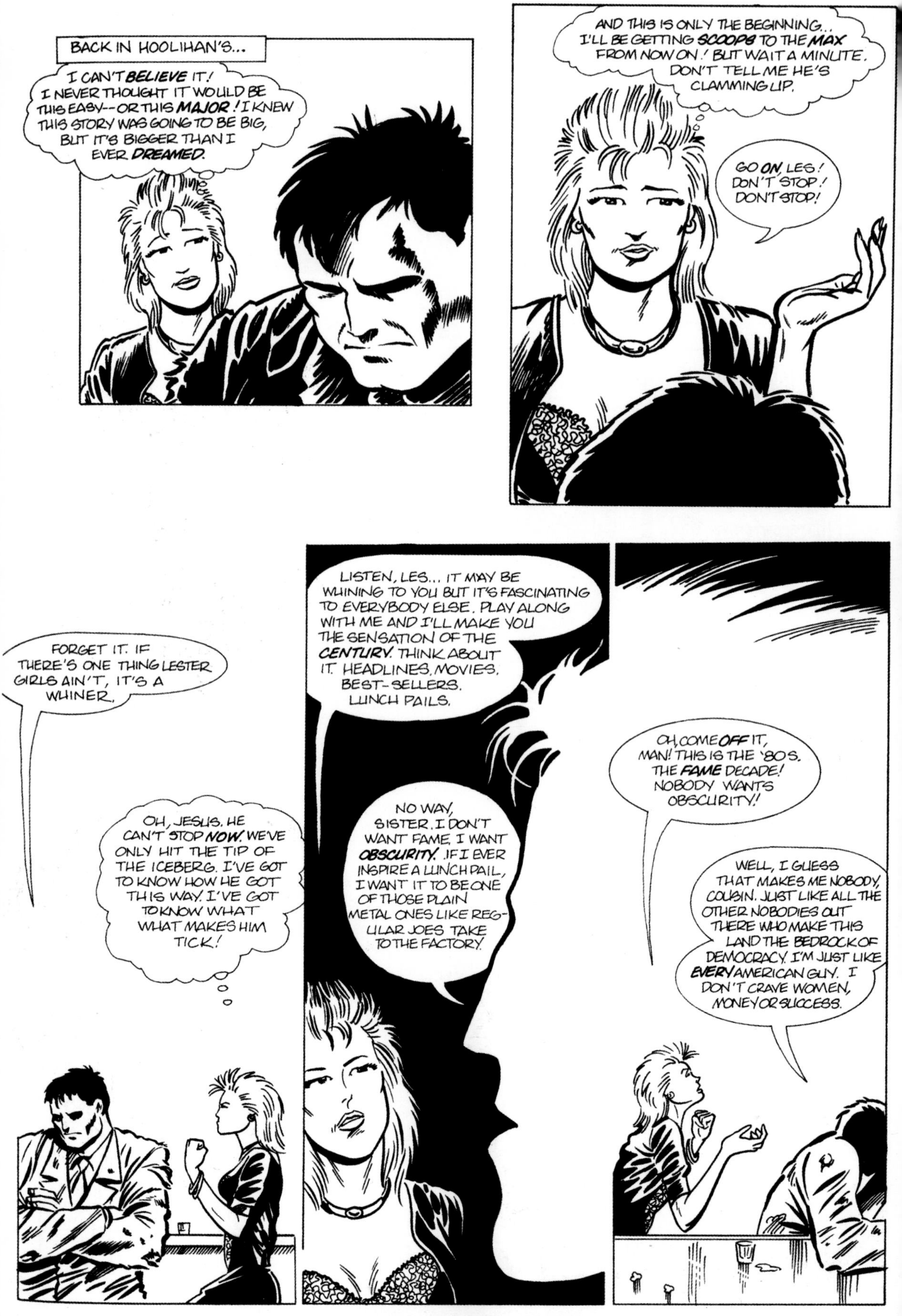
BACK IN HOOLIHAN'S...
I CAN'T **BELIEVE** IT! I NEVER THOUGHT IT WOULD BE THIS EASY--OR THIS **MAJOR**! I KNEW THIS STORY WAS GOING TO BE BIG, BUT IT'S BIGGER THAN I EVER **DREAMED**.
AND THIS IS ONLY THE BEGINNING... I'LL BE GETTING **SCOOPS** TO THE **MAX** FROM NOW ON! BUT WAIT A MINUTE. DON'T TELL ME HE'S CLAMMING UP.
GO **ON**, LES! DON'T STOP! DON'T STOP!
FORGET IT. IF THERE'S ONE THING LESTER GIRLS AIN'T, IT'S A WHINER.
OH, JESUS, HE CAN'T STOP **NOW**. WE'VE ONLY HIT THE TIP OF THE ICEBERG. I'VE GOT TO KNOW HOW HE GOT THIS WAY. I'VE GOT TO KNOW WHAT WHAT MAKES HIM TICK!
LISTEN, LES... IT MAY BE WHINING TO YOU BUT IT'S FASCINATING TO EVERYBODY ELSE. PLAY ALONG WITH ME AND I'LL MAKE YOU THE SENSATION OF THE **CENTURY**. THINK ABOUT IT. HEADLINES, MOVIES, BEST-SELLERS. LUNCH PAILS.
NO WAY, SISTER. I DON'T WANT FAME, I WANT **OBSCURITY**. IF I EVER INSPIRE A LUNCH PAIL, I WANT IT TO BE ONE OF THOSE PLAIN METAL ONES LIKE REG-ULAR JOES TAKE TO THE FACTORY.
OH, COME **OFF** IT, MAN! THIS IS THE '80S. THE **FAME** DECADE! NOBODY WANTS OBSCURITY!
WELL, I GUESS THAT MAKES ME NOBODY, COUSIN. JUST LIKE ALL THE OTHER NOBODIES OUT THERE WHO MAKE THIS LAND THE BEDROCK OF DEMOCRACY. I'M JUST LIKE **EVERY** AMERICAN GUY. I DON'T CRAVE WOMEN, MONEY OR SUCCESS.

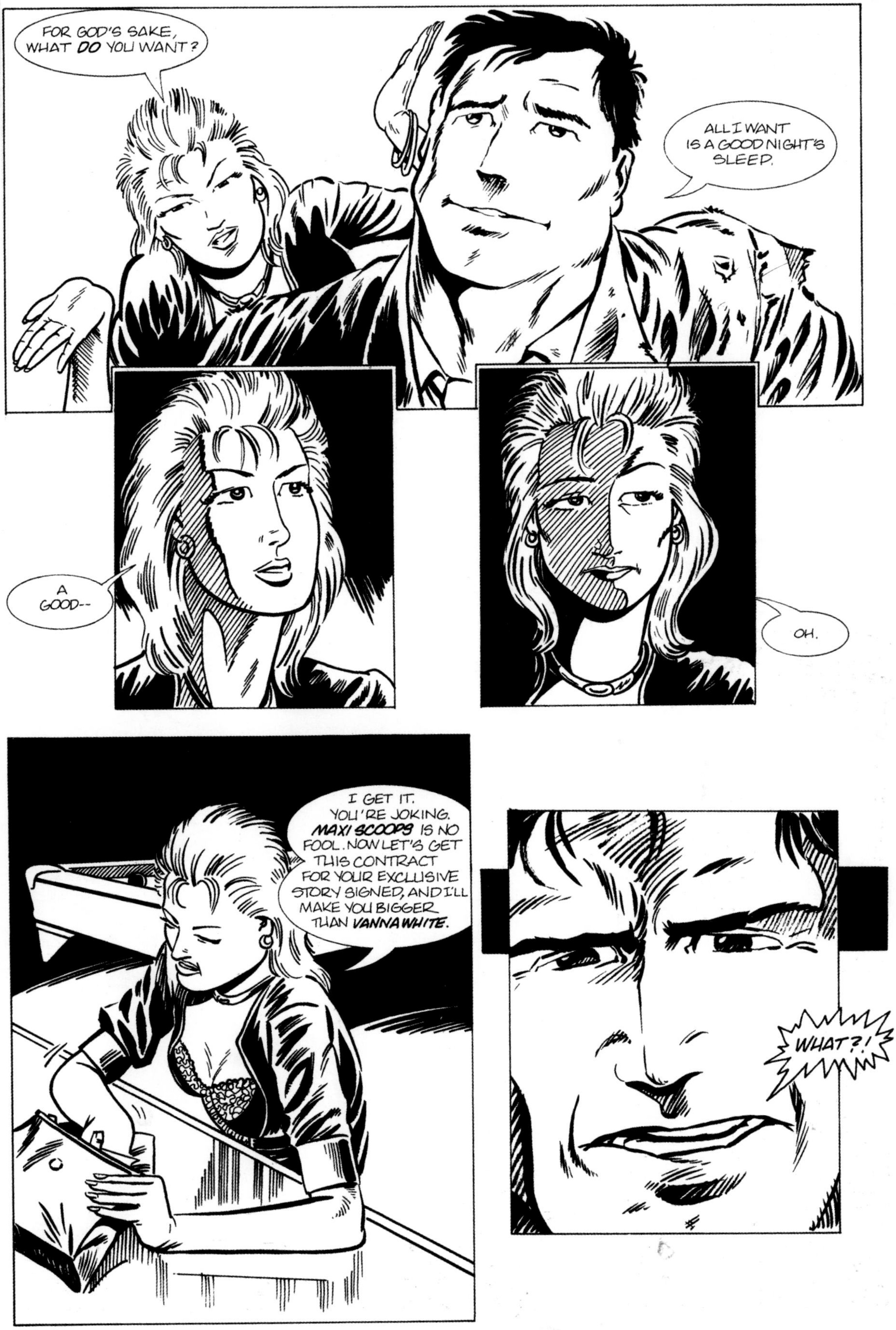
FOR GOD'S SAKE, WHAT DO YOU WANT?
ALL I WANT IS A GOOD NIGHT'S SLEEP.
A GOOD--
OH.
I GET IT. YOU'RE JOKING. MAXI SCOOPS IS NO FOOL. NOW LET'S GET THIS CONTRACT FOR YOUR EXCLUSIVE STORY SIGNED, AND I'LL MAKE YOU BIGGER THAN VANNA WHITE.
WHAT?!

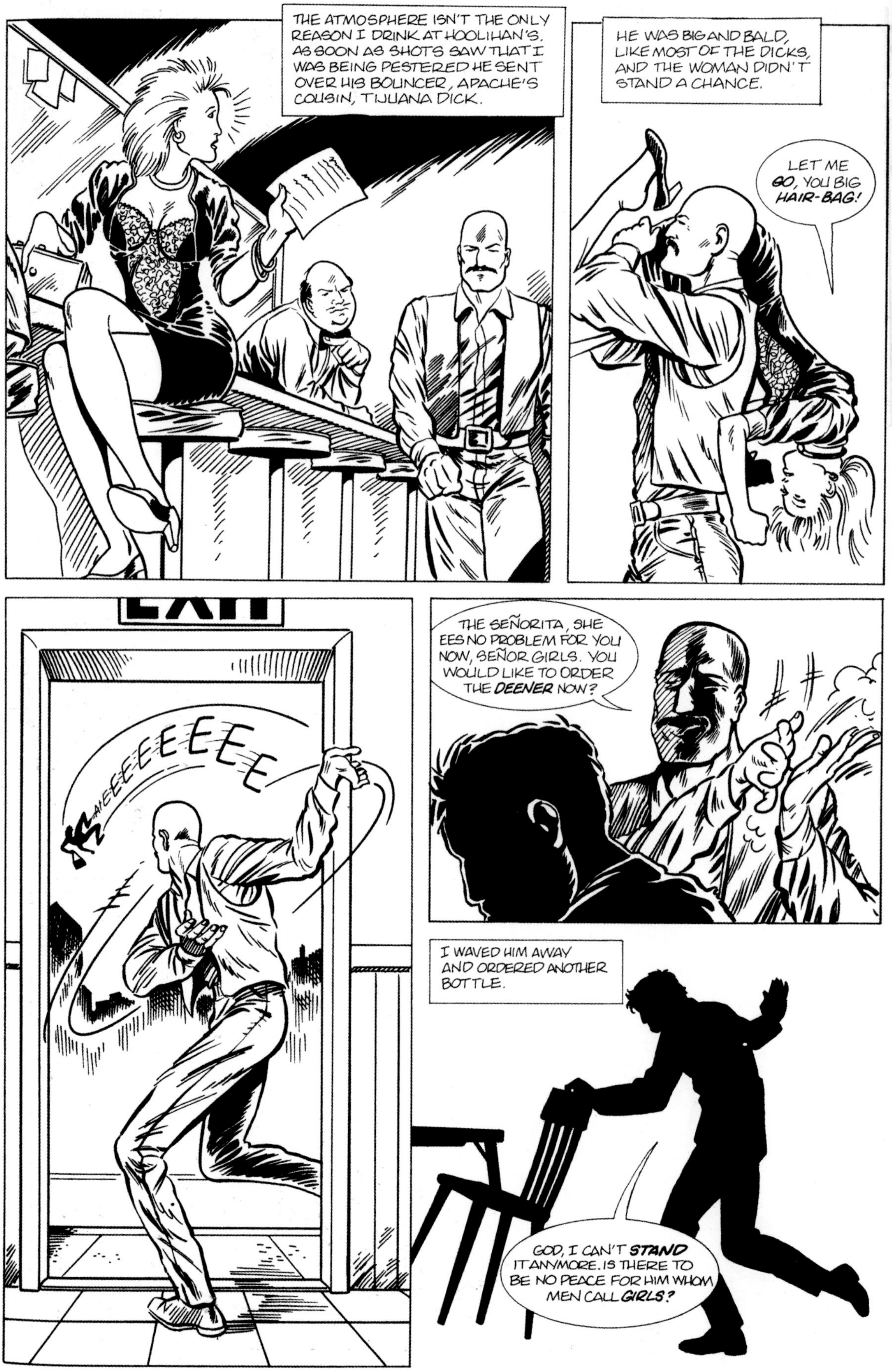
THE ATMOSPHERE ISN'T THE ONLY REASON I DRINK AT HOOLIHAN'S. AS SOON AS SHOTS SAW THAT I WAS BEING PESTERED HE SENT OVER HIS BOUNCER, APACHE'S COUSIN, TIJUANA DICK.
HE WAS BIG AND BALD, LIKE MOST OF THE DICKS, AND THE WOMAN DIDN'T STAND A CHANCE.
LET ME GO, YOU BIG HAIR-BAG!
EEEEEEE
THE SEÑORITA, SHE EES NO PROBLEM FOR YOU NOW, SEÑOR GIRLS. YOU WOULD LIKE TO ORDER THE DEENER NOW?
I WAVED HIM AWAY AND ORDERED ANOTHER BOTTLE.
GOD, I CAN'T STAND IT ANYMORE. IS THERE TO BE NO PEACE FOR HIM WHOM MEN CALL GIRLS?

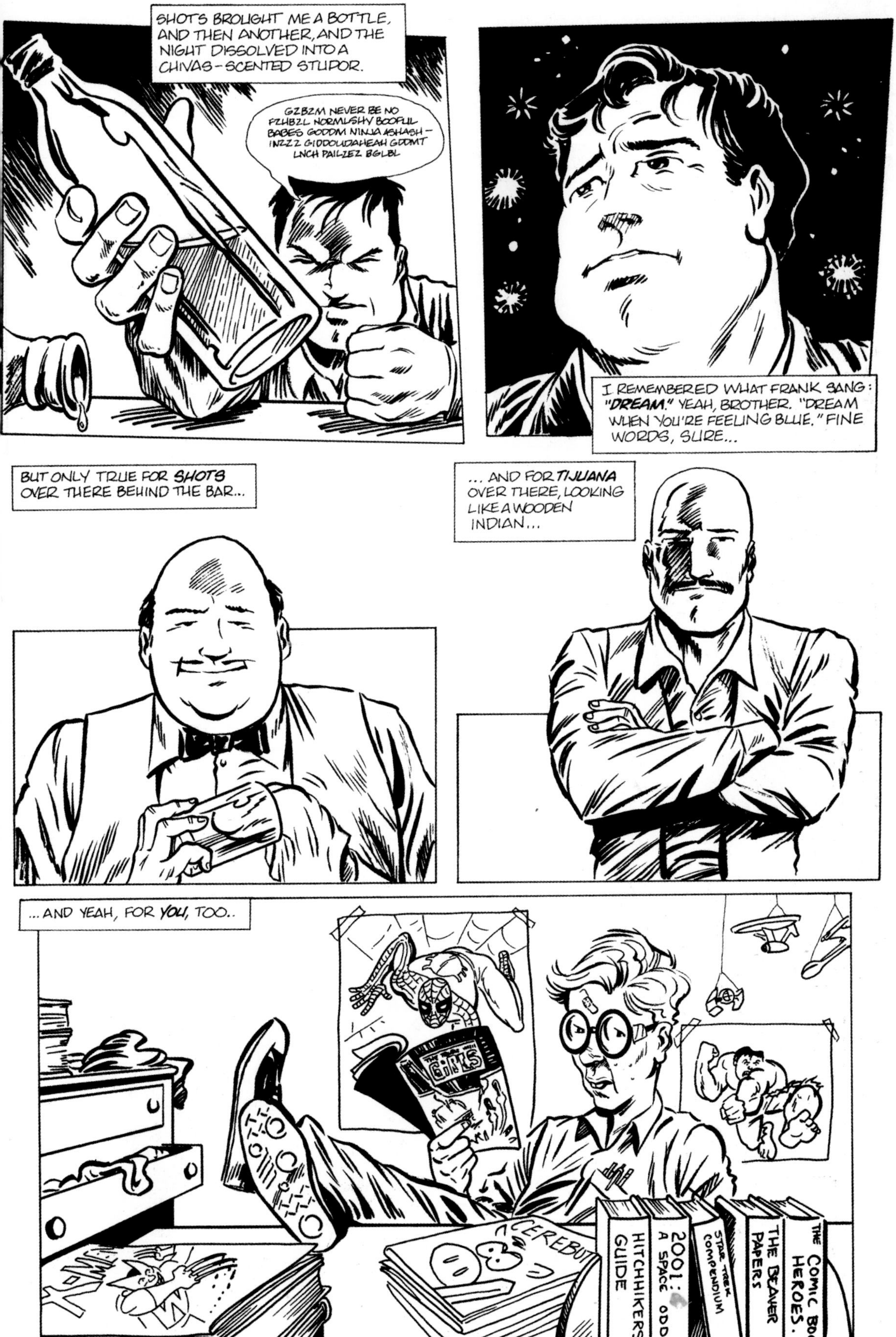
SHOTS BROUGHT ME A BOTTLE, AND THEN ANOTHER, AND THE NIGHT DISSOLVED INTO A CHIVAS-SCENTED STUPOR.
GZBZM NEVER BE NO FZHBZL NORMLSHY BOOFUL BABES GODDM NINJA ASHASH-INZZZ GIDDOUDAHEAH GDDMT LNCH PAILZEZ BGLBL
I REMEMBERED WHAT FRANK SANG: "DREAM." YEAH, BROTHER. "DREAM WHEN YOU'RE FEELING BLUE." FINE WORDS, SURE...
BUT ONLY TRUE FOR SHOTS OVER THERE BEHIND THE BAR...
... AND FOR TIJUANA OVER THERE, LOOKING LIKE A WOODEN INDIAN...
... AND YEAH, FOR YOU, TOO...
HITCHHIKERS GUIDE
2001: A SPACE ODD
STAR TREK COMPENDIUM
THE BEAVER PAPERS
THE COMIC BOO HEROES.

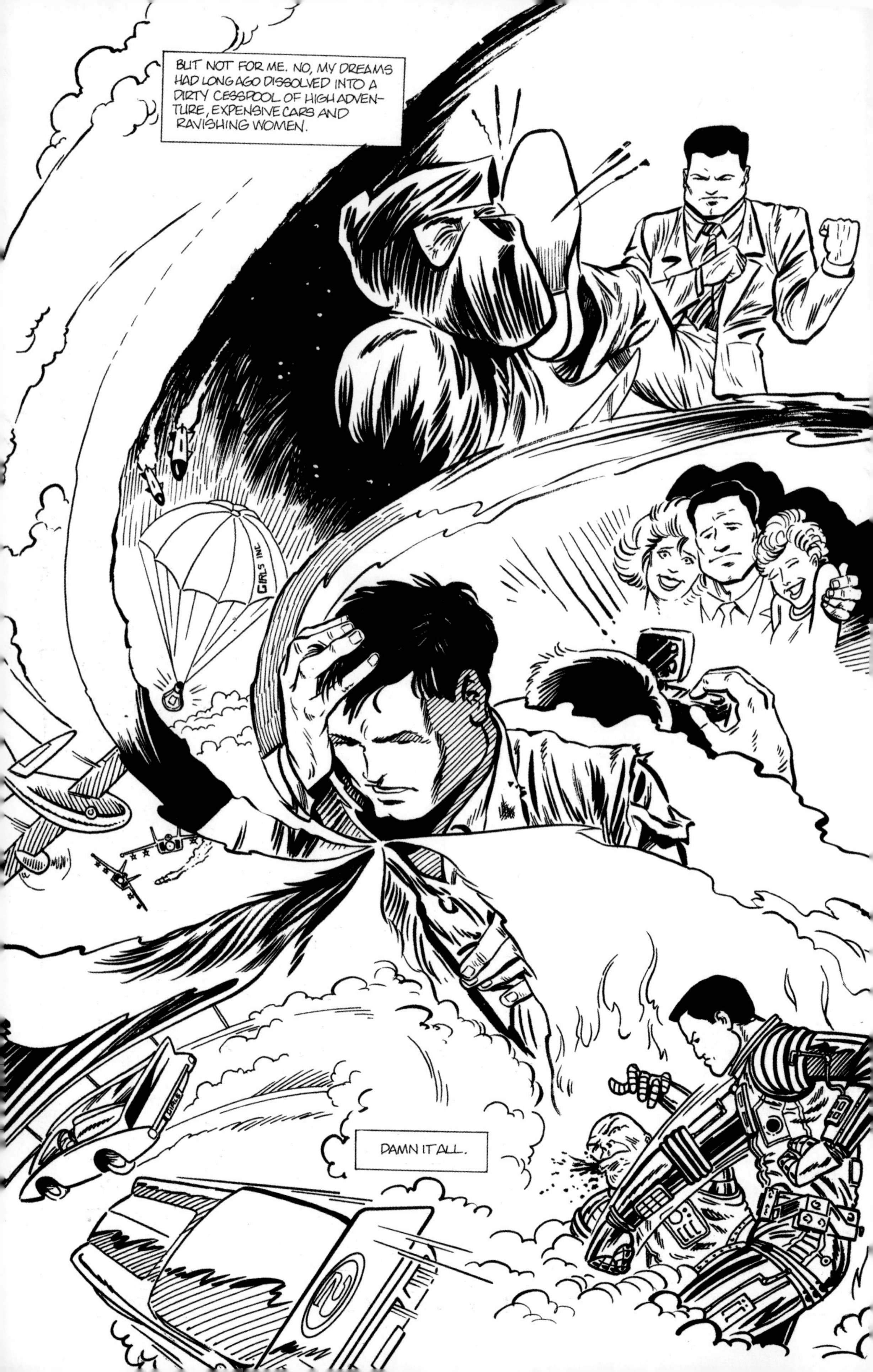
BUT NOT FOR ME. NO, MY DREAMS HAD LONG AGO DISSOLVED INTO A DIRTY CESSPOOL OF HIGH ADVENTURE, EXPENSIVE CARS AND RAVISHING WOMEN.
GIRLS INC.
DAMN IT ALL.

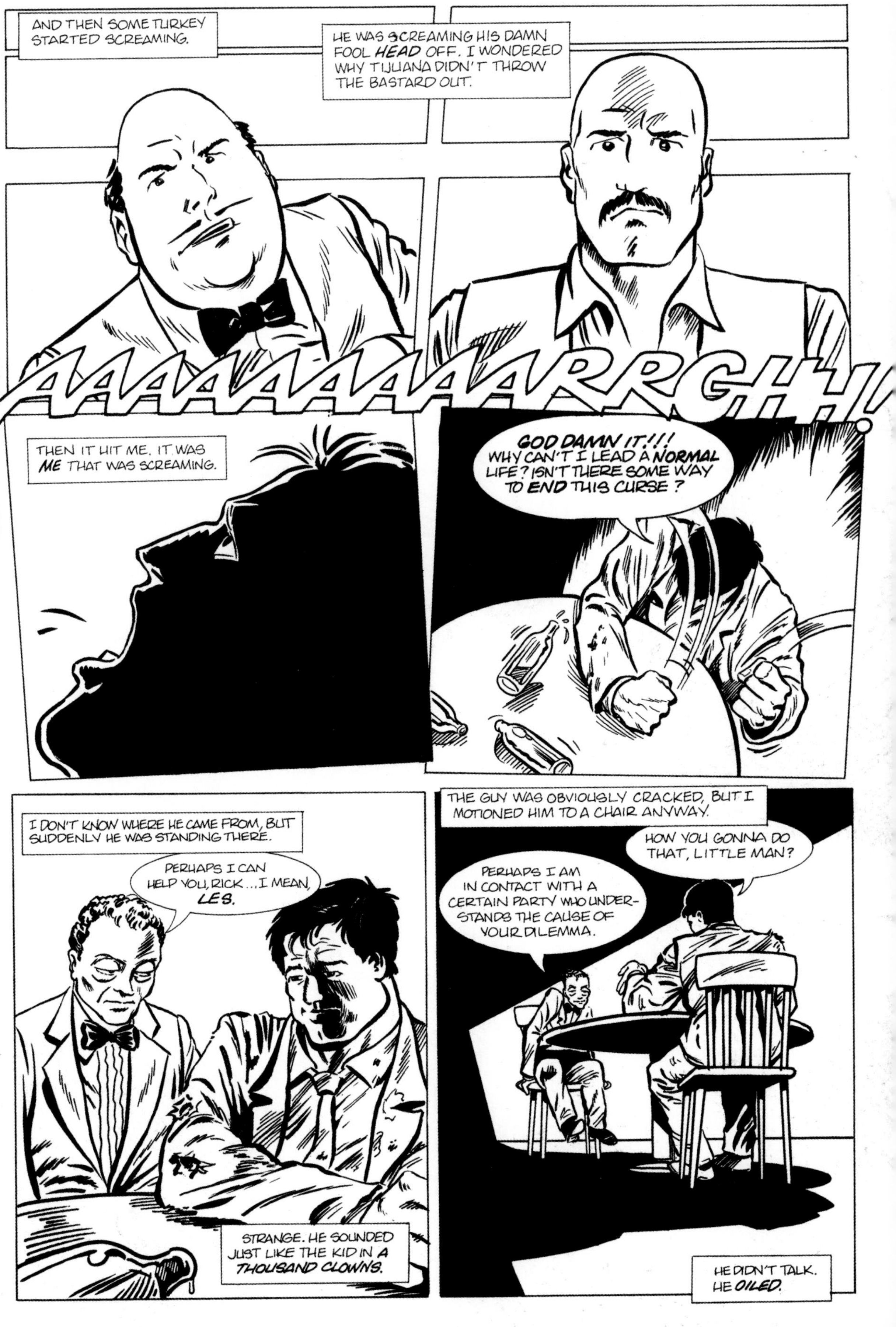
AND THEN SOME TURKEY STARTED SCREAMING.
HE WAS SCREAMING HIS DAMN FOOL HEAD OFF. I WONDERED WHY TIJUANA DIDN'T THROW THE BASTARD OUT.
AAAAAAAAARRGHH!
THEN IT HIT ME. IT WAS ME THAT WAS SCREAMING.
GOD DAMN IT!!! WHY CAN'T I LEAD A NORMAL LIFE? ISN'T THERE SOME WAY TO END THIS CURSE?
I DON'T KNOW WHERE HE CAME FROM, BUT SUDDENLY HE WAS STANDING THERE.
PERHAPS I CAN HELP YOU, RICK... I MEAN, LES.
STRANGE. HE SOUNDED JUST LIKE THE KID IN A THOUSAND CLOWNS.
THE GUY WAS OBVIOUSLY CRACKED, BUT I MOTIONED HIM TO A CHAIR ANYWAY.
HOW YOU GONNA DO THAT, LITTLE MAN?
PERHAPS I AM IN CONTACT WITH A CERTAIN PARTY WHO UNDERSTANDS THE CAUSE OF YOUR DILEMMA.
HE DIDN'T TALK. HE OILED.

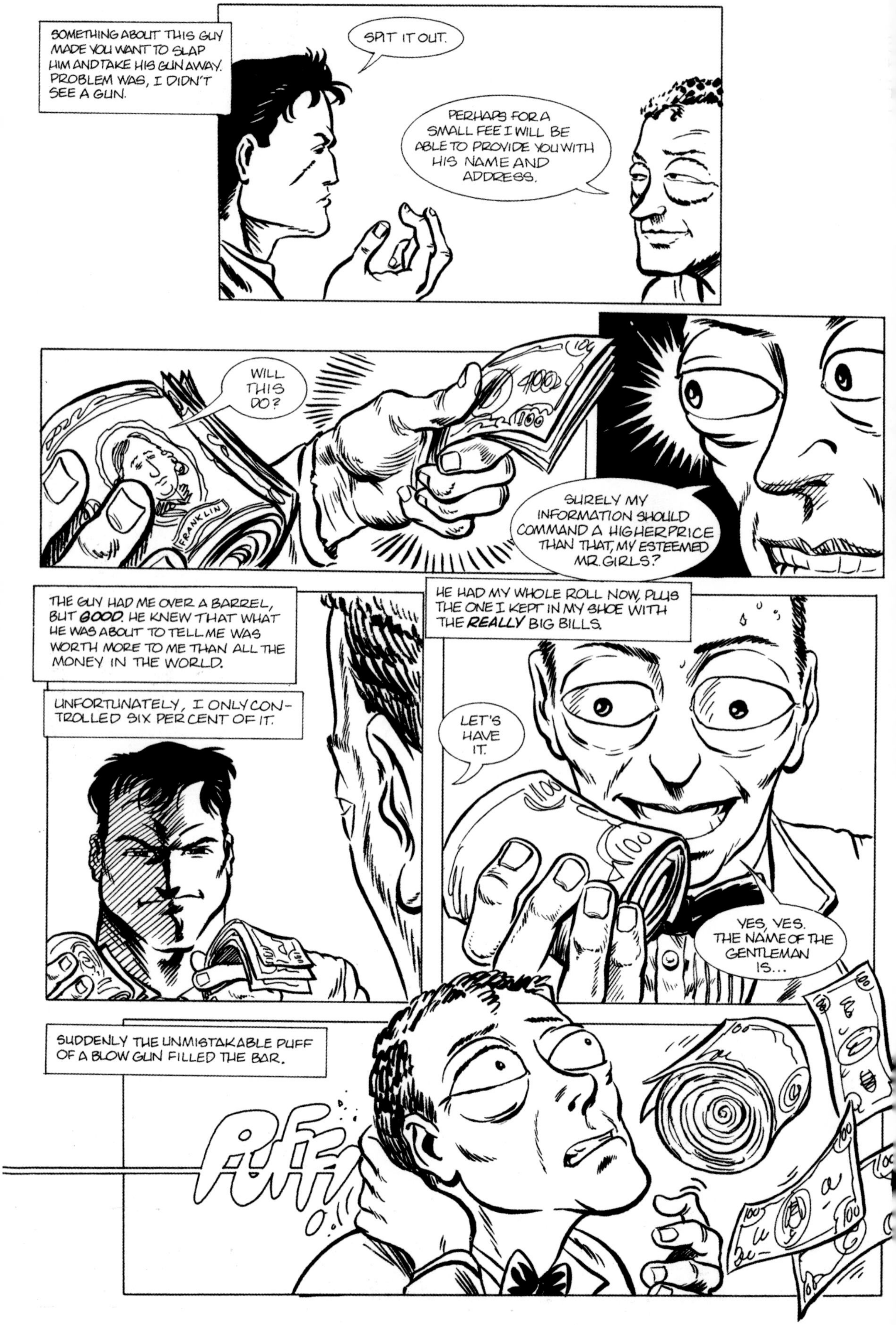
SOMETHING ABOUT THIS GUY MADE YOU WANT TO SLAP HIM AND TAKE HIS GUN AWAY. PROBLEM WAS, I DIDN'T SEE A GUN.
SPIT IT OUT.
PERHAPS FOR A SMALL FEE I WILL BE ABLE TO PROVIDE YOU WITH HIS NAME AND ADDRESS.
WILL THIS DO?
FRANKLIN
SURELY MY INFORMATION SHOULD COMMAND A HIGHER PRICE THAN THAT, MY ESTEEMED MR. GIRLS?
THE GUY HAD ME OVER A BARREL, BUT GOOD. HE KNEW THAT WHAT HE WAS ABOUT TO TELL ME WAS WORTH MORE TO ME THAN ALL THE MONEY IN THE WORLD.
UNFORTUNATELY, I ONLY CONTROLLED SIX PER CENT OF IT.
HE HAD MY WHOLE ROLL NOW, PLUS THE ONE I KEPT IN MY SHOE WITH THE REALLY BIG BILLS.
LET'S HAVE IT.
YES, YES. THE NAME OF THE GENTLEMAN IS...
SUDDENLY THE UNMISTAKABLE PUFF OF A BLOW GUN FILLED THE BAR.
PFFT!

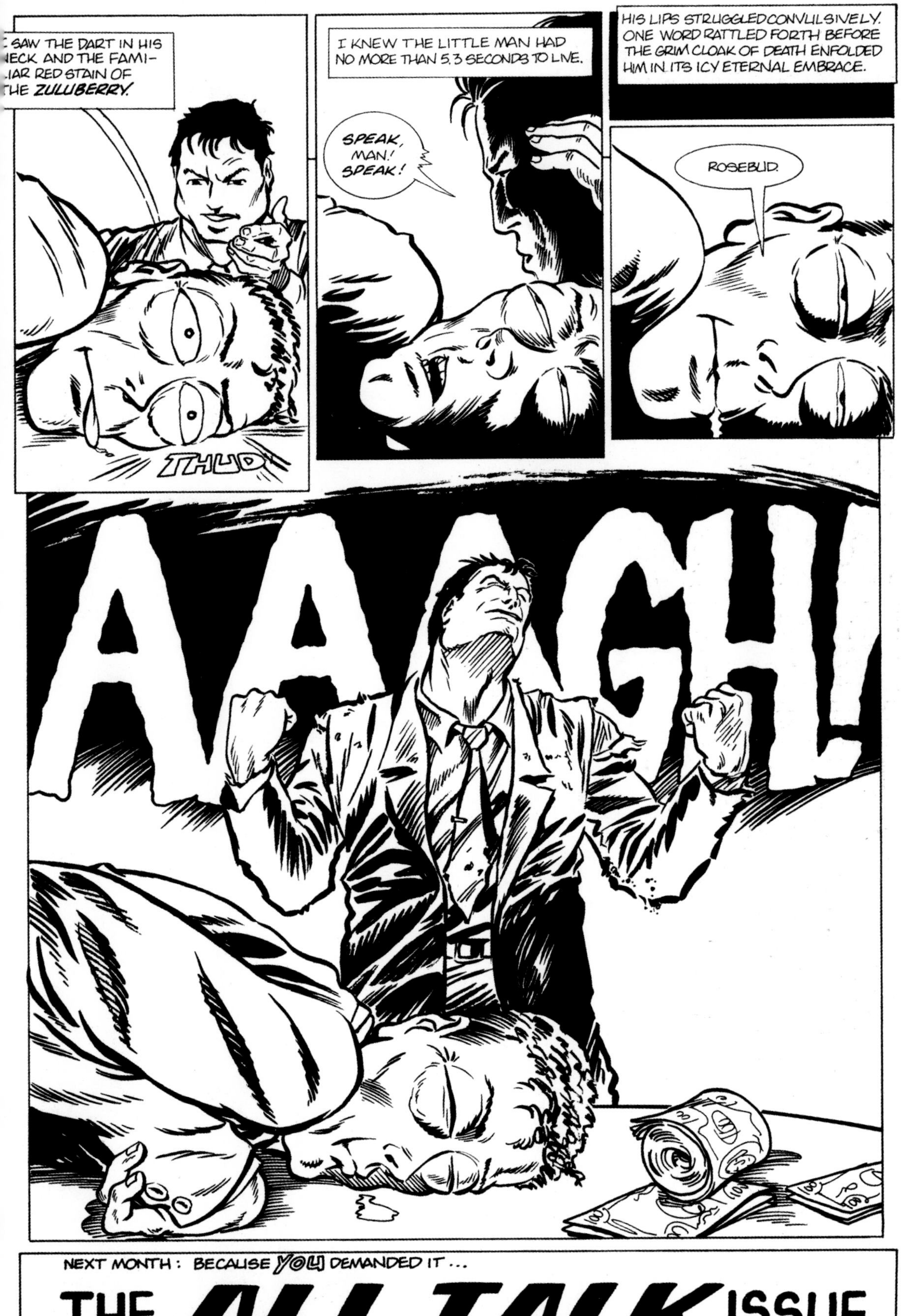
SAW THE DART IN HIS NECK AND THE FAMI- IAR RED STAIN OF THE ZULUBERRY.
THUD
I KNEW THE LITTLE MAN HAD NO MORE THAN 5.3 SECONDS TO LIVE.
SPEAK, MAN! SPEAK!
HIS LIPS STRUGGLED CONVULSIVELY. ONE WORD RATTLED FORTH BEFORE THE GRIM CLOAK OF DEATH ENFOLDED HIM IN ITS ICY ETERNAL EMBRACE.
ROSEBUD.
AAGH
NEXT MONTH: BECAUSE YOU DEMANDED IT...
THE ALL TALK ISSUE

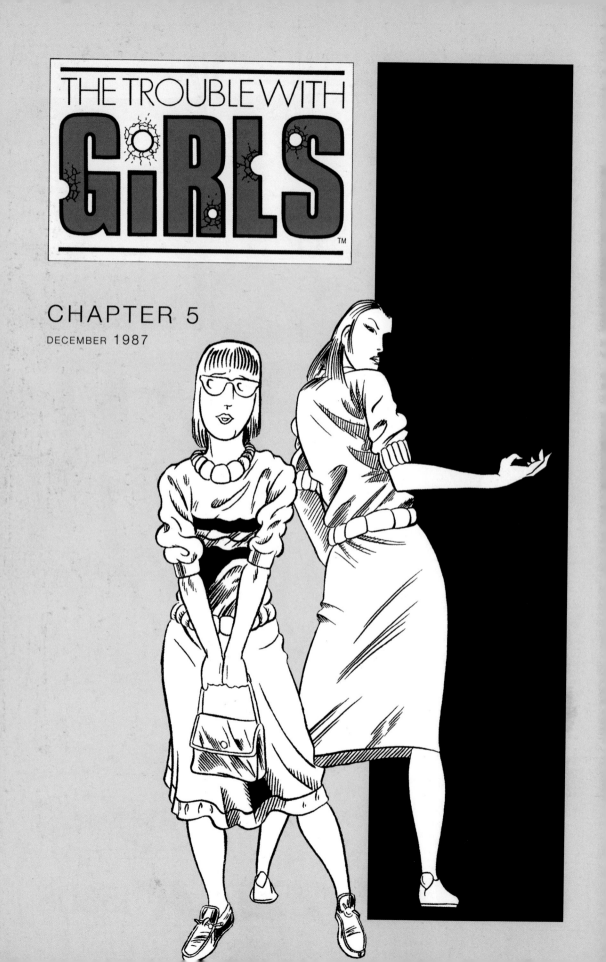

THE TROUBLE WITH GiRLS

CHAPTER 5
DECEMBER 1987

YOU KNOW HOW IT IS WHEN SOMEBODY CONKS YOU OVER THE HEAD AND JUST BEFORE YOU BLACK OUT YOU THINK, "I'M BLACKING OUT," AND THEN YOU BLACK OUT? AND HOW WHEN YOU COME TO YOU REMEMBER ALL THAT?

WELL, WHEN I RECOVERED CONSCIOUSNESS IN A DARK ALLEY FIVE MINUTES AFTER I'D LEFT HOOLIHAN'S, I DIDN'T REMEMBER A DAMN THING. YOU SEE, WHOEVER HAD RAPPED ME HAD HIT ME SO HARD THAT THE BLOW HAD GIVEN ME AMNESIA.

...AGAIN

GIRLS TALK

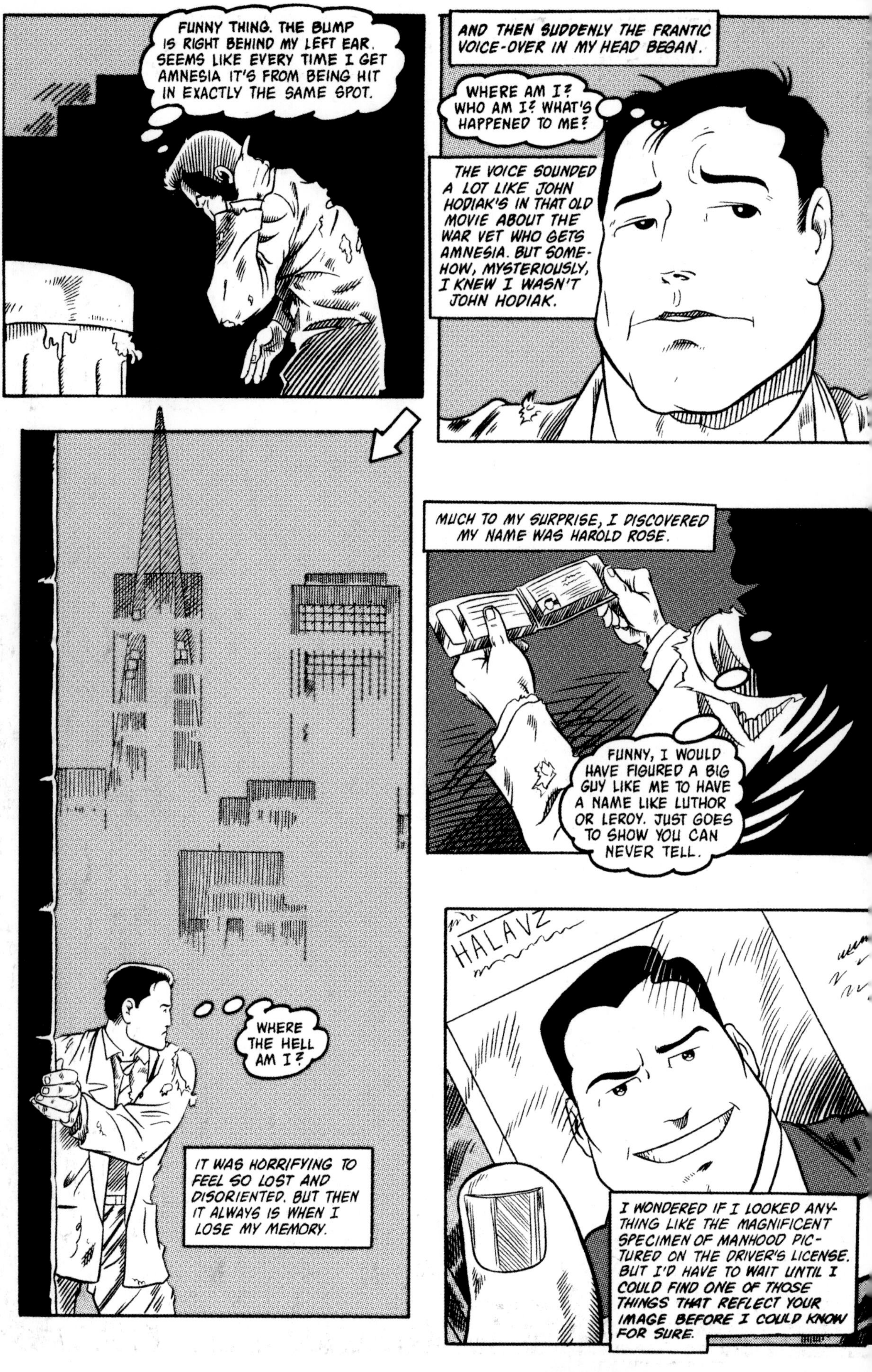
FUNNY THING. THE BUMP IS RIGHT BEHIND MY LEFT EAR. SEEMS LIKE EVERY TIME I GET AMNESIA IT'S FROM BEING HIT IN EXACTLY THE SAME SPOT.
AND THEN SUDDENLY THE FRANTIC VOICE-OVER IN MY HEAD BEGAN.
WHERE AM I? WHO AM I? WHAT'S HAPPENED TO ME?
THE VOICE SOUNDED A LOT LIKE JOHN HODIAK'S IN THAT OLD MOVIE ABOUT THE WAR VET WHO GETS AMNESIA. BUT SOME-HOW, MYSTERIOUSLY, I KNEW I WASN'T JOHN HODIAK.
WHERE THE HELL AM I?
IT WAS HORRIFYING TO FEEL SO LOST AND DISORIENTED. BUT THEN IT ALWAYS IS WHEN I LOSE MY MEMORY.
MUCH TO MY SURPRISE, I DISCOVERED MY NAME WAS HAROLD ROSE.
FUNNY, I WOULD HAVE FIGURED A BIG GUY LIKE ME TO HAVE A NAME LIKE LUTHOR OR LEROY. JUST GOES TO SHOW YOU CAN NEVER TELL.
I WONDERED IF I LOOKED ANY-THING LIKE THE MAGNIFICENT SPECIMEN OF MANHOOD PIC-TURED ON THE DRIVER'S LICENSE. BUT I'D HAVE TO WAIT UNTIL I COULD FIND ONE OF THOSE THINGS THAT REFLECT YOUR IMAGE BEFORE I COULD KNOW FOR SURE.

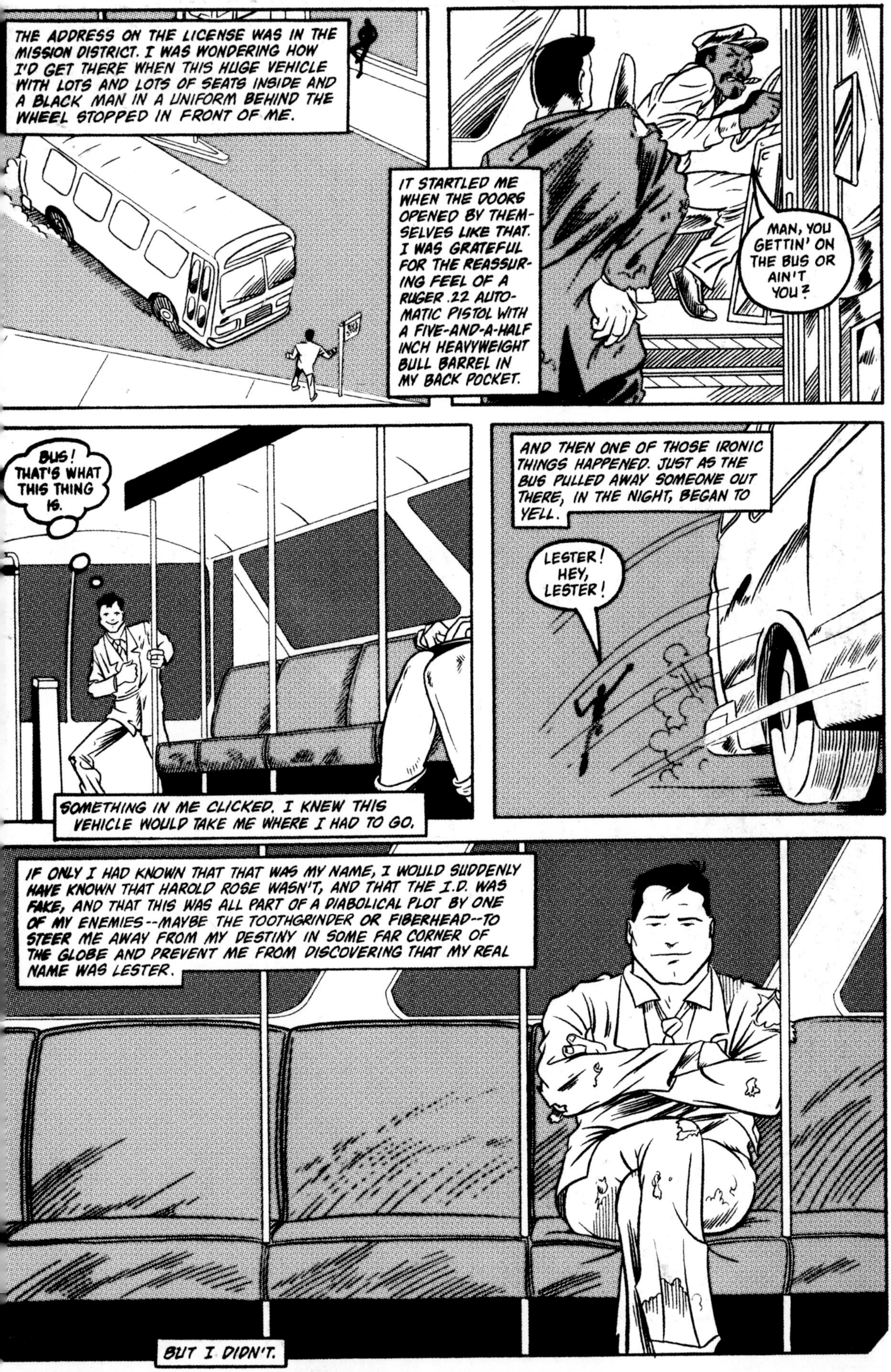
THE ADDRESS ON THE LICENSE WAS IN THE MISSION DISTRICT. I WAS WONDERING HOW I'D GET THERE WHEN THIS HUGE VEHICLE WITH LOTS AND LOTS OF SEATS INSIDE AND A BLACK MAN IN A UNIFORM BEHIND THE WHEEL STOPPED IN FRONT OF ME.
IT STARTLED ME WHEN THE DOORS OPENED BY THEMSELVES LIKE THAT. I WAS GRATEFUL FOR THE REASSURING FEEL OF A RUGER .22 AUTOMATIC PISTOL WITH A FIVE-AND-A-HALF INCH HEAVYWEIGHT BULL BARREL IN MY BACK POCKET.
MAN, YOU GETTIN' ON THE BUS OR AIN'T YOU?
BUS! THAT'S WHAT THIS THING IS.
SOMETHING IN ME CLICKED. I KNEW THIS VEHICLE WOULD TAKE ME WHERE I HAD TO GO.
AND THEN ONE OF THOSE IRONIC THINGS HAPPENED. JUST AS THE BUS PULLED AWAY SOMEONE OUT THERE, IN THE NIGHT, BEGAN TO YELL.
LESTER! HEY, LESTER!
IF ONLY I HAD KNOWN THAT THAT WAS MY NAME, I WOULD SUDDENLY HAVE KNOWN THAT HAROLD ROSE WASN'T, AND THAT THE I.D. WAS FAKE, AND THAT THIS WAS ALL PART OF A DIABOLICAL PLOT BY ONE OF MY ENEMIES--MAYBE THE TOOTHGRINDER OR FIBERHEAD--TO STEER ME AWAY FROM MY DESTINY IN SOME FAR CORNER OF THE GLOBE AND PREVENT ME FROM DISCOVERING THAT MY REAL NAME WAS LESTER.
BUT I DIDN'T.

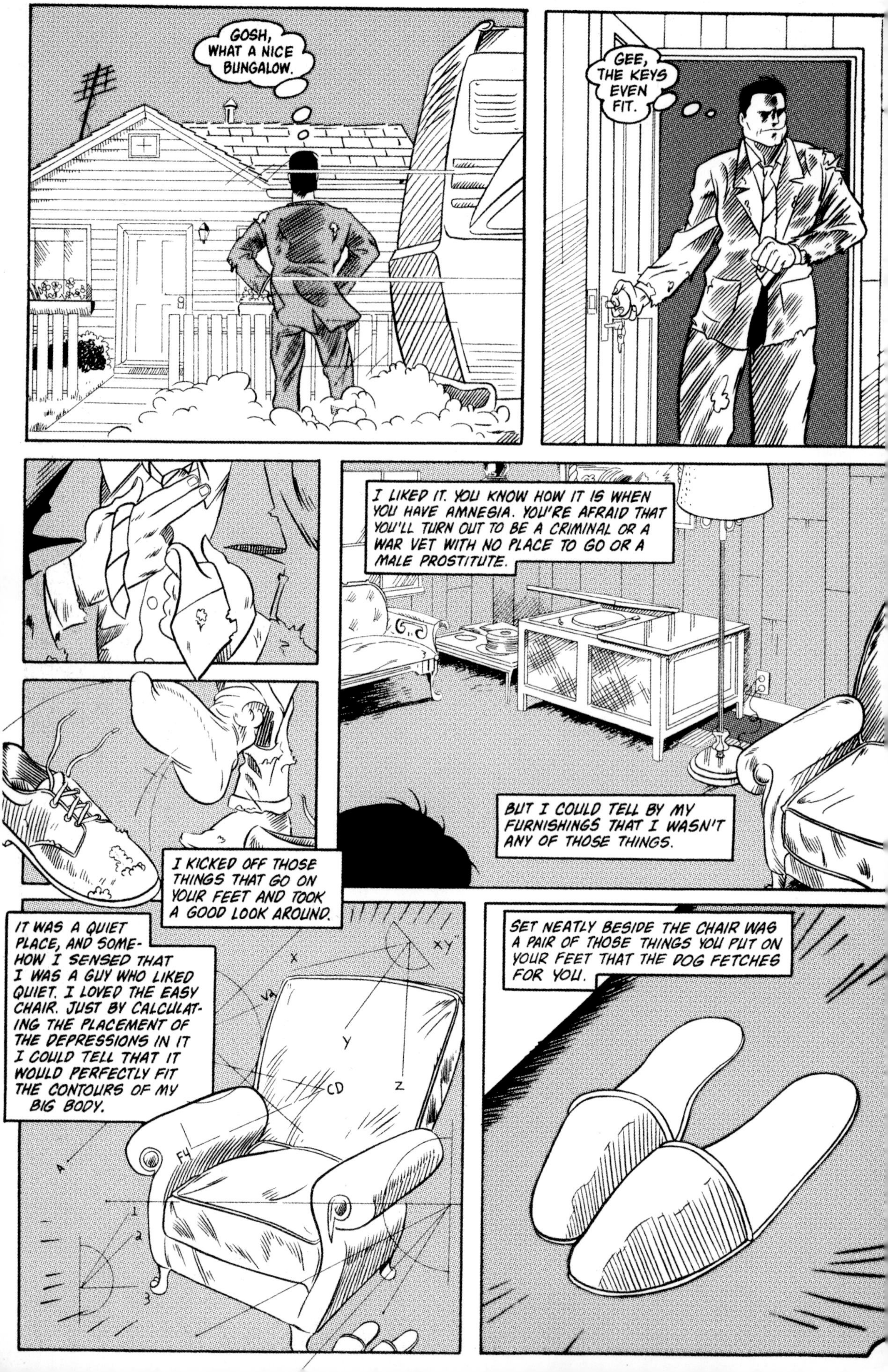
GOSH, WHAT A NICE BUNGALOW.
GEE, THE KEYS EVEN FIT.
I LIKED IT. YOU KNOW HOW IT IS WHEN YOU HAVE AMNESIA. YOU'RE AFRAID THAT YOU'LL TURN OUT TO BE A CRIMINAL OR A WAR VET WITH NO PLACE TO GO OR A MALE PROSTITUTE.
BUT I COULD TELL BY MY FURNISHINGS THAT I WASN'T ANY OF THOSE THINGS.
I KICKED OFF THOSE THINGS THAT GO ON YOUR FEET AND TOOK A GOOD LOOK AROUND.
IT WAS A QUIET PLACE, AND SOMEHOW I SENSED THAT I WAS A GUY WHO LIKED QUIET. I LOVED THE EASY CHAIR. JUST BY CALCULATING THE PLACEMENT OF THE DEPRESSIONS IN IT I COULD TELL THAT IT WOULD PERFECTLY FIT THE CONTOURS OF MY BIG BODY.
XY
X
Y
CD
Z
F4
A
1
2
3
SET NEATLY BESIDE THE CHAIR WAS A PAIR OF THOSE THINGS YOU PUT ON YOUR FEET THAT THE DOG FETCHES FOR YOU.

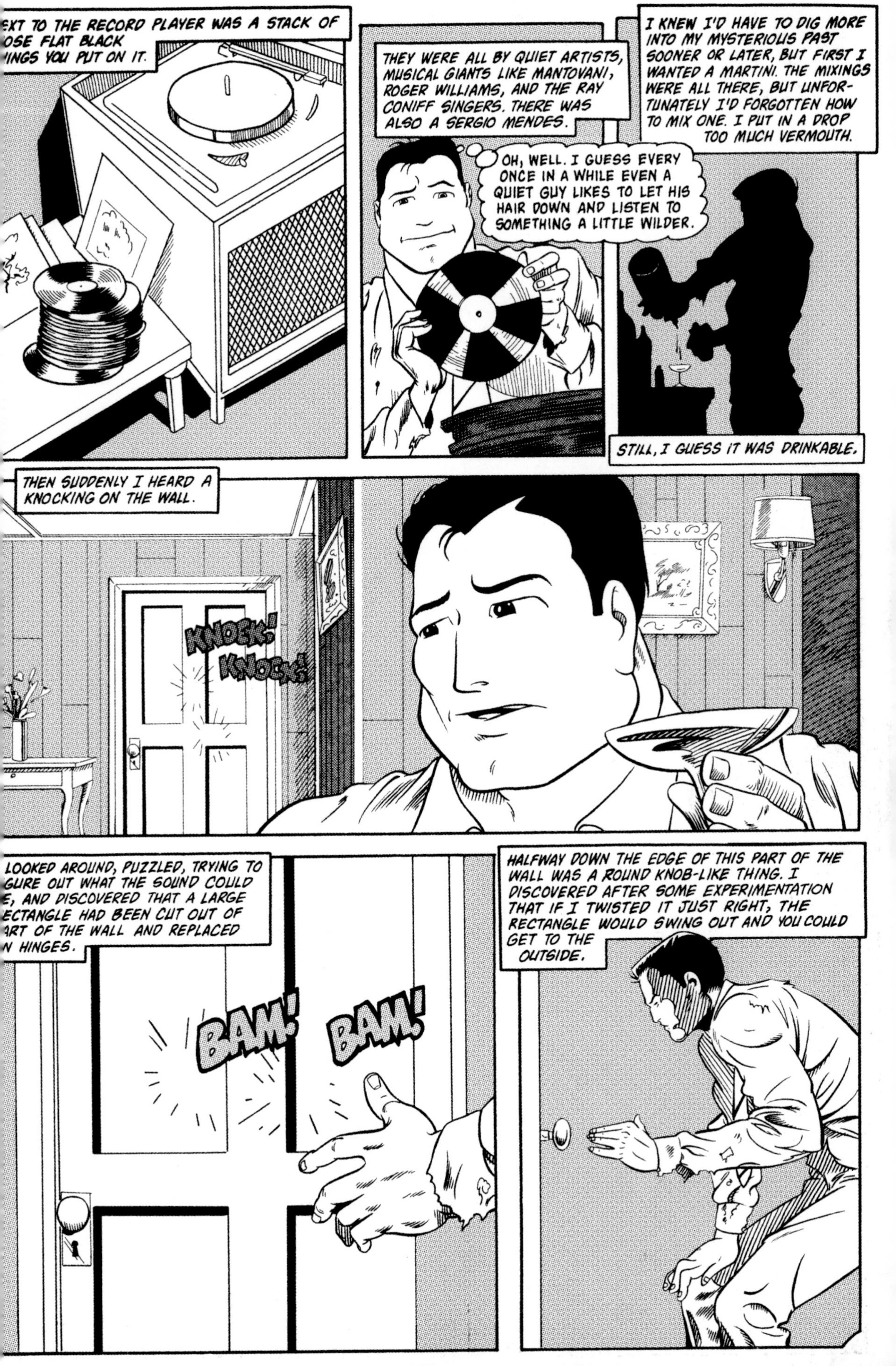

EXT TO THE RECORD PLAYER WAS A STACK OF
OSE FLAT BLACK
INGS YOU PUT ON IT.
THEY WERE ALL BY QUIET ARTISTS, MUSICAL GIANTS LIKE MANTOVANI, ROGER WILLIAMS, AND THE RAY CONIFF SINGERS. THERE WAS ALSO A SERGIO MENDES.
OH, WELL. I GUESS EVERY ONCE IN A WHILE EVEN A QUIET GUY LIKES TO LET HIS HAIR DOWN AND LISTEN TO SOMETHING A LITTLE WILDER.
I KNEW I'D HAVE TO DIG MORE INTO MY MYSTERIOUS PAST SOONER OR LATER, BUT FIRST I WANTED A MARTINI. THE MIXINGS WERE ALL THERE, BUT UNFORTUNATELY I'D FORGOTTEN HOW TO MIX ONE. I PUT IN A DROP TOO MUCH VERMOUTH.
STILL, I GUESS IT WAS DRINKABLE.
THEN SUDDENLY I HEARD A KNOCKING ON THE WALL.
KNOCK! KNOCK!
LOOKED AROUND, PUZZLED, TRYING TO
GURE OUT WHAT THE SOUND COULD
E, AND DISCOVERED THAT A LARGE
ECTANGLE HAD BEEN CUT OUT OF
ART OF THE WALL AND REPLACED
N HINGES.
BAM! BAM!
HALFWAY DOWN THE EDGE OF THIS PART OF THE WALL WAS A ROUND KNOB-LIKE THING. I DISCOVERED AFTER SOME EXPERIMENTATION THAT IF I TWISTED IT JUST RIGHT, THE RECTANGLE WOULD SWING OUT AND YOU COULD GET TO THE OUTSIDE.

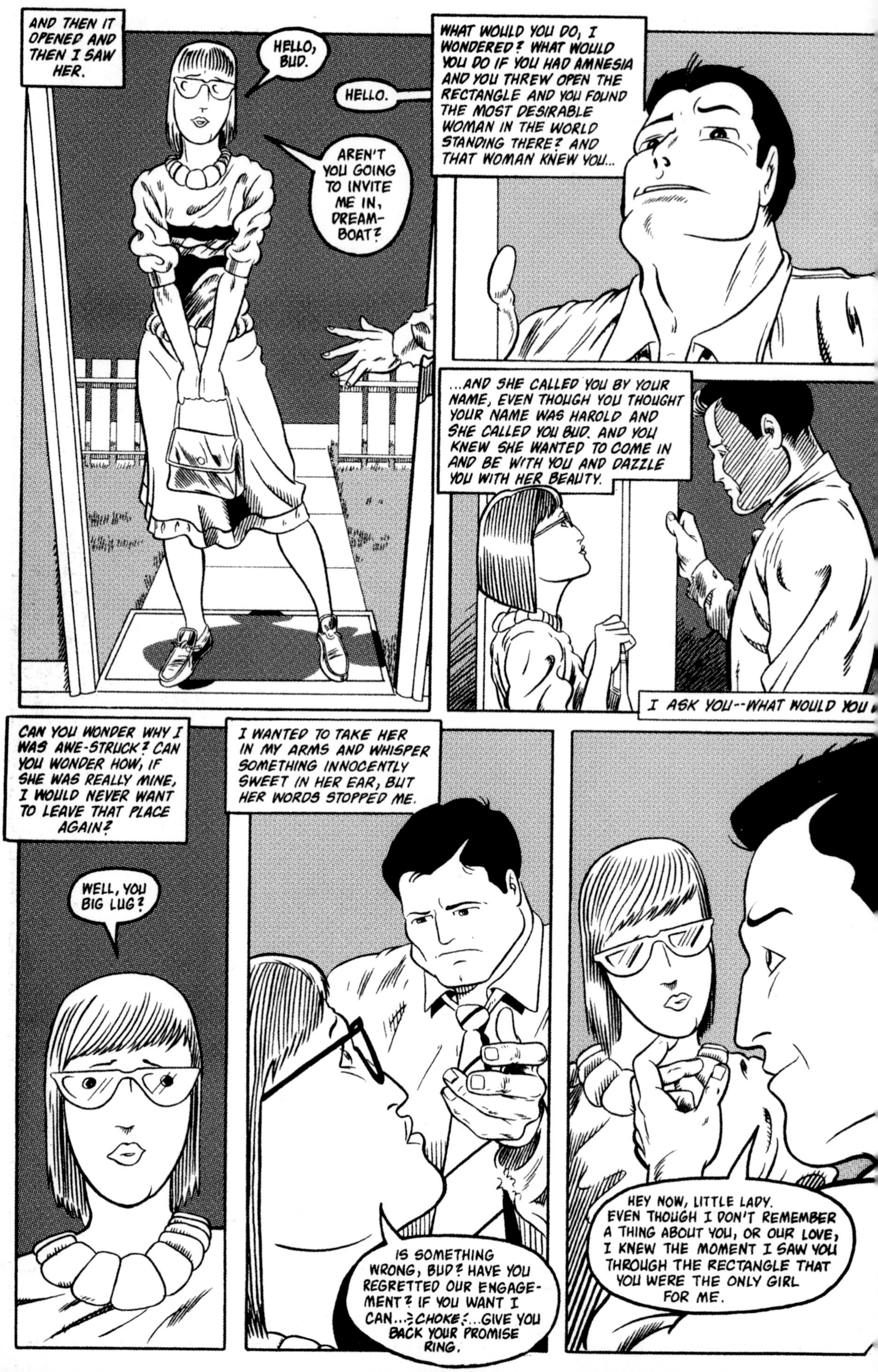
AND THEN IT OPENED AND THEN I SAW HER.
HELLO, BUD.
HELLO.
AREN'T YOU GOING TO INVITE ME IN, DREAM-BOAT?
WHAT WOULD YOU DO, I WONDERED? WHAT WOULD YOU DO IF YOU HAD AMNESIA AND YOU THREW OPEN THE RECTANGLE AND YOU FOUND THE MOST DESIRABLE WOMAN IN THE WORLD STANDING THERE? AND THAT WOMAN KNEW YOU...
...AND SHE CALLED YOU BY YOUR NAME, EVEN THOUGH YOU THOUGHT YOUR NAME WAS HAROLD AND SHE CALLED YOU BUD. AND YOU KNEW SHE WANTED TO COME IN AND BE WITH YOU AND DAZZLE YOU WITH HER BEAUTY.
I ASK YOU--WHAT WOULD YOU
CAN YOU WONDER WHY I WAS AWE-STRUCK? CAN YOU WONDER HOW, IF SHE WAS REALLY MINE, I WOULD NEVER WANT TO LEAVE THAT PLACE AGAIN?
WELL, YOU BIG LUG?
I WANTED TO TAKE HER IN MY ARMS AND WHISPER SOMETHING INNOCENTLY SWEET IN HER EAR, BUT HER WORDS STOPPED ME.
IS SOMETHING WRONG, BUD? HAVE YOU REGRETTED OUR ENGAGE-MENT? IF YOU WANT I CAN... CHOKE ...GIVE YOU BACK YOUR PROMISE RING.
HEY NOW, LITTLE LADY. EVEN THOUGH I DON'T REMEMBER A THING ABOUT YOU, OR OUR LOVE, I KNEW THE MOMENT I SAW YOU THROUGH THE RECTANGLE THAT YOU WERE THE ONLY GIRL FOR ME.

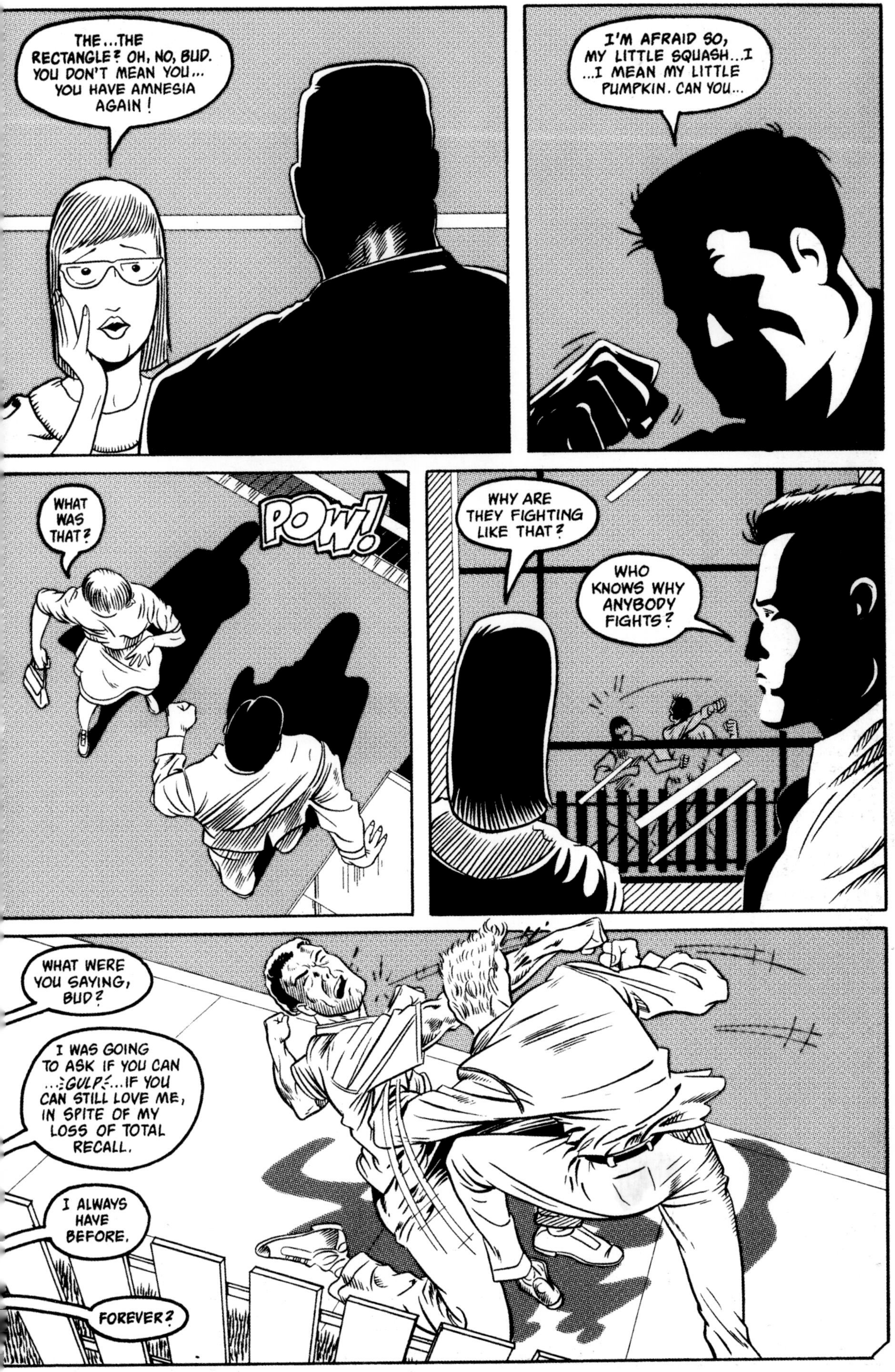
THE...THE RECTANGLE? OH, NO, BUD. YOU DON'T MEAN YOU... YOU HAVE AMNESIA AGAIN!
I'M AFRAID SO, MY LITTLE SQUASH...I ...I MEAN MY LITTLE PUMPKIN. CAN YOU...
WHAT WAS THAT?
POW!
WHY ARE THEY FIGHTING LIKE THAT?
WHO KNOWS WHY ANYBODY FIGHTS?
WHAT WERE YOU SAYING, BUD?
I WAS GOING TO ASK IF YOU CAN ...GULP...IF YOU CAN STILL LOVE ME, IN SPITE OF MY LOSS OF TOTAL RECALL.
I ALWAYS HAVE BEFORE.
FOREVER?

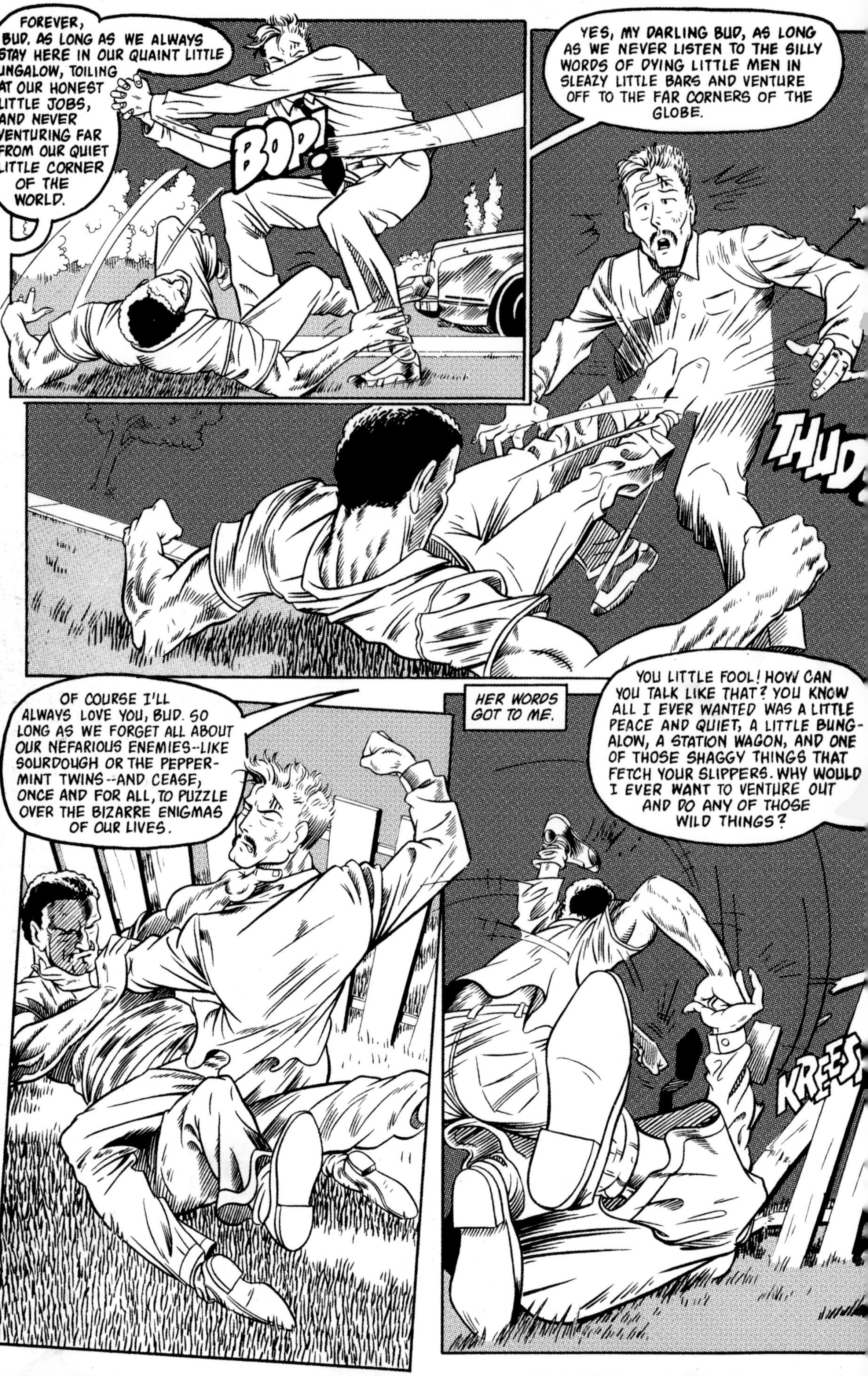

FOREVER, BUD. AS LONG AS WE ALWAYS STAY HERE IN OUR QUAINT LITTLE BUNGALOW, TOILING AT OUR HONEST LITTLE JOBS, AND NEVER VENTURING FAR FROM OUR QUIET LITTLE CORNER OF THE WORLD.
BOP!
YES, MY DARLING BUD, AS LONG AS WE NEVER LISTEN TO THE SILLY WORDS OF DYING LITTLE MEN IN SLEAZY LITTLE BARS AND VENTURE OFF TO THE FAR CORNERS OF THE GLOBE.
OF COURSE I'LL ALWAYS LOVE YOU, BUD. SO LONG AS WE FORGET ALL ABOUT OUR NEFARIOUS ENEMIES--LIKE SOURDOUGH OR THE PEPPERMINT TWINS--AND CEASE, ONCE AND FOR ALL, TO PUZZLE OVER THE BIZARRE ENIGMAS OF OUR LIVES.
HER WORDS GOT TO ME.
YOU LITTLE FOOL! HOW CAN YOU TALK LIKE THAT? YOU KNOW ALL I EVER WANTED WAS A LITTLE PEACE AND QUIET, A LITTLE BUNGALOW, A STATION WAGON, AND ONE OF THOSE SHAGGY THINGS THAT FETCH YOUR SLIPPERS. WHY WOULD I EVER WANT TO VENTURE OUT AND DO ANY OF THOSE WILD THINGS?

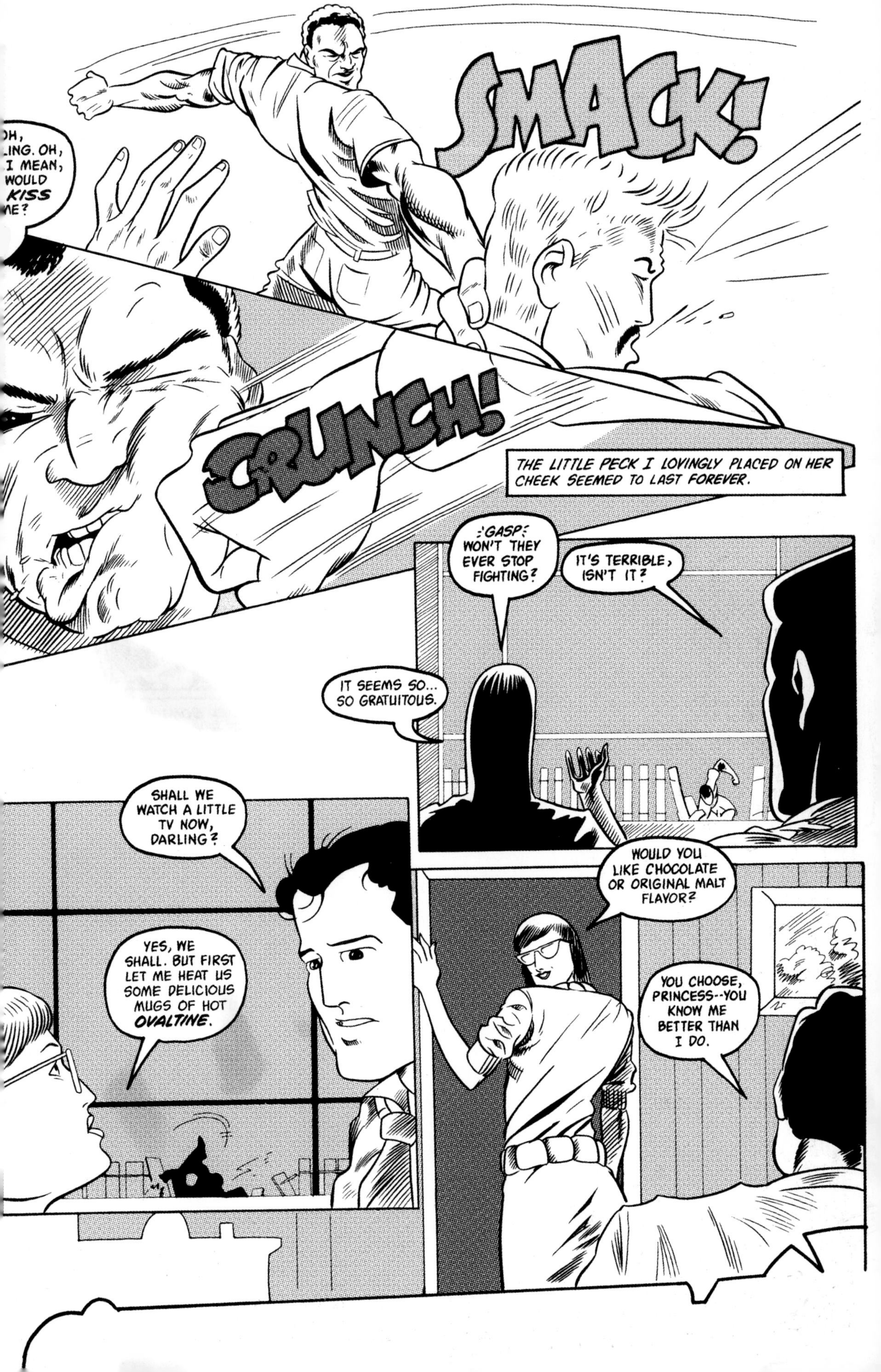

SMACK!
CRUNCH!
THE LITTLE PECK I LOVINGLY PLACED ON HER CHEEK SEEMED TO LAST FOREVER.
:GASP: WON'T THEY EVER STOP FIGHTING?
IT'S TERRIBLE, ISN'T IT?
IT SEEMS SO... SO GRATUITOUS.
SHALL WE WATCH A LITTLE TV NOW, DARLING?
YES, WE SHALL. BUT FIRST LET ME HEAT US SOME DELICIOUS MUGS OF HOT OVALTINE.
WOULD YOU LIKE CHOCOLATE OR ORIGINAL MALT FLAVOR?
YOU CHOOSE, PRINCESS--YOU KNOW ME BETTER THAN I DO.

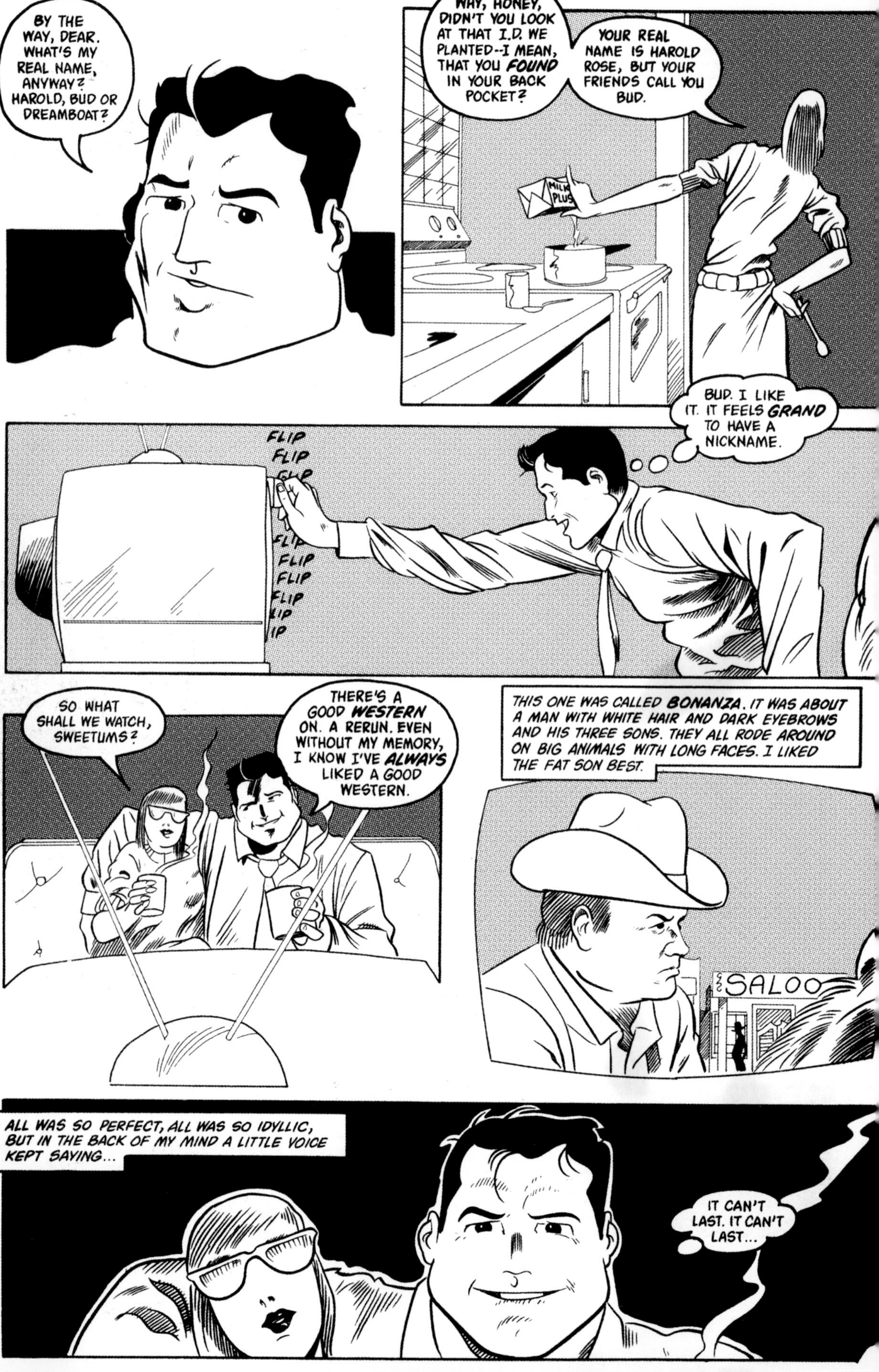
BY THE WAY, DEAR. WHAT'S MY REAL NAME, ANYWAY? HAROLD, BUD OR DREAMBOAT?
WHY, HONEY, DIDN'T YOU LOOK AT THAT I.D. WE PLANTED--I MEAN, THAT YOU FOUND IN YOUR BACK POCKET?
YOUR REAL NAME IS HAROLD ROSE, BUT YOUR FRIENDS CALL YOU BUD.
MILK PLUS
BUD. I LIKE IT. IT FEELS GRAND TO HAVE A NICKNAME.
FLIP FLIP FLIP FLIP FLIP FLIP FLIP FLIP FLIP
SO WHAT SHALL WE WATCH, SWEETUMS?
THERE'S A GOOD WESTERN ON. A RERUN. EVEN WITHOUT MY MEMORY, I KNOW I'VE ALWAYS LIKED A GOOD WESTERN.
THIS ONE WAS CALLED BONANZA. IT WAS ABOUT A MAN WITH WHITE HAIR AND DARK EYEBROWS AND HIS THREE SONS. THEY ALL RODE AROUND ON BIG ANIMALS WITH LONG FACES. I LIKED THE FAT SON BEST.
SALOO
ALL WAS SO PERFECT, ALL WAS SO IDYLLIC, BUT IN THE BACK OF MY MIND A LITTLE VOICE KEPT SAYING...
IT CAN'T LAST. IT CAN'T LAST...

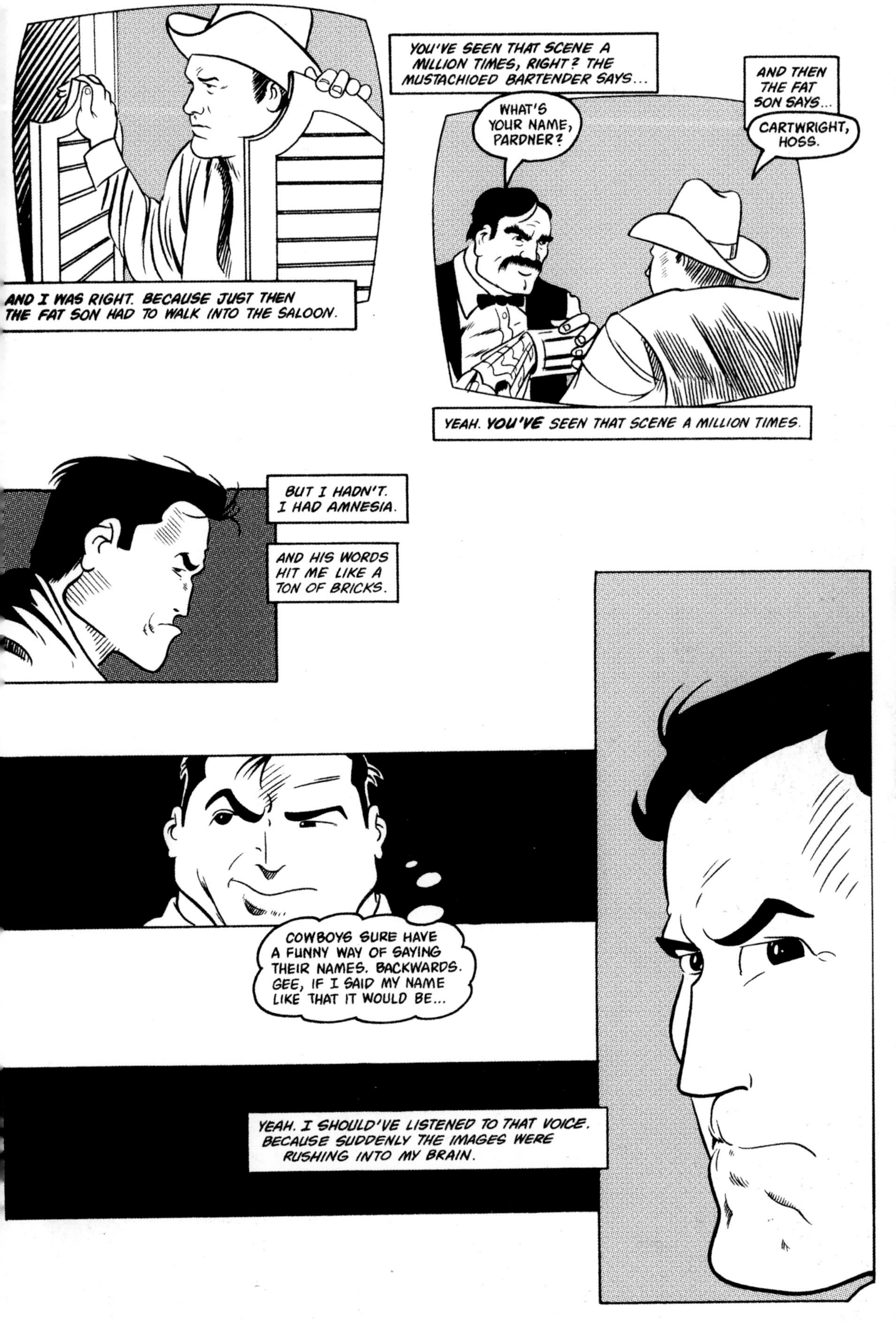
AND I WAS RIGHT. BECAUSE JUST THEN THE FAT SON HAD TO WALK INTO THE SALOON.
YOU'VE SEEN THAT SCENE A MILLION TIMES, RIGHT? THE MUSTACHIOED BARTENDER SAYS...
WHAT'S YOUR NAME, PARDNER?
AND THEN THE FAT SON SAYS...
CARTWRIGHT, HOSS.
YEAH. YOU'VE SEEN THAT SCENE A MILLION TIMES.
BUT I HADN'T. I HAD AMNESIA.
AND HIS WORDS HIT ME LIKE A TON OF BRICKS.
COWBOYS SURE HAVE A FUNNY WAY OF SAYING THEIR NAMES. BACKWARDS. GEE, IF I SAID MY NAME LIKE THAT IT WOULD BE...
YEAH. I SHOULD'VE LISTENED TO THAT VOICE. BECAUSE SUDDENLY THE IMAGES WERE RUSHING INTO MY BRAIN.

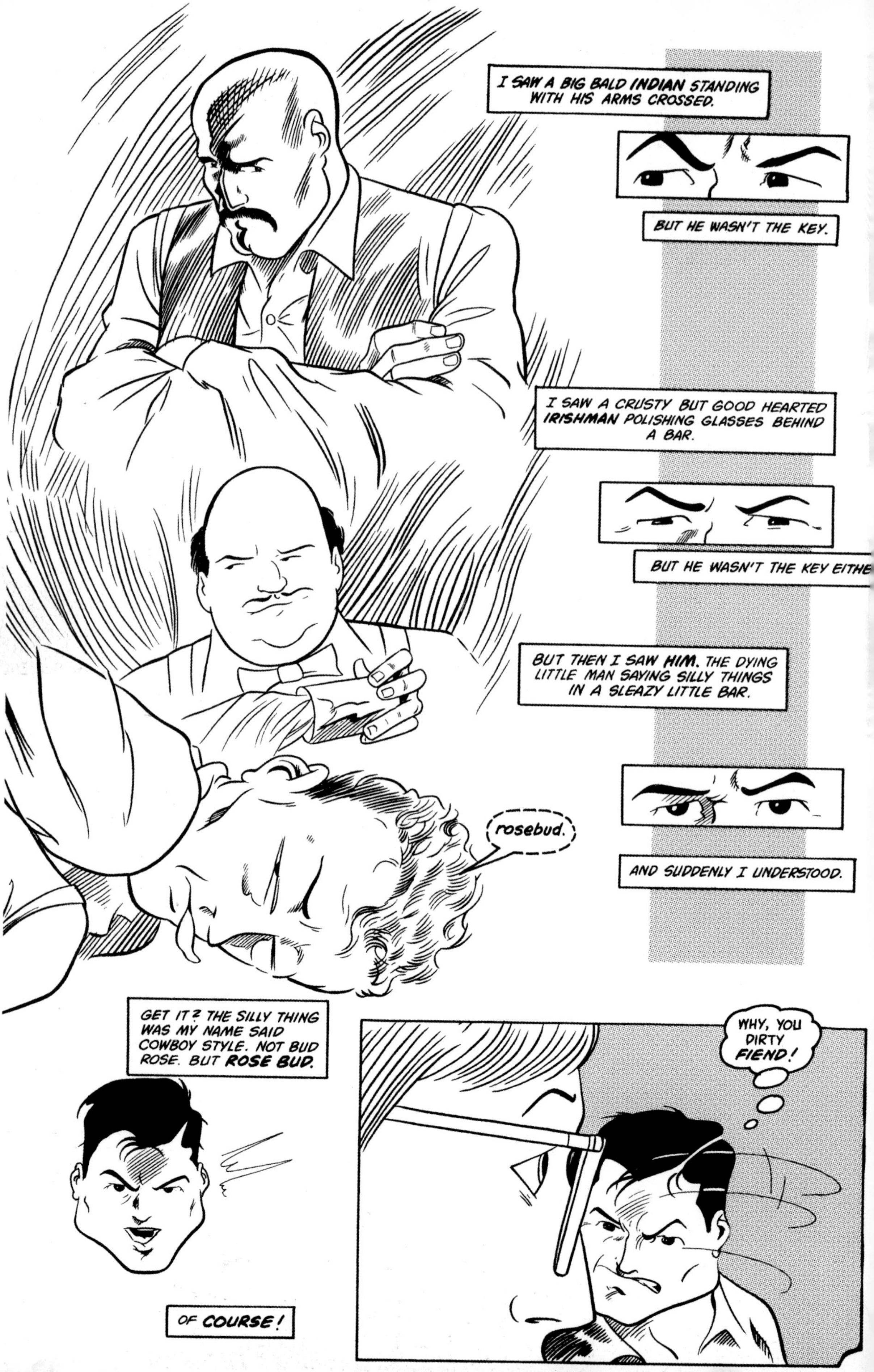

I SAW A BIG BALD INDIAN STANDING WITH HIS ARMS CROSSED.
BUT HE WASN'T THE KEY.
I SAW A CRUSTY BUT GOOD HEARTED IRISHMAN POLISHING GLASSES BEHIND A BAR.
BUT HE WASN'T THE KEY EITHE
BUT THEN I SAW HIM. THE DYING LITTLE MAN SAYING SILLY THINGS IN A SLEAZY LITTLE BAR.
rosebud.
AND SUDDENLY I UNDERSTOOD.
GET IT? THE SILLY THING WAS MY NAME SAID COWBOY STYLE. NOT BUD ROSE. BUT ROSE BUD.
OF COURSE!
WHY, YOU DIRTY FIEND!

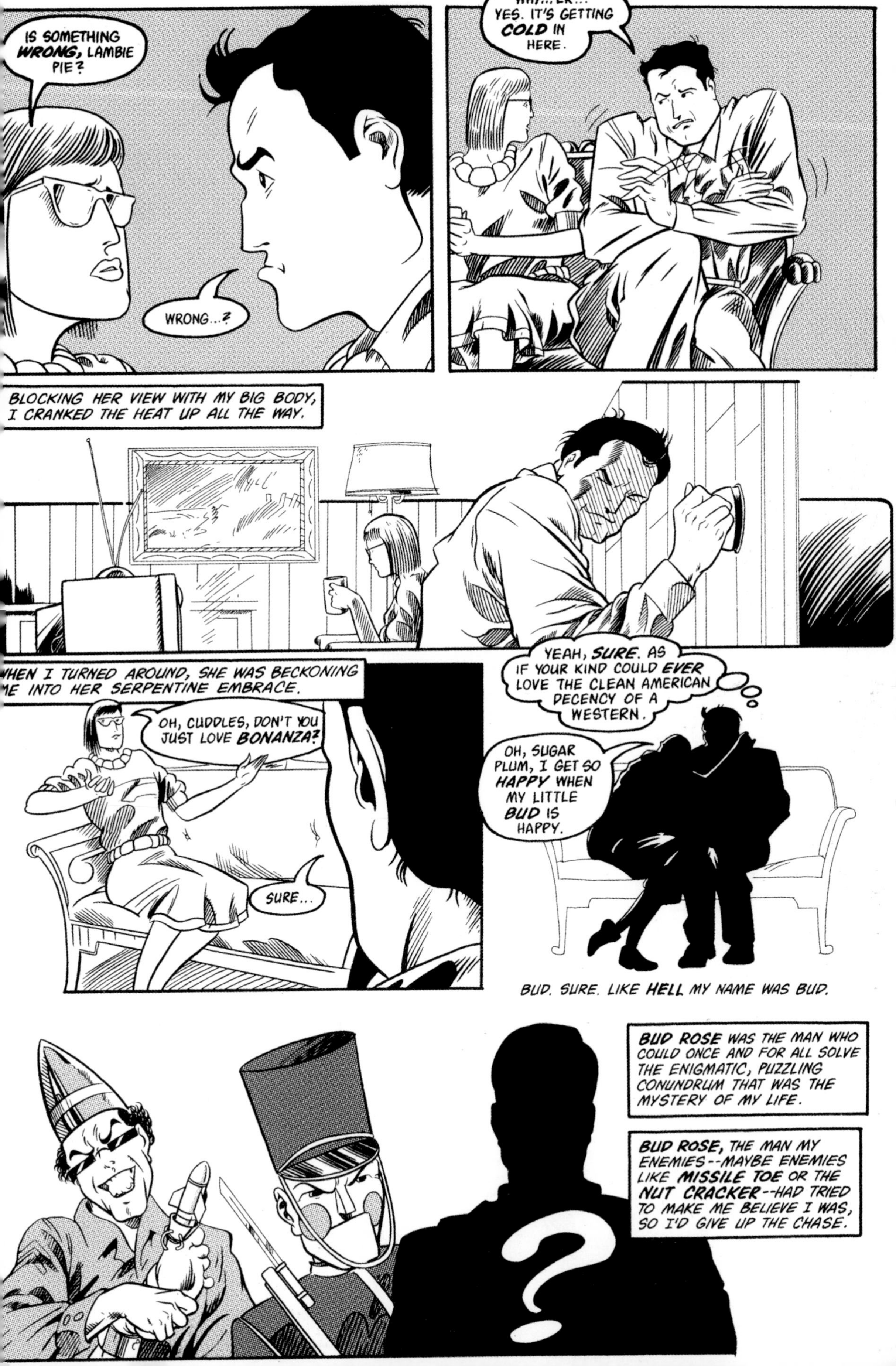
IS SOMETHING WRONG, LAMBIE PIE?
WRONG...?
WHY... ER... YES. IT'S GETTING COLD IN HERE.
BLOCKING HER VIEW WITH MY BIG BODY, I CRANKED THE HEAT UP ALL THE WAY.
WHEN I TURNED AROUND, SHE WAS BECKONING ME INTO HER SERPENTINE EMBRACE.
OH, CUDDLES, DON'T YOU JUST LOVE BONANZA?
SURE...
YEAH, SURE. AS IF YOUR KIND COULD EVER LOVE THE CLEAN AMERICAN DECENCY OF A WESTERN.
OH, SUGAR PLUM, I GET SO HAPPY WHEN MY LITTLE BUD IS HAPPY.
BUD. SURE. LIKE HELL MY NAME WAS BUD.
BUD ROSE WAS THE MAN WHO COULD ONCE AND FOR ALL SOLVE THE ENIGMATIC, PUZZLING CONUNDRUM THAT WAS THE MYSTERY OF MY LIFE.
BUD ROSE, THE MAN MY ENEMIES--MAYBE ENEMIES LIKE MISSILE TOE OR THE NUT CRACKER--HAD TRIED TO MAKE ME BELIEVE I WAS, SO I'D GIVE UP THE CHASE.

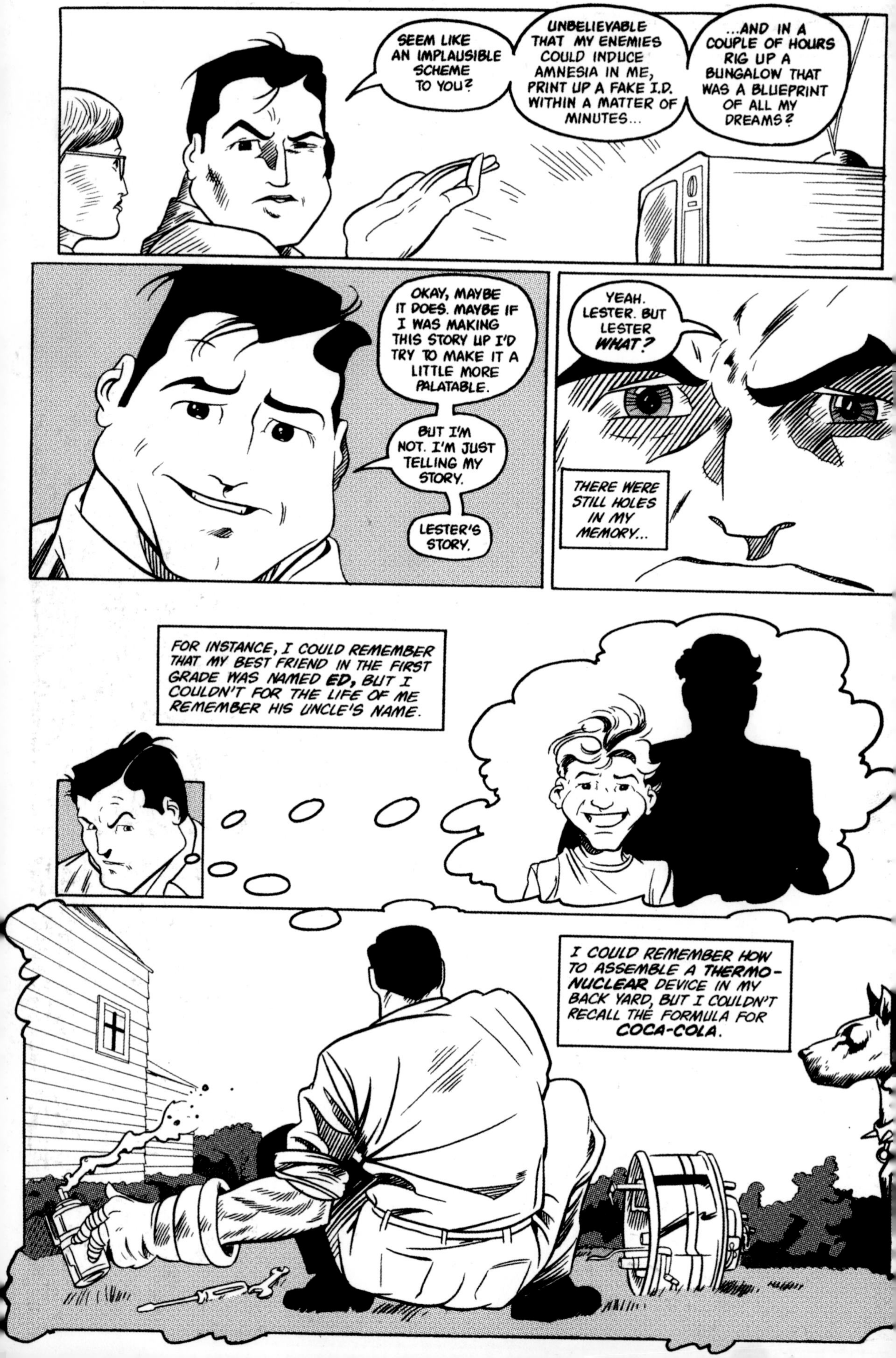
SEEM LIKE AN IMPLAUSIBLE SCHEME TO YOU?
UNBELIEVABLE THAT MY ENEMIES COULD INDUCE AMNESIA IN ME, PRINT UP A FAKE I.D. WITHIN A MATTER OF MINUTES...
...AND IN A COUPLE OF HOURS RIG UP A BUNGALOW THAT WAS A BLUEPRINT OF ALL MY DREAMS?
OKAY, MAYBE IT DOES. MAYBE IF I WAS MAKING THIS STORY UP I'D TRY TO MAKE IT A LITTLE MORE PALATABLE.
BUT I'M NOT. I'M JUST TELLING MY STORY.
LESTER'S STORY.
YEAH. LESTER. BUT LESTER WHAT?
THERE WERE STILL HOLES IN MY MEMORY...
FOR INSTANCE, I COULD REMEMBER THAT MY BEST FRIEND IN THE FIRST GRADE WAS NAMED ED, BUT I COULDN'T FOR THE LIFE OF ME REMEMBER HIS UNCLE'S NAME.
I COULD REMEMBER HOW TO ASSEMBLE A THERMONUCLEAR DEVICE IN MY BACK YARD, BUT I COULDN'T RECALL THE FORMULA FOR COCA-COLA.

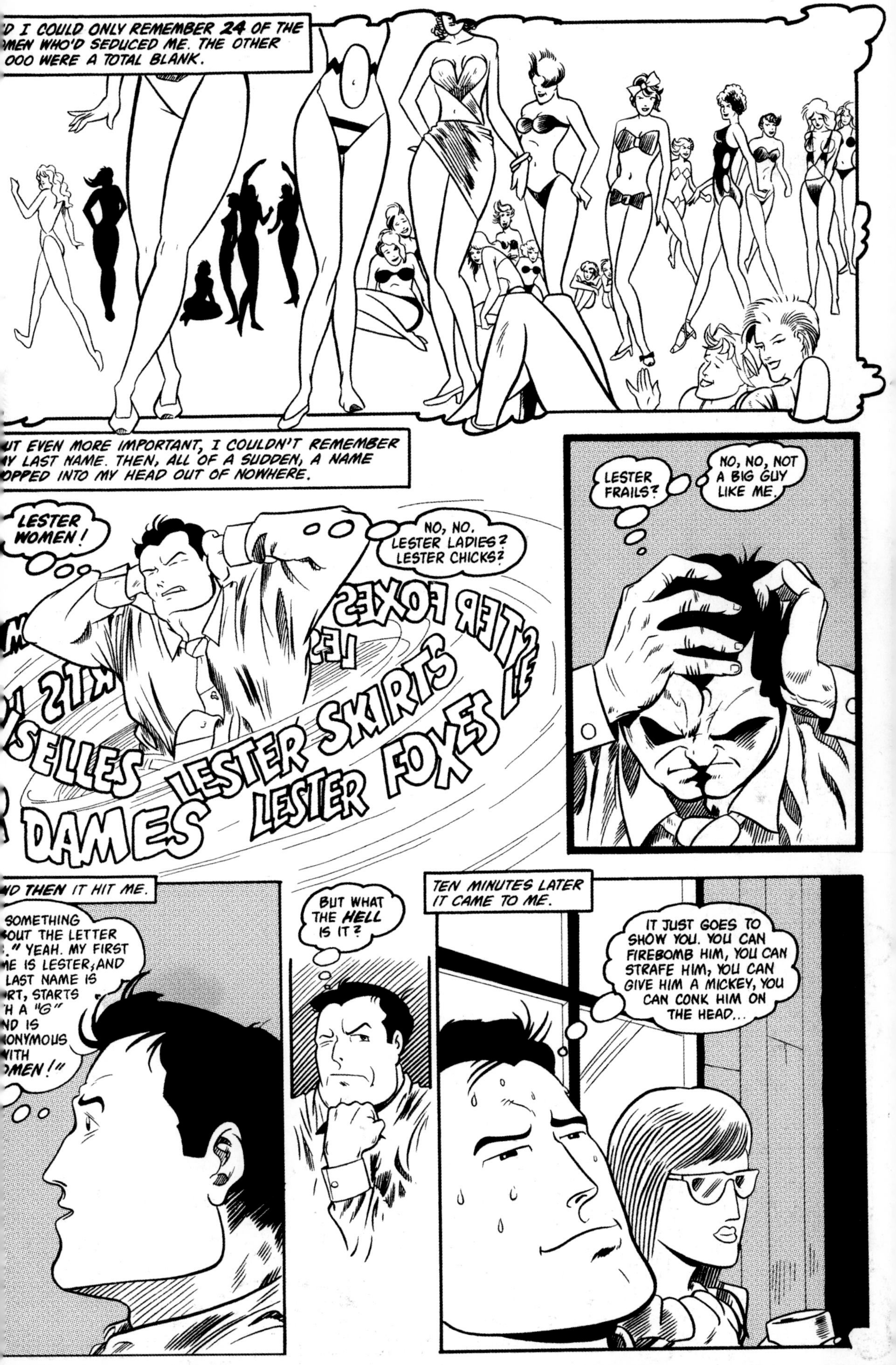

D I COULD ONLY REMEMBER 24 OF THE
OMEN WHO'D SEDUCED ME. THE OTHER
000 WERE A TOTAL BLANK.
UT EVEN MORE IMPORTANT, I COULDN'T REMEMBER
Y LAST NAME. THEN, ALL OF A SUDDEN, A NAME
OPPED INTO MY HEAD OUT OF NOWHERE.
LESTER WOMEN!
NO, NO. LESTER LADIES? LESTER CHICKS?
LESTER FOXES
LESTER SKIRTS
LESTER FOXES
DAMES
LESTER FRAILS?
NO, NO, NOT A BIG GUY LIKE ME.
D THEN IT HIT ME.
SOMETHING
OUT THE LETTER
." YEAH. MY FIRST
ME IS LESTER, AND
LAST NAME IS
RT, STARTS
H A "G"
D IS
ONYMOUS
ITH
OMEN!"
BUT WHAT THE HELL IS IT?
TEN MINUTES LATER IT CAME TO ME.
IT JUST GOES TO SHOW YOU. YOU CAN FIREBOMB HIM, YOU CAN STRAFE HIM, YOU CAN GIVE HIM A MICKEY, YOU CAN CONK HIM ON THE HEAD...

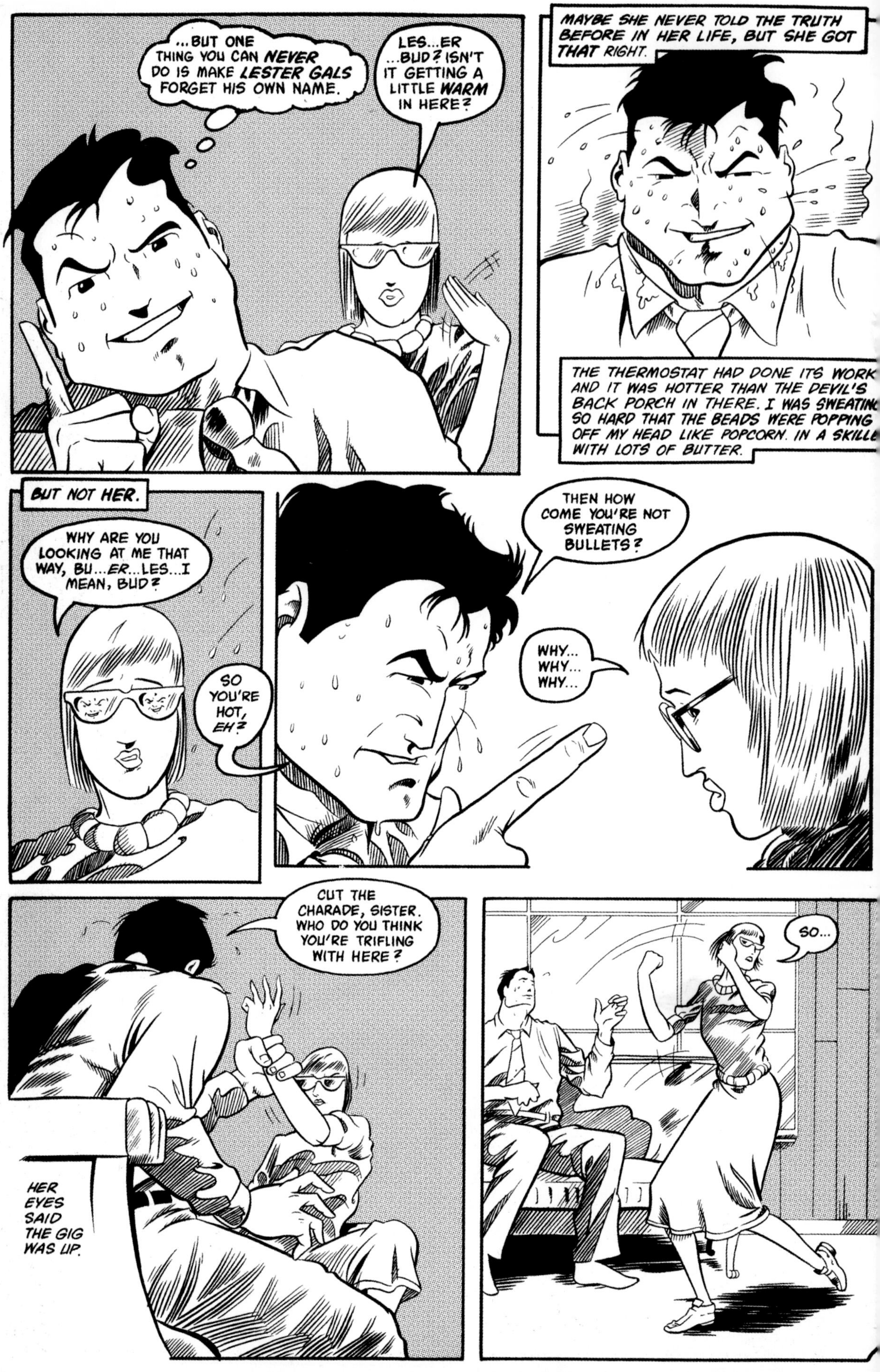
...BUT ONE THING YOU CAN NEVER DO IS MAKE LESTER GALS FORGET HIS OWN NAME.
LES...ER ...BUD? ISN'T IT GETTING A LITTLE WARM IN HERE?
MAYBE SHE NEVER TOLD THE TRUTH BEFORE IN HER LIFE, BUT SHE GOT THAT RIGHT.
THE THERMOSTAT HAD DONE ITS WORK AND IT WAS HOTTER THAN THE DEVIL'S BACK PORCH IN THERE. I WAS SWEATING SO HARD THAT THE BEADS WERE POPPING OFF MY HEAD LIKE POPCORN. IN A SKILLET WITH LOTS OF BUTTER.
BUT NOT HER.
WHY ARE YOU LOOKING AT ME THAT WAY, BU...ER...LES...I MEAN, BUD?
SO YOU'RE HOT, EH?
THEN HOW COME YOU'RE NOT SWEATING BULLETS?
WHY... WHY... WHY...
CUT THE CHARADE, SISTER. WHO DO YOU THINK YOU'RE TRIFLING WITH HERE?
HER EYES SAID THE GIG WAS UP.
SO...

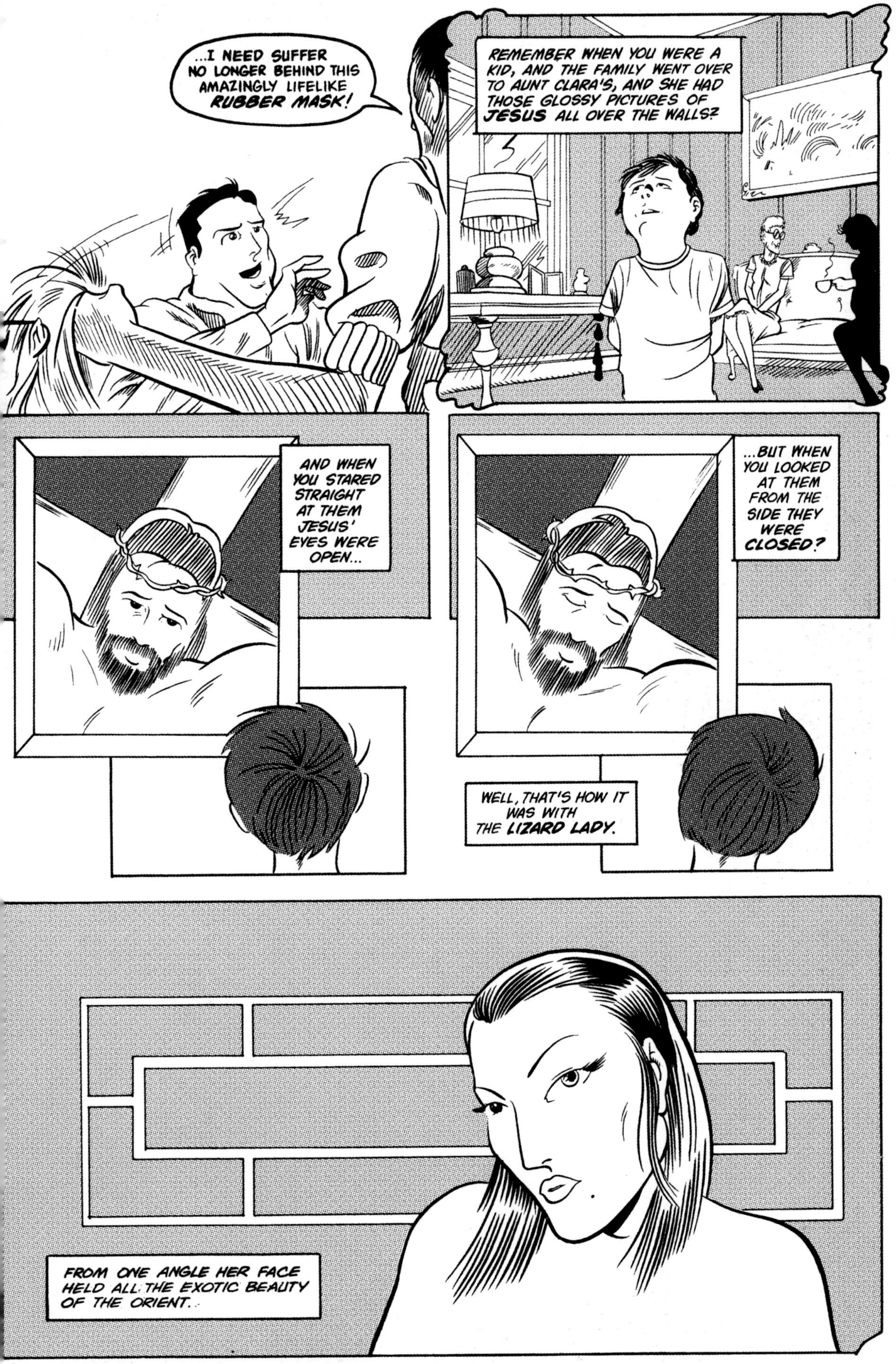
...I NEED SUFFER NO LONGER BEHIND THIS AMAZINGLY LIFELIKE RUBBER MASK!
REMEMBER WHEN YOU WERE A KID, AND THE FAMILY WENT OVER TO AUNT CLARA'S, AND SHE HAD THOSE GLOSSY PICTURES OF JESUS ALL OVER THE WALLS?
AND WHEN YOU STARED STRAIGHT AT THEM JESUS' EYES WERE OPEN...
...BUT WHEN YOU LOOKED AT THEM FROM THE SIDE THEY WERE CLOSED?
WELL, THAT'S HOW IT WAS WITH THE LIZARD LADY.
FROM ONE ANGLE HER FACE HELD ALL THE EXOTIC BEAUTY OF THE ORIENT...

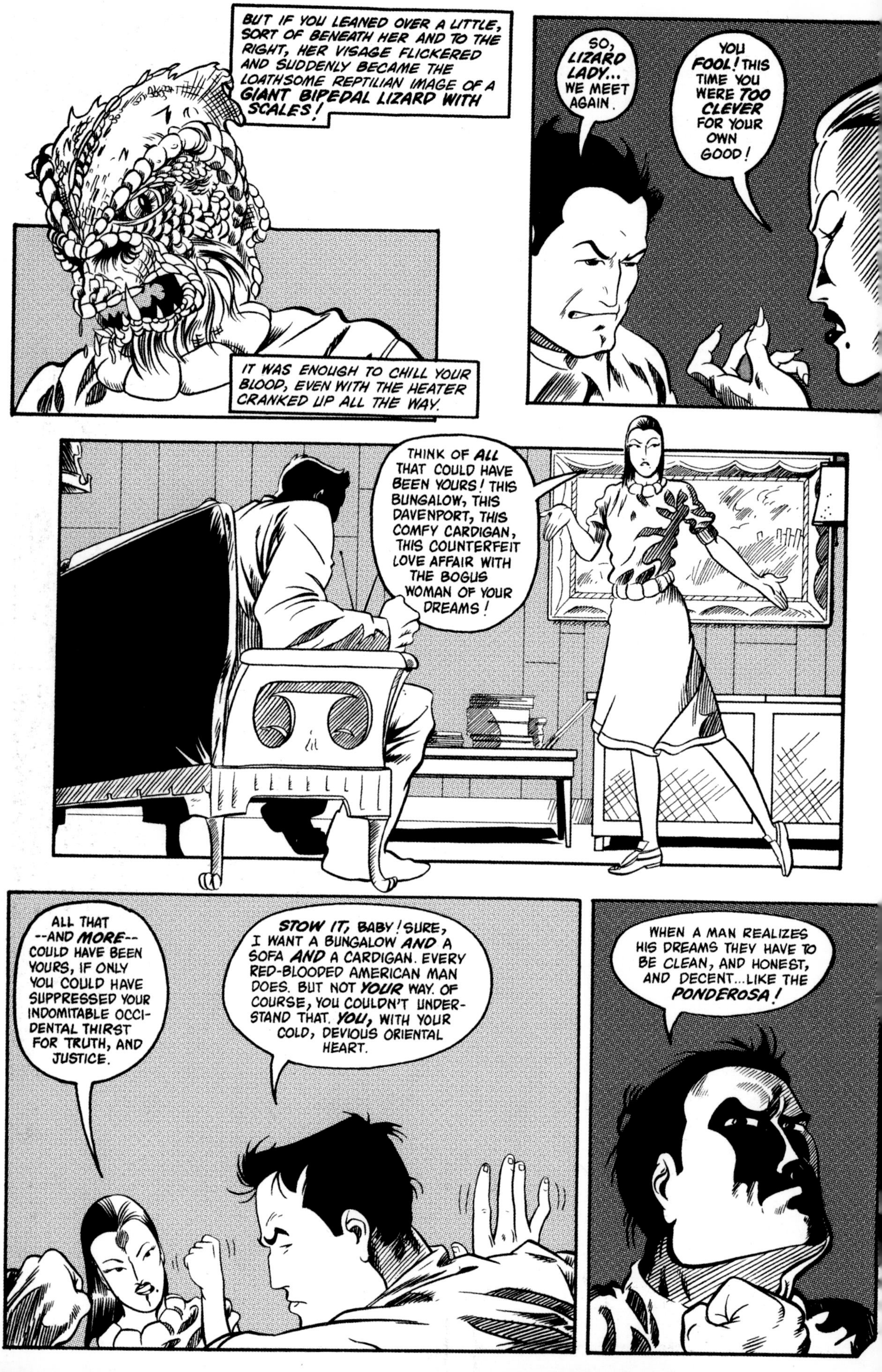

BUT IF YOU LEANED OVER A LITTLE, SORT OF BENEATH HER AND TO THE RIGHT, HER VISAGE FLICKERED AND SUDDENLY BECAME THE LOATHSOME REPTILIAN IMAGE OF A GIANT BIPEDAL LIZARD WITH SCALES!
IT WAS ENOUGH TO CHILL YOUR BLOOD, EVEN WITH THE HEATER CRANKED UP ALL THE WAY.
SO, LIZARD LADY... WE MEET AGAIN.
YOU FOOL! THIS TIME YOU WERE TOO CLEVER FOR YOUR OWN GOOD!
THINK OF ALL THAT COULD HAVE BEEN YOURS! THIS BUNGALOW, THIS DAVENPORT, THIS COMFY CARDIGAN, THIS COUNTERFEIT LOVE AFFAIR WITH THE BOGUS WOMAN OF YOUR DREAMS!
ALL THAT --AND MORE-- COULD HAVE BEEN YOURS, IF ONLY YOU COULD HAVE SUPPRESSED YOUR INDOMITABLE OCCI-DENTAL THIRST FOR TRUTH, AND JUSTICE.
STOW IT, BABY! SURE, I WANT A BUNGALOW AND A SOFA AND A CARDIGAN. EVERY RED-BLOODED AMERICAN MAN DOES. BUT NOT YOUR WAY. OF COURSE, YOU COULDN'T UNDER-STAND THAT. YOU, WITH YOUR COLD, DEVIOUS ORIENTAL HEART.
WHEN A MAN REALIZES HIS DREAMS THEY HAVE TO BE CLEAN, AND HONEST, AND DECENT...LIKE THE PONDEROSA!

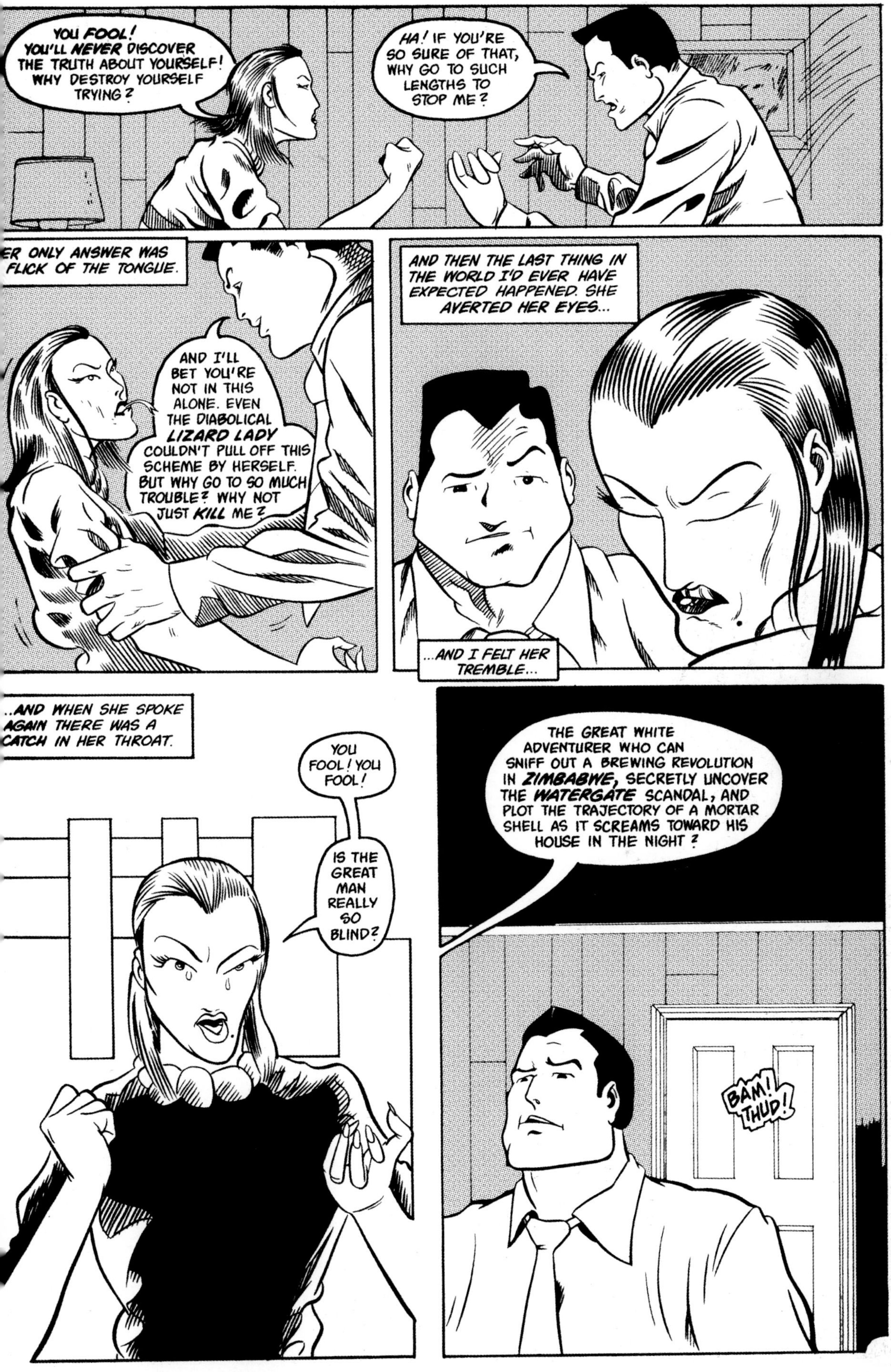
YOU FOOL! YOU'LL NEVER DISCOVER THE TRUTH ABOUT YOURSELF! WHY DESTROY YOURSELF TRYING?
HA! IF YOU'RE SO SURE OF THAT, WHY GO TO SUCH LENGTHS TO STOP ME?
ER ONLY ANSWER WAS FLICK OF THE TONGUE.
AND I'LL BET YOU'RE NOT IN THIS ALONE. EVEN THE DIABOLICAL LIZARD LADY COULDN'T PULL OFF THIS SCHEME BY HERSELF. BUT WHY GO TO SO MUCH TROUBLE? WHY NOT JUST KILL ME?
AND THEN THE LAST THING IN THE WORLD I'D EVER HAVE EXPECTED HAPPENED. SHE AVERTED HER EYES...
...AND I FELT HER TREMBLE...
..AND WHEN SHE SPOKE AGAIN THERE WAS A CATCH IN HER THROAT.
YOU FOOL! YOU FOOL!
IS THE GREAT MAN REALLY SO BLIND?
THE GREAT WHITE ADVENTURER WHO CAN SNIFF OUT A BREWING REVOLUTION IN ZIMBABWE, SECRETLY UNCOVER THE WATERGATE SCANDAL, AND PLOT THE TRAJECTORY OF A MORTAR SHELL AS IT SCREAMS TOWARD HIS HOUSE IN THE NIGHT?
BAM! THUD!

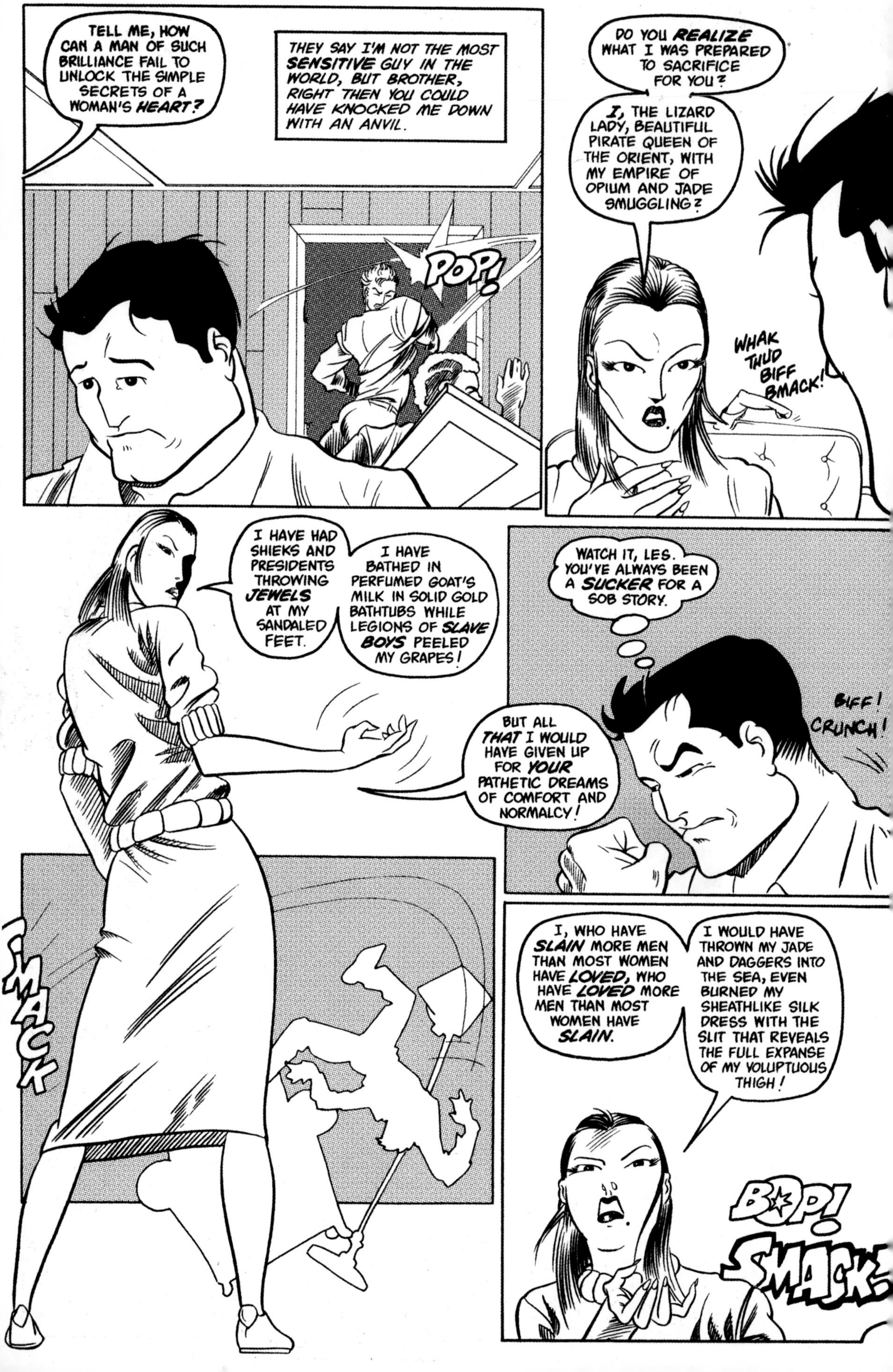
TELL ME, HOW CAN A MAN OF SUCH BRILLIANCE FAIL TO UNLOCK THE SIMPLE SECRETS OF A WOMAN'S HEART?
THEY SAY I'M NOT THE MOST SENSITIVE GUY IN THE WORLD, BUT BROTHER, RIGHT THEN YOU COULD HAVE KNOCKED ME DOWN WITH AN ANVIL.
POP!
DO YOU REALIZE WHAT I WAS PREPARED TO SACRIFICE FOR YOU?
I, THE LIZARD LADY, BEAUTIFUL PIRATE QUEEN OF THE ORIENT, WITH MY EMPIRE OF OPIUM AND JADE SMUGGLING?
WHAK THUD BIFF BMACK!
I HAVE HAD SHIEKS AND PRESIDENTS THROWING JEWELS AT MY SANDALED FEET.
I HAVE BATHED IN PERFUMED GOAT'S MILK IN SOLID GOLD BATHTUBS WHILE LEGIONS OF SLAVE BOYS PEELED MY GRAPES!
BUT ALL THAT I WOULD HAVE GIVEN UP FOR YOUR PATHETIC DREAMS OF COMFORT AND NORMALCY!
WATCH IT, LES. YOU'VE ALWAYS BEEN A SUCKER FOR A SOB STORY.
BIFF! CRUNCH!
SMACK
I, WHO HAVE SLAIN MORE MEN THAN MOST WOMEN HAVE LOVED, WHO HAVE LOVED MORE MEN THAN MOST WOMEN HAVE SLAIN.
I WOULD HAVE THROWN MY JADE AND DAGGERS INTO THE SEA, EVEN BURNED MY SHEATHLIKE SILK DRESS WITH THE SLIT THAT REVEALS THE FULL EXPANSE OF MY VOLUPTUOUS THIGH!
BOP!
SMACK

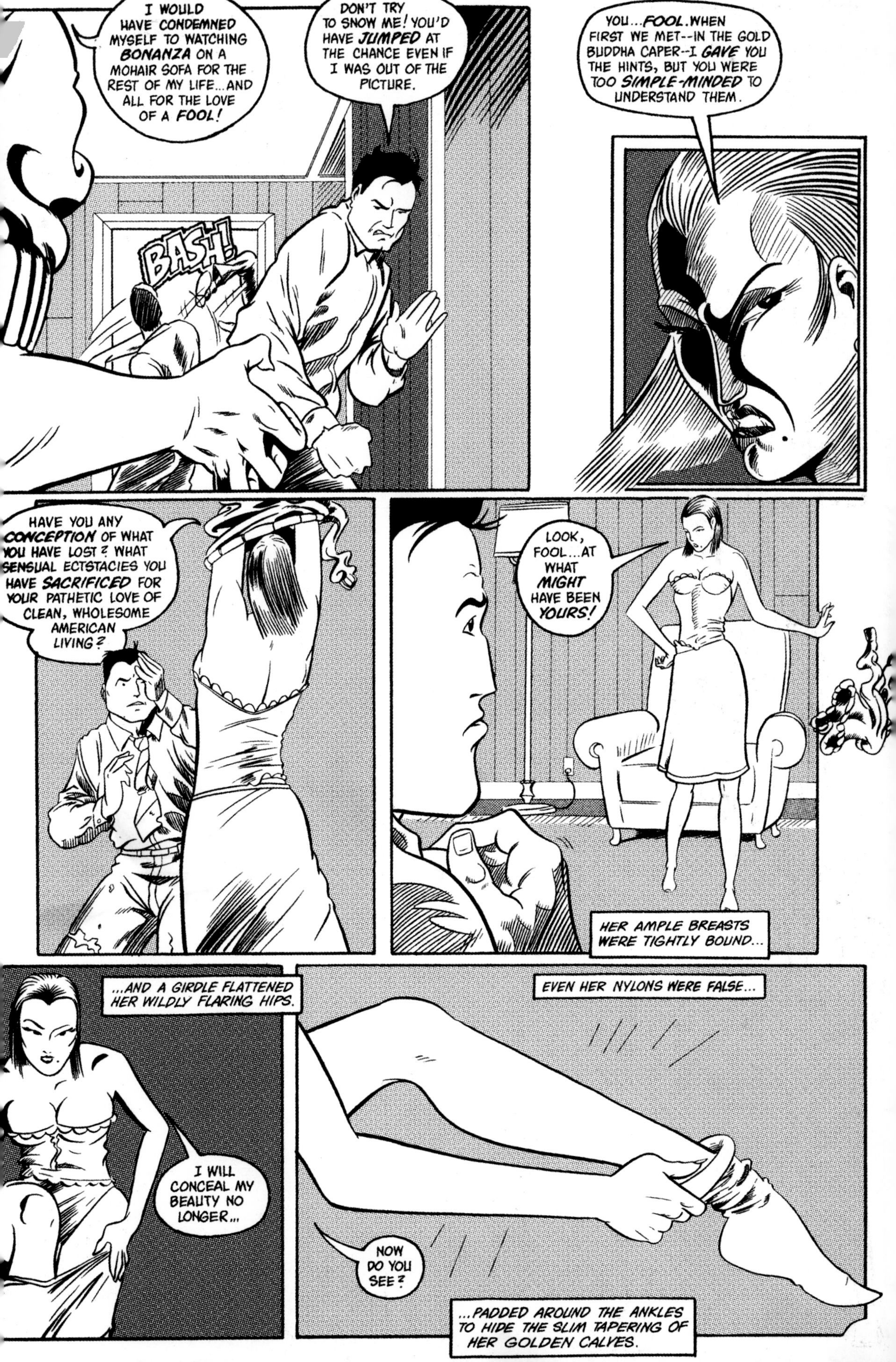
I WOULD HAVE CONDEMNED MYSELF TO WATCHING BONANZA ON A MOHAIR SOFA FOR THE REST OF MY LIFE... AND ALL FOR THE LOVE OF A FOOL!
DON'T TRY TO SNOW ME! YOU'D HAVE JUMPED AT THE CHANCE EVEN IF I WAS OUT OF THE PICTURE.
BASH!
YOU... FOOL. WHEN FIRST WE MET--IN THE GOLD BUDDHA CAPER--I GAVE YOU THE HINTS, BUT YOU WERE TOO SIMPLE-MINDED TO UNDERSTAND THEM.
HAVE YOU ANY CONCEPTION OF WHAT YOU HAVE LOST? WHAT SENSUAL ECTSTACIES YOU HAVE SACRIFICED FOR YOUR PATHETIC LOVE OF CLEAN, WHOLESOME AMERICAN LIVING?
LOOK, FOOL... AT WHAT MIGHT HAVE BEEN YOURS!
HER AMPLE BREASTS WERE TIGHTLY BOUND...
...AND A GIRDLE FLATTENED HER WILDLY FLARING HIPS.
I WILL CONCEAL MY BEAUTY NO LONGER...
EVEN HER NYLONS WERE FALSE...
NOW DO YOU SEE?
...PADDED AROUND THE ANKLES TO HIDE THE SLIM TAPERING OF HER GOLDEN CALVES.

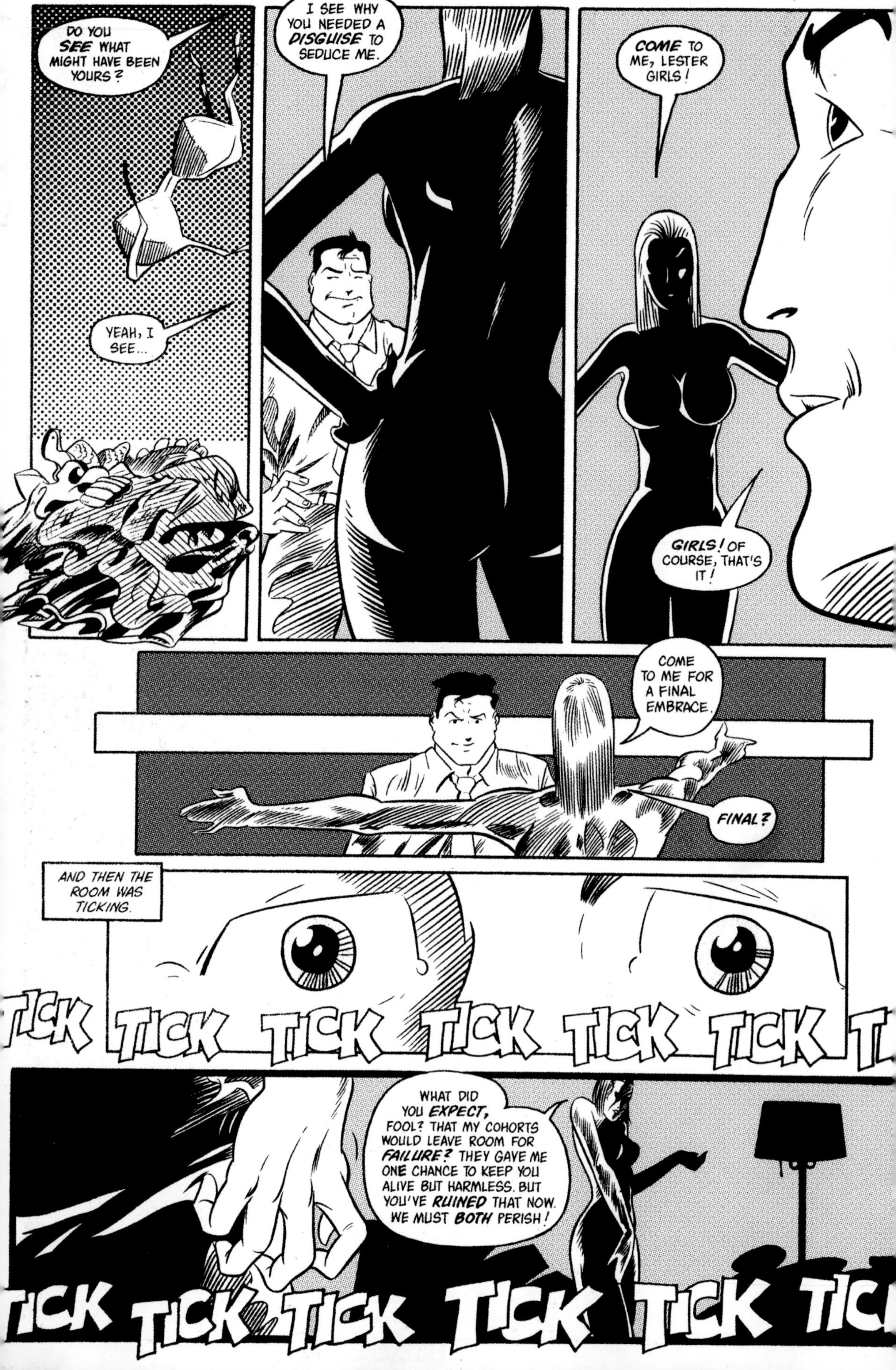
DO YOU SEE WHAT MIGHT HAVE BEEN YOURS?
YEAH, I SEE...
I SEE WHY YOU NEEDED A DISGUISE TO SEDUCE ME.
COME TO ME, LESTER GIRLS!
GIRLS! OF COURSE, THAT'S IT!
COME TO ME FOR A FINAL EMBRACE.
FINAL?
AND THEN THE ROOM WAS TICKING.
TICK TICK TICK TICK TICK TICK
WHAT DID YOU EXPECT, FOOL? THAT MY COHORTS WOULD LEAVE ROOM FOR FAILURE? THEY GAVE ME ONE CHANCE TO KEEP YOU ALIVE BUT HARMLESS. BUT YOU'VE RUINED THAT NOW. WE MUST BOTH PERISH!
TICK TICK TICK TICK TICK

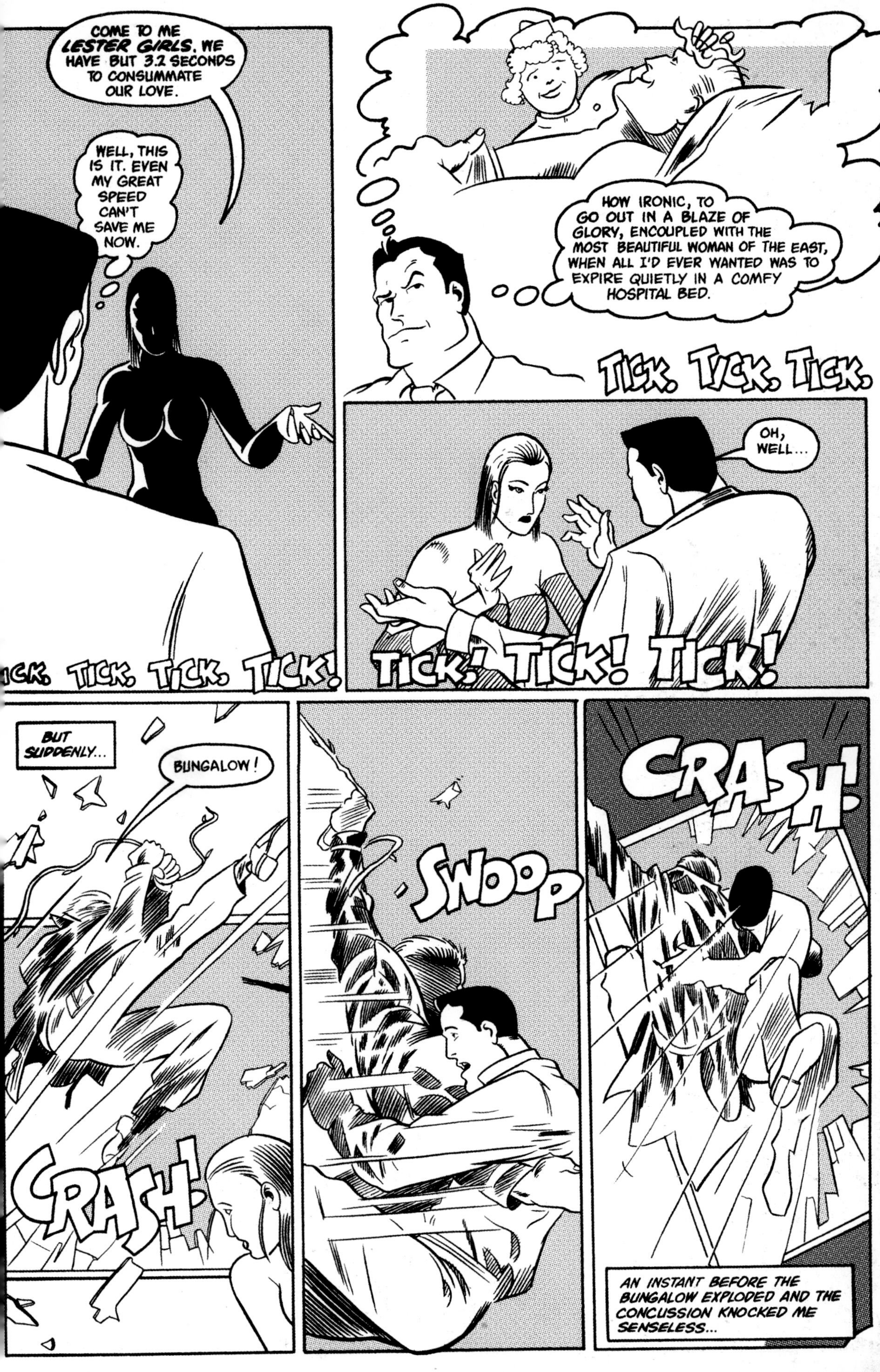
COME TO ME LESTER GIRLS. WE HAVE BUT 3.2 SECONDS TO CONSUMMATE OUR LOVE.
WELL, THIS IS IT. EVEN MY GREAT SPEED CAN'T SAVE ME NOW.
TICK. TICK. TICK. TICK!
HOW IRONIC, TO GO OUT IN A BLAZE OF GLORY, ENCOUPLED WITH THE MOST BEAUTIFUL WOMAN OF THE EAST, WHEN ALL I'D EVER WANTED WAS TO EXPIRE QUIETLY IN A COMFY HOSPITAL BED.
TICK. TICK. TICK.
OH, WELL...
TICK! TICK! TICK!
BUT SUDDENLY...
BUNGALOW!
CRASH!
SWOOP
CRASH!
AN INSTANT BEFORE THE BUNGALOW EXPLODED AND THE CONCUSSION KNOCKED ME SENSELESS...

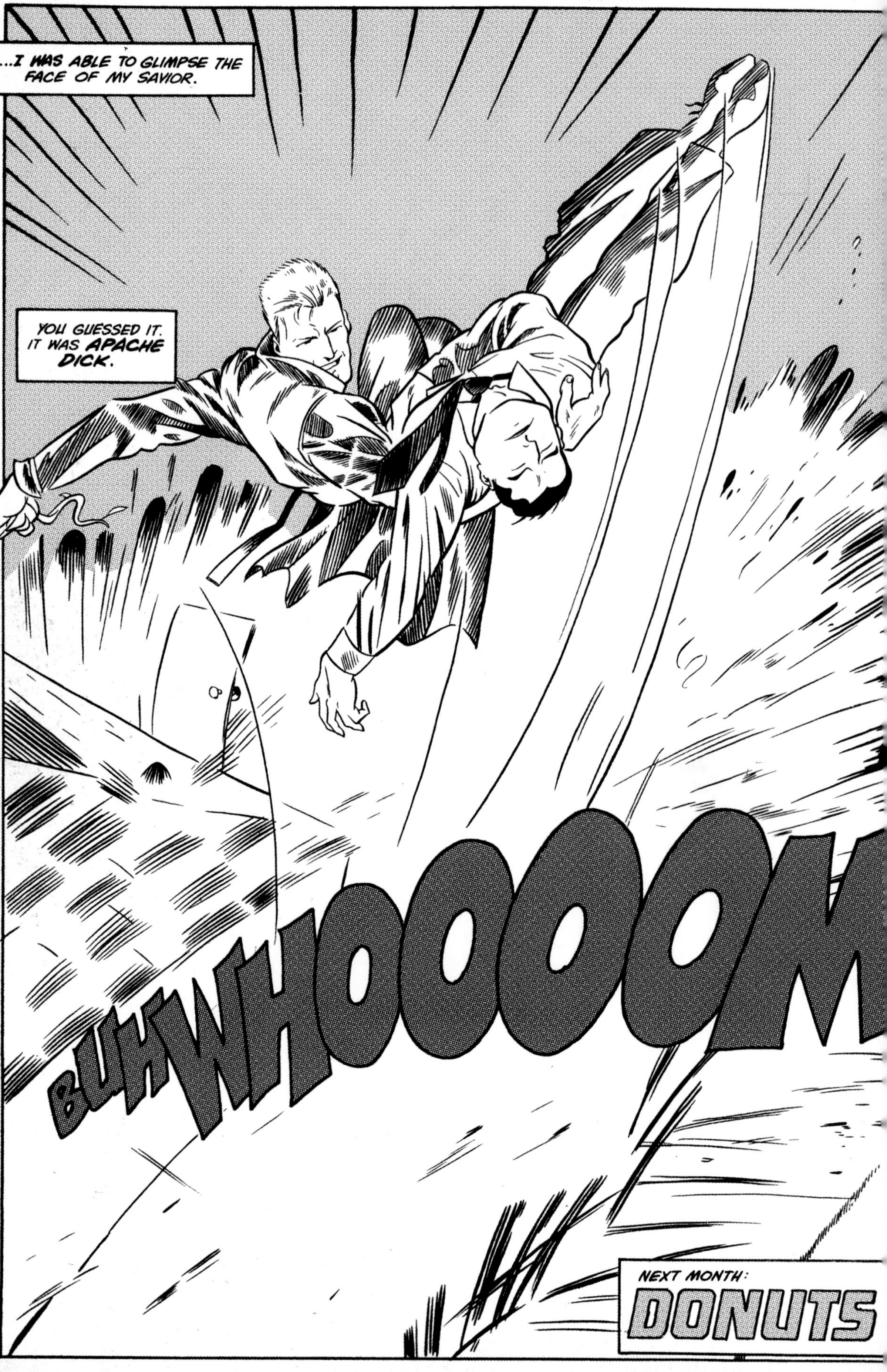

...I WAS ABLE TO GLIMPSE THE FACE OF MY SAVIOR.
YOU GUESSED IT. IT WAS APACHE DICK.
BUHWHOOOOM
NEXT MONTH: DONUTS

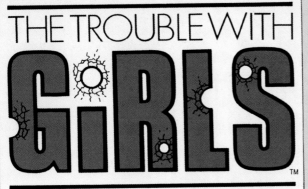

THE TROUBLE WITH GIRLS™

CHAPTER 6

JANUARY 1988

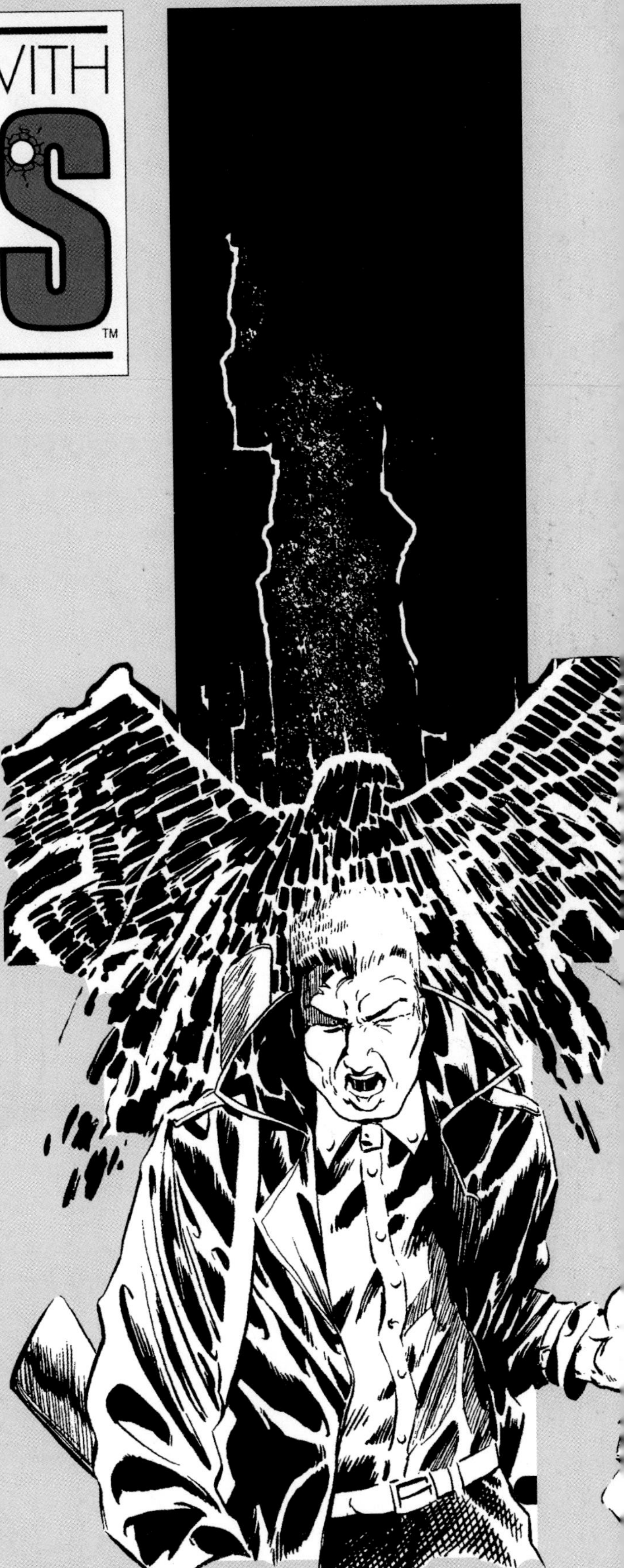

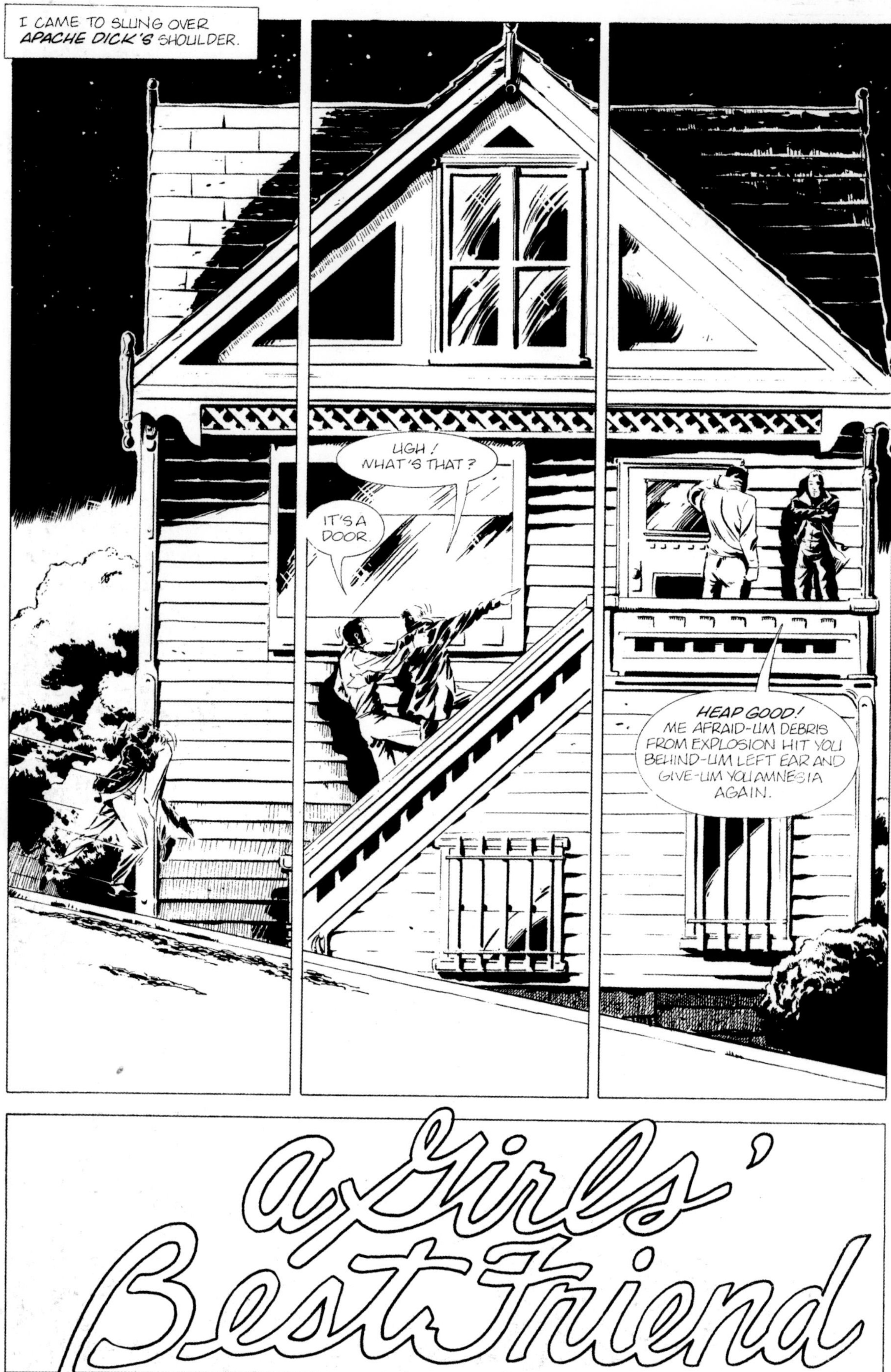
I CAME TO SLUNG OVER APACHE DICK'S SHOULDER.
UGH! WHAT'S THAT?
IT'S A DOOR.
HEAP GOOD! ME AFRAID-UM DEBRIS FROM EXPLOSION HIT YOU BEHIND-UM LEFT EAR AND GIVE-UM YOU AMNESIA AGAIN.
a Girls' Best Friend

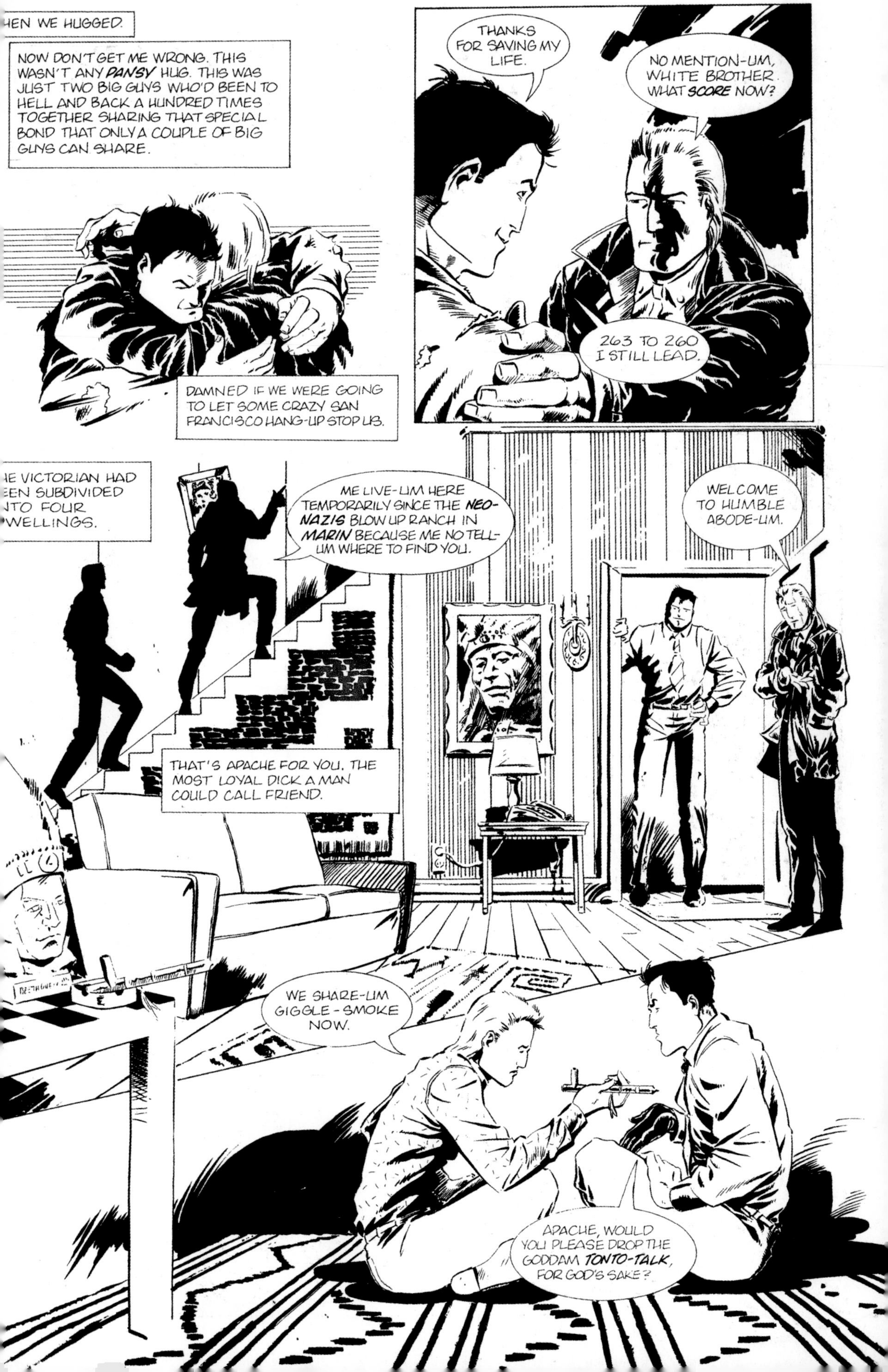
HEN WE HUGGED.
NOW DON'T GET ME WRONG. THIS WASN'T ANY PANSY HUG. THIS WAS JUST TWO BIG GUYS WHO'D BEEN TO HELL AND BACK A HUNDRED TIMES TOGETHER SHARING THAT SPECIAL BOND THAT ONLY A COUPLE OF BIG GUYS CAN SHARE.
DAMNED IF WE WERE GOING TO LET SOME CRAZY SAN FRANCISCO HANG-UP STOP US.
THANKS FOR SAVING MY LIFE.
NO MENTION-UM, WHITE BROTHER. WHAT SCORE NOW?
263 TO 260 I STILL LEAD.
HE VICTORIAN HAD EEN SUBDIVIDED NTO FOUR WELLINGS.
ME LIVE-UM HERE TEMPORARILY SINCE THE NEO-NAZIS BLOW UP RANCH IN MARIN BECAUSE ME NO TELL-UM WHERE TO FIND YOU.
THAT'S APACHE FOR YOU. THE MOST LOYAL DICK A MAN COULD CALL FRIEND.
WELCOME TO HUMBLE ABODE-UM.
WE SHARE-UM GIGGLE - SMOKE NOW.
APACHE, WOULD YOU PLEASE DROP THE GODDAM TONTO-TALK, FOR GOD'S SAKE?

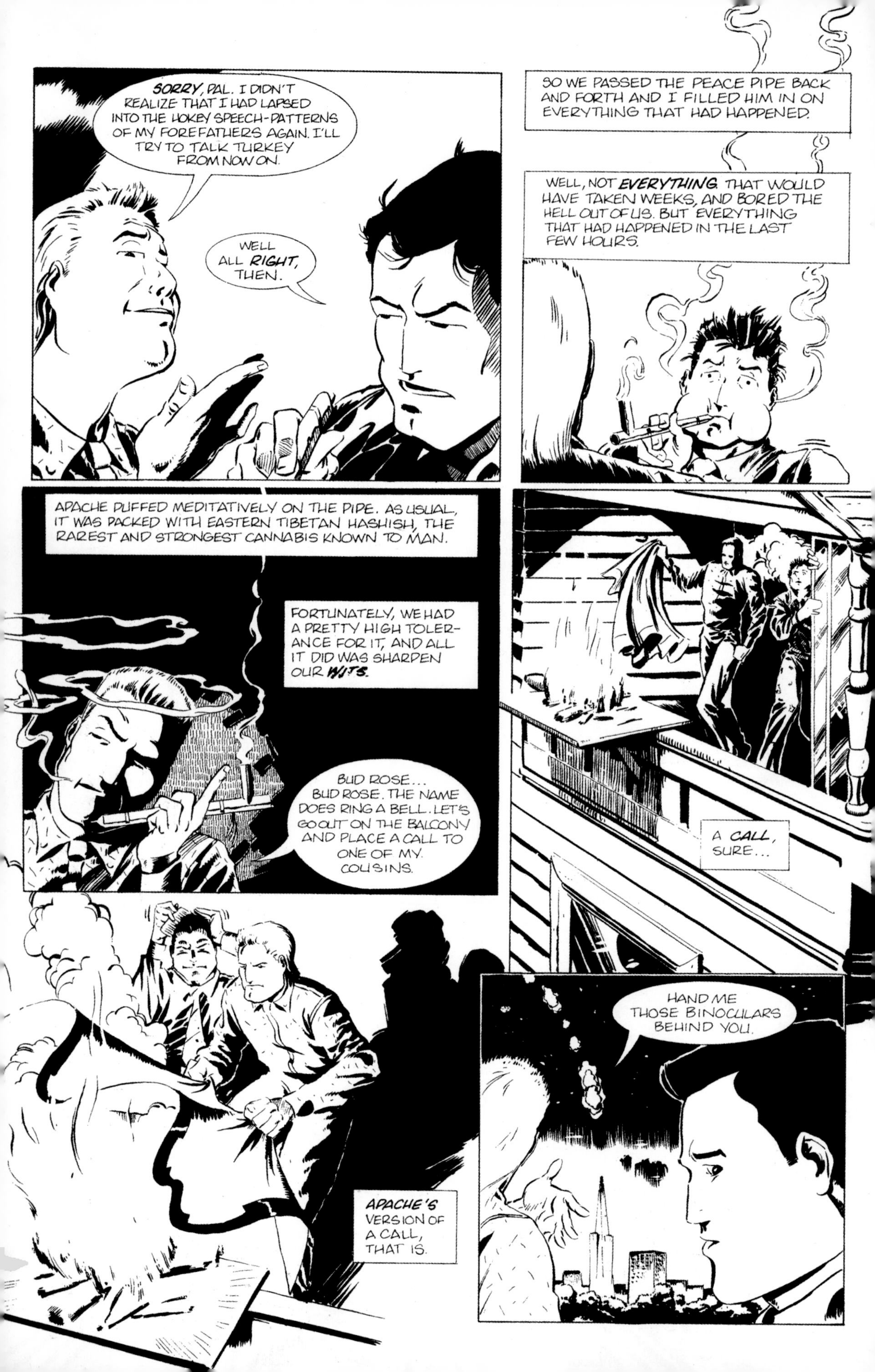
SORRY, PAL. I DIDN'T REALIZE THAT I HAD LAPSED INTO THE HOKEY SPEECH-PATTERNS OF MY FOREFATHERS AGAIN. I'LL TRY TO TALK TURKEY FROM NOW ON.
WELL ALL RIGHT, THEN.
SO WE PASSED THE PEACE PIPE BACK AND FORTH AND I FILLED HIM IN ON EVERYTHING THAT HAD HAPPENED.
WELL, NOT EVERYTHING. THAT WOULD HAVE TAKEN WEEKS, AND BORED THE HELL OUT OF US. BUT EVERYTHING THAT HAD HAPPENED IN THE LAST FEW HOURS.
APACHE PUFFED MEDITATIVELY ON THE PIPE. AS USUAL, IT WAS PACKED WITH EASTERN TIBETAN HASHISH, THE RAREST AND STRONGEST CANNABIS KNOWN TO MAN.
FORTUNATELY, WE HAD A PRETTY HIGH TOLERANCE FOR IT, AND ALL IT DID WAS SHARPEN OUR WITS.
BUD ROSE... BUD ROSE. THE NAME DOES RING A BELL. LET'S GO OUT ON THE BALCONY AND PLACE A CALL TO ONE OF MY COUSINS.
A CALL, SURE...
APACHE'S VERSION OF A CALL, THAT IS.
HAND ME THOSE BINOCULARS BEHIND YOU.

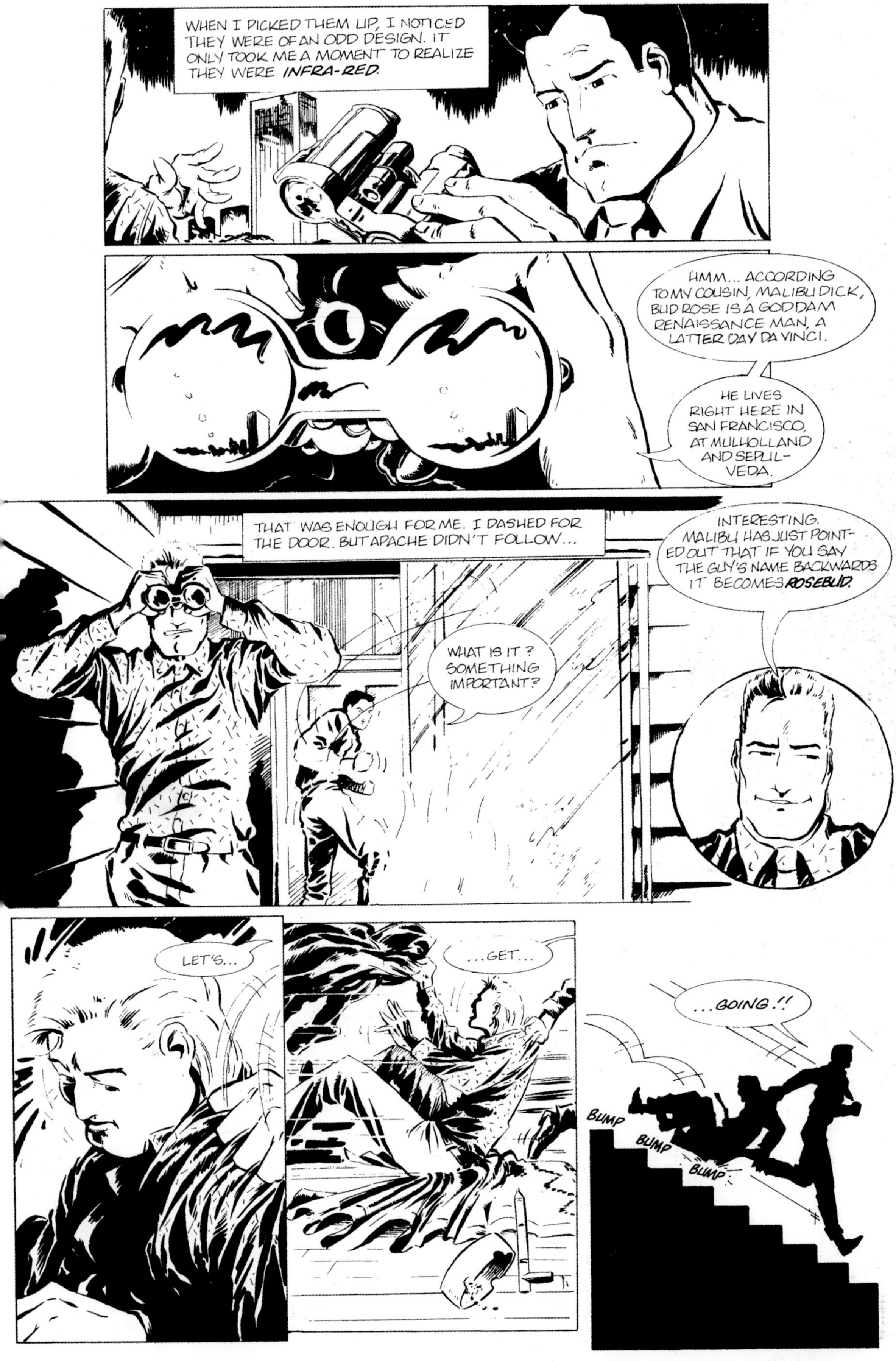

WHEN I PICKED THEM UP, I NOTICED THEY WERE OF AN ODD DESIGN. IT ONLY TOOK ME A MOMENT TO REALIZE THEY WERE INFRA-RED.
HMM... ACCORDING TO MY COUSIN, MALIBU DICK, BUD ROSE IS A GODDAM RENAISSANCE MAN, A LATTER DAY DA VINCI.
HE LIVES RIGHT HERE IN SAN FRANCISCO, AT MULHOLLAND AND SEPUL-VEDA.
THAT WAS ENOUGH FOR ME. I DASHED FOR THE DOOR. BUT APACHE DIDN'T FOLLOW...
WHAT IS IT? SOMETHING IMPORTANT?
INTERESTING. MALIBU HAS JUST POINTED OUT THAT IF YOU SAY THE GUY'S NAME BACKWARDS IT BECOMES ROSEBUD.
LET'S...
...GET...
...GOING!!
BUMP
BUMP
BUMP

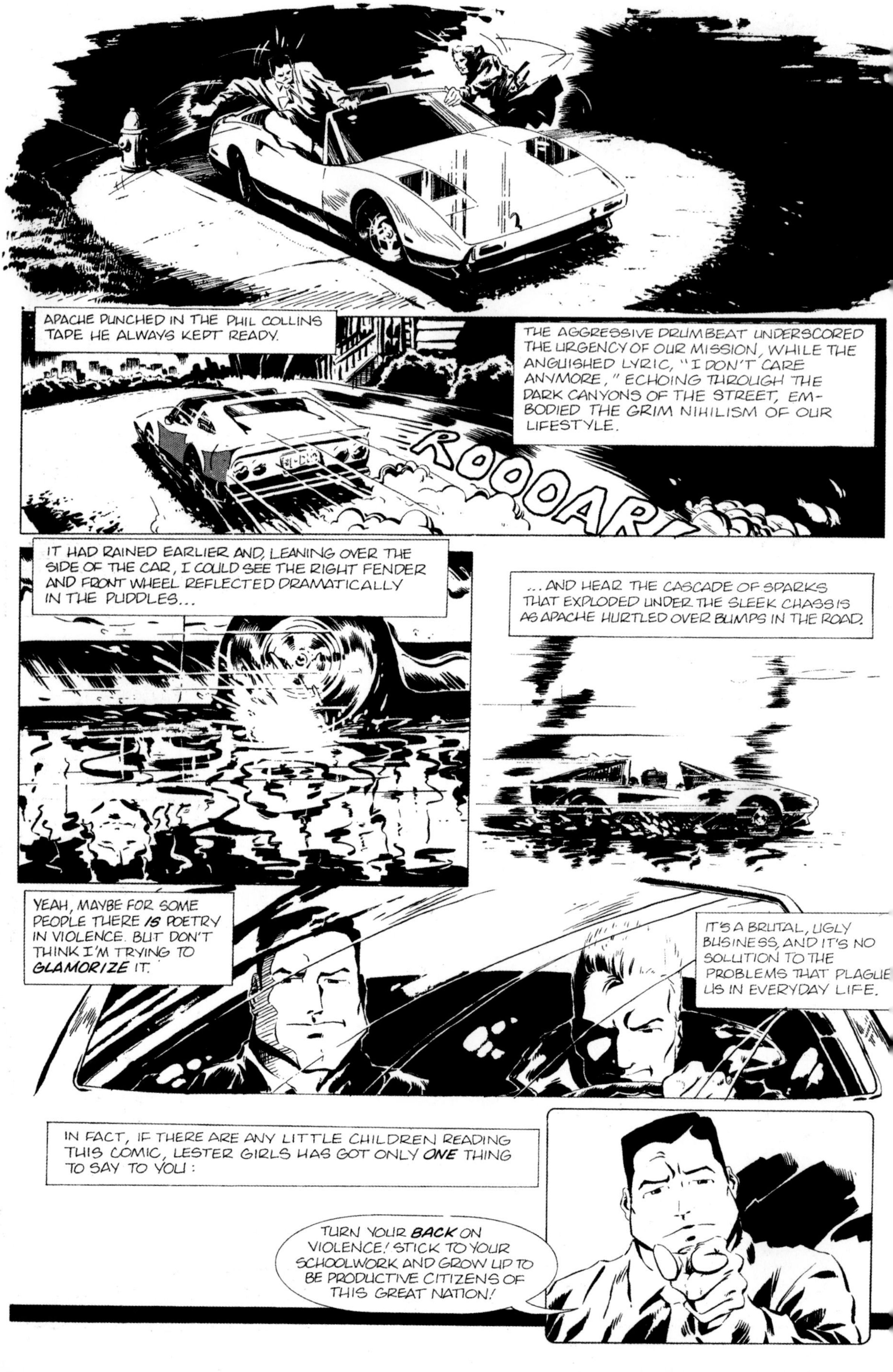
APACHE PUNCHED IN THE PHIL COLLINS TAPE HE ALWAYS KEPT READY.
THE AGGRESSIVE DRUMBEAT UNDERSCORED THE URGENCY OF OUR MISSION, WHILE THE ANGUISHED LYRIC, "I DON'T CARE ANYMORE," ECHOING THROUGH THE DARK CANYONS OF THE STREET, EMBODIED THE GRIM NIHILISM OF OUR LIFESTYLE.
ROOOAR
IT HAD RAINED EARLIER AND, LEANING OVER THE SIDE OF THE CAR, I COULD SEE THE RIGHT FENDER AND FRONT WHEEL REFLECTED DRAMATICALLY IN THE PUDDLES...
...AND HEAR THE CASCADE OF SPARKS THAT EXPLODED UNDER THE SLEEK CHASSIS AS APACHE HURTLED OVER BUMPS IN THE ROAD.
YEAH, MAYBE FOR SOME PEOPLE THERE ***IS*** POETRY IN VIOLENCE. BUT DON'T THINK I'M TRYING TO ***GLAMORIZE*** IT.
IT'S A BRUTAL, UGLY BUSINESS, AND IT'S NO SOLUTION TO THE PROBLEMS THAT PLAGUE US IN EVERYDAY LIFE.
IN FACT, IF THERE ARE ANY LITTLE CHILDREN READING THIS COMIC, LESTER GIRLS HAS GOT ONLY ***ONE*** THING TO SAY TO YOU:
TURN YOUR **BACK** ON VIOLENCE! STICK TO YOUR SCHOOLWORK AND GROW UP TO BE PRODUCTIVE CITIZENS OF THIS GREAT NATION!

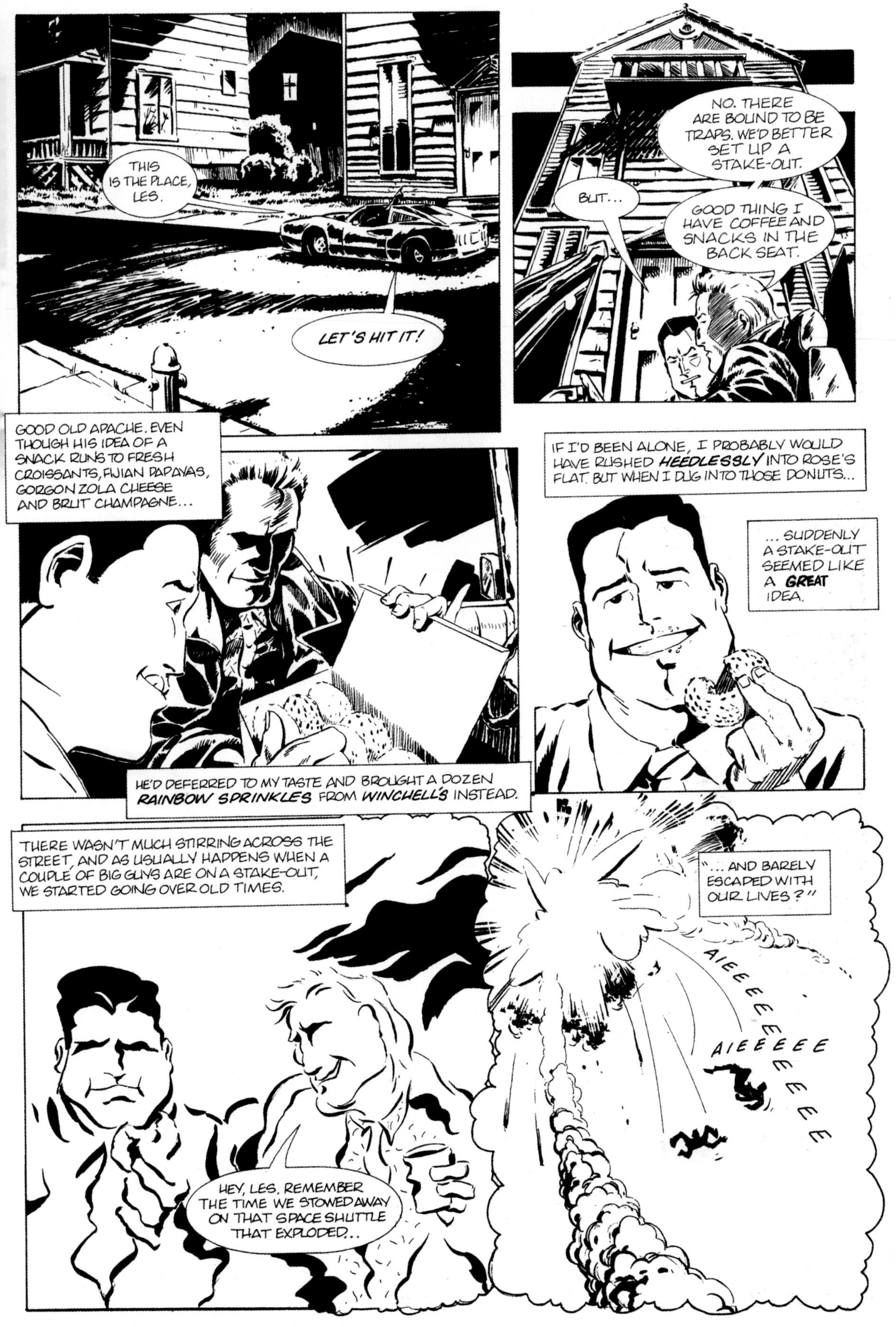
THIS IS THE PLACE, LES.
LET'S HIT IT!
NO. THERE ARE BOUND TO BE TRAPS. WE'D BETTER SET UP A STAKE-OUT.
BUT...
GOOD THING I HAVE COFFEE AND SNACKS IN THE BACK SEAT.
GOOD OLD APACHE. EVEN THOUGH HIS IDEA OF A SNACK RUNS TO FRESH CROISSANTS, FIJIAN PAPAYAS, GORGON ZOLA CHEESE AND BRUT CHAMPAGNE...
HE'D DEFERRED TO MY TASTE AND BROUGHT A DOZEN RAINBOW SPRINKLES FROM WINCHELL'S INSTEAD.
IF I'D BEEN ALONE, I PROBABLY WOULD HAVE RUSHED HEEDLESSLY INTO ROSE'S FLAT. BUT WHEN I DUG INTO THOSE DONUTS...
... SUDDENLY A STAKE-OUT SEEMED LIKE A GREAT IDEA.
THERE WASN'T MUCH STIRRING ACROSS THE STREET, AND AS USUALLY HAPPENS WHEN A COUPLE OF BIG GUYS ARE ON A STAKE-OUT, WE STARTED GOING OVER OLD TIMES.
HEY, LES. REMEMBER THE TIME WE STOWED AWAY ON THAT SPACE SHUTTLE THAT EXPLODED...
"... AND BARELY ESCAPED WITH OUR LIVES?"
AIEEEEEEEE
AIEEEEEEEEEEE

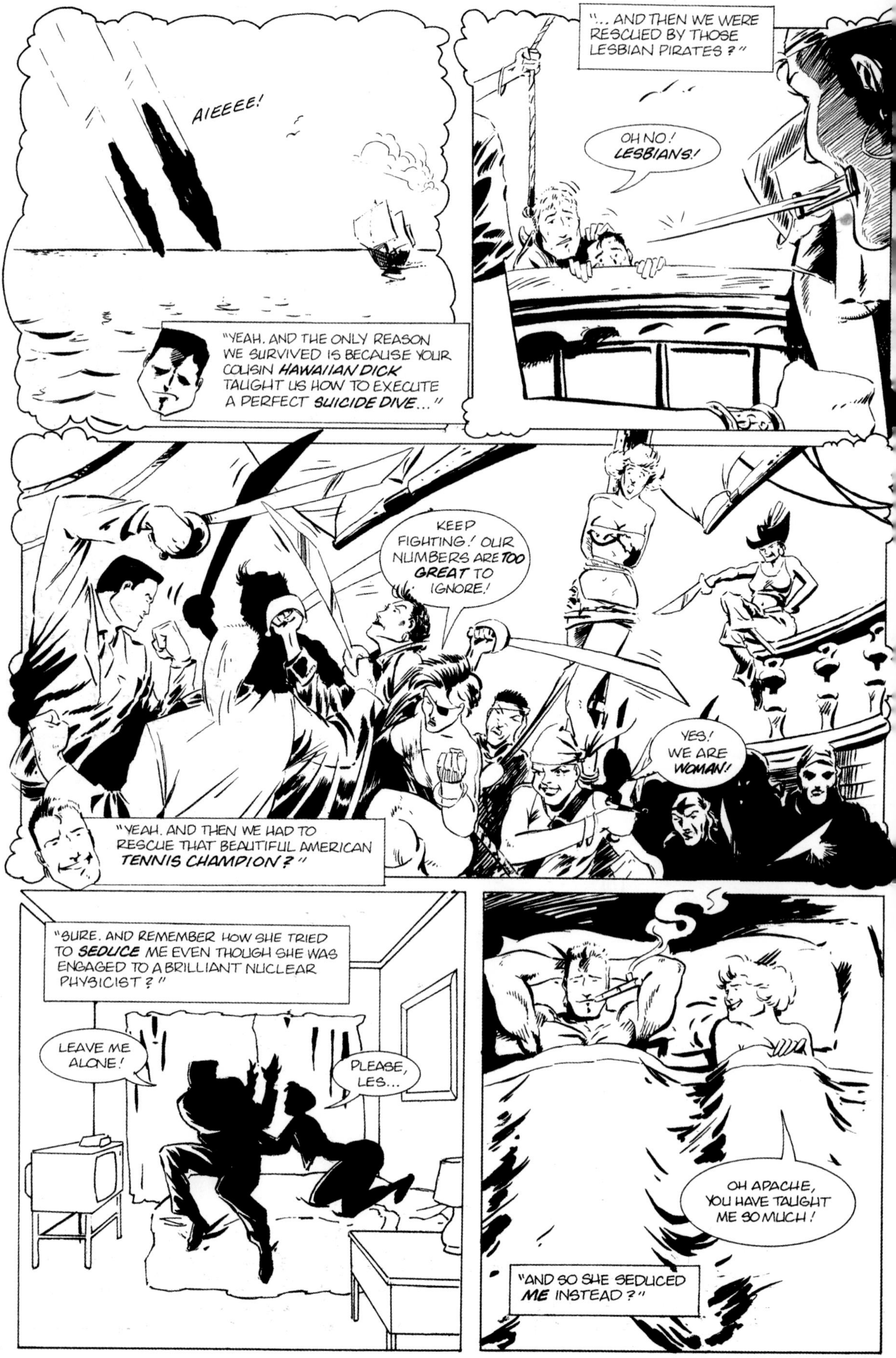

AIEEEE!
"YEAH. AND THE ONLY REASON WE SURVIVED IS BECAUSE YOUR COUSIN HAWAIIAN DICK TAUGHT US HOW TO EXECUTE A PERFECT SUICIDE DIVE..."
"... AND THEN WE WERE RESCUED BY THOSE LESBIAN PIRATES ?"
OH NO! LESBIANS!
KEEP FIGHTING! OUR NUMBERS ARE TOO GREAT TO IGNORE!
YES! WE ARE WOMAN!
"YEAH. AND THEN WE HAD TO RESCUE THAT BEAUTIFUL AMERICAN TENNIS CHAMPION ?"
"SURE. AND REMEMBER HOW SHE TRIED TO SEDUCE ME EVEN THOUGH SHE WAS ENGAGED TO A BRILLIANT NUCLEAR PHYSICIST ?"
LEAVE ME ALONE!
PLEASE, LES...
OH APACHE, YOU HAVE TAUGHT ME SO MUCH!
"AND SO SHE SEDUCED ME INSTEAD ?"

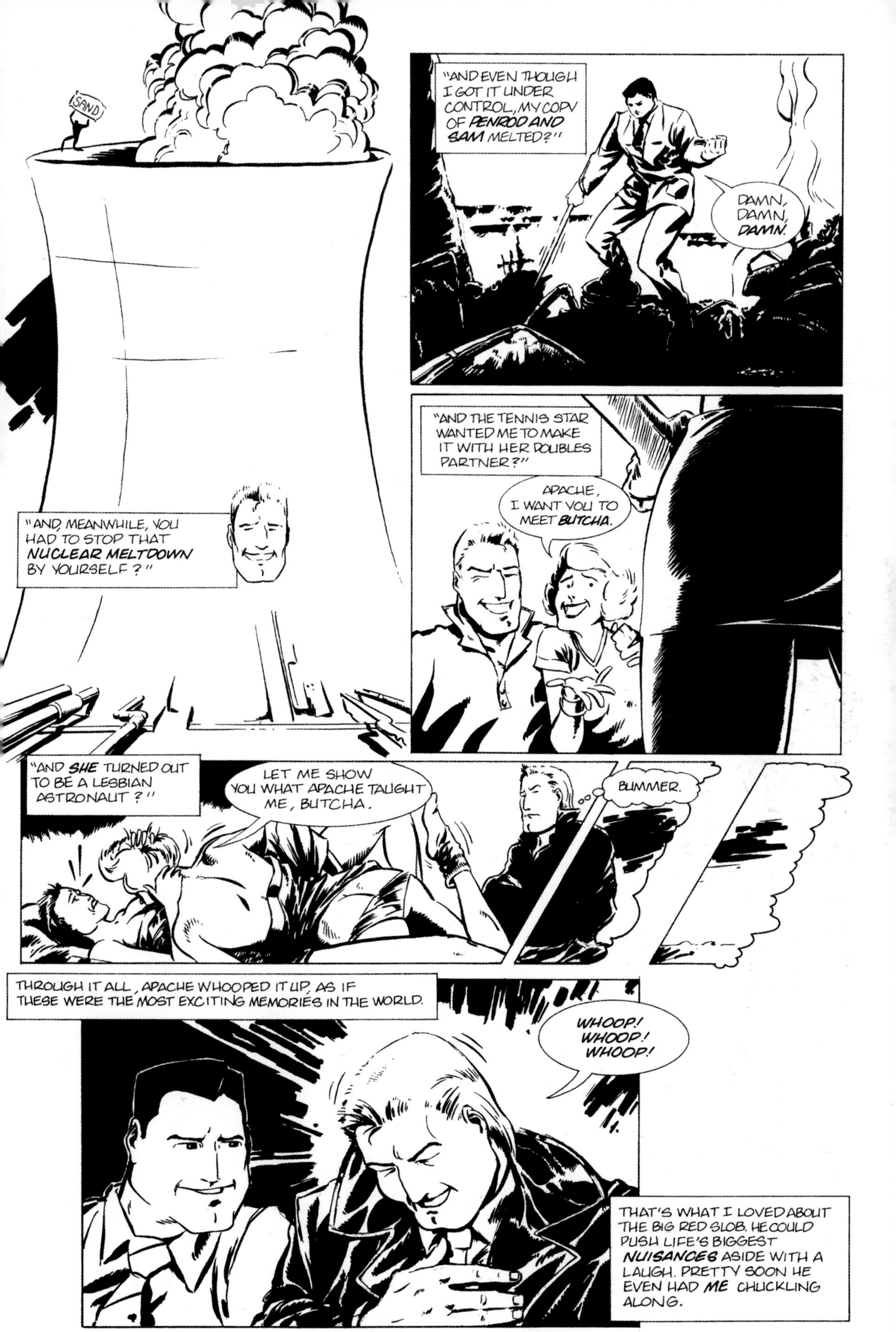
"AND EVEN THOUGH I GOT IT UNDER CONTROL, MY COPY OF PENROD AND SAM MELTED?"
DAMN, DAMN, DAMN.
SAND
"AND, MEANWHILE, YOU HAD TO STOP THAT NUCLEAR MELTDOWN BY YOURSELF?"
"AND THE TENNIS STAR WANTED ME TO MAKE IT WITH HER DOUBLES PARTNER?"
APACHE, I WANT YOU TO MEET BUTCHA.
"AND SHE TURNED OUT TO BE A LESBIAN ASTRONAUT?"
LET ME SHOW YOU WHAT APACHE TAUGHT ME, BUTCHA.
BUMMER.
THROUGH IT ALL, APACHE WHOOPED IT UP, AS IF THESE WERE THE MOST EXCITING MEMORIES IN THE WORLD.
WHOOP! WHOOP! WHOOP!
THAT'S WHAT I LOVED ABOUT THE BIG RED SLOB. HE COULD PUSH LIFE'S BIGGEST NUISANCES ASIDE WITH A LAUGH. PRETTY SOON HE EVEN HAD ME CHUCKLING ALONG.

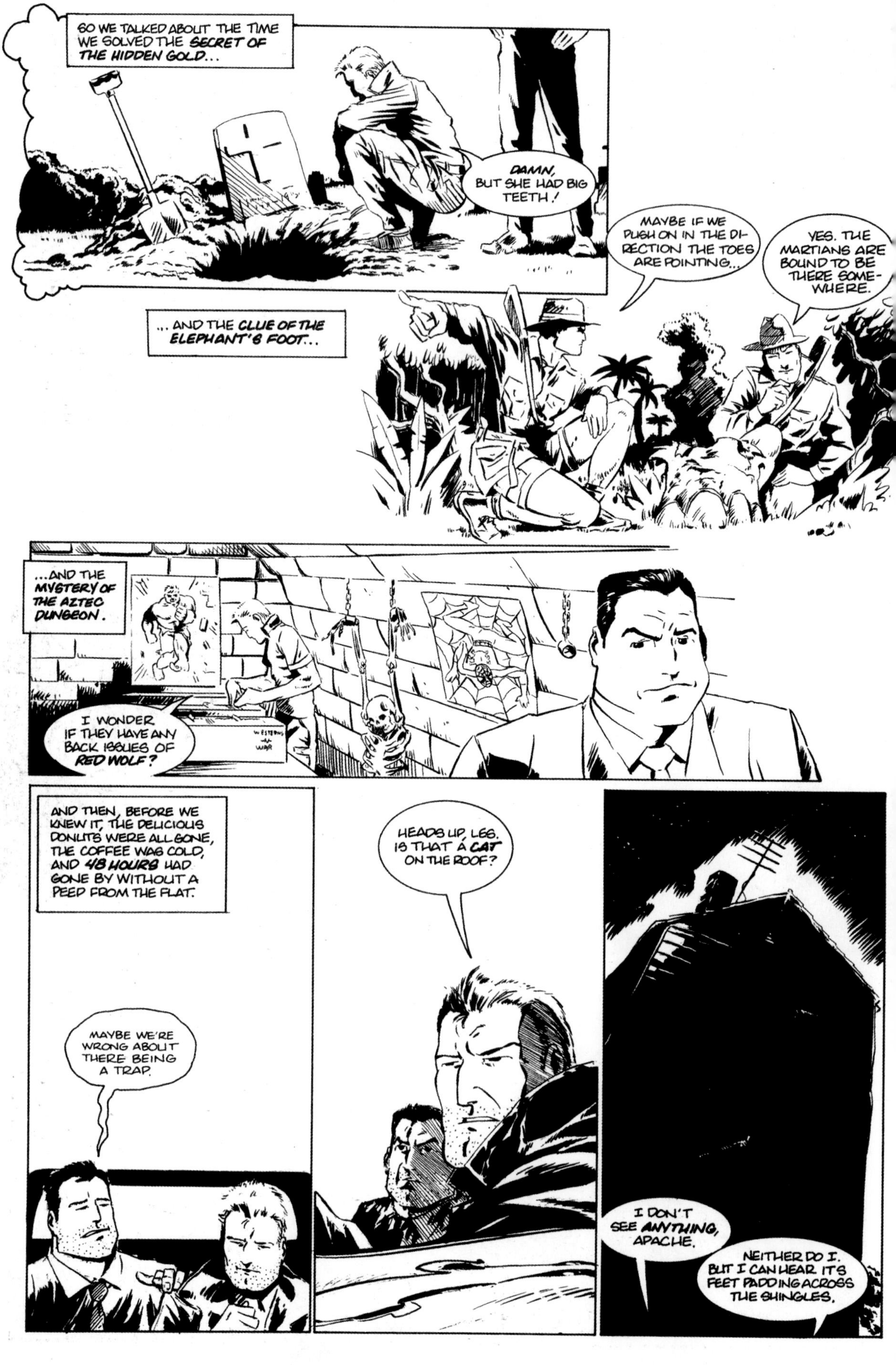
SO WE TALKED ABOUT THE TIME WE SOLVED THE SECRET OF THE HIDDEN GOLD...
DAMN, BUT SHE HAD BIG TEETH!
... AND THE CLUE OF THE ELEPHANT'S FOOT...
MAYBE IF WE PUSH ON IN THE DIRECTION THE TOES ARE POINTING...
YES. THE MARTIANS ARE BOUND TO BE THERE SOMEWHERE.
...AND THE MYSTERY OF THE AZTEC DUNGEON.
I WONDER IF THEY HAVE ANY BACK ISSUES OF RED WOLF?
AND THEN, BEFORE WE KNEW IT, THE DELICIOUS DONUTS WERE ALL GONE, THE COFFEE WAS COLD, AND 48 HOURS HAD GONE BY WITHOUT A PEEP FROM THE FLAT.
MAYBE WE'RE WRONG ABOUT THERE BEING A TRAP.
HEADS UP, LES. IS THAT A CAT ON THE ROOF?
I DON'T SEE ANYTHING, APACHE.
NEITHER DO I. BUT I CAN HEAR ITS FEET PADDING ACROSS THE SHINGLES.

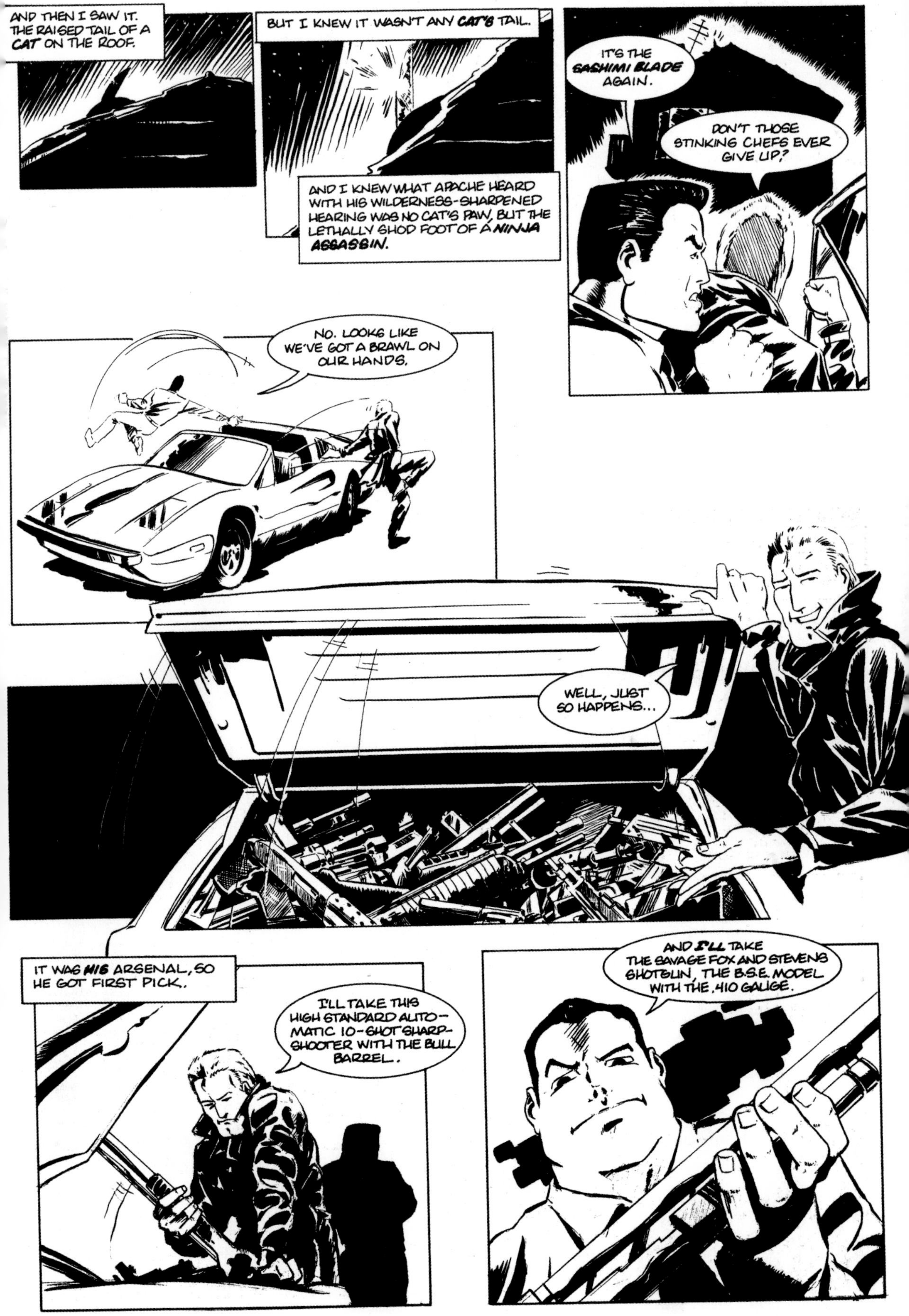
AND THEN I SAW IT. THE RAISED TAIL OF A CAT ON THE ROOF.
BUT I KNEW IT WASN'T ANY CAT'S TAIL.
AND I KNEW WHAT APACHE HEARD WITH HIS WILDERNESS-SHARPENED HEARING WAS NO CAT'S PAW, BUT THE LETHALLY SHOD FOOT OF A NINJA ASSASSIN.
IT'S THE SASHIMI BLADE AGAIN.
DON'T THOSE STINKING CHEFS EVER GIVE UP?
NO. LOOKS LIKE WE'VE GOT A BRAWL ON OUR HANDS.
WELL, JUST SO HAPPENS...
IT WAS HIS ARSENAL, SO HE GOT FIRST PICK.
I'LL TAKE THIS HIGH STANDARD AUTO-MATIC 10-SHOT SHARP-SHOOTER WITH THE BULL BARREL.
AND I'LL TAKE THE SAVAGE FOX AND STEVENS SHOTGUN, THE B.S.E. MODEL WITH THE .410 GAUGE.

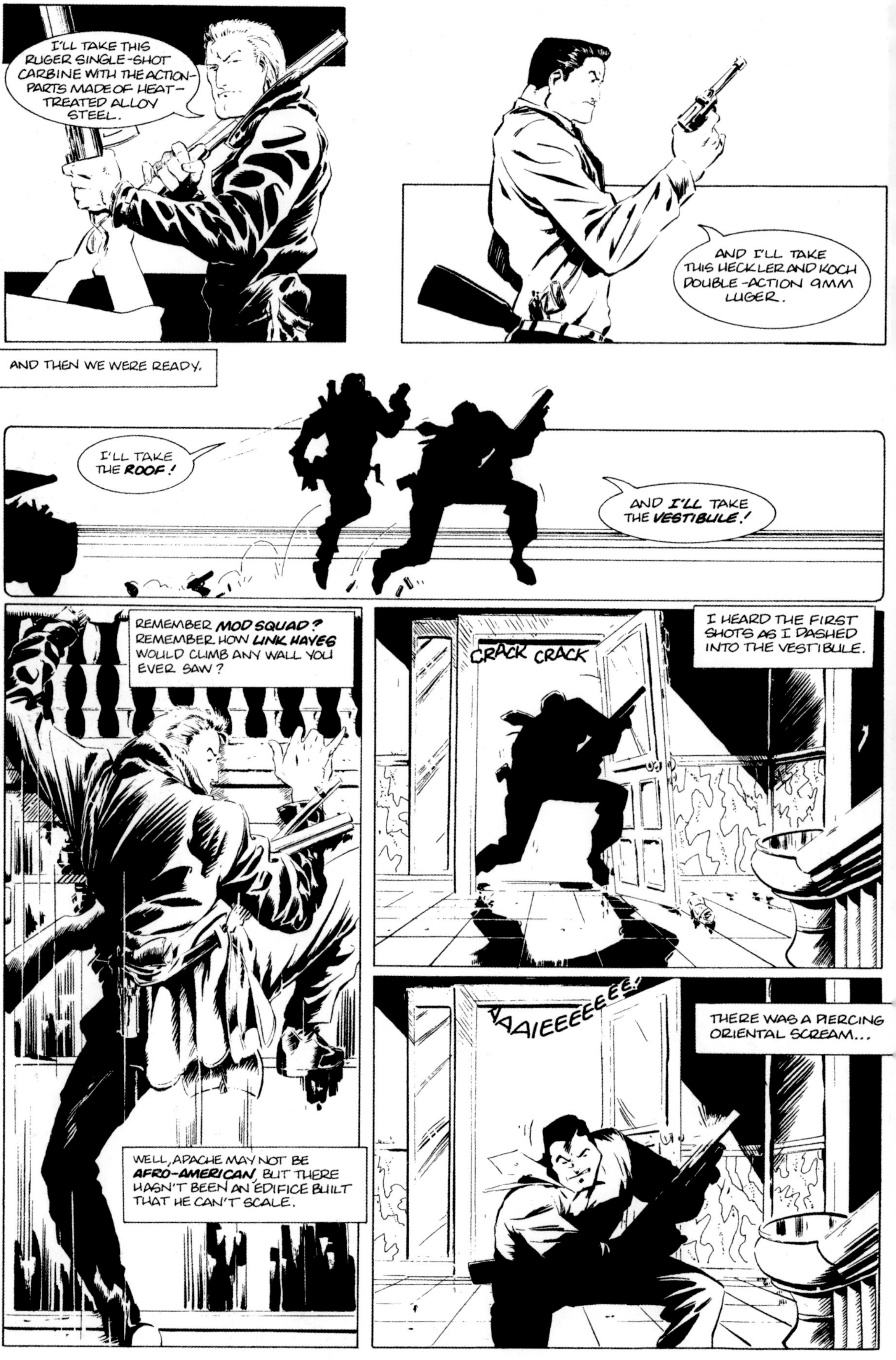
I'LL TAKE THIS RUGER SINGLE-SHOT CARBINE WITH THE ACTION-PARTS MADE OF HEAT-TREATED ALLOY STEEL.
AND I'LL TAKE THIS HECKLER AND KOCH DOUBLE-ACTION 9MM LUGER.
AND THEN WE WERE READY.
I'LL TAKE THE ROOF!
AND I'LL TAKE THE VESTIBULE!
REMEMBER MOD SQUAD? REMEMBER HOW LINK HAYES WOULD CLIMB ANY WALL YOU EVER SAW?
WELL, APACHE MAY NOT BE AFRO-AMERICAN, BUT THERE HASN'T BEEN AN EDIFICE BUILT THAT HE CAN'T SCALE.
I HEARD THE FIRST SHOTS AS I DASHED INTO THE VESTIBULE.
CRACK CRACK
THERE WAS A PIERCING ORIENTAL SCREAM...
YAAIEEEEEEEEE!

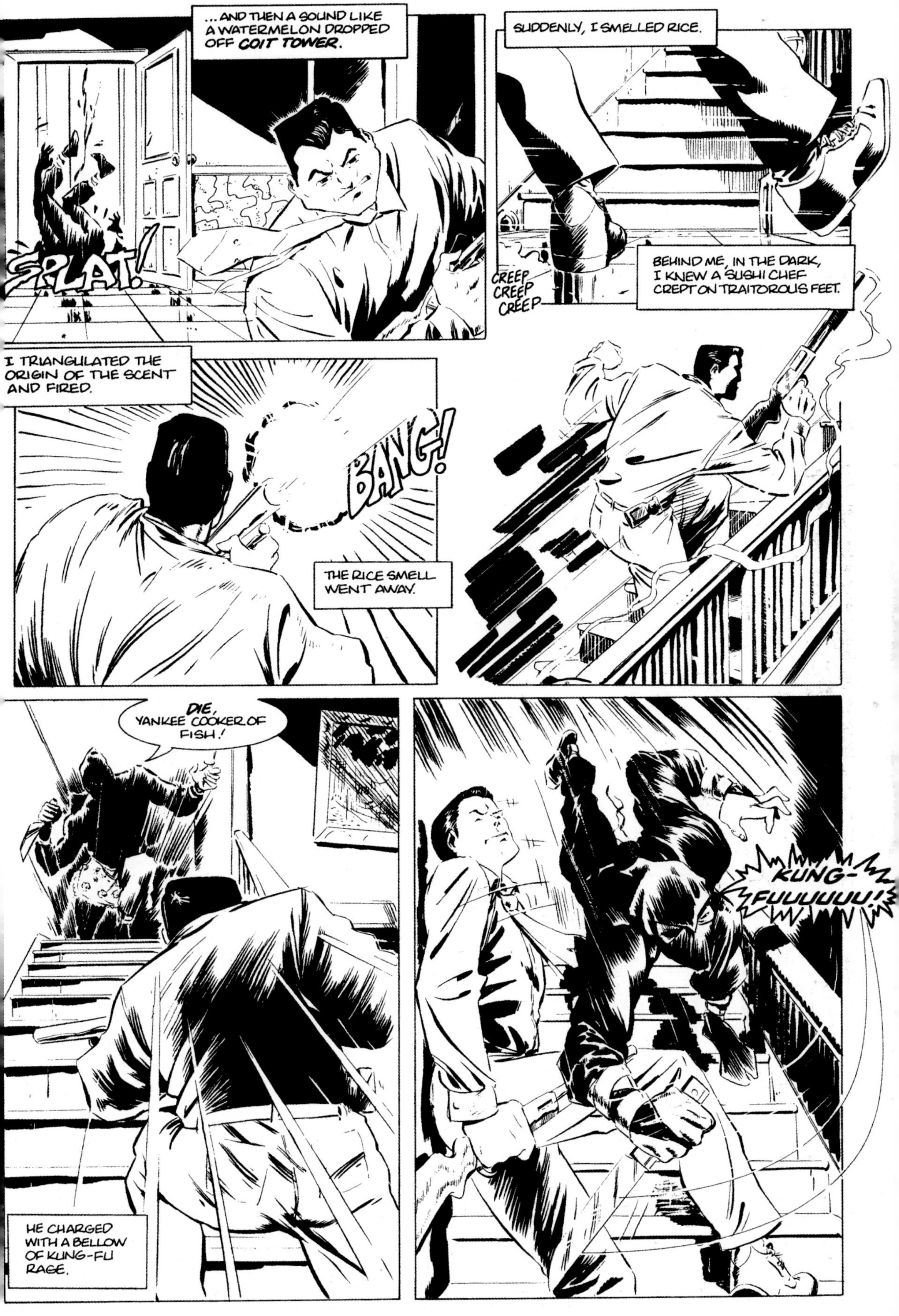

...AND THEN A SOUND LIKE A WATERMELON DROPPED OFF COIT TOWER.
SPLAT!
SUDDENLY, I SMELLED RICE.
BEHIND ME, IN THE DARK, I KNEW A SUSHI CHEF CREPT ON TRAITOROUS FEET.
CREEP CREEP CREEP
I TRIANGULATED THE ORIGIN OF THE SCENT AND FIRED.
BANG!
THE RICE SMELL WENT AWAY.
DIE, YANKEE COOKER OF FISH!
HE CHARGED WITH A BELLOW OF KUNG-FU RAGE.
KUNG-FUUUUUU!

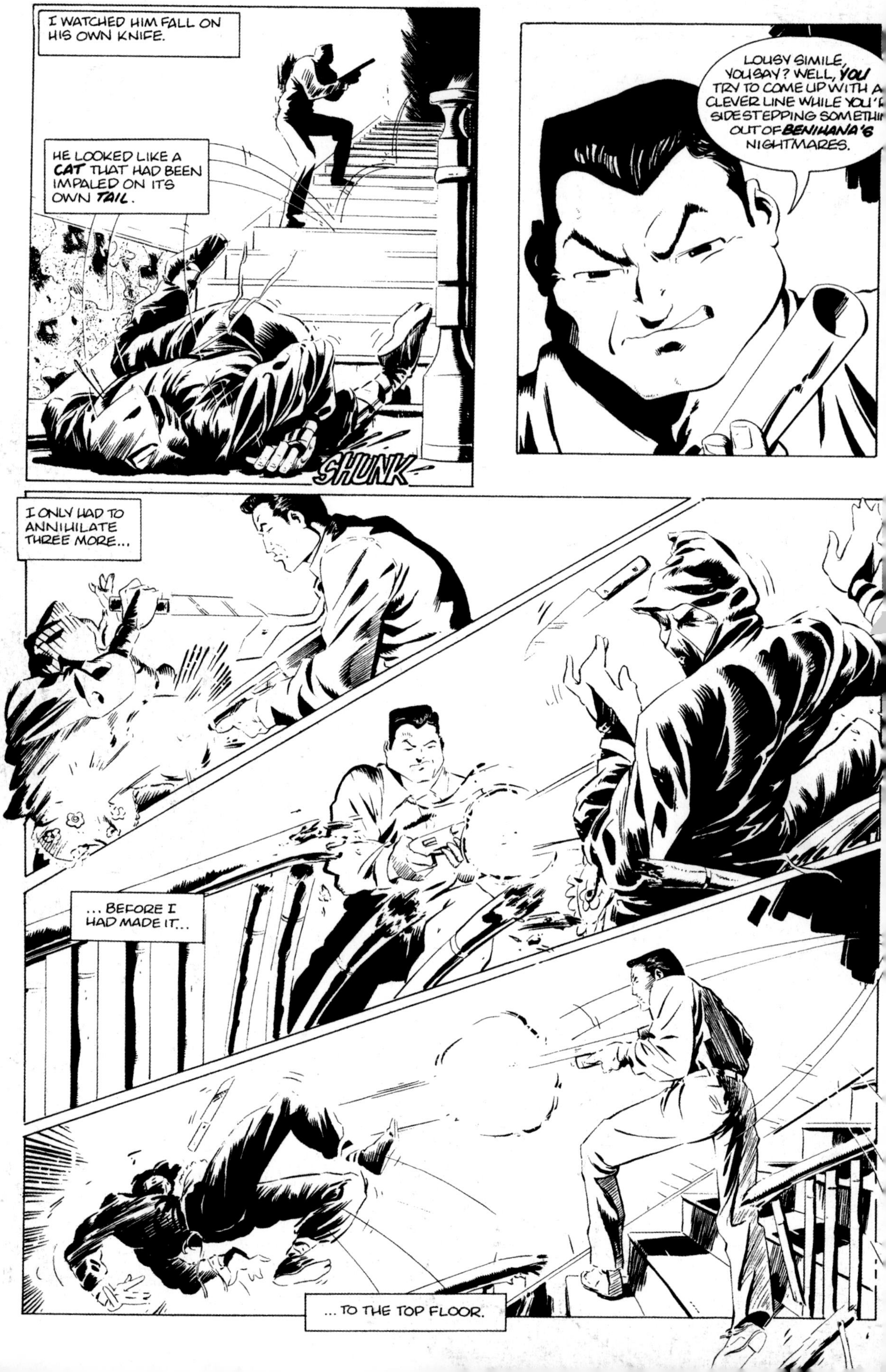
I WATCHED HIM FALL ON HIS OWN KNIFE.
HE LOOKED LIKE A CAT THAT HAD BEEN IMPALED ON ITS OWN TAIL.
SHUNK
LOUSY SIMILE, YOU SAY? WELL, YOU TRY TO COME UP WITH A CLEVER LINE WHILE YOU'RE SIDESTEPPING SOMETHING OUT OF BENIHANA'S NIGHTMARES.
I ONLY HAD TO ANNIHILATE THREE MORE...
... BEFORE I HAD MADE IT...
... TO THE TOP FLOOR.

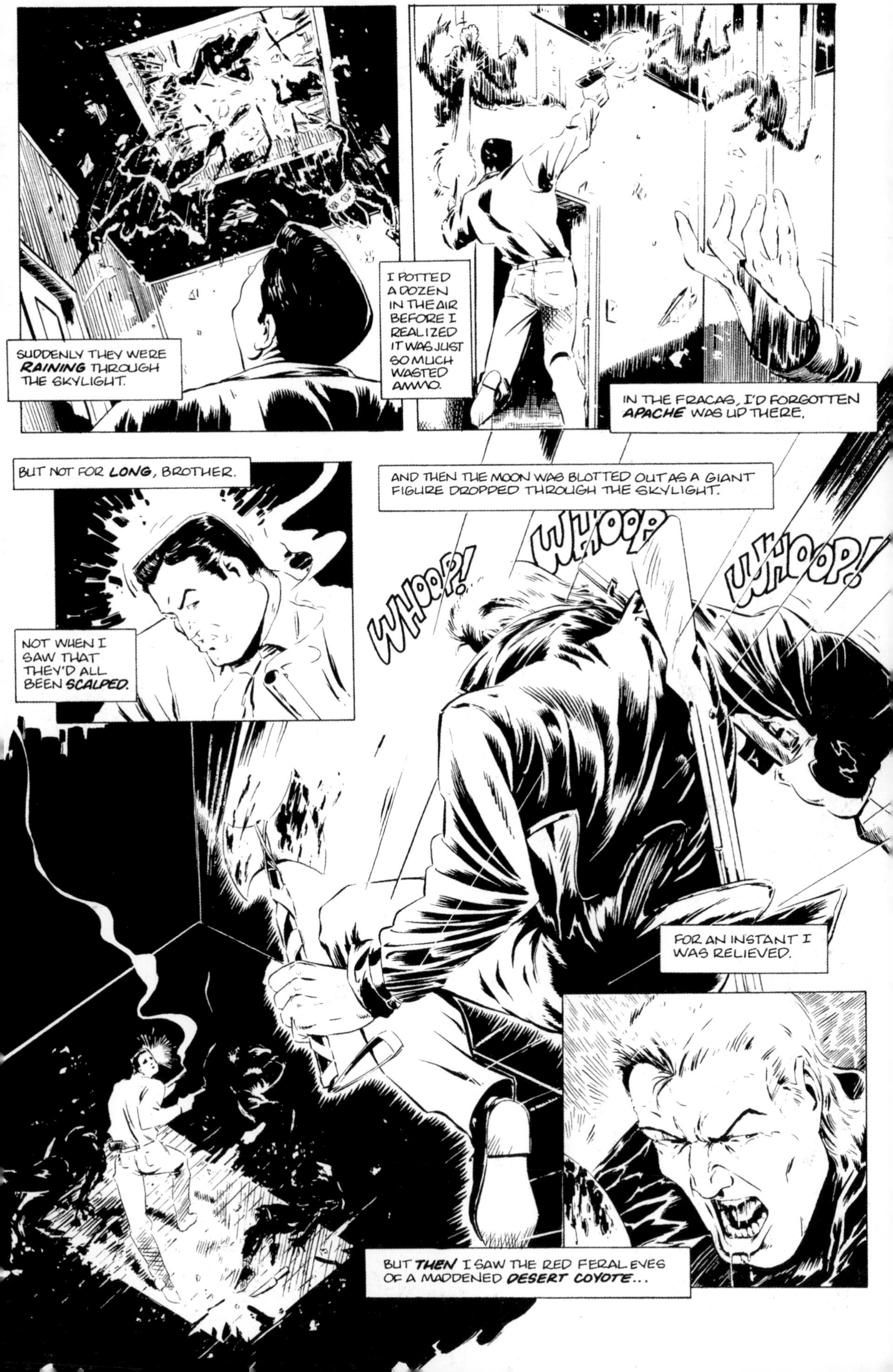
SUDDENLY THEY WERE RAINING THROUGH THE SKYLIGHT.
I POTTED A DOZEN IN THE AIR BEFORE I REALIZED IT WAS JUST SO MUCH WASTED AMMO.
IN THE FRACAS, I'D FORGOTTEN APACHE WAS UP THERE.
BUT NOT FOR LONG, BROTHER.
NOT WHEN I SAW THAT THEY'D ALL BEEN SCALPED.
AND THEN THE MOON WAS BLOTTED OUT AS A GIANT FIGURE DROPPED THROUGH THE SKYLIGHT.
WHOOP!
WHOOP!
WHOOP!
WHOOP!
FOR AN INSTANT I WAS RELIEVED.
BUT THEN I SAW THE RED FERAL EYES OF A MADDENED DESERT COYOTE...

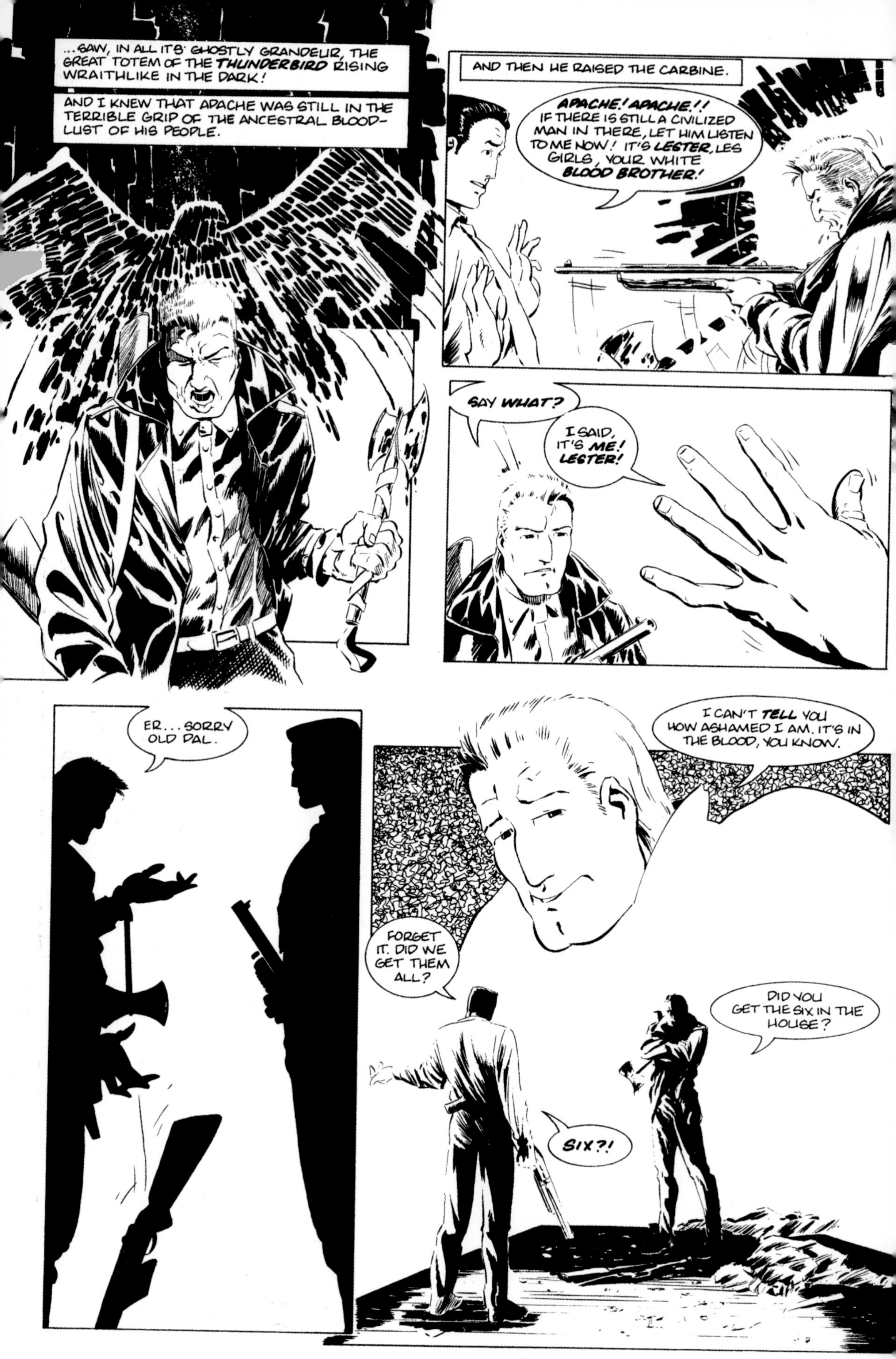

...SAW, IN ALL ITS GHOSTLY GRANDEUR, THE GREAT TOTEM OF THE THUNDERBIRD RISING WRAITHLIKE IN THE DARK!
AND I KNEW THAT APACHE WAS STILL IN THE TERRIBLE GRIP OF THE ANCESTRAL BLOOD-LUST OF HIS PEOPLE.
AND THEN HE RAISED THE CARBINE.
APACHE! APACHE!! IF THERE IS STILL A CIVILIZED MAN IN THERE, LET HIM LISTEN TO ME NOW! IT'S LESTER, LES GIRLS, YOUR WHITE BLOOD BROTHER!
SAY WHAT?
I SAID, IT'S ME! LESTER!
ER... SORRY OLD PAL.
I CAN'T TELL YOU HOW ASHAMED I AM. IT'S IN THE BLOOD, YOU KNOW.
FORGET IT. DID WE GET THEM ALL?
DID YOU GET THE SIX IN THE HOUSE?
SIX?!

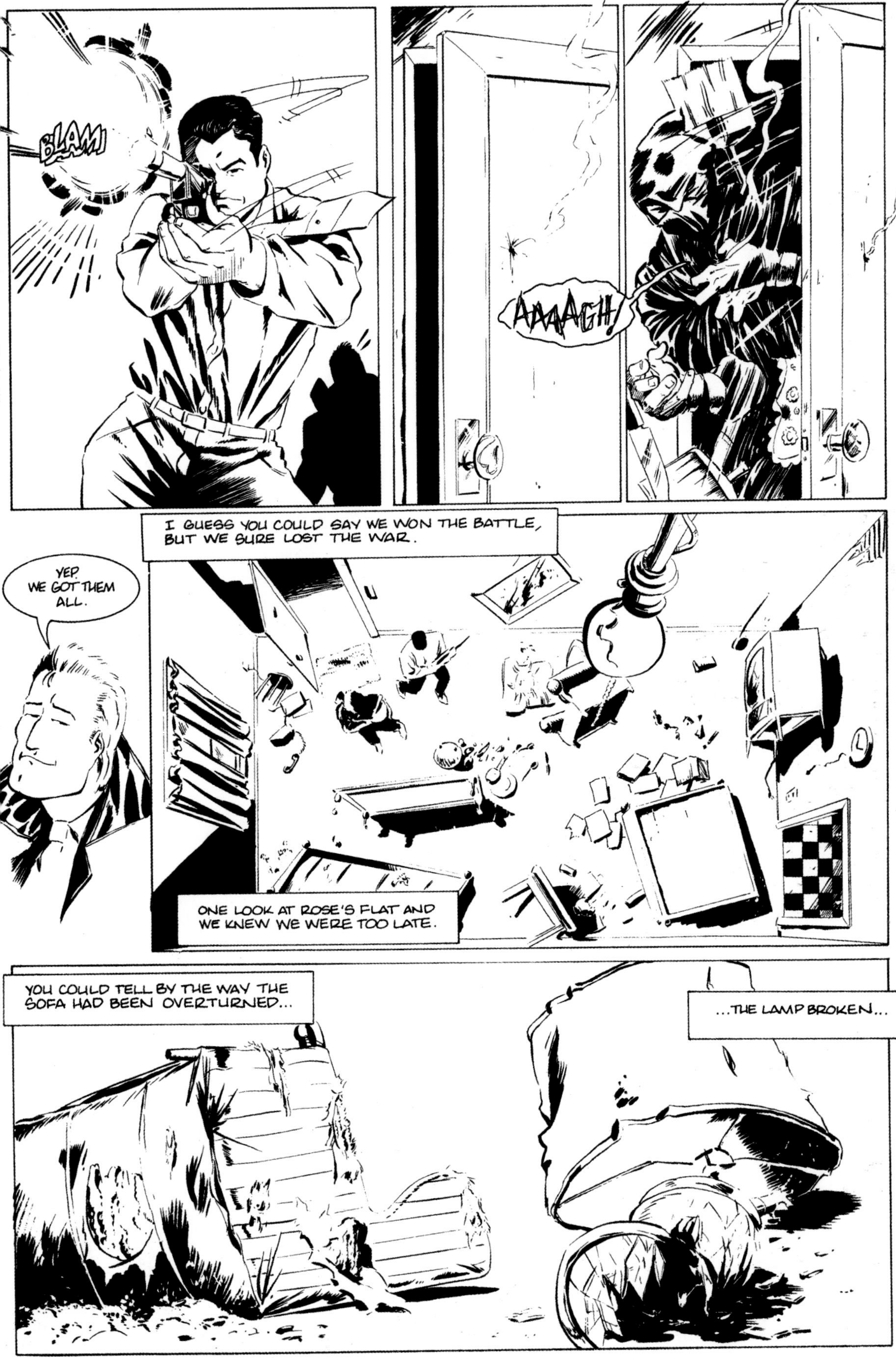
BLAM!
AAAAGH!
I GUESS YOU COULD SAY WE WON THE BATTLE, BUT WE SURE LOST THE WAR.
YEP. WE GOT THEM ALL.
ONE LOOK AT ROSE'S FLAT AND WE KNEW WE WERE TOO LATE.
YOU COULD TELL BY THE WAY THE SOFA HAD BEEN OVERTURNED...
...THE LAMP BROKEN...

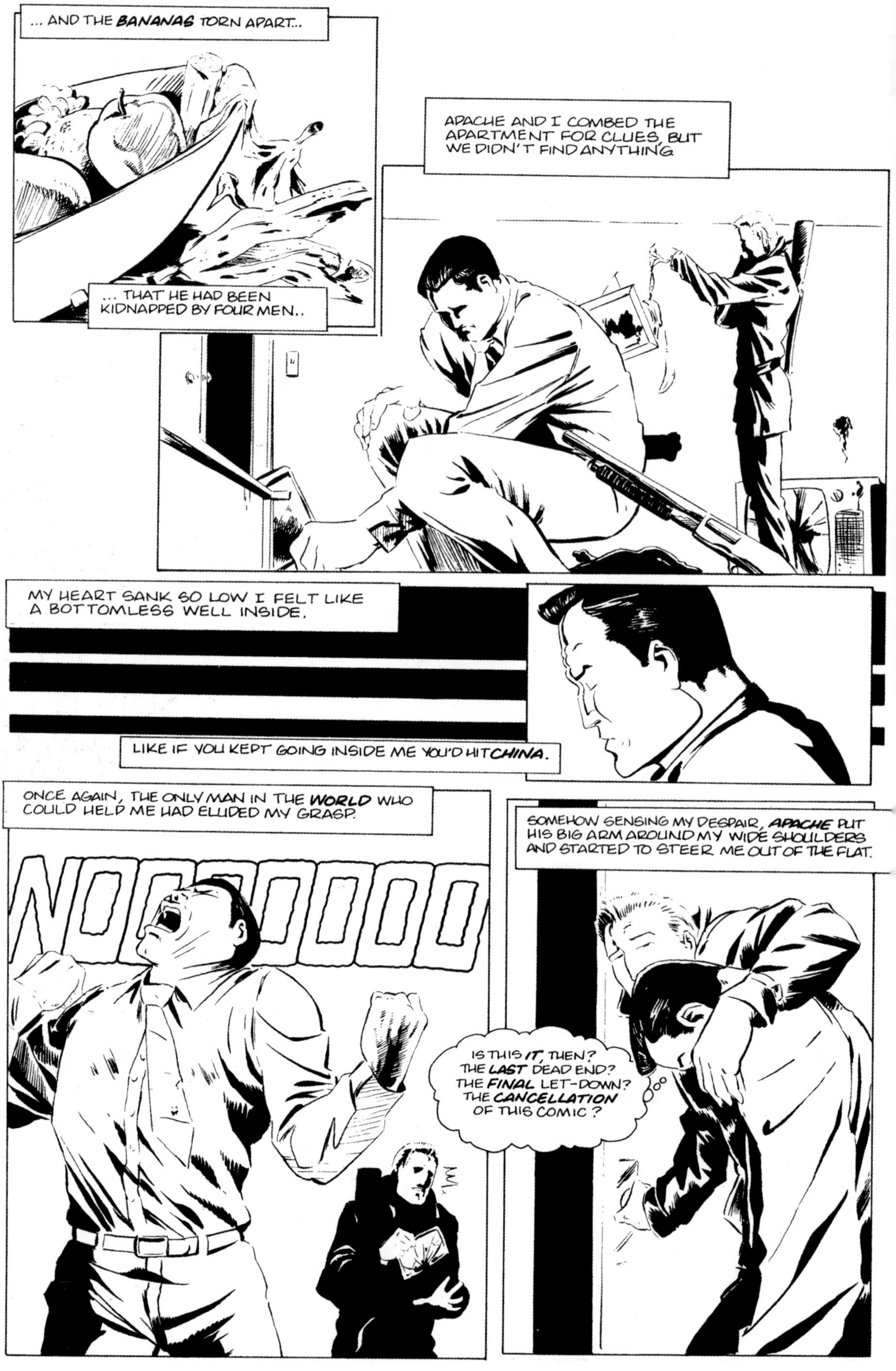
... AND THE BANANAS TORN APART...
... THAT HE HAD BEEN KIDNAPPED BY FOUR MEN..
APACHE AND I COMBED THE APARTMENT FOR CLUES, BUT WE DIDN'T FIND ANYTHING.
MY HEART SANK SO LOW I FELT LIKE A BOTTOMLESS WELL INSIDE.
LIKE IF YOU KEPT GOING INSIDE ME YOU'D HIT CHINA.
ONCE AGAIN, THE ONLY MAN IN THE WORLD WHO COULD HELP ME HAD ELUDED MY GRASP.
NOOOOOOO
SOMEHOW SENSING MY DESPAIR, APACHE PUT HIS BIG ARM AROUND MY WIDE SHOULDERS AND STARTED TO STEER ME OUT OF THE FLAT.
IS THIS IT, THEN? THE LAST DEAD END? THE FINAL LET-DOWN? THE CANCELLATION OF THIS COMIC?

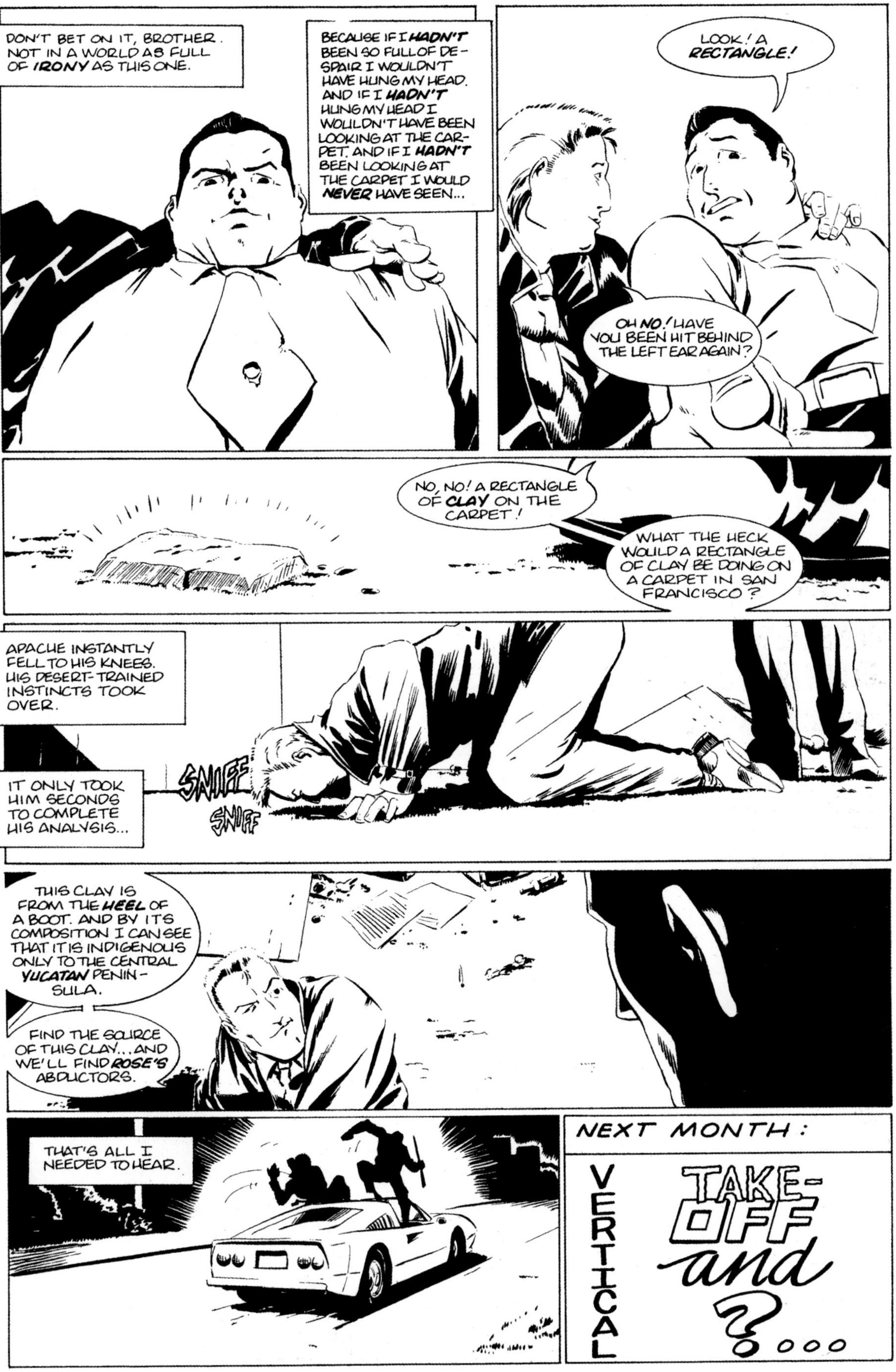
DON'T BET ON IT, BROTHER. NOT IN A WORLD AS FULL OF IRONY AS THIS ONE.
BECAUSE IF I HADN'T BEEN SO FULL OF DE-SPAIR I WOULDN'T HAVE HUNG MY HEAD. AND IF I HADN'T HUNG MY HEAD I WOULDN'T HAVE BEEN LOOKING AT THE CAR-PET. AND IF I HADN'T BEEN LOOKING AT THE CARPET I WOULD NEVER HAVE SEEN...
LOOK! A RECTANGLE!
OH NO! HAVE YOU BEEN HIT BEHIND THE LEFT EAR AGAIN?
NO, NO! A RECTANGLE OF CLAY ON THE CARPET!
WHAT THE HECK WOULD A RECTANGLE OF CLAY BE DOING ON A CARPET IN SAN FRANCISCO?
APACHE INSTANTLY FELL TO HIS KNEES. HIS DESERT-TRAINED INSTINCTS TOOK OVER.
IT ONLY TOOK HIM SECONDS TO COMPLETE HIS ANALYSIS...
SNIFF
SNIFF
THIS CLAY IS FROM THE HEEL OF A BOOT. AND BY ITS COMPOSITION I CAN SEE THAT IT IS INDIGENOUS ONLY TO THE CENTRAL YUCATAN PENIN-SULA.
FIND THE SOURCE OF THIS CLAY... AND WE'LL FIND ROSE'S ABDUCTORS.
THAT'S ALL I NEEDED TO HEAR.
NEXT MONTH:
VERTICAL TAKE-OFF and ?...

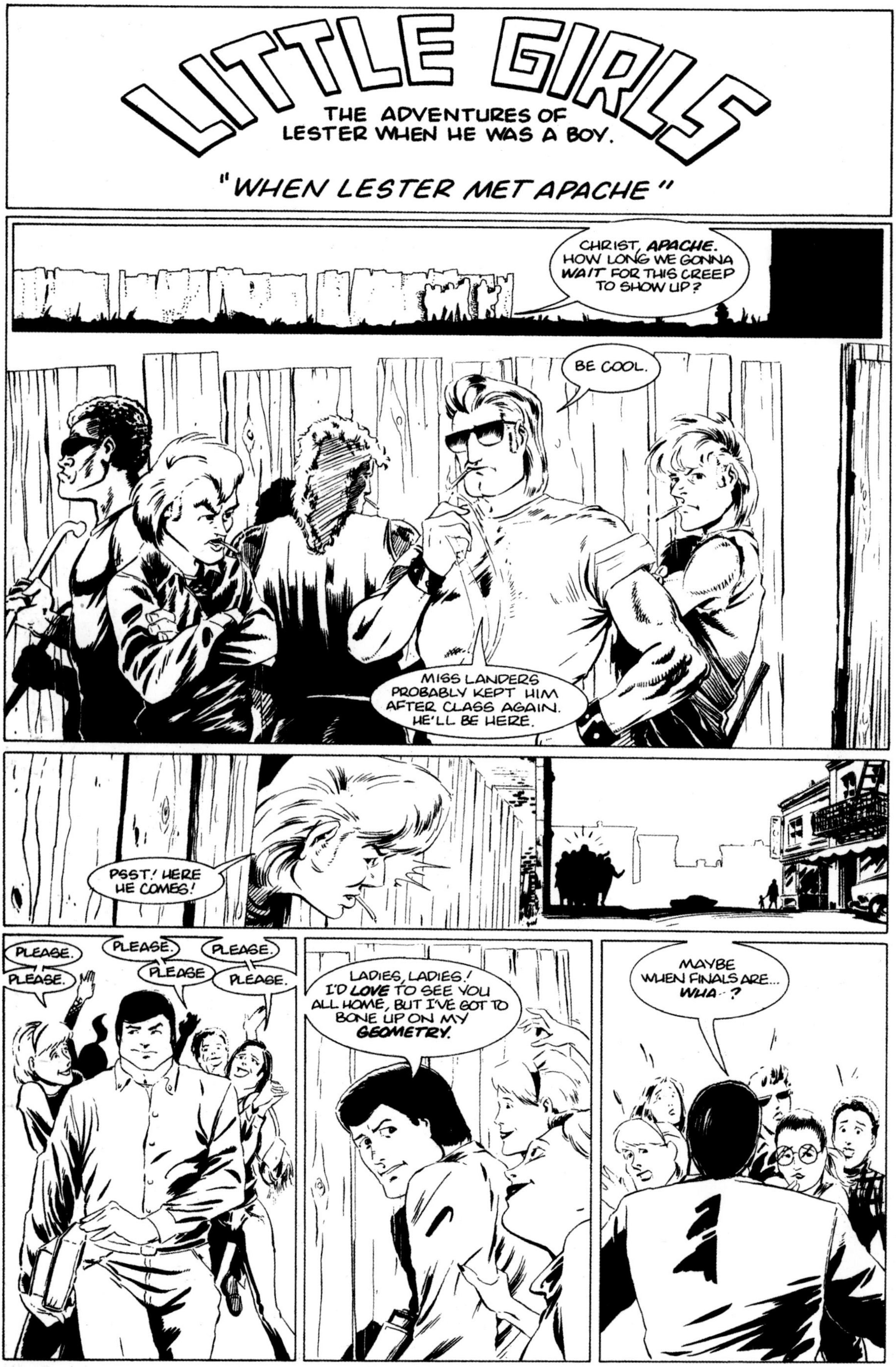
LITTLE GIRLS
THE ADVENTURES OF LESTER WHEN HE WAS A BOY.
"WHEN LESTER MET APACHE"
CHRIST, APACHE. HOW LONG WE GONNA WAIT FOR THIS CREEP TO SHOW UP?
BE COOL.
MISS LANDERS PROBABLY KEPT HIM AFTER CLASS AGAIN. HE'LL BE HERE.
PSST! HERE HE COMES!
PLEASE.
PLEASE.
PLEASE.
PLEASE
PLEASE.
PLEASE.
LADIES, LADIES! I'D LOVE TO SEE YOU ALL HOME, BUT I'VE GOT TO BONE UP ON MY GEOMETRY.
MAYBE WHEN FINALS ARE... WHA--?

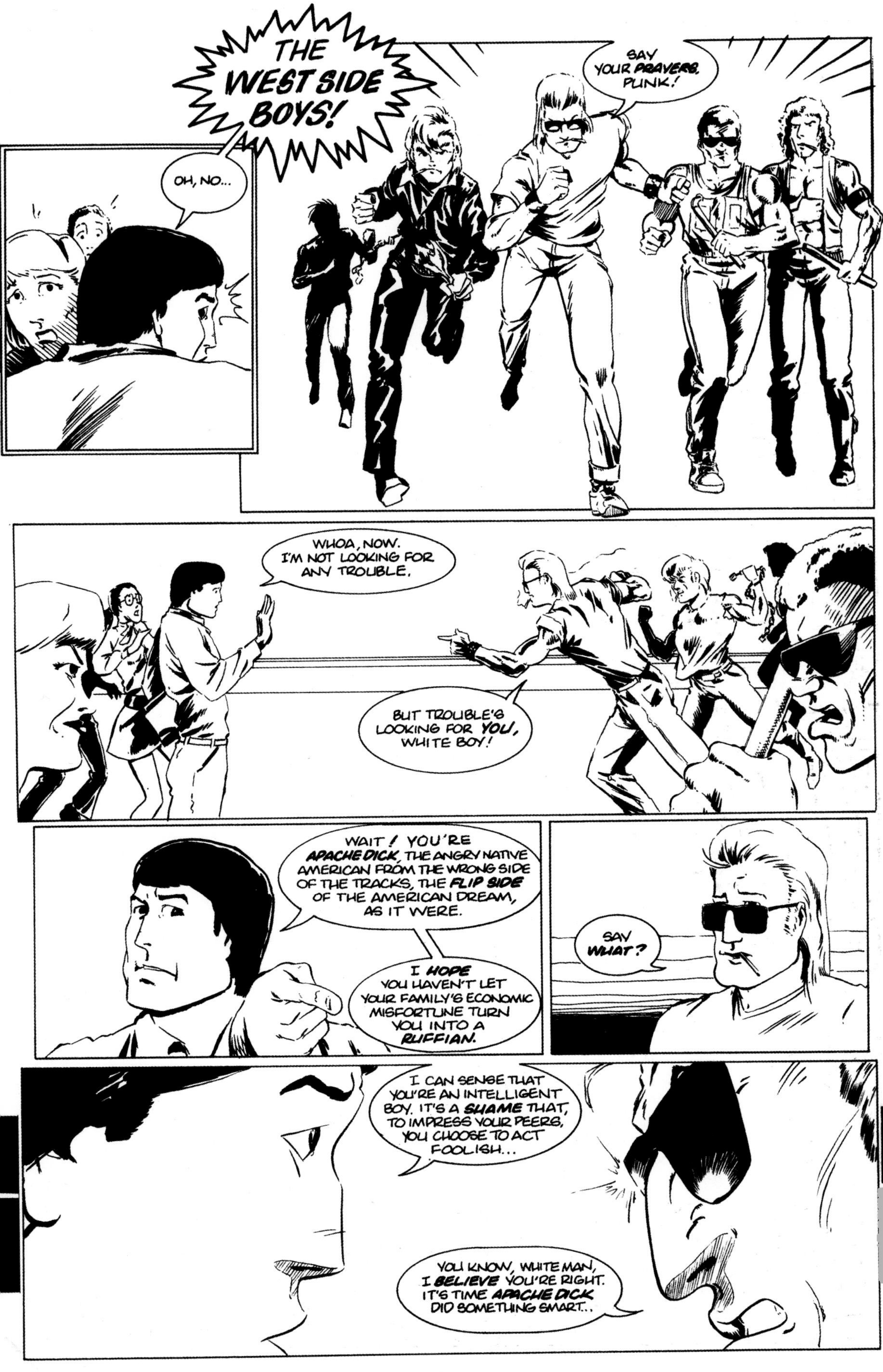
THE WEST SIDE BOYS!
OH, NO...
SAY YOUR PRAYERS, PUNK!
WHOA, NOW. I'M NOT LOOKING FOR ANY TROUBLE.
BUT TROUBLE'S LOOKING FOR YOU, WHITE BOY!
WAIT! YOU'RE APACHE DICK, THE ANGRY NATIVE AMERICAN FROM THE WRONG SIDE OF THE TRACKS, THE FLIP SIDE OF THE AMERICAN DREAM, AS IT WERE.
I HOPE YOU HAVEN'T LET YOUR FAMILY'S ECONOMIC MISFORTUNE TURN YOU INTO A RUFFIAN.
SAY WHAT?
I CAN SENSE THAT YOU'RE AN INTELLIGENT BOY. IT'S A SHAME THAT, TO IMPRESS YOUR PEERS, YOU CHOOSE TO ACT FOOLISH...
YOU KNOW, WHITE MAN, I BELIEVE YOU'RE RIGHT. IT'S TIME APACHE DICK DID SOMETHING SMART...

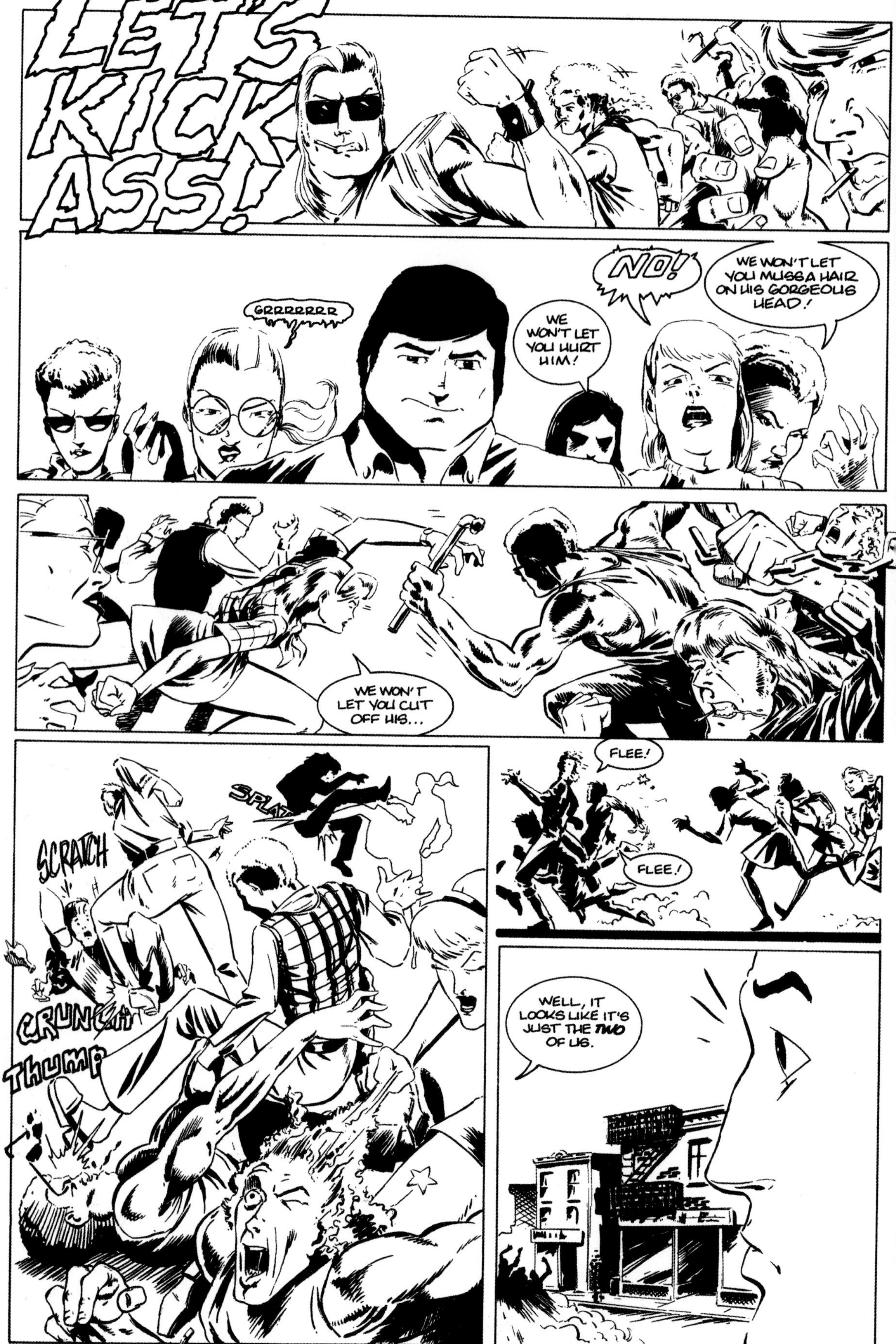
LET'S KICK ASS!
GRRRRRRR
WE WON'T LET YOU HURT HIM!
NO!
WE WON'T LET YOU MUSSA HAIR ON HIS GORGEOUS HEAD!
WE WON'T LET YOU CUT OFF HIS...
SCRATCH
SPLAT
CRUNCH
THUMP
FLEE!
FLEE!
WELL, IT LOOKS LIKE IT'S JUST THE TWO OF US.

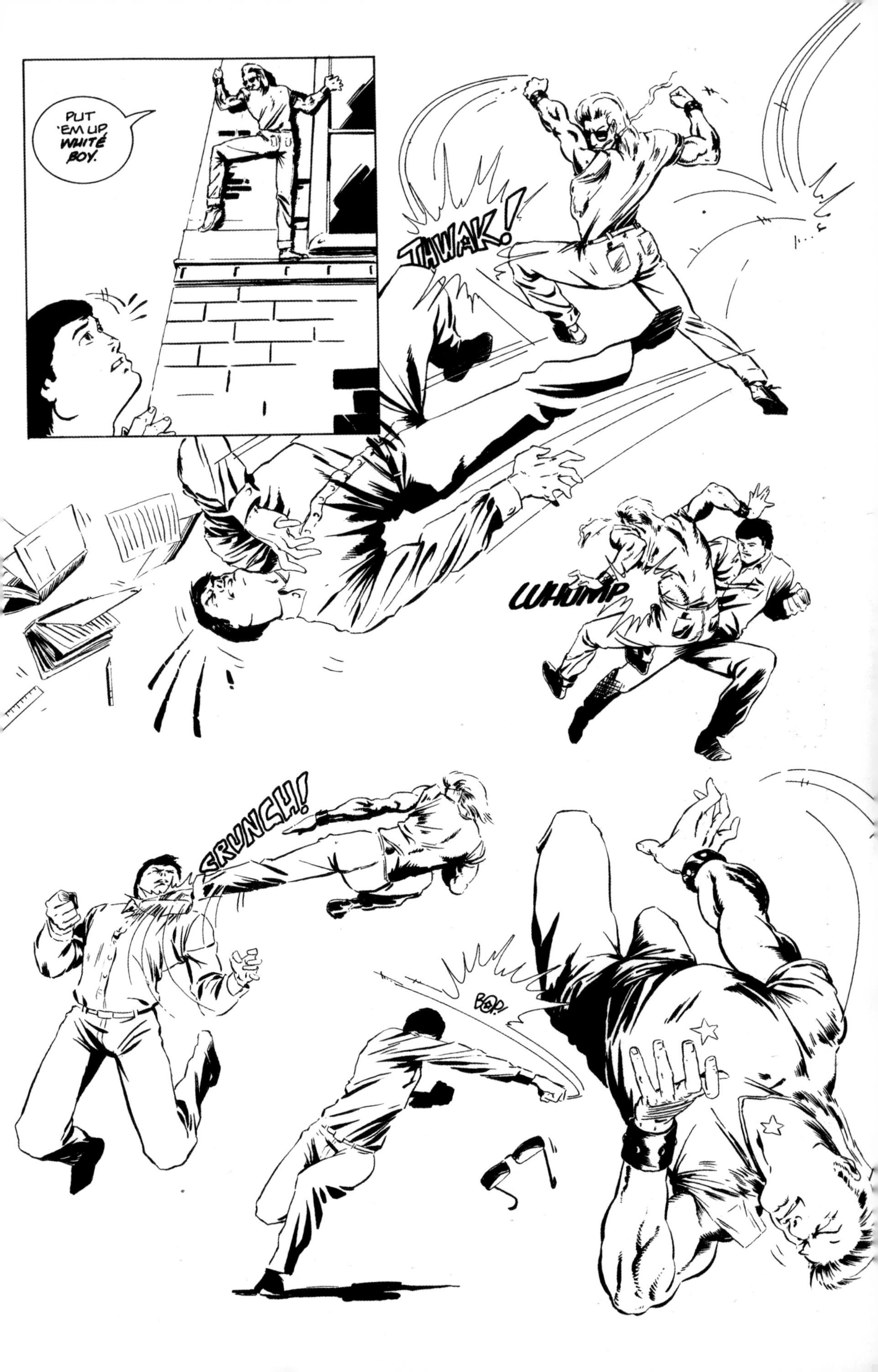
PUT 'EM UP WHITE BOY.
THWAK!
WHUMP
CRUNCH!
BOP!

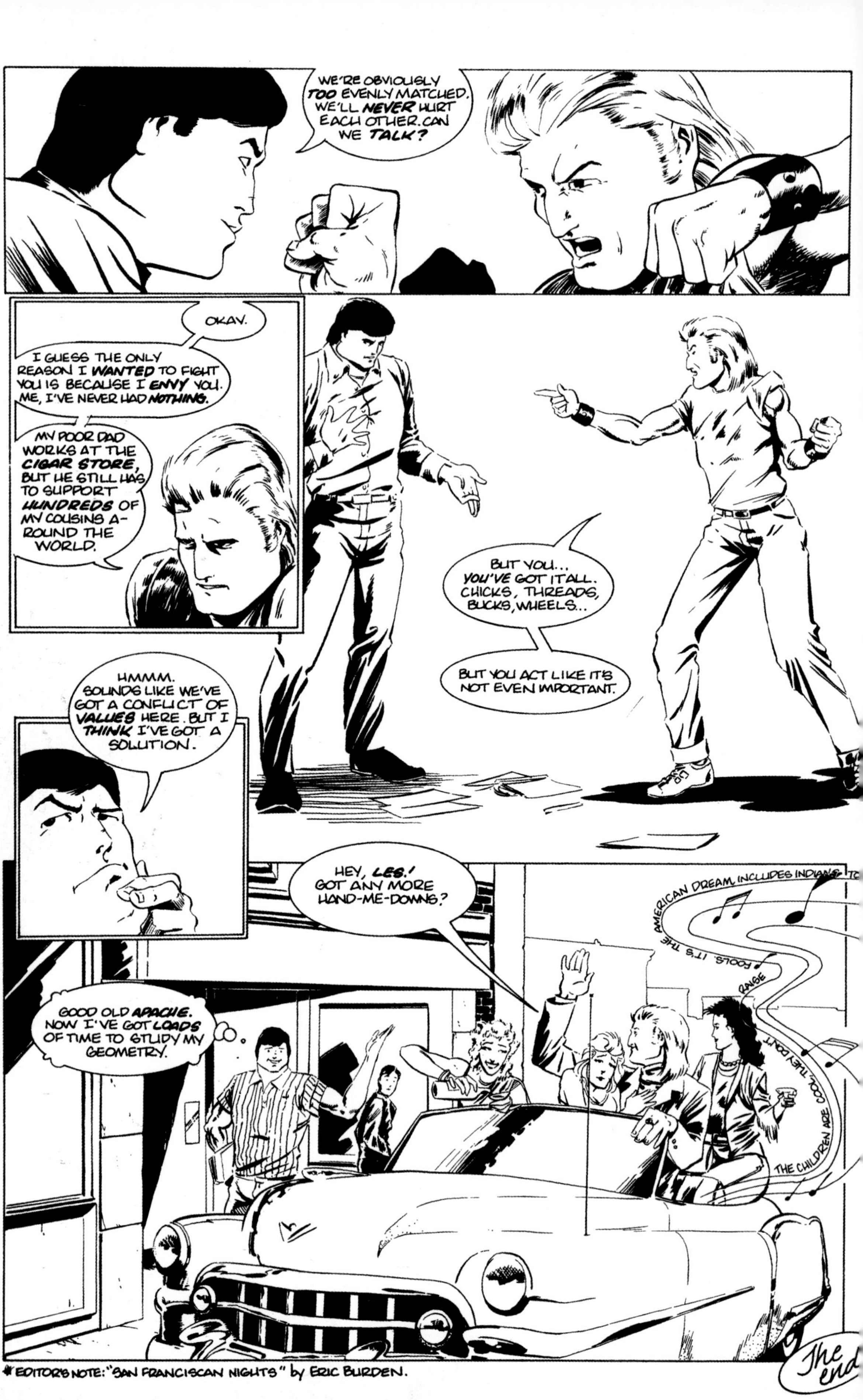
WE'RE OBVIOUSLY TOO EVENLY MATCHED. WE'LL NEVER HURT EACH OTHER. CAN WE TALK?
OKAY.
I GUESS THE ONLY REASON I WANTED TO FIGHT YOU IS BECAUSE I ENVY YOU. ME, I'VE NEVER HAD NOTHING.
MY POOR DAD WORKS AT THE CIGAR STORE, BUT HE STILL HAS TO SUPPORT HUNDREDS OF MY COUSINS A-ROUND THE WORLD.
BUT YOU... YOU'VE GOT IT ALL. CHICKS, THREADS, BUCKS, WHEELS...
BUT YOU ACT LIKE IT'S NOT EVEN IMPORTANT.
HMMM. SOUNDS LIKE WE'VE GOT A CONFLICT OF VALUES HERE. BUT I THINK I'VE GOT A SOLUTION.
HEY, LES! GOT ANY MORE HAND-ME-DOWNS?
THE AMERICAN DREAM INCLUDES INDIANS TO
FOOLS. IT'S THE
RAISE
THE CHILDREN ARE COOL, THEY DON'T
GOOD OLD APACHE. NOW I'VE GOT LOADS OF TIME TO STUDY MY GEOMETRY.
The end

*EDITOR'S NOTE: "SAN FRANCISCAN NIGHTS" by ERIC BURDEN.

THE TROUBLE WITH GIRLS™

CHAPTER 7

FEBRUARY 1988

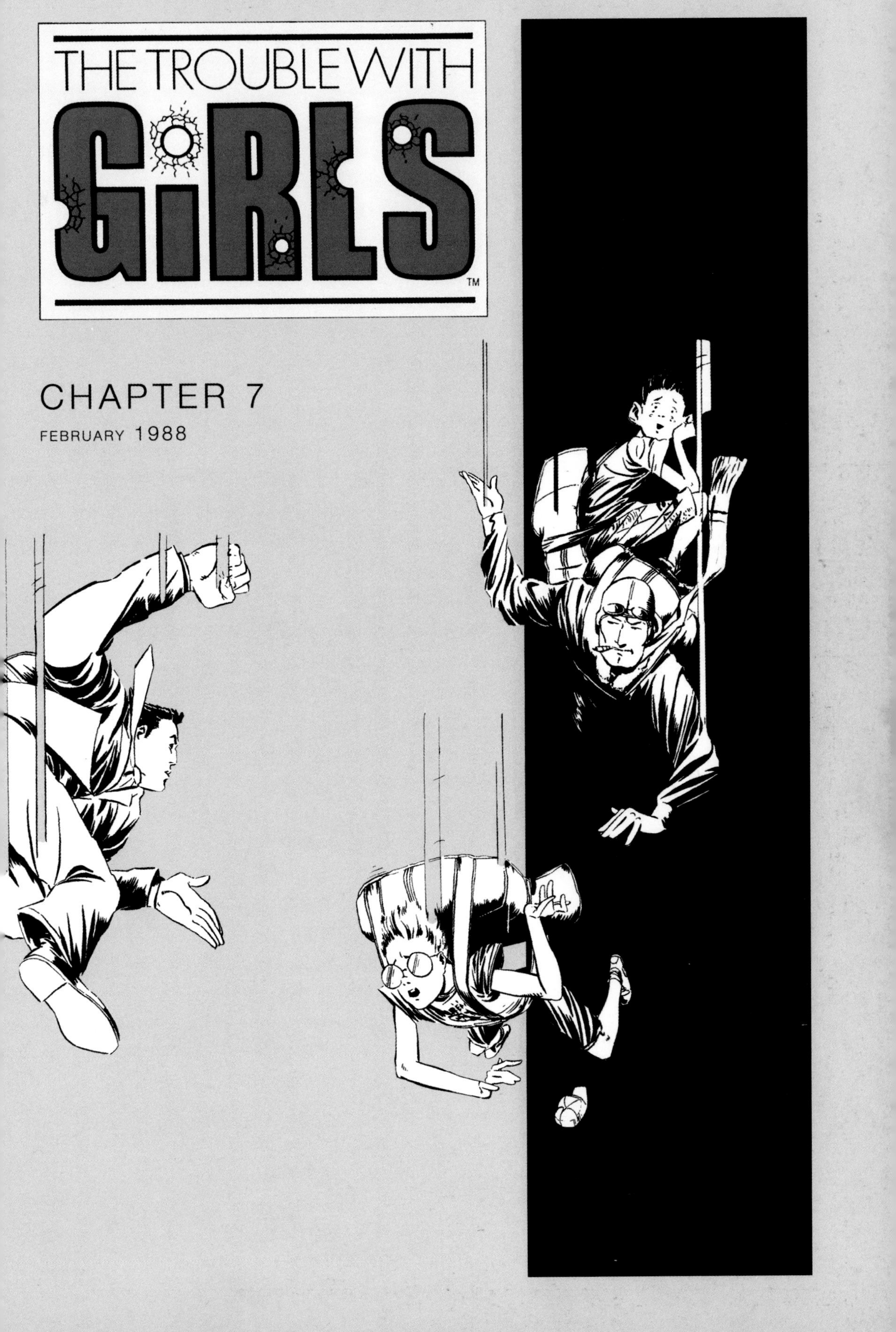

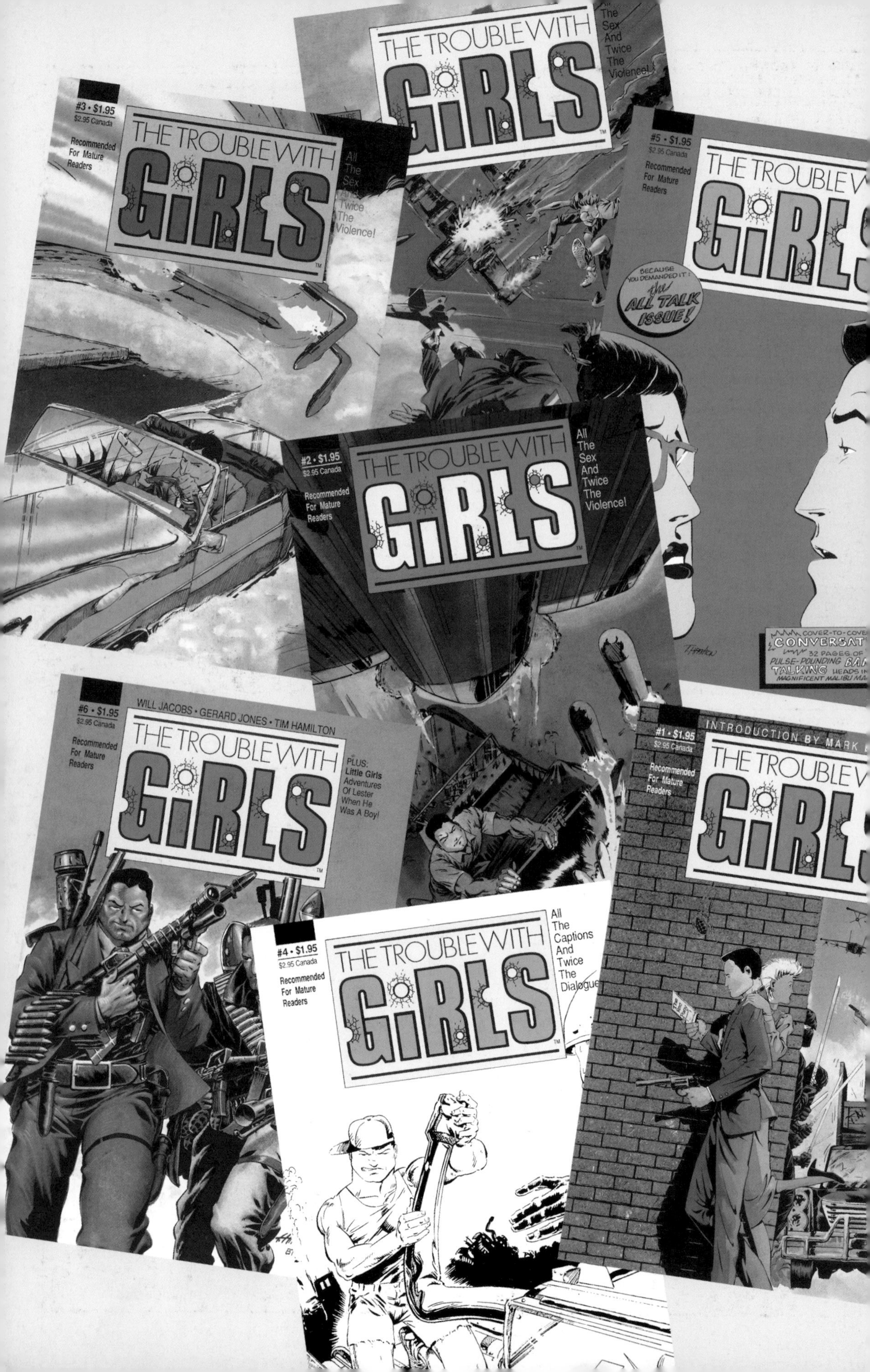
THE TROUBLE WITH GiRLS
All The Sex And Twice The Violence!
#3 • $1.95
$2.95 Canada
Recommended For Mature Readers
THE TROUBLE WITH GiRLS
All The Sex And Twice The Violence!
#5 • $1.95
$2.95 Canada
Recommended For Mature Readers
THE TROUBLE WI
GiRLS
BECAUSE YOU DEMANDED IT: the ALL TALK ISSUE!
COVER-TO-COVER CONVERSAT
32 PAGES OF PULSE-POUNDING BAN
TALKING HEADS IN
MAGNIFICENT MALIBU MA
#2 • $1.95
$2.95 Canada
Recommended For Mature Readers
THE TROUBLE WITH GiRLS
All The Sex And Twice The Violence!
#6 • $1.95
$2.95 Canada
Recommended For Mature Readers
WILL JACOBS • GERARD JONES • TIM HAMILTON
THE TROUBLE WITH GiRLS
PLUS: Little Girls Adventures Of Lester When He Was A Boy!
#1 • $1.95
$2.95 Canada
Recommended For Mature Readers
INTRODUCTION BY MARK
THE TROUBLE W
GiRLS
#4 • $1.95
$2.95 Canada
Recommended For Mature Readers
THE TROUBLE WITH GiRLS
All The Captions And Twice The Dialogue

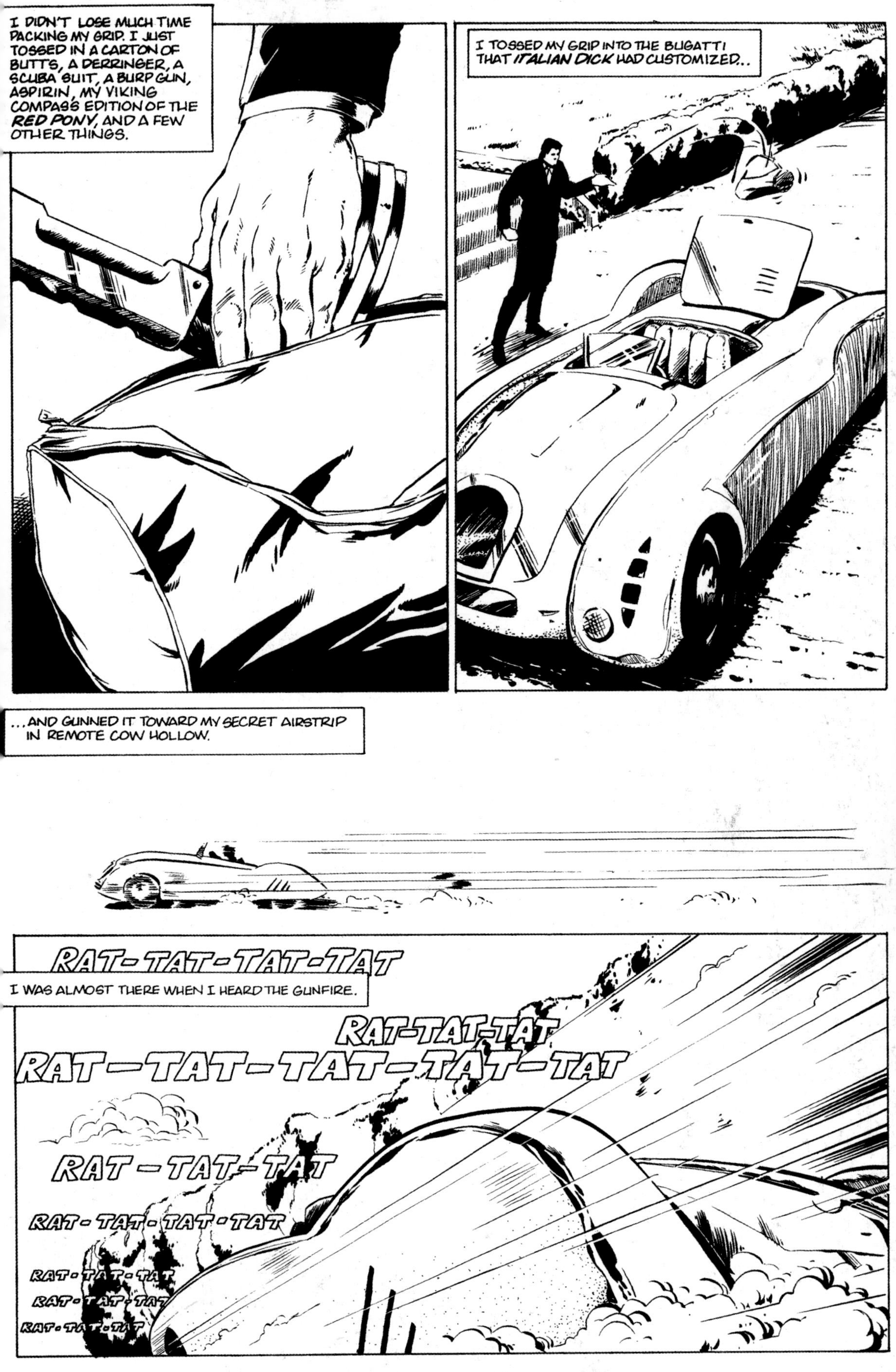
I DIDN'T LOSE MUCH TIME PACKING MY GRIP. I JUST TOSSED IN A CARTON OF BUTTS, A DERRINGER, A SCUBA SUIT, A BURP GUN, ASPIRIN, MY VIKING COMPASS EDITION OF THE RED PONY, AND A FEW OTHER THINGS.
I TOSSED MY GRIP INTO THE BUGATTI THAT ITALIAN DICK HAD CUSTOMIZED..
...AND GUNNED IT TOWARD MY SECRET AIRSTRIP IN REMOTE COW HOLLOW.
RAT-TAT-TAT-TAT
I WAS ALMOST THERE WHEN I HEARD THE GUNFIRE.
RAT-TAT-TAT
RAT-TAT-TAT-TAT-TAT
RAT-TAT-TAT
RAT-TAT-TAT-TAT
RAT-TAT-TAT
RAT-TAT-TAT
RAT-TAT-TAT

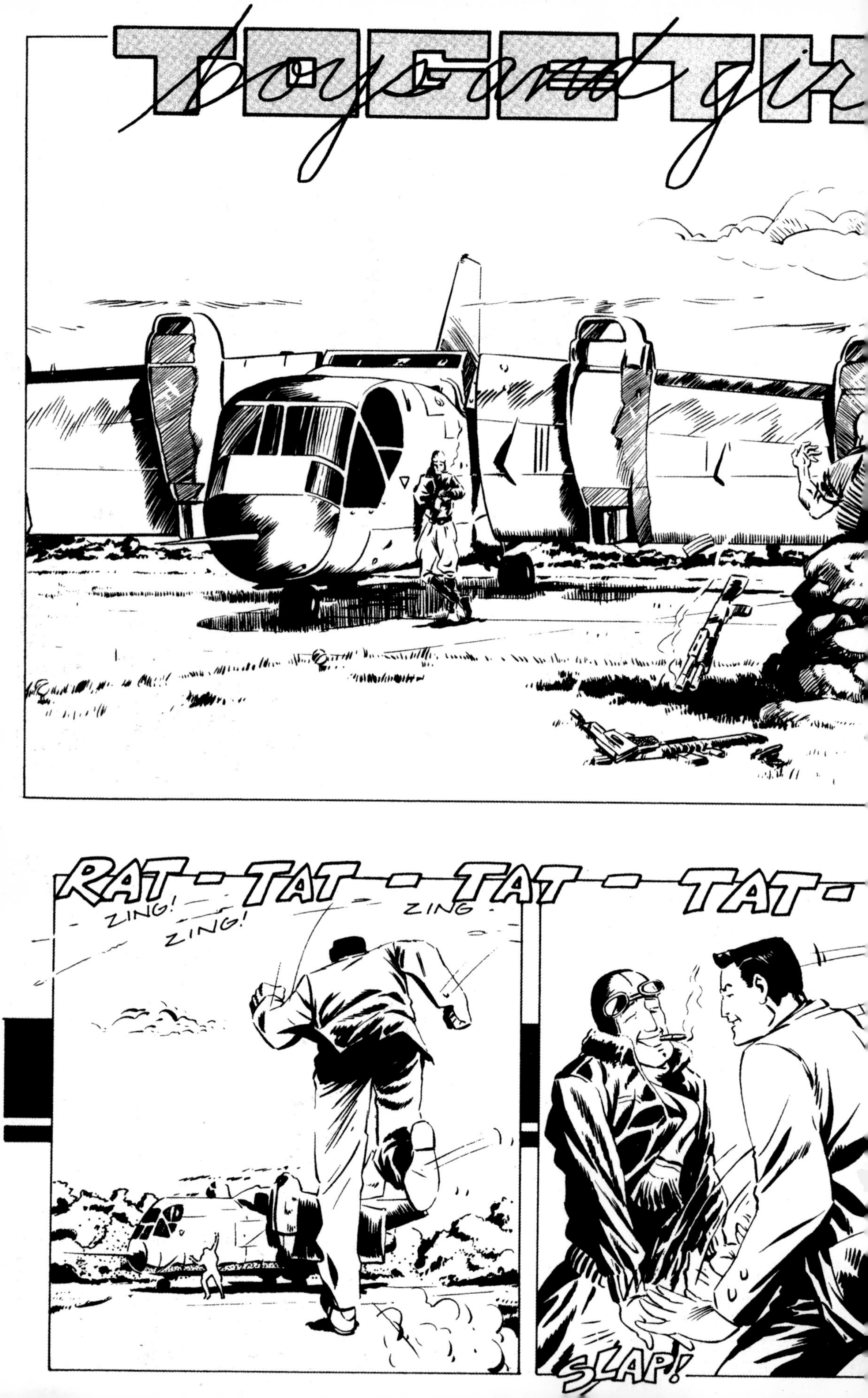
RAT - TAT - TAT - TAT -
ZING!
ZING!
ZING
SLAP!

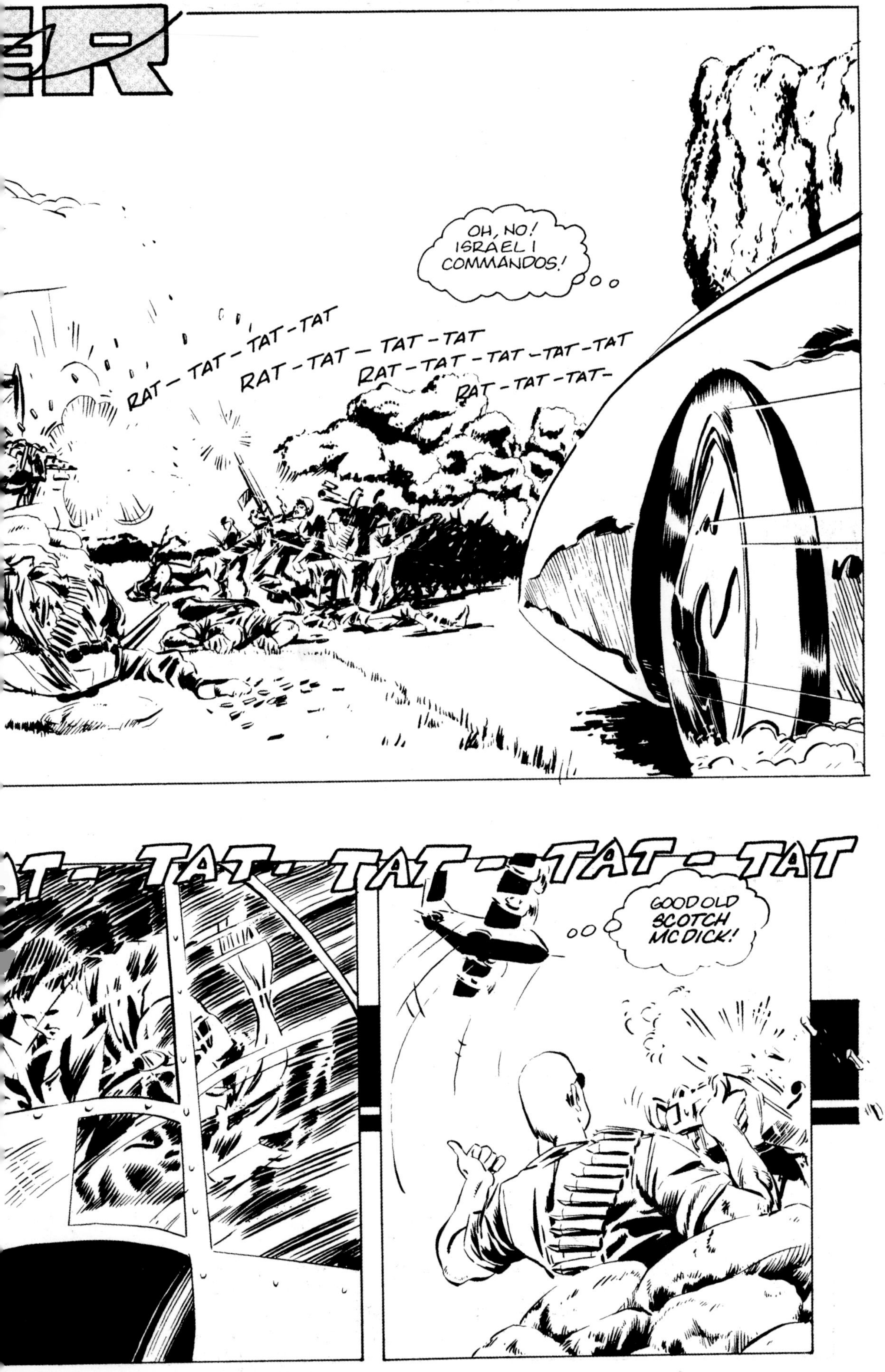
OH, NO! ISRAELI COMMANDOS!
RAT-TAT-TAT-TAT
RAT-TAT-TAT-TAT
RAT-TAT-TAT-TAT-TAT
RAT-TAT-TAT-
TAT-TAT-TAT-TAT
GOOD OLD SCOTCH MC DICK!

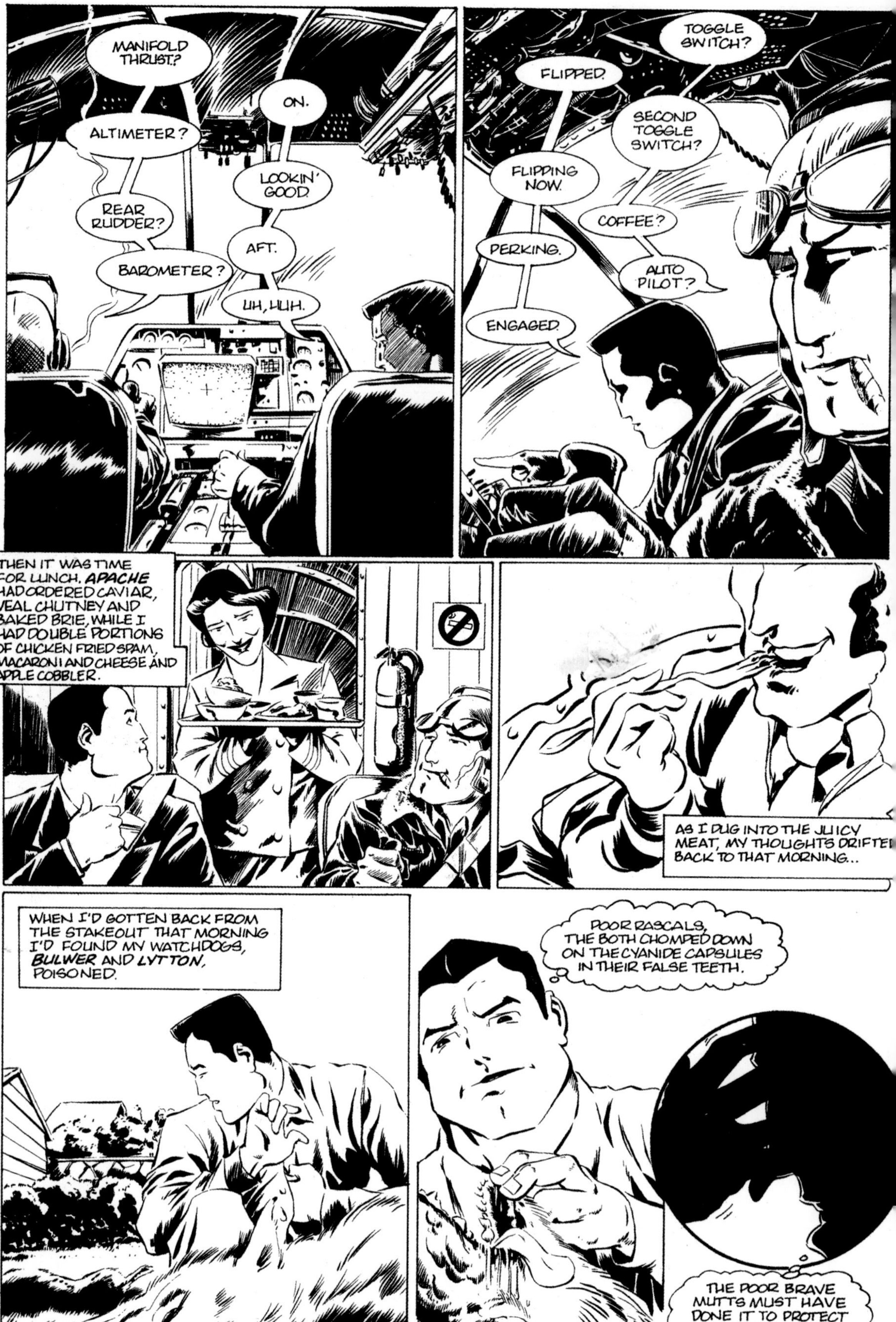
MANIFOLD THRUST?
ALTIMETER?
ON.
REAR RUDDER?
LOOKIN' GOOD.
BAROMETER?
AFT.
UH, HUH.
TOGGLE SWITCH?
FLIPPED.
SECOND TOGGLE SWITCH?
FLIPPING NOW.
COFFEE?
PERKING.
AUTO PILOT?
ENGAGED.
THEN IT WAS TIME FOR LUNCH. APACHE HAD ORDERED CAVIAR, VEAL CHUTNEY AND BAKED BRIE, WHILE I HAD DOUBLE PORTIONS OF CHICKEN FRIED SPAM, MACARONI AND CHEESE AND APPLE COBBLER.
AS I DUG INTO THE JUICY MEAT, MY THOUGHTS DRIFTED BACK TO THAT MORNING...
WHEN I'D GOTTEN BACK FROM THE STAKEOUT THAT MORNING I'D FOUND MY WATCHDOGS, BULWER AND LYTTON, POISONED.
POOR RASCALS, THE BOTH CHOMPED DOWN ON THE CYANIDE CAPSULES IN THEIR FALSE TEETH.
THE POOR BRAVE MUTTS MUST HAVE DONE IT TO PROTECT ME.

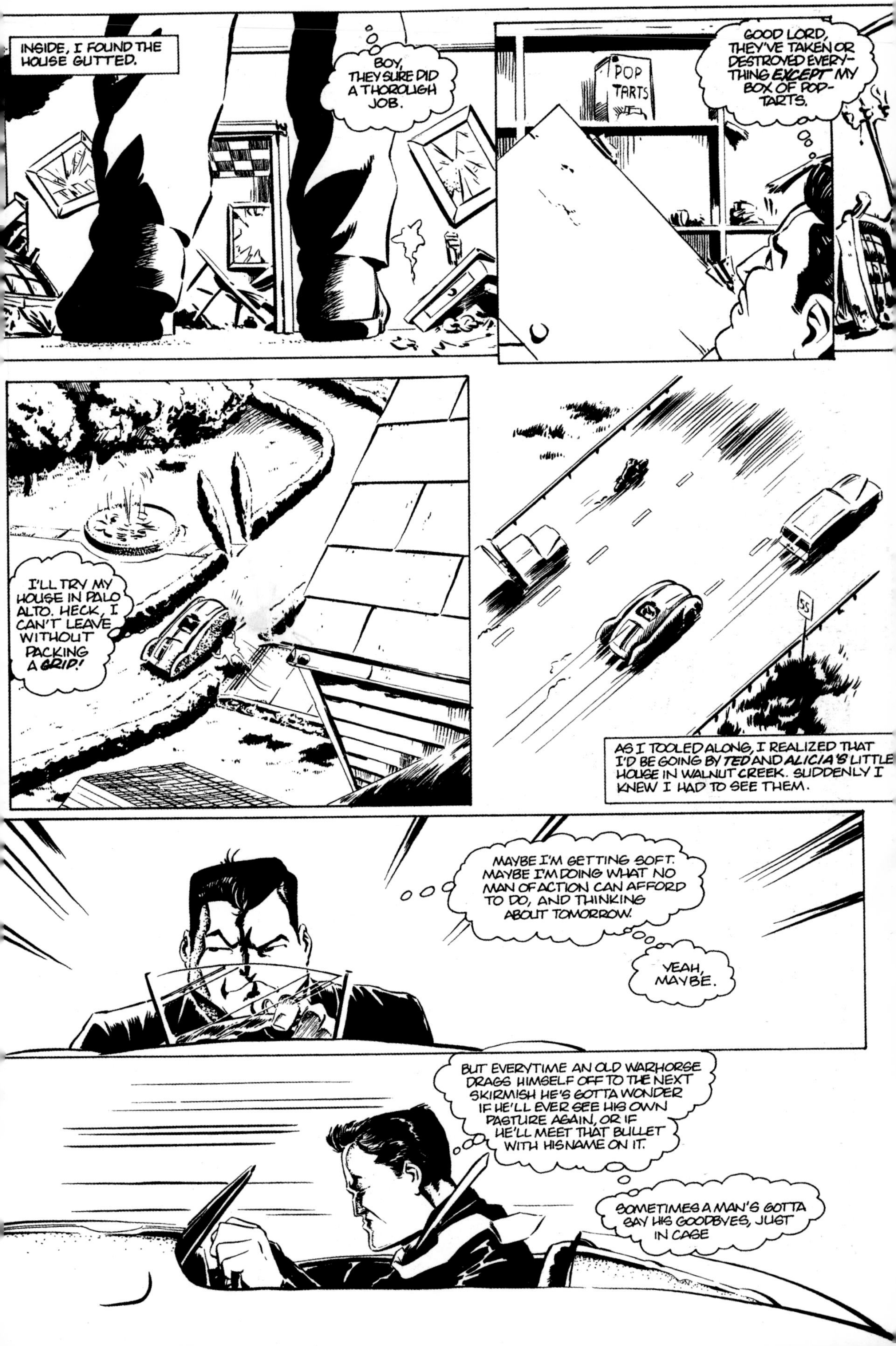
INSIDE, I FOUND THE HOUSE GUTTED.
BOY, THEY SURE DID A THOROUGH JOB.
POP TARTS
GOOD LORD, THEY'VE TAKEN OR DESTROYED EVERYTHING *EXCEPT* MY BOX OF POP-TARTS.
I'LL TRY MY HOUSE IN PALO ALTO. HECK, I CAN'T LEAVE WITHOUT PACKING A *GRID!*
55
AS I TOOLED ALONG, I REALIZED THAT I'D BE GOING BY *TED* AND *ALICIA'S* LITTLE HOUSE IN WALNUT CREEK. SUDDENLY I KNEW I HAD TO SEE THEM.
MAYBE I'M GETTING SOFT. MAYBE I'M DOING WHAT NO MAN OF ACTION CAN AFFORD TO DO, AND THINKING ABOUT TOMORROW.
YEAH, MAYBE.
BUT EVERYTIME AN OLD WARHORSE DRAGS HIMSELF OFF TO THE NEXT SKIRMISH HE'S GOTTA WONDER IF HE'LL EVER SEE HIS OWN PASTURE AGAIN, OR IF HE'LL MEET THAT BULLET WITH HIS NAME ON IT.
SOMETIMES A MAN'S GOTTA SAY HIS GOODBYES, JUST IN CASE

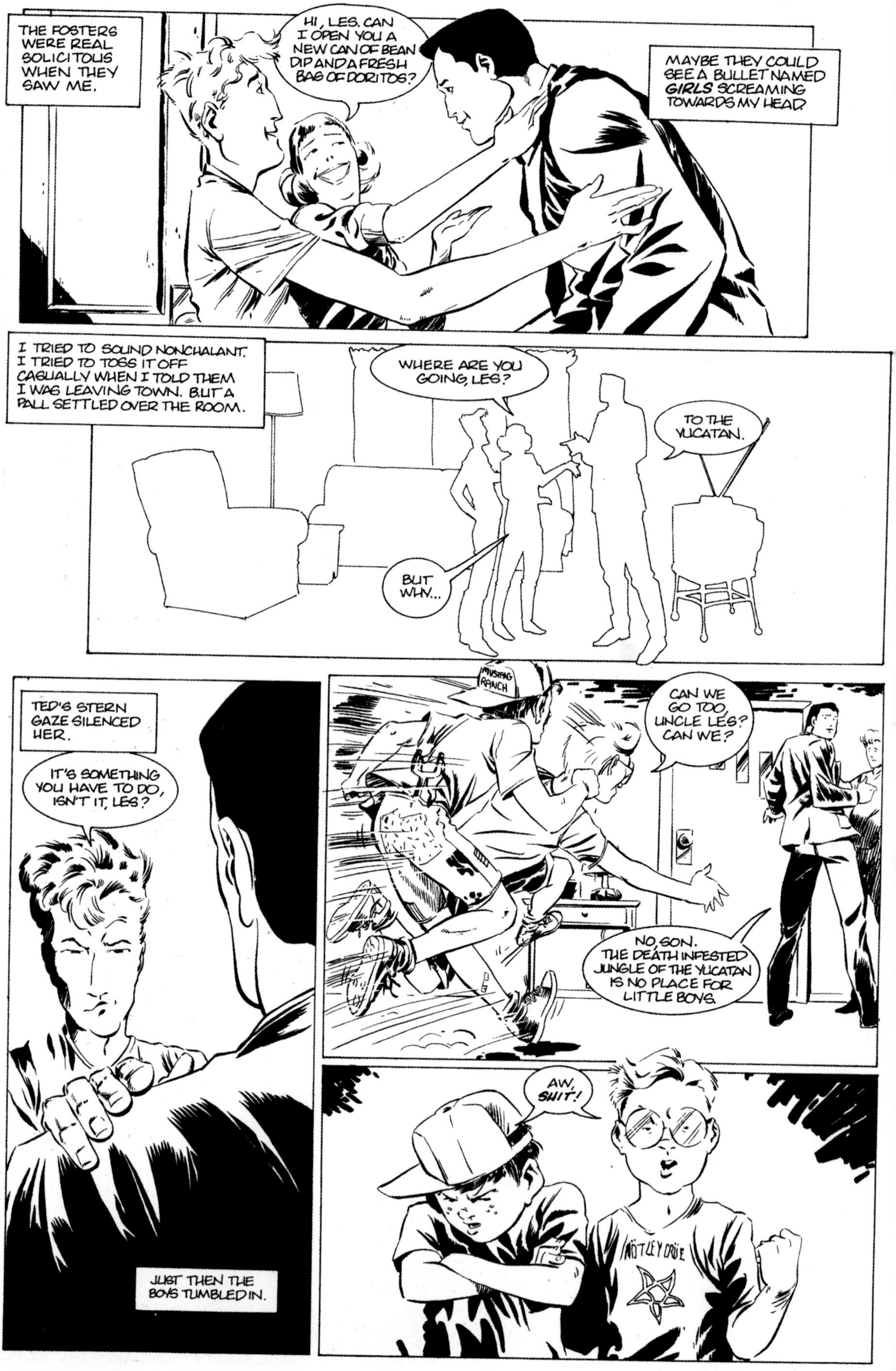
THE FOSTERS WERE REAL SOLICITOUS WHEN THEY SAW ME.
HI, LES. CAN I OPEN YOU A NEW CAN OF BEAN DIP AND A FRESH BAG OF DORITOS?
MAYBE THEY COULD SEE A BULLET NAMED GIRLS SCREAMING TOWARDS MY HEAD.
I TRIED TO SOUND NONCHALANT. I TRIED TO TOSS IT OFF CASUALLY WHEN I TOLD THEM I WAS LEAVING TOWN. BUT A PALL SETTLED OVER THE ROOM.
WHERE ARE YOU GOING, LES?
TO THE YUCATAN.
BUT WHY...
TED'S STERN GAZE SILENCED HER.
IT'S SOMETHING YOU HAVE TO DO, ISN'T IT, LES?
JUST THEN THE BOYS TUMBLED IN.
MUSTANG RANCH
CAN WE GO TOO, UNCLE LES? CAN WE?
NO, SON. THE DEATH INFESTED JUNGLE OF THE YUCATAN IS NO PLACE FOR LITTLE BOYS.
AW, SHIT!
MÖTLEY CRÜE

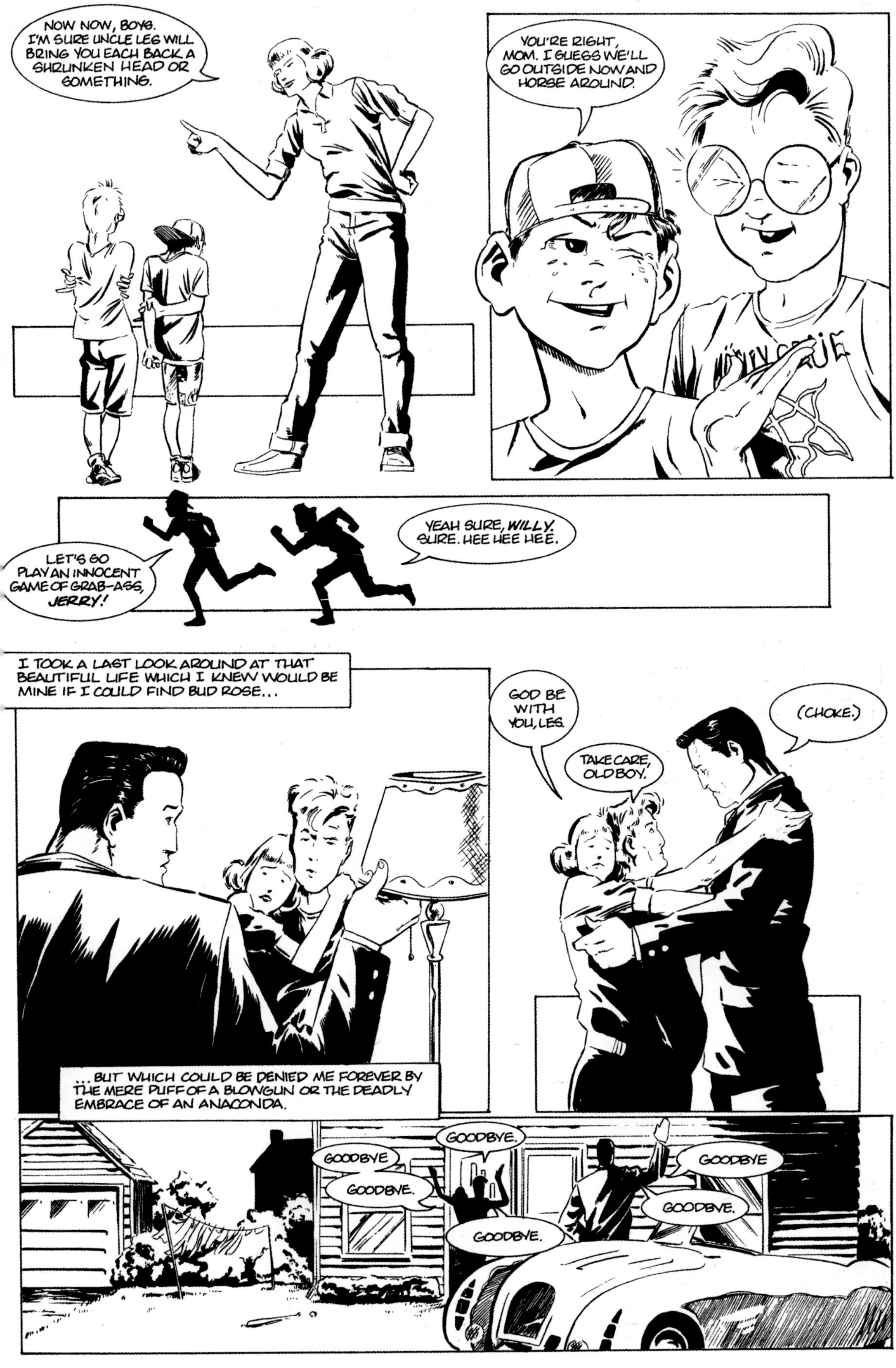
NOW NOW, BOYS. I'M SURE UNCLE LES WILL BRING YOU EACH BACK A SHRUNKEN HEAD OR SOMETHING.
YOU'RE RIGHT, MOM. I GUESS WE'LL GO OUTSIDE NOW AND HORSE AROUND.
LET'S GO PLAY AN INNOCENT GAME OF GRAB-ASS, JERRY!
YEAH SURE, WILLY. SURE. HEE HEE HEE.
I TOOK A LAST LOOK AROUND AT THAT BEAUTIFUL LIFE WHICH I KNEW WOULD BE MINE IF I COULD FIND BUD ROSE...
...BUT WHICH COULD BE DENIED ME FOREVER BY THE MERE PUFF OF A BLOWGUN OR THE DEADLY EMBRACE OF AN ANACONDA.
GOD BE WITH YOU, LES.
TAKE CARE, OLD BOY.
(CHOKE.)
GOODBYE
GOODBYE.
GOODBYE.
GOODBYE.
GOODBYE
GOODBYE.

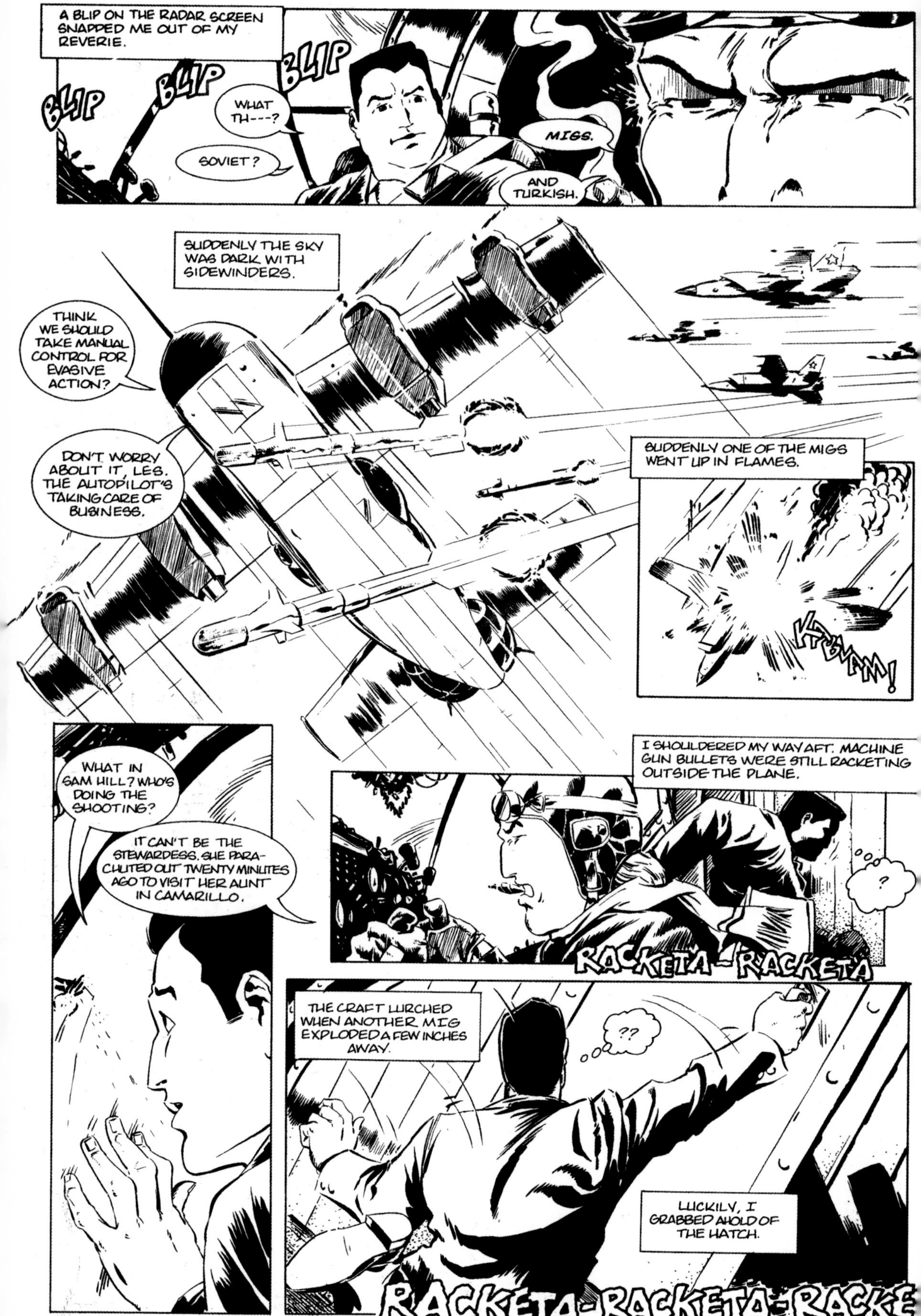
A BLIP ON THE RADAR SCREEN SNAPPED ME OUT OF MY REVERIE.
BLIP
BLIP
BLIP
WHAT TH---?
SOVIET?
MIGS.
AND TURKISH.
SUDDENLY THE SKY WAS DARK WITH SIDEWINDERS.
THINK WE SHOULD TAKE MANUAL CONTROL FOR EVASIVE ACTION?
DON'T WORRY ABOUT IT, LES. THE AUTOPILOT'S TAKING CARE OF BUSINESS.
SUDDENLY ONE OF THE MIGS WENT UP IN FLAMES.
KABLAM!
WHAT IN SAM HILL? WHO'S DOING THE SHOOTING?
IT CAN'T BE THE STEWARDESS. SHE PARACHUTED OUT TWENTY MINUTES AGO TO VISIT HER AUNT IN CAMARILLO.
I SHOULDERED MY WAY AFT. MACHINE GUN BULLETS WERE STILL RACKETING OUTSIDE THE PLANE.
?
RACKETA-RACKETA
THE CRAFT LURCHED WHEN ANOTHER MIG EXPLODED A FEW INCHES AWAY.
??
LUCKILY, I GRABBED AHOLD OF THE HATCH.
RACKETA-RACKETA-RACKE

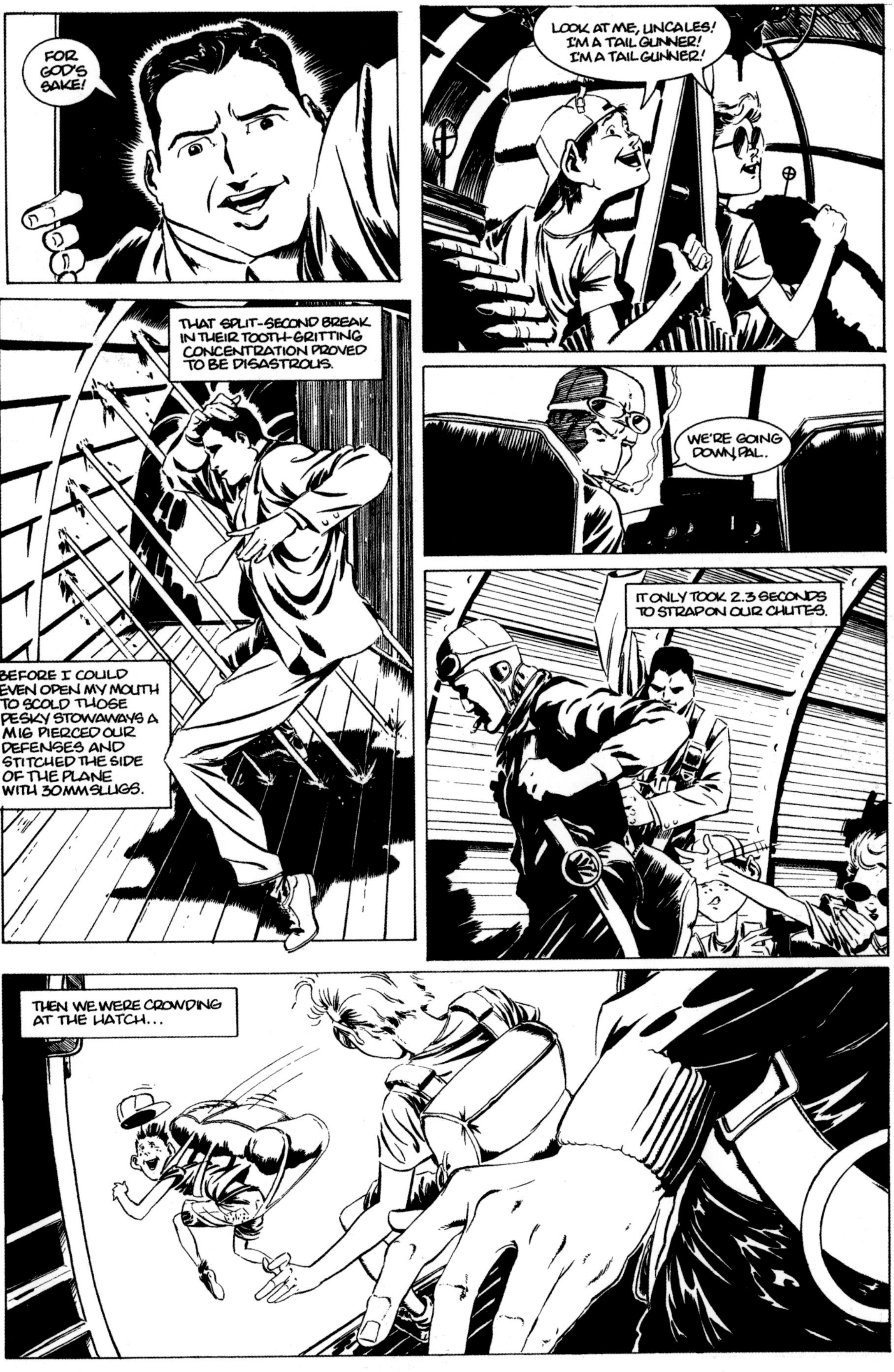

FOR GOD'S SAKE!
LOOK AT ME, UNCALES! I'M A TAIL GUNNER! I'M A TAIL GUNNER!
THAT SPLIT-SECOND BREAK IN THEIR TOOTH-GRITTING CONCENTRATION PROVED TO BE DISASTROUS.
BEFORE I COULD EVEN OPEN MY MOUTH TO SCOLD THOSE PESKY STOWAWAYS A MIG PIERCED OUR DEFENSES AND STITCHED THE SIDE OF THE PLANE WITH 30MM SLUGS.
WE'RE GOING DOWN, PAL.
IT ONLY TOOK 2.3 SECONDS TO STRAP ON OUR CHUTES.
THEN WE WERE CROWDING AT THE HATCH...

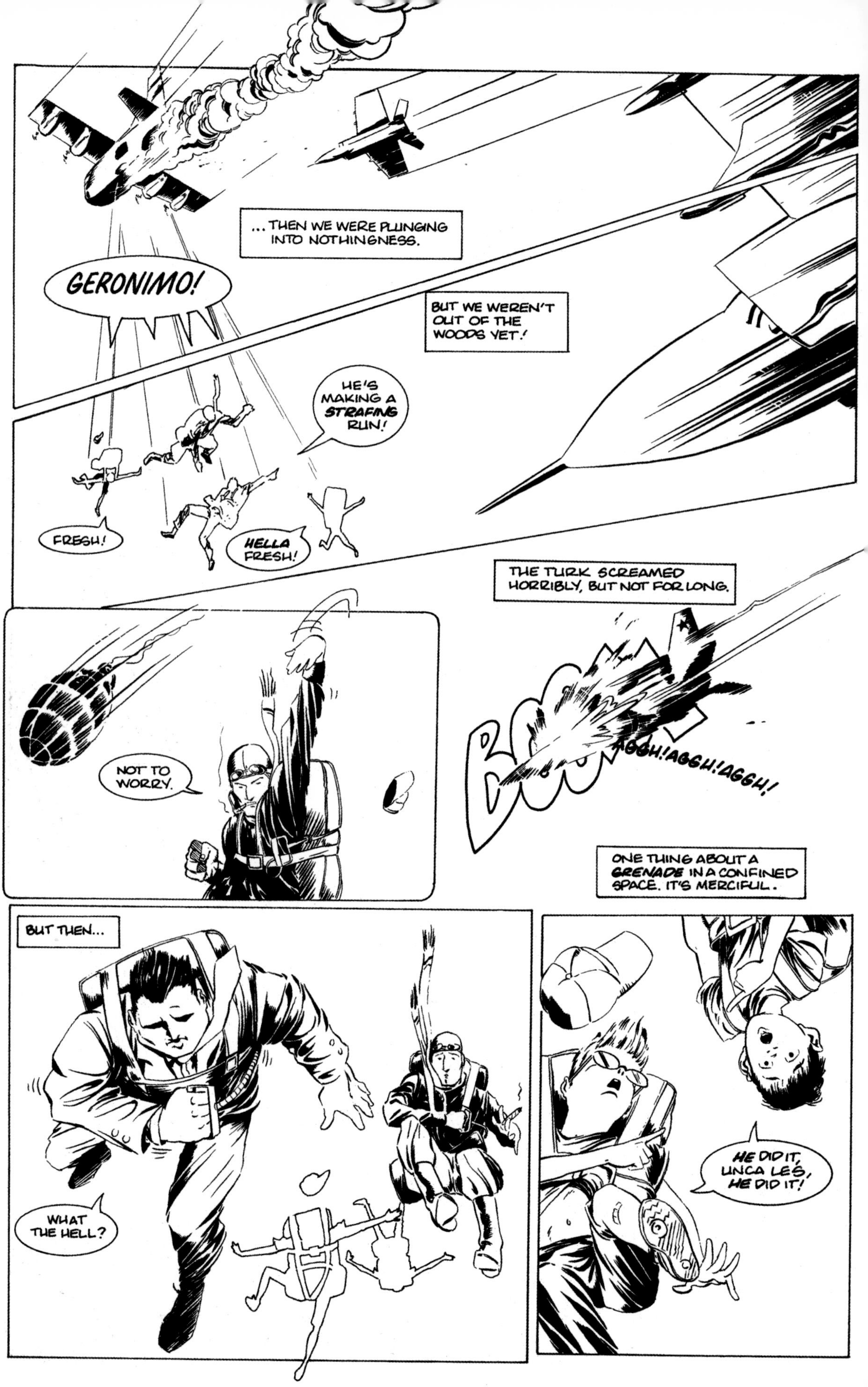
...THEN WE WERE PLUNGING INTO NOTHINGNESS.
GERONIMO!
BUT WE WEREN'T OUT OF THE WOODS YET!
HE'S MAKING A STRAFING RUN!
FRESH!
HELLA FRESH!
NOT TO WORRY.
THE TURK SCREAMED HORRIBLY, BUT NOT FOR LONG.
BOOM!
AGGH!AGGH!AGGH!
ONE THING ABOUT A GRENADE IN A CONFINED SPACE. IT'S MERCIFUL.
BUT THEN...
WHAT THE HELL?
HE DID IT, UNCA LES, HE DID IT!

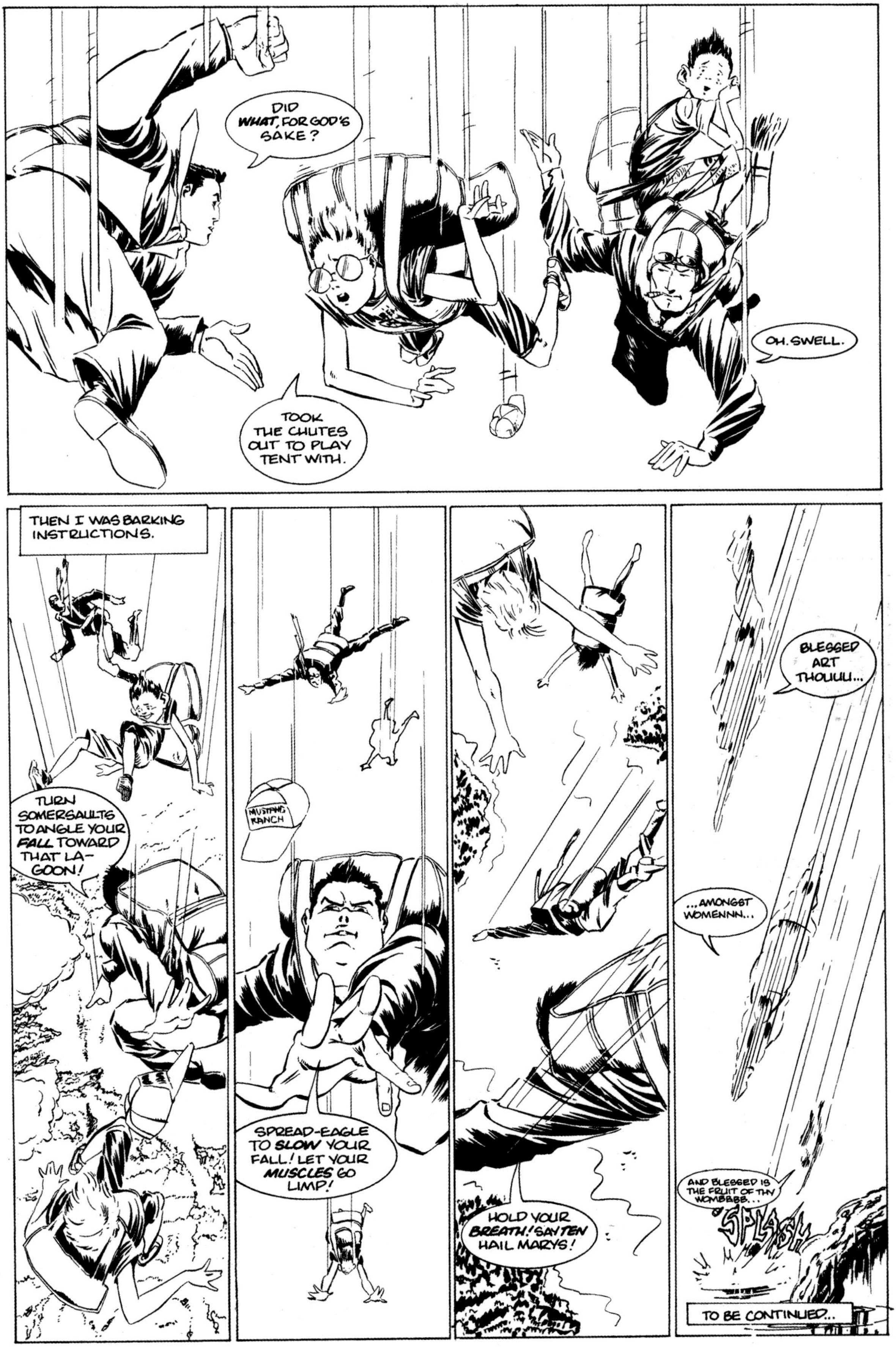
DID WHAT, FOR GOD'S SAKE?
TOOK THE CHUTES OUT TO PLAY TENT WITH.
OH. SWELL.
THEN I WAS BARKING INSTRUCTIONS.
TURN SOMERSAULTS TO ANGLE YOUR FALL TOWARD THAT LA-GOON!
MUSTANG RANCH
SPREAD-EAGLE TO SLOW YOUR FALL! LET YOUR MUSCLES GO LIMP!
HOLD YOUR BREATH! SAY TEN HAIL MARYS!
BLESSED ART THOUUU...
...AMONGST WOMENNN...
AND BLESSED IS THE FRUIT OF THY WOMBBBB...
SPLASH
TO BE CONTINUED...

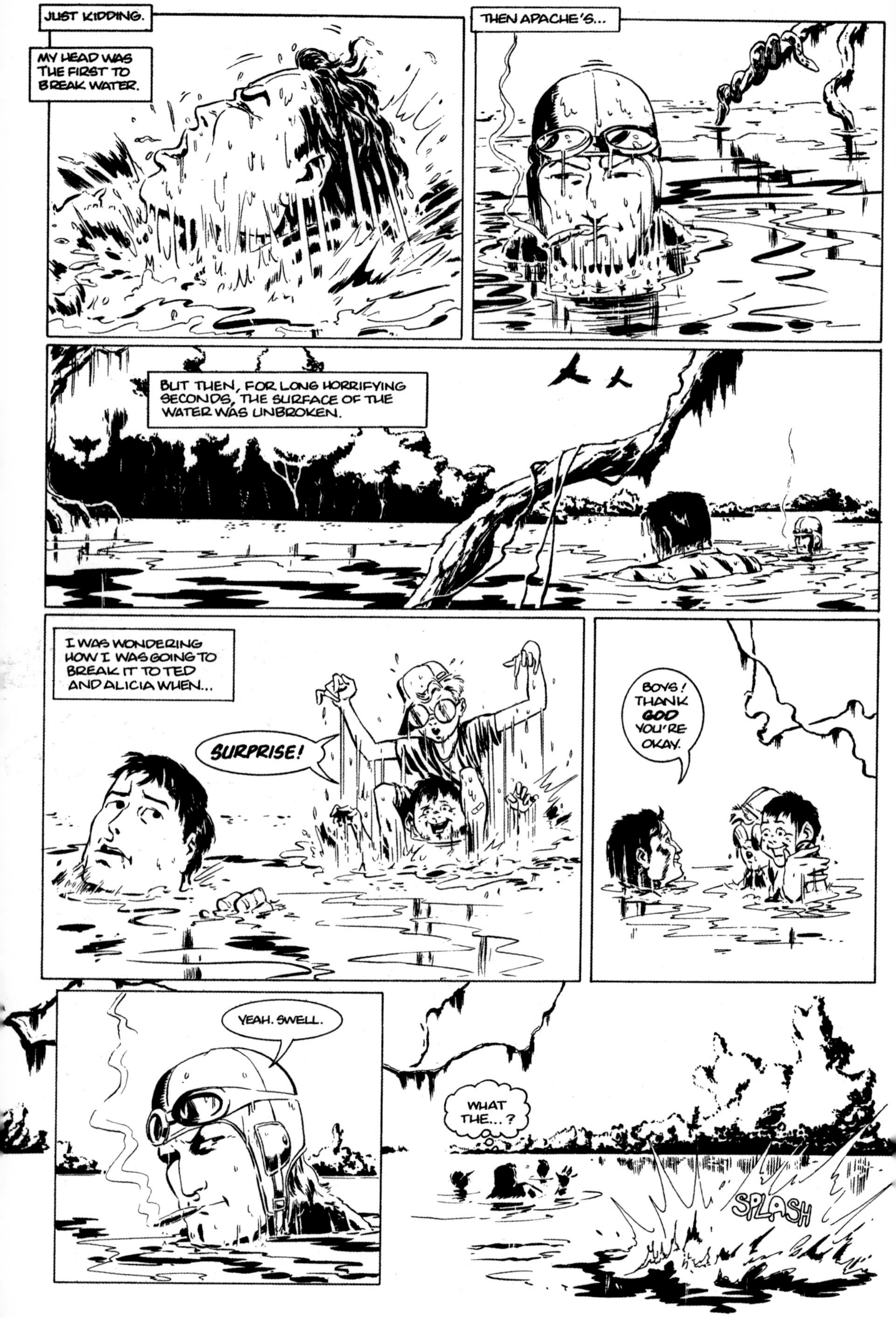
JUST KIDDING.
MY HEAD WAS THE FIRST TO BREAK WATER.
THEN APACHE'S...
BUT THEN, FOR LONG HORRIFYING SECONDS, THE SURFACE OF THE WATER WAS UNBROKEN.
I WAS WONDERING HOW I WAS GOING TO BREAK IT TO TED AND ALICIA WHEN...
SURPRISE!
BOYS! THANK GOD YOU'RE OKAY.
YEAH. SWELL.
WHAT THE...?
SPLASH

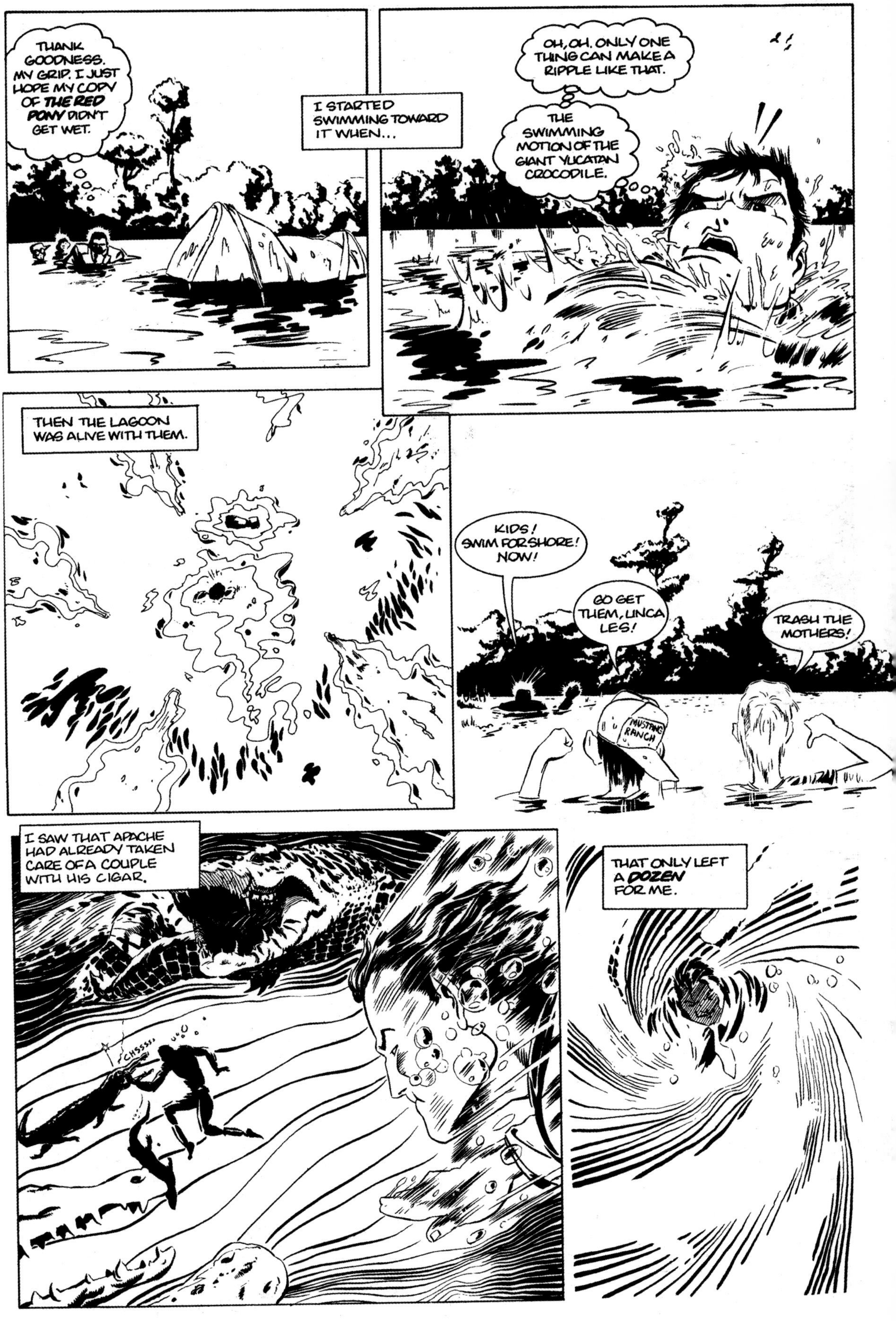
THANK GOODNESS. MY GRIP. I JUST HOPE MY COPY OF THE RED PONY DIDN'T GET WET.
I STARTED SWIMMING TOWARD IT WHEN...
OH, OH. ONLY ONE THING CAN MAKE A RIPPLE LIKE THAT.
THE SWIMMING MOTION OF THE GIANT YUCATAN CROCODILE.
THEN THE LAGOON WAS ALIVE WITH THEM.
KIDS! SWIM FOR SHORE! NOW!
GO GET THEM, LINCA LES!
TRASH THE MOTHERS!
MUSTANG RANCH
I SAW THAT APACHE HAD ALREADY TAKEN CARE OF A COUPLE WITH HIS CIGAR.
CHSSSSS
THAT ONLY LEFT A DOZEN FOR ME.

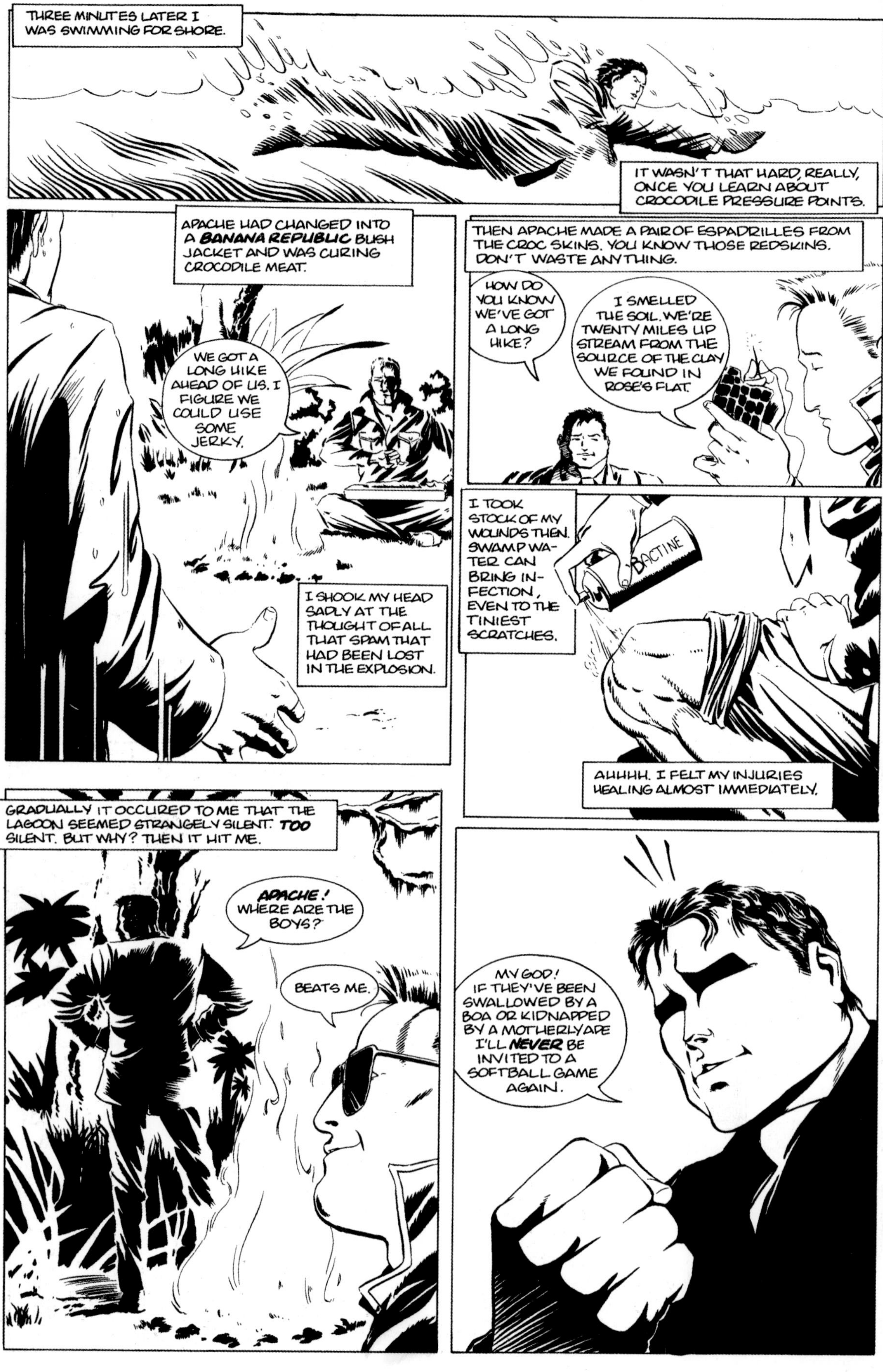
THREE MINUTES LATER I WAS SWIMMING FOR SHORE.
IT WASN'T THAT HARD, REALLY, ONCE YOU LEARN ABOUT CROCODILE PRESSURE POINTS.
APACHE HAD CHANGED INTO A BANANA REPUBLIC BUSH JACKET AND WAS CURING CROCODILE MEAT.
WE GOT A LONG HIKE AHEAD OF US. I FIGURE WE COULD USE SOME JERKY.
I SHOOK MY HEAD SADLY AT THE THOUGHT OF ALL THAT SPAM THAT HAD BEEN LOST IN THE EXPLOSION.
THEN APACHE MADE A PAIR OF ESPADRILLES FROM THE CROC SKINS. YOU KNOW THOSE REDSKINS. DON'T WASTE ANYTHING.
HOW DO YOU KNOW WE'VE GOT A LONG HIKE?
I SMELLED THE SOIL. WE'RE TWENTY MILES UP STREAM FROM THE SOURCE OF THE CLAY WE FOUND IN ROSE'S FLAT.
I TOOK STOCK OF MY WOUNDS THEN. SWAMP WATER CAN BRING INFECTION, EVEN TO THE TINIEST SCRATCHES.
BACTINE
AHHHH. I FELT MY INJURIES HEALING ALMOST IMMEDIATELY.
GRADUALLY IT OCCURED TO ME THAT THE LAGOON SEEMED STRANGELY SILENT. TOO SILENT. BUT WHY? THEN IT HIT ME.
APACHE! WHERE ARE THE BOYS?
BEATS ME.
MY GOD! IF THEY'VE BEEN SWALLOWED BY A BOA OR KIDNAPPED BY A MOTHERLY APE I'LL NEVER BE INVITED TO A SOFTBALL GAME AGAIN.

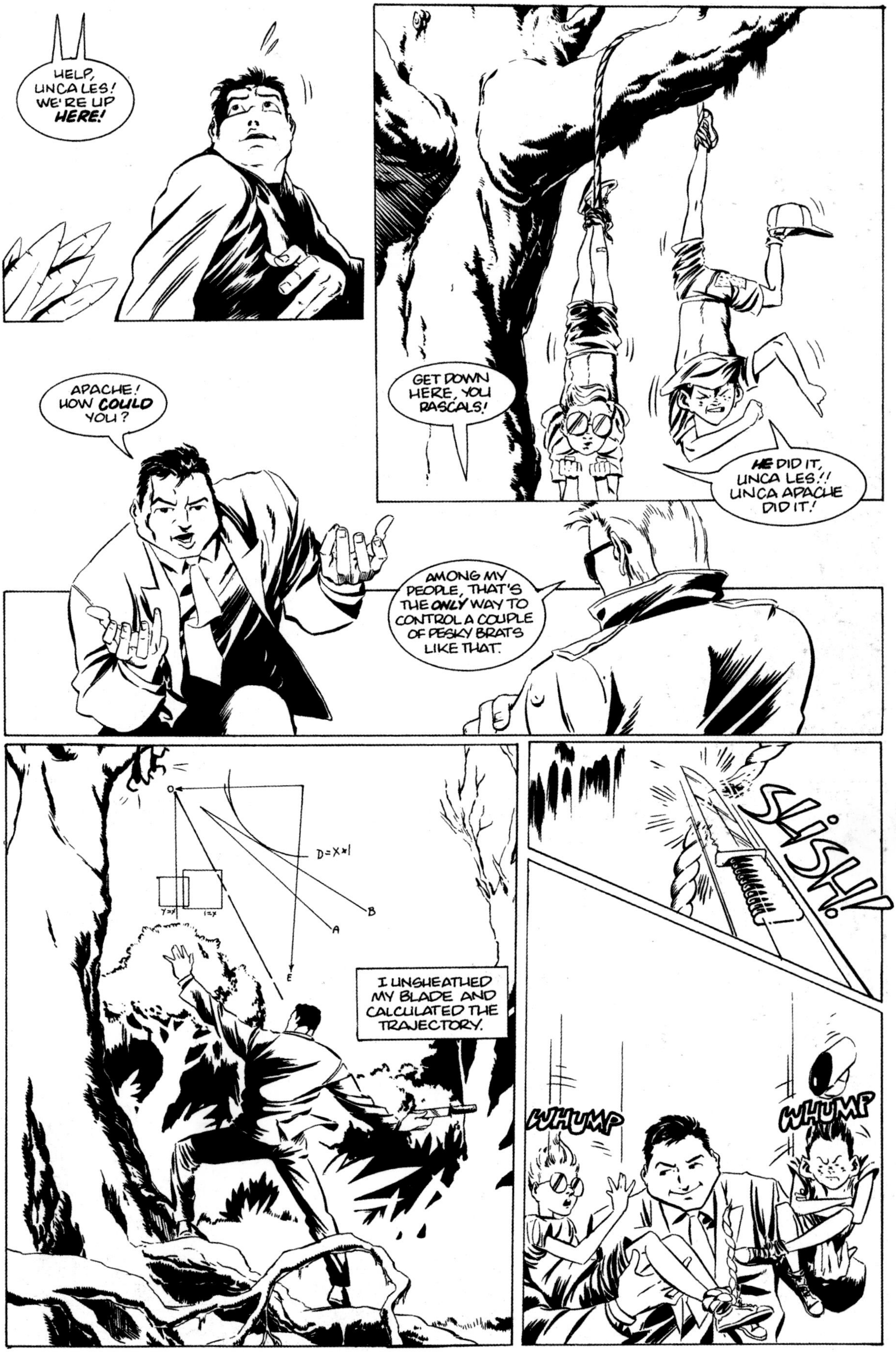

HELP, UNCA LES! WE'RE UP HERE!
GET DOWN HERE, YOU RASCALS!
HE DID IT, UNCA LES!! UNCA APACHE DID IT!
APACHE! HOW COULD YOU?
AMONG MY PEOPLE, THAT'S THE ONLY WAY TO CONTROL A COUPLE OF PESKY BRATS LIKE THAT.
D=X×1
A
B
E
I UNSHEATHED MY BLADE AND CALCULATED THE TRAJECTORY.
SLISH!
WHUMP
WHUMP

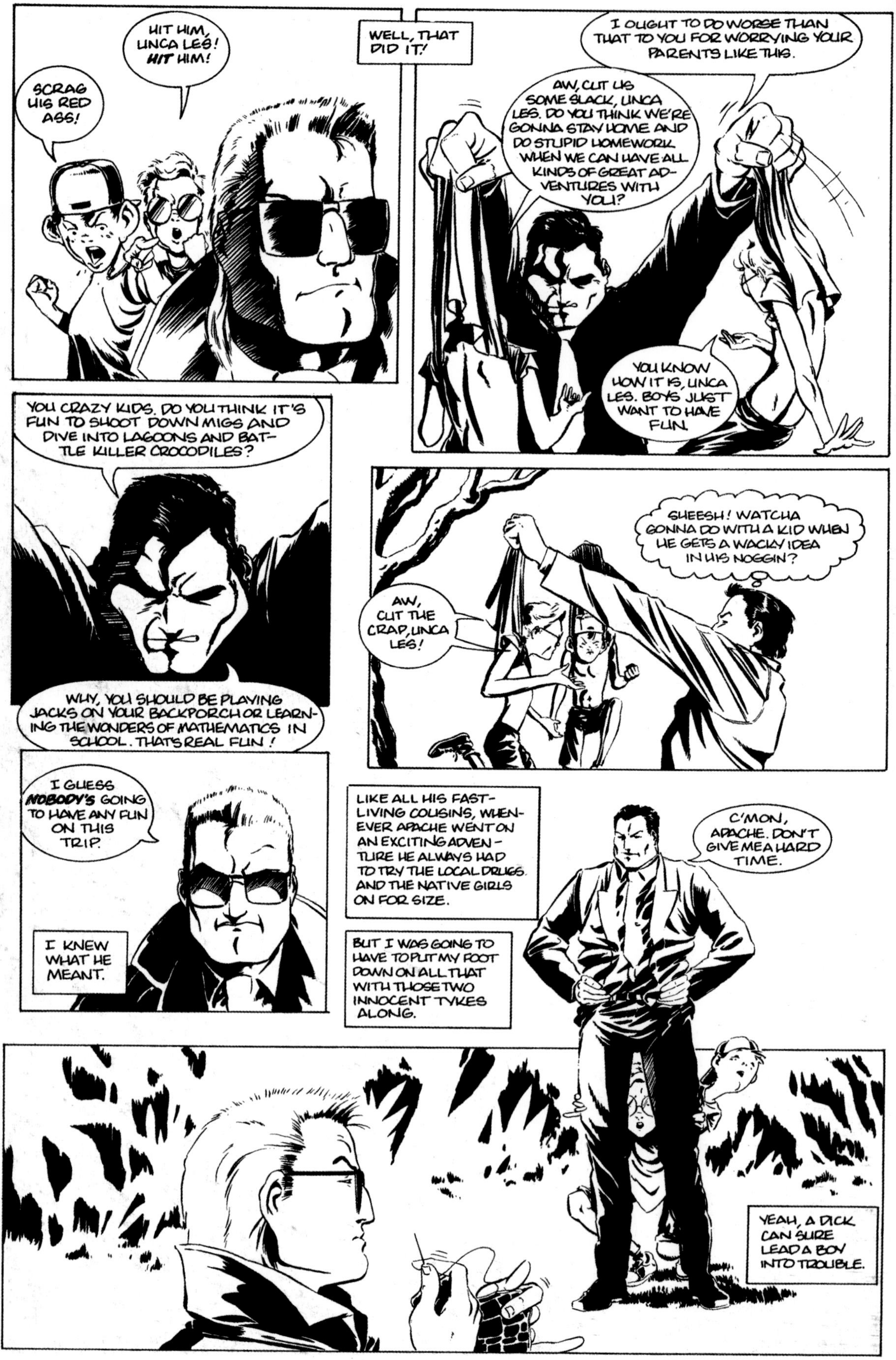
SCRAG HIS RED ASS!
HIT HIM, UNCA LES! HIT HIM!
WELL, THAT DID IT!
I OUGHT TO DO WORSE THAN THAT TO YOU FOR WORRYING YOUR PARENTS LIKE THIS.
AW, CUT US SOME SLACK, UNCA LES. DO YOU THINK WE'RE GONNA STAY HOME AND DO STUPID HOMEWORK WHEN WE CAN HAVE ALL KINDS OF GREAT AD-VENTURES WITH YOU?
YOU KNOW HOW IT IS, UNCA LES. BOYS JUST WANT TO HAVE FUN.
YOU CRAZY KIDS. DO YOU THINK IT'S FUN TO SHOOT DOWN MIGS AND DIVE INTO LAGOONS AND BAT-TLE KILLER CROCODILES?
WHY, YOU SHOULD BE PLAYING JACKS ON YOUR BACKPORCH OR LEARN-ING THE WONDERS OF MATHEMATICS IN SCHOOL. THAT'S REAL FUN!
SHEESH! WATCHA GONNA DO WITH A KID WHEN HE GETS A WACKY IDEA IN HIS NOGGIN?
AW, CUT THE CRAP, UNCA LES!
I GUESS NOBODY'S GOING TO HAVE ANY FUN ON THIS TRIP.
I KNEW WHAT HE MEANT.
LIKE ALL HIS FAST-LIVING COUSINS, WHEN-EVER APACHE WENT ON AN EXCITING ADVEN-TURE HE ALWAYS HAD TO TRY THE LOCAL DRUGS. AND THE NATIVE GIRLS ON FOR SIZE.
BUT I WAS GOING TO HAVE TO PUT MY FOOT DOWN ON ALL THAT WITH THOSE TWO INNOCENT TYKES ALONG.
C'MON, APACHE. DON'T GIVE ME A HARD TIME.
YEAH, A DICK CAN SURE LEAD A BOY INTO TROUBLE.

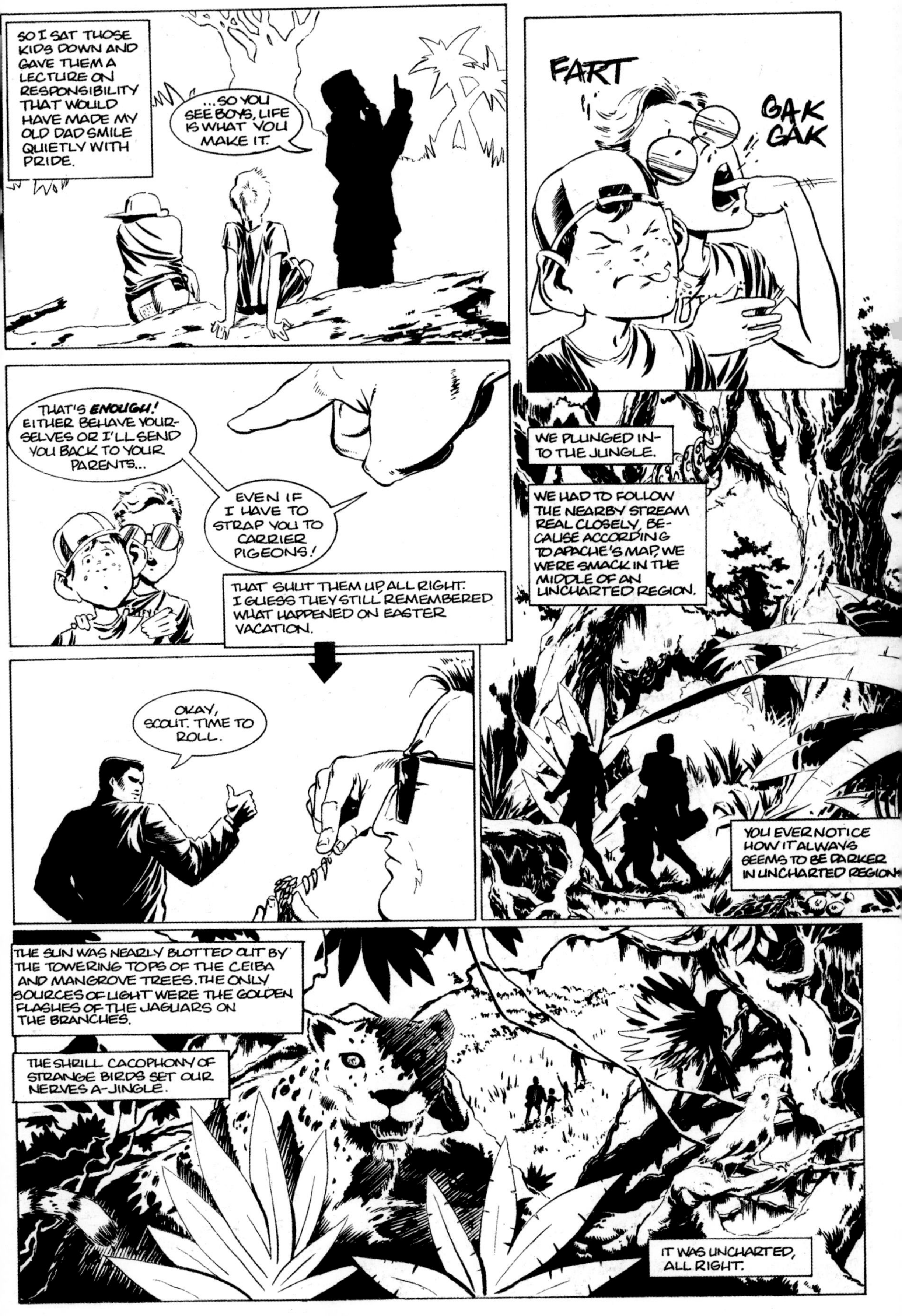
SO I SAT THOSE KIDS DOWN AND GAVE THEM A LECTURE ON RESPONSIBILITY THAT WOULD HAVE MADE MY OLD DAD SMILE QUIETLY WITH PRIDE.
...SO YOU SEE BOYS, LIFE IS WHAT YOU MAKE IT.
FART
GAK GAK
THAT'S ENOUGH! EITHER BEHAVE YOURSELVES OR I'LL SEND YOU BACK TO YOUR PARENTS...
EVEN IF I HAVE TO STRAP YOU TO CARRIER PIGEONS!
THAT SHUT THEM UP, ALL RIGHT. I GUESS THEY STILL REMEMBERED WHAT HAPPENED ON EASTER VACATION.
OKAY, SCOUT. TIME TO ROLL.
WE PLUNGED INTO THE JUNGLE.
WE HAD TO FOLLOW THE NEARBY STREAM REAL CLOSELY, BECAUSE ACCORDING TO APACHE'S MAP, WE WERE SMACK IN THE MIDDLE OF AN UNCHARTED REGION.
YOU EVER NOTICE HOW IT ALWAYS SEEMS TO BE DARKER IN UNCHARTED REGIONS
THE SUN WAS NEARLY BLOTTED OUT BY THE TOWERING TOPS OF THE CEIBA AND MANGROVE TREES. THE ONLY SOURCES OF LIGHT WERE THE GOLDEN FLASHES OF THE JAGUARS ON THE BRANCHES.
THE SHRILL CACOPHONY OF STRANGE BIRDS SET OUR NERVES A-JINGLE.
IT WAS UNCHARTED, ALL RIGHT.

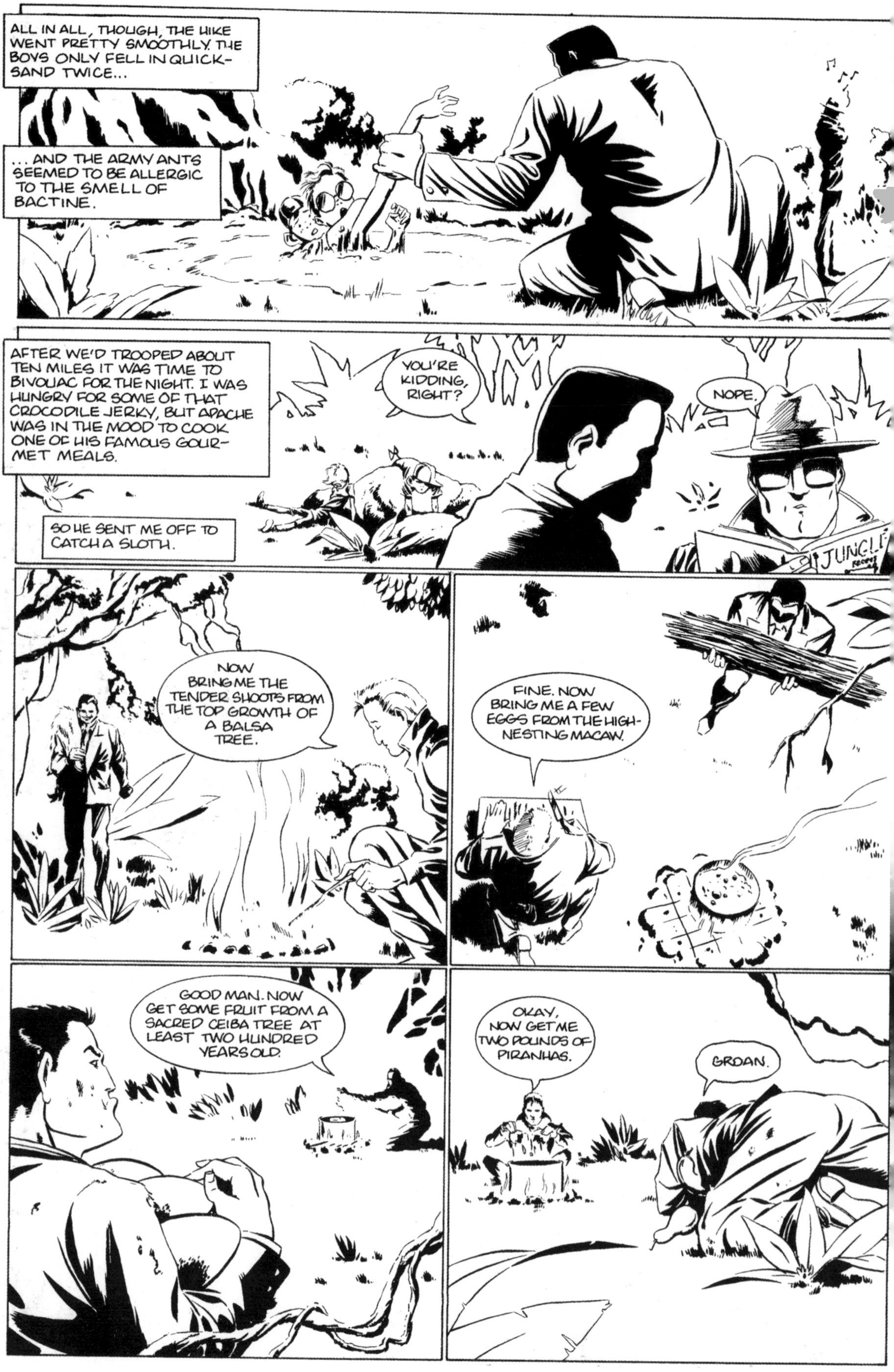
ALL IN ALL, THOUGH, THE HIKE WENT PRETTY SMOOTHLY. THE BOYS ONLY FELL IN QUICK-SAND TWICE...
...AND THE ARMY ANTS SEEMED TO BE ALLERGIC TO THE SMELL OF BACTINE.
AFTER WE'D TROOPED ABOUT TEN MILES IT WAS TIME TO BIVOUAC FOR THE NIGHT. I WAS HUNGRY FOR SOME OF THAT CROCODILE JERKY, BUT APACHE WAS IN THE MOOD TO COOK ONE OF HIS FAMOUS GOURMET MEALS.
SO HE SENT ME OFF TO CATCH A SLOTH.
YOU'RE KIDDING, RIGHT?
NOPE.
JUNGLE
NOW BRING ME THE TENDER SHOOTS FROM THE TOP GROWTH OF A BALSA TREE.
FINE. NOW BRING ME A FEW EGGS FROM THE HIGH-NESTING MACAW.
GOOD MAN. NOW GET SOME FRUIT FROM A SACRED CEIBA TREE AT LEAST TWO HUNDRED YEARS OLD.
OKAY, NOW GET ME TWO POUNDS OF PIRANHAS.
GROAN.

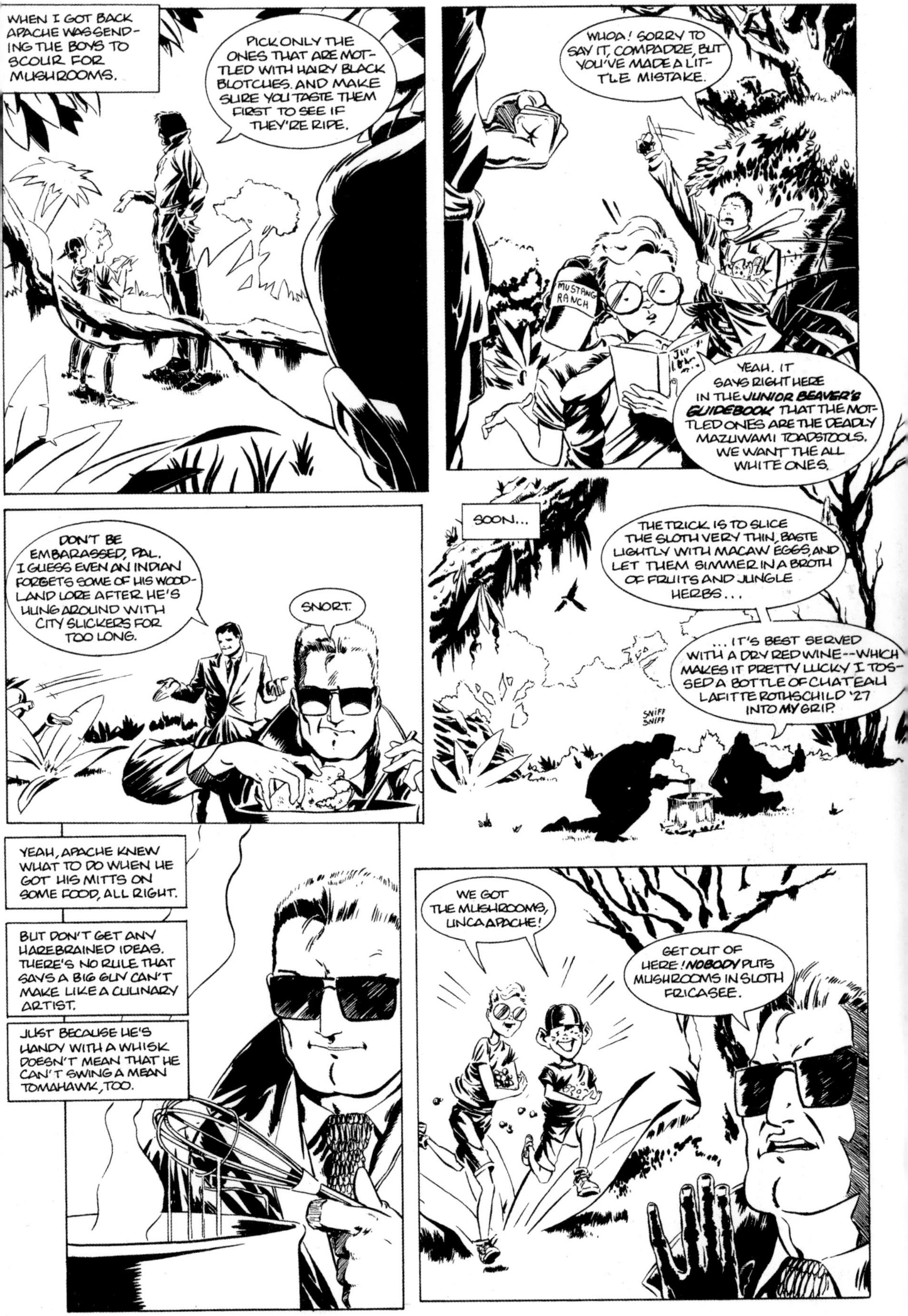
WHEN I GOT BACK APACHE WAS SENDING THE BOYS TO SCOUR FOR MUSHROOMS.
PICK ONLY THE ONES THAT ARE MOTTLED WITH HAIRY BLACK BLOTCHES. AND MAKE SURE YOU TASTE THEM FIRST TO SEE IF THEY'RE RIPE.
WHOA! SORRY TO SAY IT, COMPADRE, BUT YOU'VE MADE A LITTLE MISTAKE.
MUSTANG RANCH
YEAH. IT SAYS RIGHT HERE IN THE JUNIOR BEAVER'S GUIDEBOOK THAT THE MOTTLED ONES ARE THE DEADLY MAZUWAMI TOADSTOOLS. WE WANT THE ALL WHITE ONES.
DON'T BE EMBARASSED, PAL. I GUESS EVEN AN INDIAN FORGETS SOME OF HIS WOODLAND LORE AFTER HE'S HUNG AROUND WITH CITY SLICKERS FOR TOO LONG.
SNORT.
SOON...
THE TRICK IS TO SLICE THE SLOTH VERY THIN, BASTE LIGHTLY WITH MACAW EGGS, AND LET THEM SIMMER IN A BROTH OF FRUITS AND JUNGLE HERBS...
...IT'S BEST SERVED WITH A DRY RED WINE--WHICH MAKES IT PRETTY LUCKY I TOSSED A BOTTLE OF CHATEAU LAFITTE ROTHSCHILD '27 INTO MY GRIP.
SNIFF SNIFF
YEAH, APACHE KNEW WHAT TO DO WHEN HE GOT HIS MITTS ON SOME FOOD, ALL RIGHT.
BUT DON'T GET ANY HAREBRAINED IDEAS. THERE'S NO RULE THAT SAYS A BIG GUY CAN'T MAKE LIKE A CULINARY ARTIST.
JUST BECAUSE HE'S HANDY WITH A WHISK DOESN'T MEAN THAT HE CAN'T SWING A MEAN TOMAHAWK, TOO.
WE GOT THE MUSHROOMS, UNCA APACHE!
GET OUT OF HERE! NOBODY PUTS MUSHROOMS IN SLOTH FRICASEE.

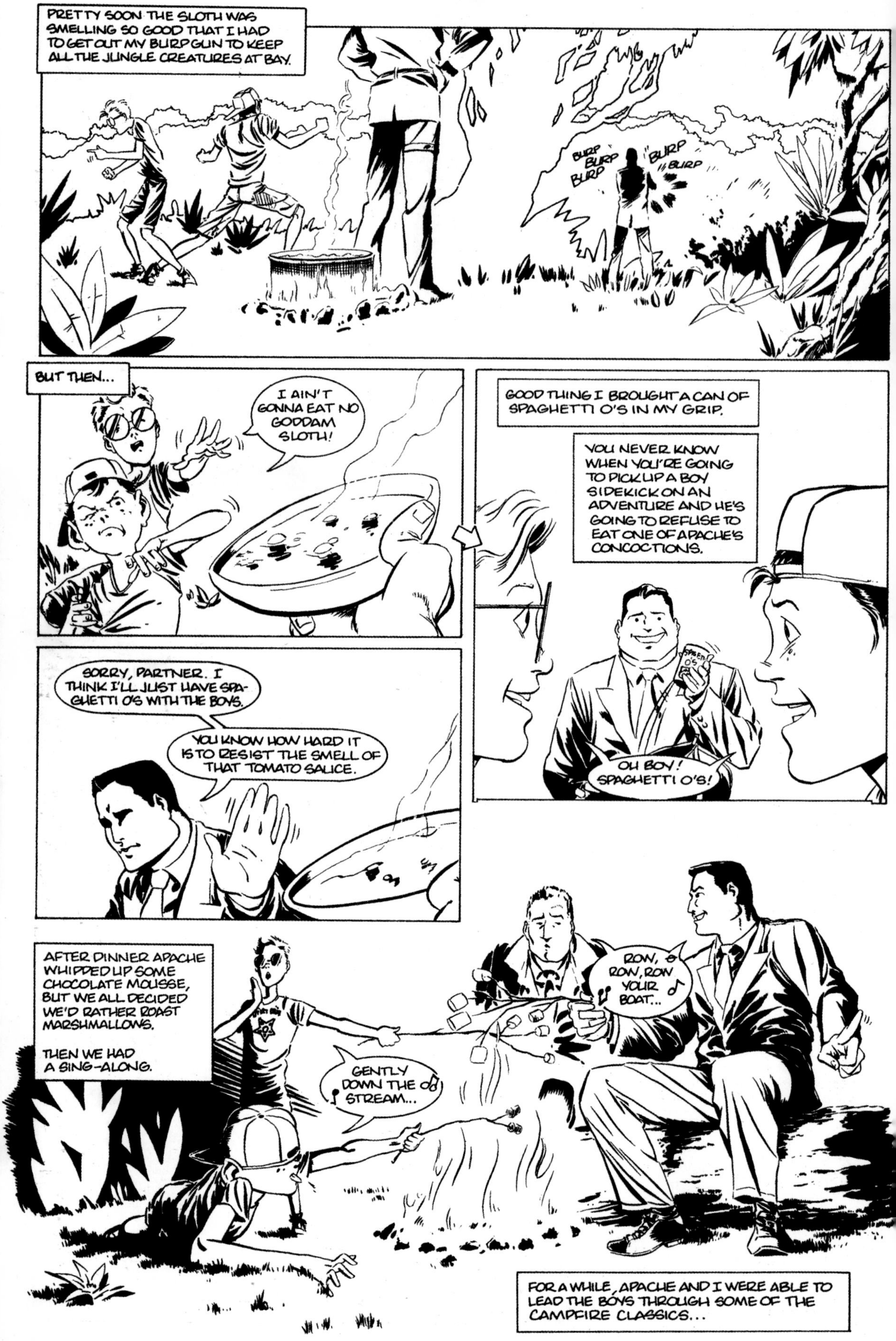
PRETTY SOON THE SLOTH WAS SMELLING SO GOOD THAT I HAD TO GET OUT MY BURP GUN TO KEEP ALL THE JUNGLE CREATURES AT BAY.
BURP BURP BURP BURP BURP
BUT THEN...
I AIN'T GONNA EAT NO GODDAM SLOTH!
GOOD THING I BROUGHT A CAN OF SPAGHETTI O'S IN MY GRIP.
YOU NEVER KNOW WHEN YOU'RE GOING TO PICK UP A BOY SIDEKICK ON AN ADVENTURE AND HE'S GOING TO REFUSE TO EAT ONE OF APACHE'S CONCOCTIONS.
SPAGETTI O'S
OH BOY! SPAGHETTI O'S!
SORRY, PARTNER. I THINK I'LL JUST HAVE SPAGHETTI O'S WITH THE BOYS.
YOU KNOW HOW HARD IT IS TO RESIST THE SMELL OF THAT TOMATO SAUCE.
AFTER DINNER APACHE WHIPPED UP SOME CHOCOLATE MOUSSE, BUT WE ALL DECIDED WE'D RATHER ROAST MARSHMALLOWS.
THEN WE HAD A SING-ALONG.
ROW, ROW, ROW YOUR BOAT...
GENTLY DOWN THE STREAM...
FOR A WHILE, APACHE AND I WERE ABLE TO LEAD THE BOYS THROUGH SOME OF THE CAMPFIRE CLASSICS...

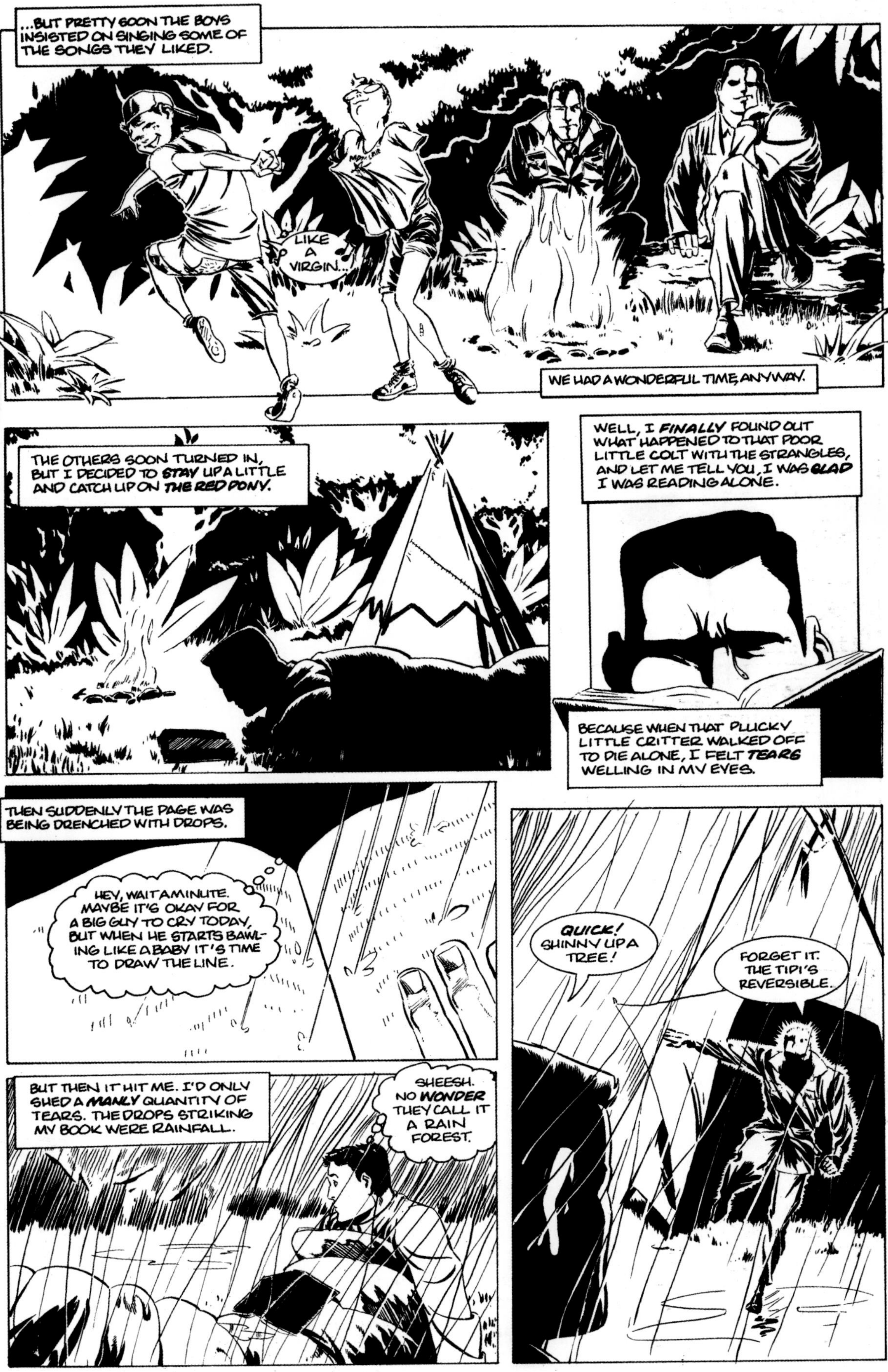
...BUT PRETTY SOON THE BOYS INSISTED ON SINGING SOME OF THE SONGS THEY LIKED.
LIKE A VIRGIN...
WE HAD A WONDERFUL TIME, ANYWAY.
THE OTHERS SOON TURNED IN, BUT I DECIDED TO STAY UP A LITTLE AND CATCH UP ON THE RED PONY.
WELL, I FINALLY FOUND OUT WHAT HAPPENED TO THAT POOR LITTLE COLT WITH THE STRANGLES, AND LET ME TELL YOU, I WAS GLAD I WAS READING ALONE.
BECAUSE WHEN THAT PLUCKY LITTLE CRITTER WALKED OFF TO DIE ALONE, I FELT TEARS WELLING IN MY EYES.
THEN SUDDENLY THE PAGE WAS BEING DRENCHED WITH DROPS.
HEY, WAIT A MINUTE. MAYBE IT'S OKAY FOR A BIG GUY TO CRY TODAY, BUT WHEN HE STARTS BAWLING LIKE A BABY IT'S TIME TO DRAW THE LINE.
BUT THEN IT HIT ME. I'D ONLY SHED A MANLY QUANTITY OF TEARS. THE DROPS STRIKING MY BOOK WERE RAINFALL.
SHEESH. NO WONDER THEY CALL IT A RAIN FOREST.
QUICK! SHINNY UP A TREE!
FORGET IT. THE TIPI'S REVERSIBLE.

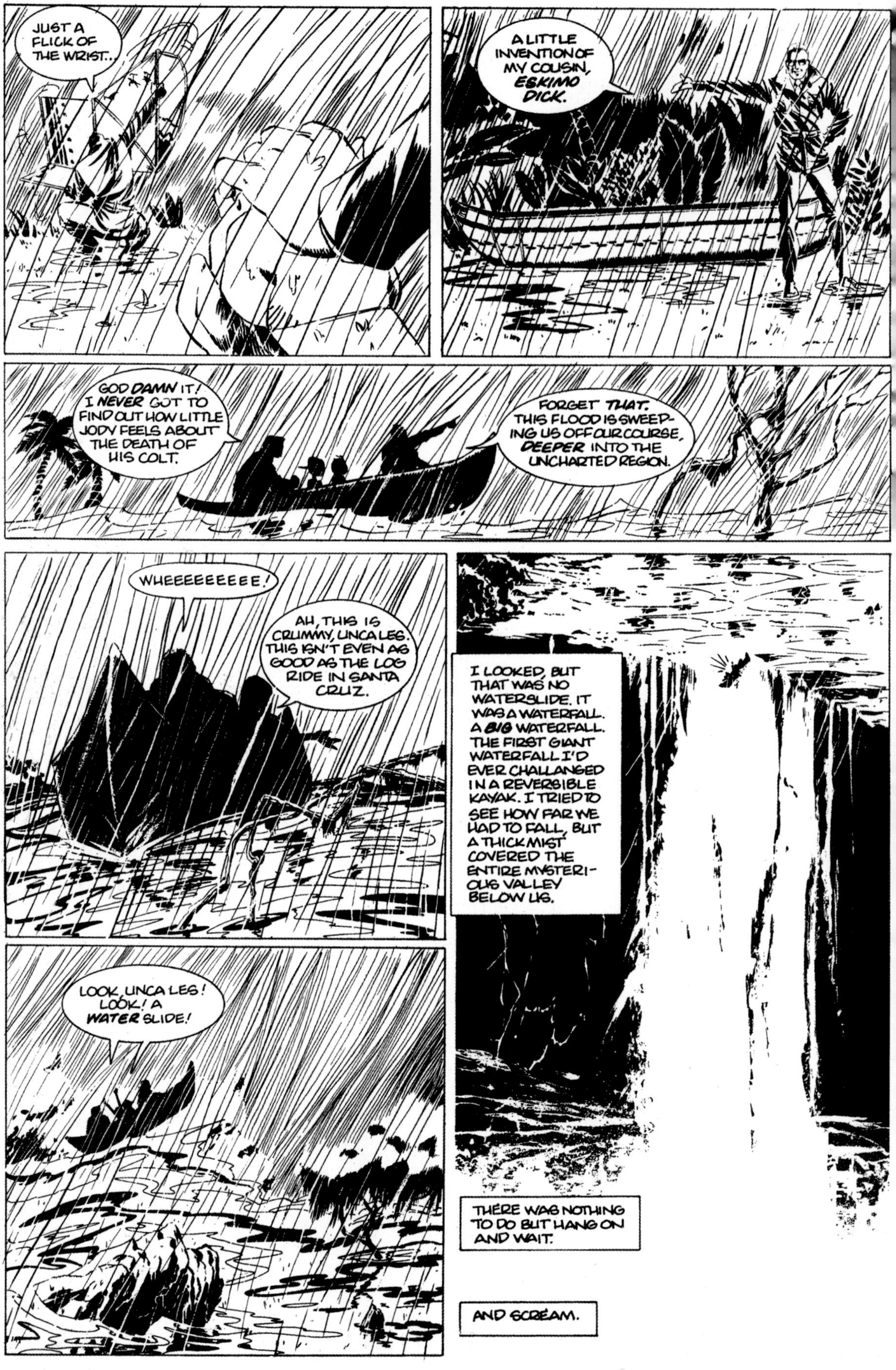
JUST A FLICK OF THE WRIST...
A LITTLE INVENTION OF MY COUSIN, ESKIMO DICK.
GOD DAMN IT! I NEVER GOT TO FIND OUT HOW LITTLE JODY FEELS ABOUT THE DEATH OF HIS COLT.
FORGET THAT. THIS FLOOD IS SWEEPING US OFF OUR COURSE, DEEPER INTO THE UNCHARTED REGION.
LOOK, UNCA LES! LOOK! A WATER SLIDE!
WHEEEEEEEEE!
AH, THIS IS CRUMMY, UNCA LES. THIS ISN'T EVEN AS GOOD AS THE LOG RIDE IN SANTA CRUZ.
I LOOKED, BUT THAT WAS NO WATERSLIDE. IT WAS A WATERFALL. A BIG WATERFALL. THE FIRST GIANT WATERFALL I'D EVER CHALLANGED IN A REVERSIBLE KAYAK. I TRIED TO SEE HOW FAR WE HAD TO FALL, BUT A THICK MIST COVERED THE ENTIRE MYSTERIOUS VALLEY BELOW US.
THERE WAS NOTHING TO DO BUT HANG ON AND WAIT.
AND SCREAM.

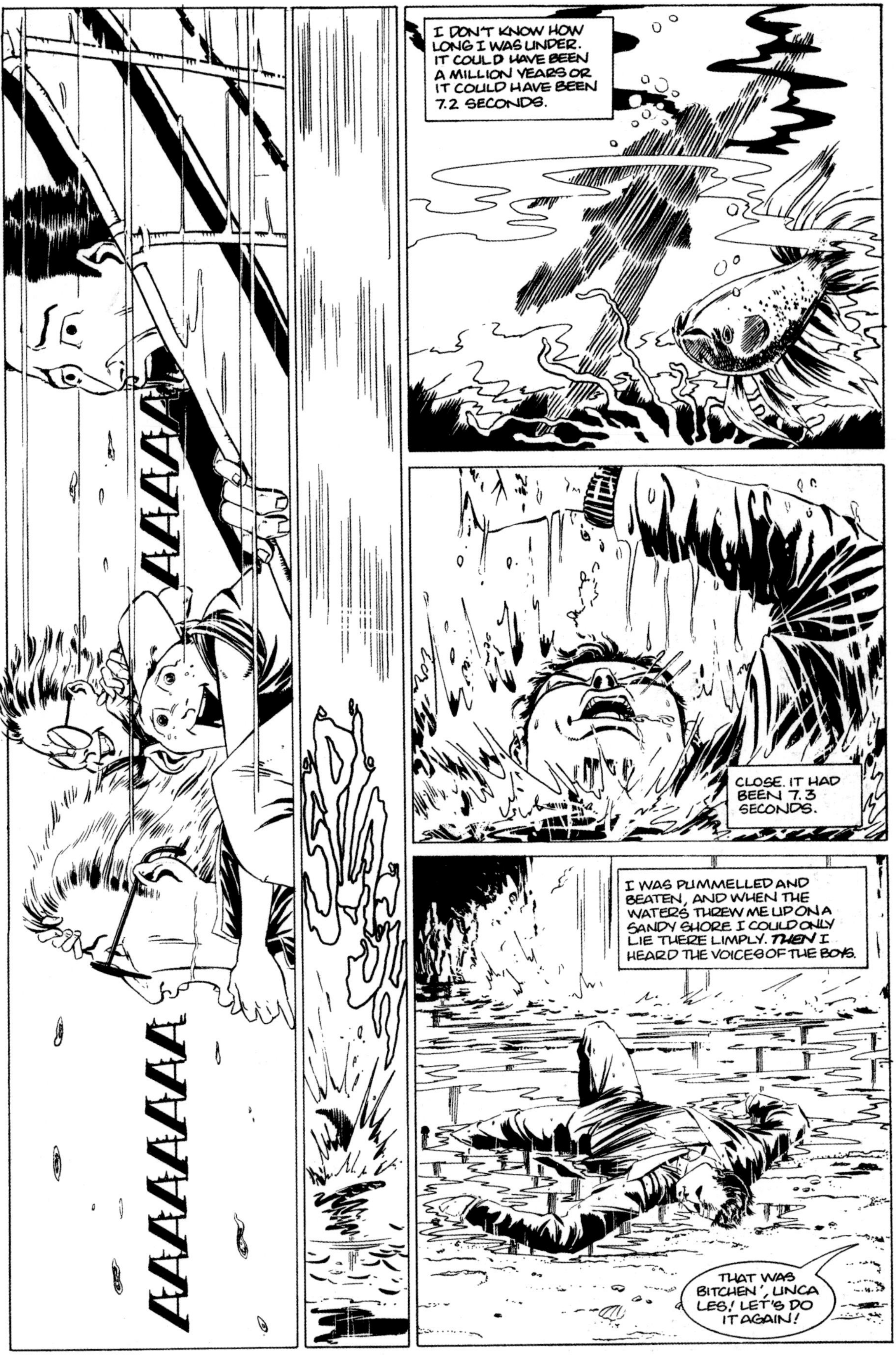
I DON'T KNOW HOW LONG I WAS UNDER. IT COULD HAVE BEEN A MILLION YEARS OR IT COULD HAVE BEEN 7.2 SECONDS.
CLOSE. IT HAD BEEN 7.3 SECONDS.
I WAS PUMMELLED AND BEATEN, AND WHEN THE WATERS THREW ME UP ON A SANDY SHORE I COULD ONLY LIE THERE LIMPLY. THEN I HEARD THE VOICES OF THE BOYS.
THAT WAS BITCHEN', UNCA LES! LET'S DO IT AGAIN!
AAAAAAAAAAAAAAA

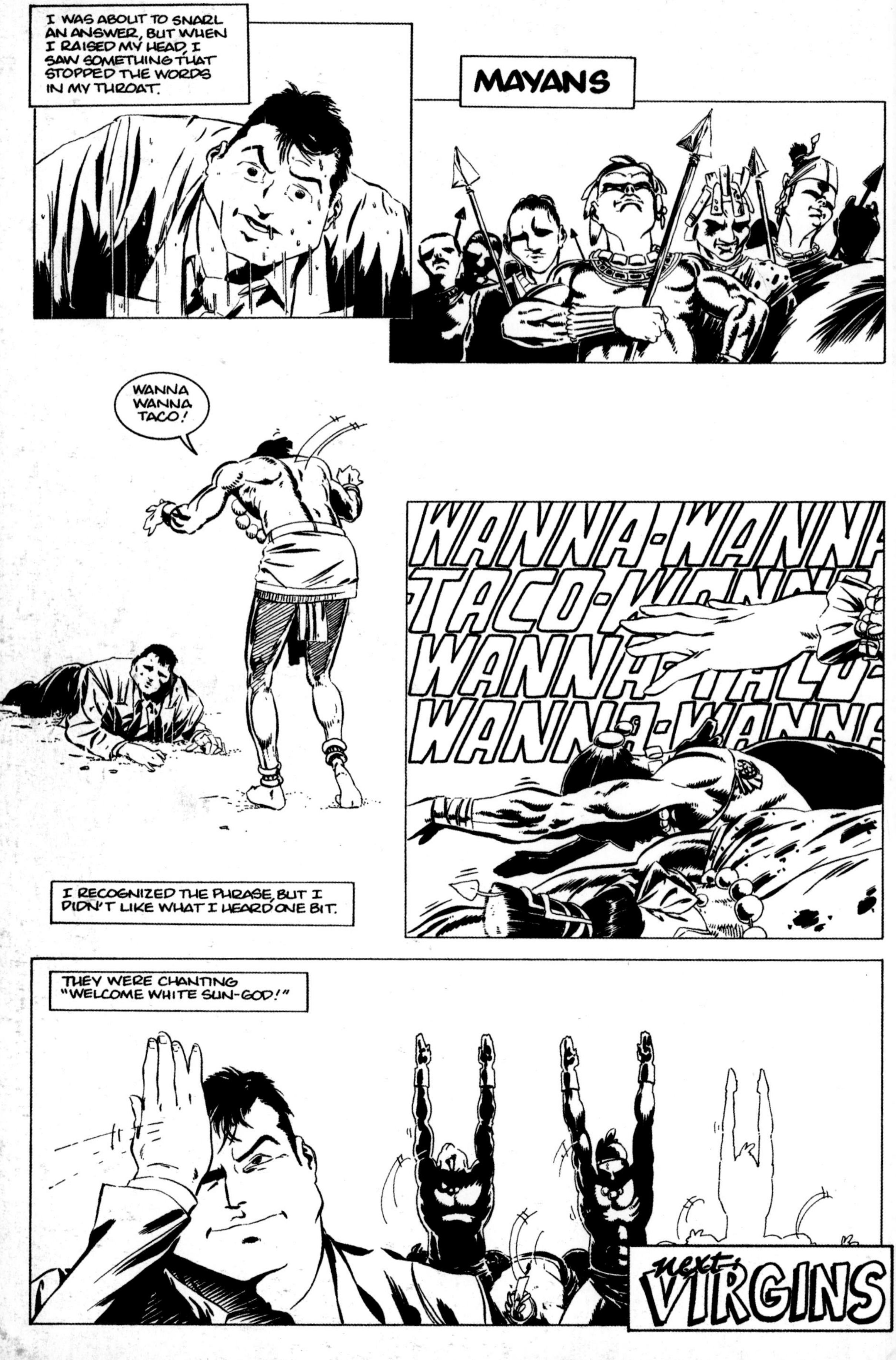
I WAS ABOUT TO SNARL AN ANSWER, BUT WHEN I RAISED MY HEAD, I SAW SOMETHING THAT STOPPED THE WORDS IN MY THROAT.
MAYANS
WANNA WANNA TACO!
WANNA-WANNA
TACO-WANNA-
WANNA-TACO-
WANNA-WANNA
I RECOGNIZED THE PHRASE, BUT I DIDN'T LIKE WHAT I HEARD ONE BIT.
THEY WERE CHANTING "WELCOME WHITE SUN-GOD!"
next: VIRGINS

ALIEN LEGION

ALIEN LEGION
FORCE·NOMAD
ALIEN LEGION
PIECEMAKER
CHUCK DIXON
LARRY STROMAN
CARL POTTS
ALIEN LEGION

Alien Legion: Force Nomad
A premium collection of the first eleven issues of this critically acclaimed comic series about a fighting force a la the French Foreign Legion.

Alien Legion: Piecemaker
The follow-up to Force Nomad, the Alien Legion resumes duty in a series of far-flung combat zones.

Alien Legion: Footsloggers
Collects the first six comics from the original incarnation of the series in 1984.

Brought to you by

checker
BOOK PUBLISHING GROUP

Alien Legion: Force Nomad
ISBN: 0-9710249-0-1

Alien Legion: Piecemaker
ISBN: 0-9710249-4-4

Alien Legion: Footsloggers
ISBN: 0-9753808-7-7

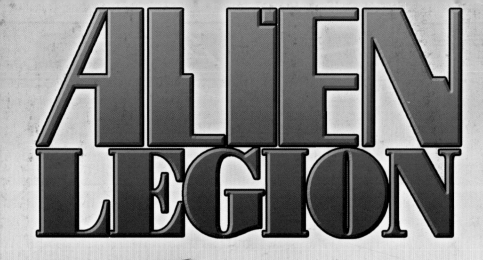

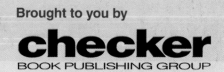

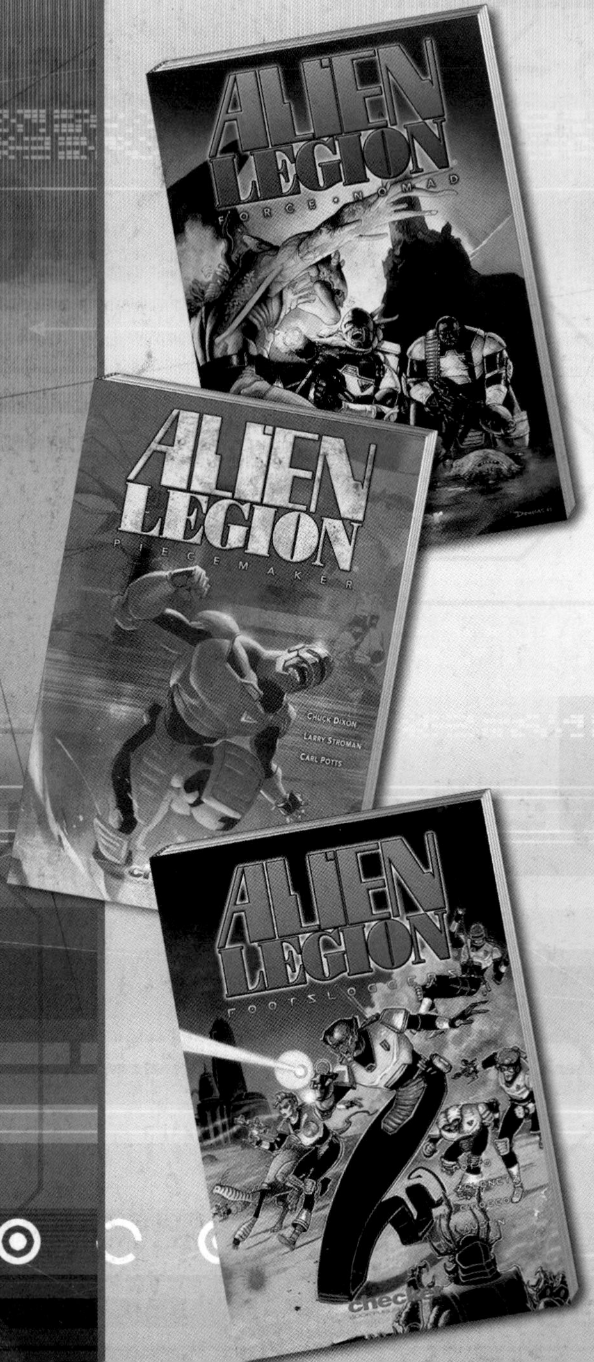

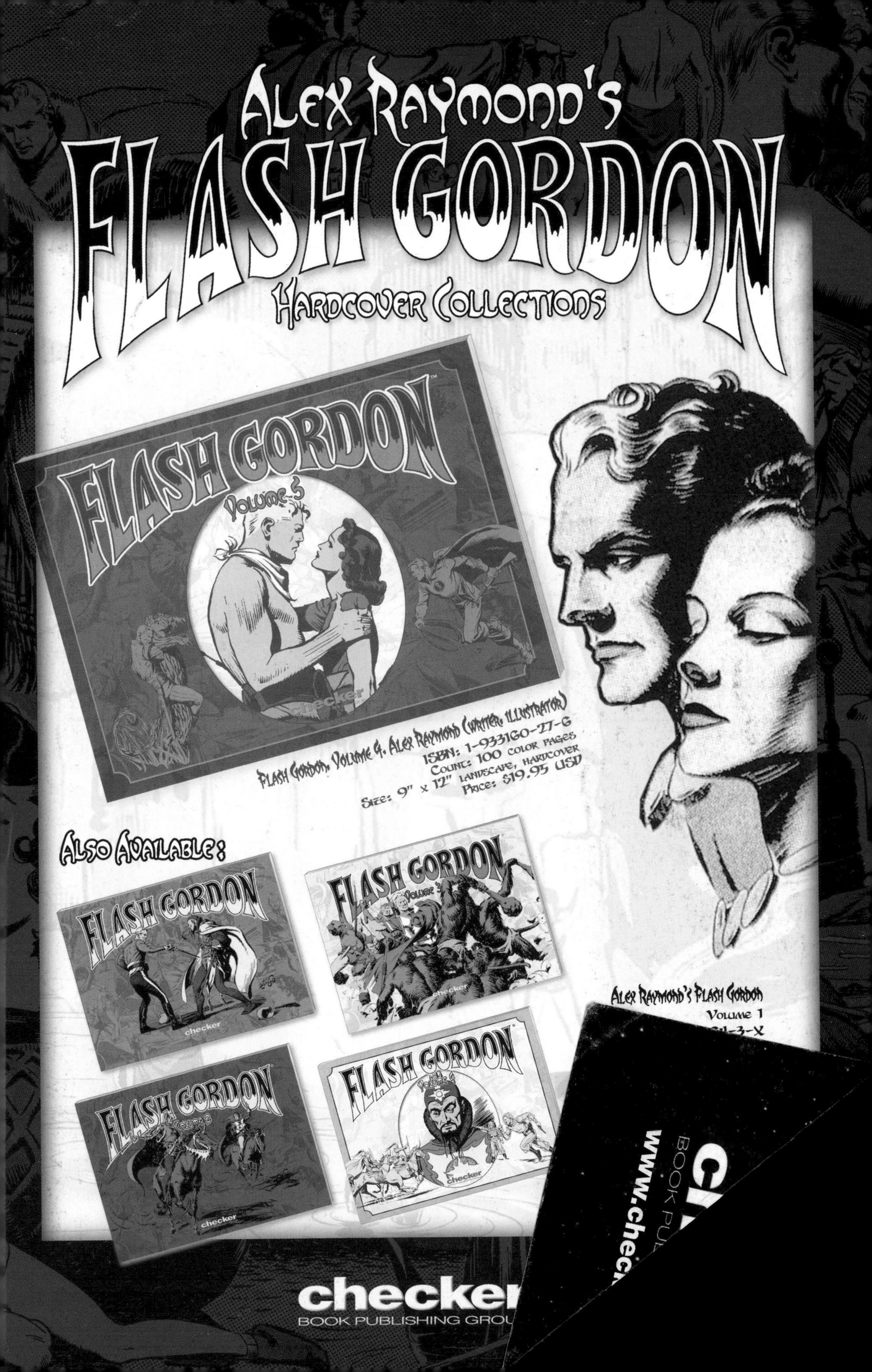

Alex Raymond's
Flash Gordon
Hardcover Collections
Flash Gordon
Volume 5
Flash Gordon, Volume 4. Alex Raymond (Writer, Illustrator)
ISBN: 1-933160-27-6
Count: 100 color pages
Size: 9" x 12" landscape, hardcover
Price: $19.95 USD
Also Available:
Flash Gordon
Flash Gordon
Flash Gordon
Flash Gordon
Alex Raymond's Flash Gordon
Volume 1
checker
BOOK PUBLISHING GROU

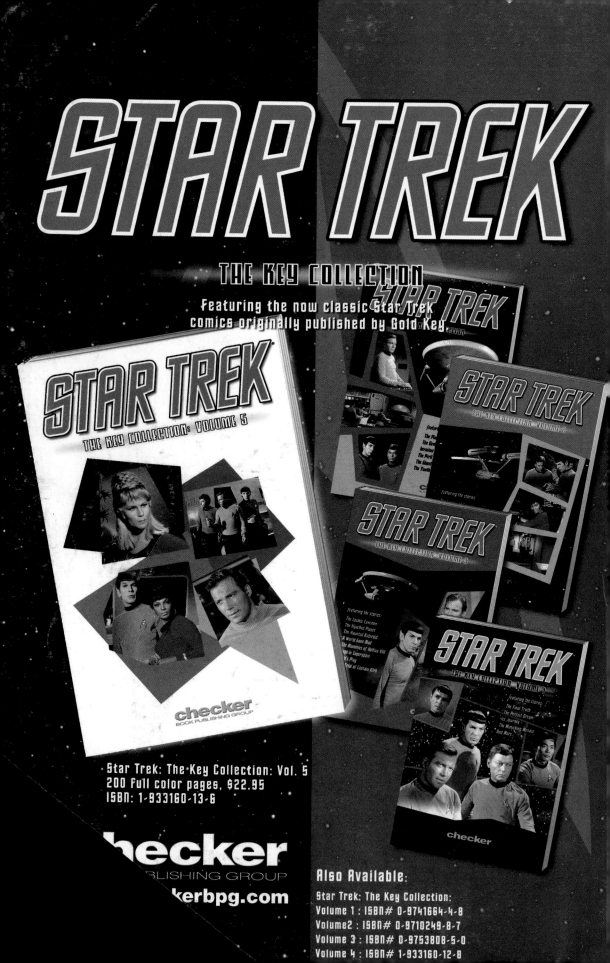